INTERACTIONS

Collaboration Skills for School Professionals

FOURTH EDITION

Marilyn Friend

University of North Carolina, Greensboro

Lynne Cook

California State University, Northridge

Allyn and Bacon

Boston • New York • San Francisco

Mexico City • Montreal • Toronto • London • Madrid • Munich • Paris

Hong Kong • Singapore • Tokyo • Cape Town • Sydney

Vice President and Editor in Chief: Paul A. Smith
Executive Editor, Special Education and Counseling: Virginia Lanigan
Editorial Assistant: Robert Champagne
Executive Marketing Manager: Amy Cronin
Editorial–Production Service: Matrix Productions Inc.
Composition and Prepress Buyer: Linda Cox
Manufacturing Buyer: JoAnne Sweeney
Cover Administrator: Linda Knowles
Interior Designer: Cynthia Bassett
Photo Researcher: Liz Wood
Illustrations: Omegatype Typography, Inc.
Electronic Composition: Omegatype Typography, Inc.

For related titles and support materials, visit our online catalog at www.ablongman.com.

Between the time Website information is gathered and then published, it is not
unusual for some sites to have closed. Also, the transcription of URLs can result
in unintended typographical errors. The publisher would appreciate notification
where these errors occur so that they may be corrected in subsequent editions.

Library of Congress Cataloging-in-Publication Data

Friend, Marilyn Penovich.
    Interactions : collaboration skills for school professionals / Marilyn Friend, Lynne
Cook.— 4th ed.
        p. cm.
    Includes bibliographical references and index.
    ISBN 0-205-35903-5
        1. Special education teachers—Training of.   2. Interpersonal relations.
3. Communication in education.   I. Cook, Lynne.   II. Title.

LC3969.45 .F75 2003
371.9—dc21   2002066587

Photo credits appear on page 364, which constitutes a continuation of the copyright
page.

Printed in the United States of America

10 9 8 7 6 5 4   RRD-VA   07 06 05 04

To Joseph Percy Price
1934–2001

*An extraordinary educator who lives on through those, like us,
who were blessed by his life and teachings.*

———————————

Contents

Features at a Glance

Perspectives on Diversity

Putting Ideas into Practice

Preface

When the first edition of *Interactions* was published in 1992, it was a slender volume with fewer than 200 pages, no photographs, and a principal focus on communication and interaction skills. In many ways, its small physical size and narrow substantive coverage reflected the place of collaboration in schools at that time: Collaboration was acknowledged as important but was still primarily a small concern pertaining mostly to special educators, it was viewed by many as a luxury within the context of classroom instruction, and its study within an education framework was somewhat limited.

Much has changed since then. The Individuals with Disabilities Education Act, the legislation governing the provision of services for students with disabilities, now carries a clear assumption that most students will be educated in typical classrooms with their peers. Further, access to the general education curriculum for students with special needs has become an expectation at the same time that accountability for all students' learning has continued to grow. These changes have led to a third: Services delivered to students within the general education classroom have become more and more common. Collaboration also has moved far beyond the school setting. There is increasing recognition that all of the agencies that work on behalf of families and children—for example, education, social service, mental health, and medical—must share their efforts and resources in order to have any long-lasting positive impact on poverty, homelessness, and other issues that affect children and their families. The vastly increased breadth of concern for collaboration and depth of its examination are seen in the thousands of websites that now exist on the topic and in the explosion of professional literature about it.

This fourth edition of *Interactions* is intended to be responsive to the changes in school policies and practices that have led to today's focused attention on collaboration as an essential skill for meeting the ever-increasing diversity of student needs. It is a guide for preprofessionals and professionals to help them understand and participate effectively in their interactions with other professionals and parents. This book was written for a broad audience, but especially for preservice and in-service special educators, general educators, and related services professionals who educate students with disabilities. Although the examples and activities focus on providers of special services, they are not unique to that group. We continue to believe that the principles for effective interaction are not dependent on roles or settings—they are universal. Our experiences in schools tell us that the concepts and skills in *Interactions* are thus equally applicable to individuals who educate English language learners, to those who work in early intervention and preschool programs, to site-based school management groups, to middle school teams, and to many other situations in which educators come together to work toward a common goal.

Over the past decade, we have received much positive feedback about the practicality of this book (and we thank you for that and the suggestions you have made for improvement). In this edition, we continue to use the principles we believe lead to instructional effectiveness: a measured amount of theory and concept heavily seasoned with examples, cases, and applied activities. *Interactions* was written specifically to enable readers to quickly use the knowledge and skills they acquire in their professional settings. In addition, because many interaction situations are complex with many possible variations and outcomes, we have tried to present possibilities but leave the reader thinking critically about personal applications and alternative options.

Overview of the Book

Collaboration is truly a topic for lifelong learning. As we interact with our colleagues at the university and in the field, we continue to grow in our own understanding of the fundamentals and subtleties of professional interpersonal relationships. We have had the good fortune of working and learning with talented teachers, administrators, parents, paraprofessionals, and providers of related services as they developed collaboration skills and put specific applications of collaboration in place. The lessons we have learned from them have helped us immensely in preparing the fourth edition of *Interactions*. Specifically, we have maintained our core of information about collaboration concepts, communication, and interaction process skills; we have expanded some material from the third edition; we have omitted a few topics that we learned have a lower priority in today's schools; we have reorganized the order of the chapters in response to student and instructor feedback; and we have augmented again the practical applications of the textbook's ideas.

Chapter 1 presents a conceptual foundation for understanding collaborative interactions and activities as well as the settings and structures that support them. In this chapter we define collaboration and highlight its benefits and risks. In addition, we distinguish collaboration from other terms that are sometimes used interchangeably, and we explore the development of collaboration as it relates to special education, including the current trend to educate students with disabilities in general education classrooms.

The next three chapters of the book comprise a unit on communication skills. These chapters existed in the third edition, but they have been updated and moved forward in the book so that students are introduced to effective communication skills earlier in their coursework. Chapter 2 serves as an introduction and overview of principles of clear and constructive communication. Concepts are presented that underlie communication and interaction skills, including recognizing diverse frames of reference and preparing to listen. This chapter also summarizes the principles of interpersonal communication, both verbal and non-verbal. An in-depth discussion of verbal communication occurs in the next two chapters. Chapter 3 provides the reader with knowledge and skills regarding using statements. Chapter 4 provides similar information about asking questions. In these two chapters, verbal strategies in using statements or asking questions are examined according to their intent to provide, solicit, or clarify information.

Chapter 5 introduces interpersonal problem solving as the most central interaction process of collaboration and one in which effective communication skills must be applied to achieve successful outcomes. It draws on but differs from professionals' skills for individual problem solving. The chapter has been moved forward in the book so that students will understand the problem-solving process that they will use later as they learn about services for students.

The next three chapters of *Interactions* explore services and applications in schools whose success relies heavily on collaboration. Chapter 6 addresses the topic of teaming, including ideas for establishing and maintaining teams and problem solving to help teams work effectively. Chapter 7 considers the service of consultation. It examines the various models through which consultation can be delivered, and it also offers a variety of suggestions for making consultation a viable means of supporting students and teachers. Chapter 8 takes up the topic of co-teaching, the service delivery option in which two educators share instructional responsibility in a single classroom. Suggestions for setting up co-teaching programs and specific information about how such arrangements should function are provided.

Chapter 9 is new. Although the topic of paraeducators has been mentioned in previous editions of *Interactions,* we decided that the increased use of paraeducators in providing services to students with disabilities and the issues that accompany that increase warranted significant attention. This chapter outlines appropriate and inappropriate roles for paraeducators, professionals' supervision responsibilities when working with paraeducators, and issues that may arise when paraeducators are part of an educational team.

Chapter 10 is also new. Although we have always believed that professionals' interactions with parents and family members are critically important in student success, we have never before dedicated an entire chapter to this topic. The chapter emphasizes understanding families, particularly their developmental stages and the unique perspectives that families from various cultures may bring to school environments, and facilitating family participation in decision making about their children.

A somewhat different direction is taken in Chapter 11, which deals with awkward and adversarial interactions by focusing on both conflict and resistance. Strategies such as negotiation and persuasion are emphasized. These require the use of many of the interactive processes and communication skills addressed earlier in the text.

The final two chapters of *Interactions* form the final essential components of collaboration. In Chapter 12, special issues related to collaboration in specific contexts are outlined. Collaborative efforts are influenced by the roles of the persons who collaborate as well as the contexts in which they work, and these topics are explored in the chapter. For example, the issues of student collaboration and collaboration for transition planning are explored. Also in Chapter 12 is a discussion of some of the critical ethical issues that arise when professionals collaborate. The final chapter, Chapter 13, addresses the practical matters that affect collaboration in all of its many applications. Topics include finding and managing time for planning, scheduling, program development and evaluation, and staff development. The chapter emphasizes the issues that arise when professionals collaborate "in the real world." For readers struggling in situations in which collaboration seems nearly impossible because of constraints on logistics, this chapter may be an appropriate starting point.

Most of the features of earlier editions of *Interactions* have been kept in the fourth edition, and others have been added. The features include the following:

- *Advance Organizers.* Each chapter begins with a section titled **Connections,** which is designed to assist the reader in understanding how the specific chapter content relates to the overall organization of the book.
- *Learner Objectives.* Each Connections section is followed by **Learner Objectives,** which inform the reader about the main purposes of the chapter. The objectives also help the reader to set expectations for what he or she will be able to do after studying the chapter.
- *Photographs.* In the fourth edition, more photographs have been added, and they more clearly illustrate collaboration in action.
- *Case Materials.* Case studies are presented throughout the text to illustrate relevant concepts and principles. These often include descriptions of specific school situations and extended dialogue between professionals or parents.
- *Putting Ideas into Practice.* In each chapter additional elaboration of concepts or skills practice is offered in boxes called **Putting Ideas into Practice.** These boxes are another means of making written ideas come to life for application in real school settings.
- *Addressing Diversity.* We have tried in this edition to pay even closer attention to matters of diversity that may arise in the context of collaboration. Each chapter contains a feature called **Perspectives on Diversity** that highlights pertinent issues and considerations.
- *Skill Models.* Chapters 2 through 5 provide instructional formats that give concrete models or examples of specific skills. This feature is designed to help the reader to discriminate between different elements of skills.
- *Application/Practice.* Application items are embedded throughout the chapters to involve the reader in analyzing the principles described and applying them to actual interpersonal situations. These items are also found at the end of each chapter; they assess the reader's understanding of important information in the chapter and provide suggestions for skill

development activities. These exercises may be used independently or as part of organized training experiences.

◆ *Chapter Summaries.* Each chapter concludes with a summary that briefly recaps the major points addressed in the chapter. The summaries are intended to assist the reader in assessing his or her understanding of the primary concepts within each chapter.

◆ *For Further Reading.* A brief list of additional readings is included at the end of each chapter. These references enable the reader who wants more detailed information about a particular topic to access that information quickly.

◆ *Instructor's Manual.* For the first time, *Interactions* is accompanied by an *Instructor's Manual* that includes chapter outlines, overhead transparency masters, additional activities and cases, and a test bank. The intent is to provide for readers and instructors more of the resources we like to use in teaching about collaboration than can be placed within the pages of the book itself.

We hope you enjoy the fourth edition of *Interactions: Collaboration Skills for School Professionals.* We continue to hold to our belief that collaboration is the foundation on which successful contemporary public schools are based as well as the only effective means through which to provide services to students with disabilities and other special needs. We hope this edition of *Interactions* helps you to further understand collaboration as it occurs in your workplace and enables you to refine your skills as a collaborative educator.

Acknowledgments

We often tell our students that collaboration is the epitome of lifelong learning, and we are reminded of this fact ourselves when we work with teachers, administrators, related service personnel, families, paraeducators, and others in schools. We are indebted to them and to our students and colleagues who have contributed in many direct and indirect ways to the creation of this book. Even though we cannot name them all, we hope they see their influence reflected in this volume and know of our appreciation.

We would also like to thank the following colleagues who provided professional reviews of the third edition of *Interactions* to make suggestions for the fourth edition: Susan M. Bruce, Boston College; Kathryn Calabrese, Wittenberg University; John W. Filler, University of Nevada, Las Vegas; and Linda A. Pehlman, University of Tennessee at Chattanooga. We know that being asked to review a manuscript means making time in already-crowded schedules. We sincerely appreciate your commitment to the field and to collaboration, and we are grateful for the detailed and insightful comments you provided. We also are thankful to our colleagues who offered informal feedback.

Throughout the development of *Interactions,* Fourth Edition, we received guidance, encouragement, and advice from the professional staff at Allyn & Bacon. We are very appreciative of Virginia Lanigan, who encouraged us through the writing process and listened patiently and responded promptly to our authoring crises and explanations for delays. We thank her for her gentle and persistent prodding, careful reviews, and continuing support. We also feel fortunate indeed to have worked with Donna Simons, Production Administrator at Allyn & Bacon, and Merrill Peterson, project manager at Matrix Productions. They managed to guide all stages of production expertly, keep track of our whereabouts, correct our errors, and provide us with strong support.

Our families also played a critical role in supporting us in our efforts. Our moms, Florence Cook and Mary Ellen Penovich, as always did the sorts of things that only wonderful moms can do—listened as we agonized over decisions and deadlines, consoled us when we were discouraged, and encouraged us to be realistic in reaching our goals. They offered to help however they could; we hope they know that just caring and being there was sometimes what we needed most. Thanks, Moms. Bruce Brandon (Marilyn's spouse) and Fred Weintraub (Lynne's spouse) deserve medals for their patience as we disappeared into our respective offices for hours on end, their willingness to help us frame our organization of the book, and their ability to help us keep a healthy perspective on the funny (but frustrating) parts of preparing the new edition of a textbook. We don't tell them often enough how much we appreciate the offers to cook and clean up, the reading of pages that are just not coming together, and the understanding that sometimes a walk is more important than a book chapter. They both also patiently tolerated our long phone conversations and our late-night faxes and e-mails. Thanks, Fred and Bruce—how could we have done this without you?

Marilyn Friend
Lynne Cook

Foreword

Even since the last edition of *Interactions,* the demands on educators, whatever their roles, to collaborate effectively have continued to increase. And few educational personnel have been prepared for this new educational way of life, a transition from the closed-door isolation of classroom and office to the communal school. A case in point is the increasing inclusion of students with disabilities in the general education classroom and the co-teaching that often accompanies this shifting placement trend. The collegial experience is fraught with both promise and danger depending on the quality of the collaboration. Another example is the pressure for accountability, which demands a new level of collaboration between school and family to insure students' educational progress and social development. The growing number of students from culturally and linguistically diverse families compels professionals to upgrade their skills in collaboration with parents. Thus, collaboration is moving away from being a helpful accompaniment to instructional and therapeutic skills: It is becoming the professional educator's most important skill to provide quality education; it even sometimes becomes a survival skill.

The fourth edition of *Interactions,* updated to reflect contemporary issues, is a guide for those who are engaged in the daunting task of building communities of learning. *Interactions* provides a road map of the essential concepts that special educators, general educators, speech/language therapists, administrators, psychologists, and others must have in order to work together effectively on behalf of students. Only by learning, practicing, and implementing the skills of collaboration can schools of this decade accomplish their mission. The increasing emphasis on accountability also requires additional emphasis on collaboration.

Educators who know what is happening in other fields recognize that the search for new ways of human exchange pervades the culture. Acknowledgment now exists that human beings must find new ways to interconnect if we are to survive. Espousing independence in lieu of collaboration is no longer an option. Mental health workers have accepted this as have juvenile justice personnel, social services providers, and public health educators. Families in poverty cannot be supported unless service providers work in concert to streamline procedures, make the most efficient use of funds, and employ the best available expertise. Schools are, of course, a central partner in this collaboration. As the authors make clear, collaboration goes beyond compromise and cooperation to shared understanding, meaning, decision making, and accountability for outcomes. It is a transformation replete with risks but also opportunities.

Because the authors continue to relate the collaboration enterprise to the foundations of individual and group psychology, infused with an ethical base, the book retains its vitality. They have not only read widely in the literature but also have evaluated the relevance of the research and applied the results to clarify particular issues. However, they also have addressed emerging developments in the study and implementation of collaborative practice. For example, they have devoted a full chapter to paraeducators, essential school personnel for whom collaboration can be a particularly complex endeavor. Likewise, this new edition focuses attention on parents and families, particularly those from diverse groups. These additions are reflective of their conviction that families are at the center of professionals' work on behalf of students.

The book continues to be user friendly and focused on practical applications. I am particularly pleased that Drs. Friend and Cook have maintained a high number and variety of examples in *Interactions*. These examples provide a means for novice and experienced practitioners alike to reflect on actual practice of effective collaboration. It is clear that these examples come from the authors' own continuing experience working in schools: Upon reading the examples the reader will probably say, "I have experienced that very situation!" A hallmark that distinguishes this book from others addressing the same topic, continuing from the very first edition, is an admirable blend of theory and practice. Readers at all levels are offered a clear grounding for the skills presented, but they are simultaneously provided applications that enable the immediate use even the next day at school. Theory-practice complementary coverage lends usefulness not only for self-study and staff development but also for undergraduate and graduate college classes.

Readers of *Interactions* also will find that it continues to address in a realistic manner the complexities of collaboration. The dilemmas caused by professionals' need for control, the sometimes hostile environment where collaboration is undertaken, and the paucity of time available for collaboration are recognized. The authors do not run away from these realities. Instead, they explicate the challenges so that they can be examined and addressed.

I applaud this fourth edition of *Interactions*. Given the increasing diversity of our students and our society, we need to strive for constructive partnerships that will assist in the goal of improving the lives of children. The challenge is to use the knowledge and skills presented in this book to transform the way we think about our work with others and to value what we accomplish together.

William C. Morse
Professor Emeritus
University of Michigan

1

The Fundamentals of Collaboration

Connections

Chapter 1 provides an overview of collaboration and lays the groundwork for all the subsequent chapters. In this chapter you will learn what collaboration is, why it can be challenging, and how it fits into broader societal and school contexts. You will also find out about a framework for studying collaboration that serves as the structure for this textbook.

Learner Objectives

After reading this chapter you will be able to:

1. Provide examples of formal and informal collaboration occurring in schools, as well as evidence of the growing importance of collaboration for professional educators.
2. Value collaboration as a tool for working in twenty-first-century schools.
3. Define collaboration and describe its critical characteristics.
4. Outline the place of collaboration from the perspectives of disciplines outside education, including business, health, and human services.
5. Describe the place of collaboration in current public school reform and other initiatives.
6. Explain how current special education legislation and policy fosters collaboration among professionals and between professionals and parents/families.
7. Describe a framework for studying collaboration.

INTRODUCTION

There was a time in education when highly trained teachers at all school levels and in all disciplines functioned largely on their own to educate the students assigned to them—instructing them, fostering their learning, and resolving academic and behavior problems as they arose. Only in extraordinary circumstances was professional advice sought from others. That era is over. Now general education teachers work in grade-level or interdisciplinary teaching teams with special education teachers, other classroom teachers, teaching assistants, reading specialists, speech/language therapists, and others. Special education teachers provide support to students in general education settings and interact closely with other professionals and parents/family members to ensure that students receive an appropriate education. Other professionals, including physical therapists, psychologists, social workers, and counselors, divide their time between traditional responsibilities and working with general and special education teachers.

Of all the many complex challenges facing schools in the early years of the twenty-first century, none is as demanding nor as critical as creating in education a culture of collaboration and ensuring that everyone who works there has the dispositions, knowledge, and skills to collaborate. Consider these examples of the many ways in which collaboration is emerging in education settings:

◆ Wednesday is a busy day for Ms. Maharrin. In addition to her daily teaching responsibilities and all the work that surrounds that most critical part of her job, she is a member of her school's leadership team, and so she has agreed to meet from 7:30–8:15 A.M. to discuss several issues, including the staff development plan for the next school year. At lunch, Ms. Maharrin has arranged to meet with Mr. Newby, the school psychologist, to design an intervention for the new student who is experiencing much frustration in the classroom. During her preparation period, Ms. Maharrin needs to call two parents and touch base with Mrs. Knox, the special education teacher. After school, she plans to meet with a colleague for instructional planning. At the end of the day Ms. Maharrin wryly thinks to herself that teaching her students seems to be the smallest part of her day on Wednesdays—an idea that she never would have imagined would be true when she entered the teaching profession 19 years ago.

◆ Mr. Mendez is a student support teacher (SST) at Hawthorne Middle School. Until last year, he was called a special education resource teacher, but his job title was changed to reflect his changed job responsibilities. Mr. Mendez begins each day meeting with his teammates, the four academic teachers with responsibility for the students on his caseload. Once classes begin at 7:50 A.M., he spends the morning co-teaching in English and math. During student lunch periods, he and several general education teachers help to staff a resource center where any student can receive academic assistance. In the afternoon, Mr. Mendez co-teaches in social studies and also provides special education instruction during an intensive study hall, his only opportunity to ensure that students have assignments started, home-work recorded, and test preparation completed. Mr. Mendez often notes that a large part of his job is public relations. He considers himself an advo-cate for students on his caseload, but he also knows that he influences teach-ers' thinking about students who are at risk. He encourages teachers to use adapted materials he prepares with any student who might benefit, and most do this. Mr. Mendez also tries to keep teachers apprised of the adaptations students are entitled to receive.

◆ Mrs. Penny is an inclusive practices consultant with responsibilities for stu-dents at Southside High School. Her job does not include directly teaching students unless it is to model a technique or demonstrate a strategy. With the help of two teaching assistants, she is responsible for the educational programs of 12 students with moderate or severe disabilities. She ensures that their teachers understand the students' needs, that communication systems are in place, that teaching assistants know what their responsibili-ties are, and that the vocational components of the students' educational programs are implemented successfully. Mrs. Penny usually has two or three meetings each day with teachers, parents, students, employers, representa-tives from various community agencies, and administrators. Sometimes she misses her direct work with students, but she often comments to others that her job is always a challenge and never boring.

Each of the professionals just described has adult-adult interactions as a signif-icant job responsibility. As a classroom teacher, Ms. Maharrin, whose primary re-sponsibility is instruction, also is expected to work with colleagues and parents. Mr. Mendez's position is so different from that of a traditional special education teacher that even his job title has changed. Most of his teaching occurs in partnership with general education teachers. Mrs. Penny's job probably would not even have existed until recently. However, with the growing recognition that students with significant disabilities can learn in typical classrooms, including in high school, the need for professionals to support students and teachers has grown. Taken together, these professional interactions illustrate three critical points for understanding the premise of this text.

First, collaboration has become an integral part of today's schools. In the past, educators who were not very effective in working with other adults were often ex-cused with a comment like this: "But she's really good with students." Although working effectively with students obviously is still the most important aspect of ed-ucators' jobs, it is not enough. Everyone in schools, including general education teachers, needs the knowledge and skills to work with colleagues, assistants, and parents. This is true in early childhood programs, in elementary schools, and in middle and high schools. It is true in schools that are still regarded as traditional in terms of programs and services as well as in those leading the way in educa-tional innovation.

Second, the examples of professionals' collaborative activities demonstrate that such interactions occur both formally and informally. School leader-ship teams, middle school teams, co-teaching, and consultative meetings are representative of the growth of formal structures and activities in schools that rely on collaboration for success. Meetings to respond to particular student needs and phone calls to parents are examples of informal collaboration. Both types of collaboration are important. However, informal collaboration often occurs whether or not a context for collaboration has been fostered and whether or not any formal structures needing collaboration are in place. Formal collaboration typically requires that strong leadership has ensured that a collaborative school culture—one that values collegial interactions—has been created.

Third, this text is based on the belief that collaboration is the common thread in the many innovations in schools. Collaboration is crucial as educators move to differentiate curriculum, meet standards of accountability for student achievement as measured through high-stakes testing, design local professional development plans, and address multicultural issues. Collaboration is also part of special education through intervention teams, multifactored assessments, IEP development, in-class service delivery approaches, and parent participation.

This book, then, is about effective interactions. It presents the generic concepts, principles, skills, and strategies that all school professionals can use to enhance their shared efforts to educate their students. Although many of the examples relate to special education, the information is not limited to those applications.

COLLABORATION CONCEPTS

The term *collaboration* has become something of an educational buzzword. One can easily get the sense that collaboration is viewed as the preferred approach in nearly any school situation. It is touted as the mechanism through which school reform can be accomplished (Pipho, 1997) and the instrument through which full-service schools can be created (Leonard & Leonard, 1999; Tourse & Mooney, 1999). Principals are admonished to use a collaborative leadership style (Chrispeels, Strait, & Brown, 1999), and teachers are encouraged to use collaboration to address diverse student needs (e.g., Howells, 2000; Krebs, 2000; Snell & Janney, 2000). Unfortunately, the term *collaboration* often is carelessly used and occasionally misapplied, as suggested in Figure 1.1.

Despite all the current discussion about collaboration, few clear definitions of it have been presented. In fact, some dictionary definitions of collaboration include reference to treason or working together for sinister purposes! In the human services, some authors have described the benefits of collaboration without defining it (e.g., Glickman, Gordon, & Ross-Gordon, 1998; Johnston, Brosnan, Cramer, & Dove, 2000; Scott & Smith, 1987), while others (e.g., Fishbaugh, 1997; Idol, Nevin, & Paolucci, 2000) have mistakenly treated collaboration as a synonym for other concepts, such as consultation, or failed to acknowledge the importance of precision in defining concepts as a prelude to effective school practice. Most authors include in their discussions of collaboration a sense of working together for mutual benefit, but since we firmly believe that a precise understanding of the term *collaboration* is far more than semantics, we begin by

Figure 1.1   Not everything people do together in schools is collaborative. . . .

carefully defining it. Knowing what collaboration is and is not and how it applies to school initiatives can help you to articulate your practices, set appropriate expectations for yourself, and positively influence others to interact collaboratively.

Definition

Given our commitment to presenting key concepts clearly, we begin our discussion of interpersonal collaboration with a technical definition that characterizes it as a unique concept:

> Interpersonal **collaboration** is a style for direct interaction between at least two coequal parties voluntarily engaged in shared decision making as they work toward a common goal.

Notice that we call collaboration a **style.** In the same way that writers use various styles to convey information to readers so, too, do individuals use interpersonal styles or approaches for their interactions with one another (Pugach & Johnson, 2002). Some professionals may choose to be directive when they interact; others may choose to be accommodative or facilitative; still others may choose to be collaborative. At first glance, referring to collaboration as a style may appear to detract from its significance by equating it to something ephemeral and seemingly lacking in substance. However, using this term enables you to distinguish the nature of the interpersonal relationship, that is, collaboration, occurring during shared interactions from the activities themselves, for example, teaming or problem solving.

As just implied, because collaboration is a style of interaction it cannot exist in isolation. It can only occur when it is used by people who are engaged in a specific process, task, or activity. To clarify this point, consider the following: If colleagues mentioned to you that they were collaborating, would you know what they were doing? Probably not. They could be collaboratively planning an educational program for a student with a disability, sharing the responsibilities for an academic lesson in a co-teaching arrangement, or planning a school social event. What the term *collaboration* conveys is *how* the activity is occurring, that is, the nature of the interpersonal relationship occurring during the interaction and the ways in which individuals communicate with each other.

Defining Characteristics for Collaboration

Considered alone, the definition we have presented only hints at the subtleties of collaboration. Through our writing (e.g., Cook & Friend, 1990b; Friend, 2000; Friend & Cook, 1990), our own ongoing collaboration, and our experience facilitating the collaboration of others, we have identified several elements of collaboration that we call **defining characteristics** since they more fully explain the basic definition.

Collaboration Is Voluntary

It is not possible to force people to use a particular style in their interactions with others. States may pass legislation, school districts may adopt policy, and site administrators may implement programs, but unless school professionals and their colleagues choose to collaborate, they will not do so. Perhaps the best illustration of this notion is the current trend for schools to mandate that professionals collaborate in designing and implementing programs for students with special needs in general education classes. If you are familiar with such a situation, you are probably also aware that some individuals are unwilling to collaborate, regardless of the mandate. For example, a professional may spend a significant amount of time complaining about the demands of teaching the student, time that could be spent collaboratively designing instruction that would help the student to succeed. If that professional attends meetings as required but undermines the special educator's efforts to support the student, he or she is not collaborating in the sense outlined in this chapter. The professional relationship is constrained, the student is still in the classroom, and the special educator bears the most responsibility for making adaptations. Alternatively, a professional unsure about inclusive practices can express anxiety and uncertainty, but that person may also work closely with others to support students with disabilities. In essence, education agencies can mandate administrative arrangements that require staff to work in close proximity, but only the individuals involved can decide if a collaborative style will be used in their interactions. In our work in schools, we frequently find ourselves emphasizing that there is no such thing as collaboration by coercion!

Does this mean that people *cannot* collaborate if programs are mandated? Not at all. Consider the situation at Harmony Middle School, where classroom teachers have been notified that they will probably need to increase collaboration to support the increased numbers of students with disabilities who will be

Collaboration can be challenging, but the benefits far outweigh the risks.

attending their school during the next two years. An eighth-grade science teacher may say, "I think there may be possibilities for student success in my classes, but I'm not sure about this. I'm glad I'll have another teacher to work with as we try to make this work." The mandate is present, but so is the teacher's voluntariness to carry out the mandate, even though others may be voicing objections to it or ignoring it.

Collaboration Requires Parity among Participants

Parity is a situation in which each person's contribution to an interaction is equally valued, and each person has equal power in decision making. If one or several individuals are perceived by others as having significantly greater decision-making power or more valuable knowledge or information, collaboration cannot occur. To illustrate, think about a principal's participation on a multidisciplinary team. If the principal is considered to have equal, not disproportionately greater, power in the decision-making process, other team members may disagree with the principal's position, and the team's ultimate decision may be one the principal did not support. Without parity, it is likely that some team members will acquiesce to the principal's preferences because of concern about repercussions for disagreeing. Another example can provide further illustration: In an interdisciplinary teaching team, when one content-area (e.g., biology) teacher believes that another (e.g., English) does not have expertise to contribute to the instructional planning, parity is unlikely to develop.

It is important to understand that individuals may have parity as they work together on a specific collaborative activity even though they do not have parity in other situations. For example, you may have parity in interactions with a paraprofessional to plan a community-based activity, but may interact directively and with appropriately greater authority and decision-making power when giving instructions to the same paraprofessional about working with students. Similarly, administrators and staff on a curriculum committee may have parity; outside of the committee, though, the relationship among the members may be markedly different.

Collaboration Is Based on Mutual Goals

Individuals who collaborate must share at least one goal. Imagine a meeting at which a decision must be reached about what specialized services a student should receive and the setting in which those services should be delivered. In one sense, the mutual goal of designing an appropriate education program seems to be obvious. In reality, however, there may be at least two goals present. The parents, social worker, and principal might think that the student should be in a general education setting for most of the day, whereas the special education teacher, classroom teacher, and psychologist might believe, because of professional literature they have read, that great care needs to be taken before there is any discussion of inclusion. In this case, a collaborative group will look at the greater goal of designing a program in the best interests of the student and will resolve their differences. In a group without a strong commitment to collaboration, the focus is likely to remain on the apparently disparate goals, and the matter is likely to become contentious.

Professionals do not have to share many or all goals in order to collaborate, just one that is specific and important enough to maintain their shared commitment. They may differ in their opinions about a student's achievement potential, but share the goal of arranging convenient transportation for the student. Their differences can be set aside as not being essential to the immediate issue. They may agree that a student with multiple needs coming to the school should spend most of the school day with typical peers, but disagree about who should have primary teaching responsibility for the student and how appropriate supports should be arranged.

Collaboration Depends on Shared Responsibility for Participation and Decision Making

If you collaborate with a colleague, you are assuming the responsibility of actively engaging in the activity and the decision making it involves. We have found it useful to distinguish between responsibility for completing tasks associated with the collaborative activity and responsibility for the decision making involved in that activity. Shared participation in task completion does *not* imply that the individuals involved must divide tasks equally or participate fully in each task required to achieve their goal. In fact, participation in the activity often involves a convenient division of labor. For instance, as a speech and language therapist you might collaborate with a kindergarten teacher to plan a series of language lessons for all the students. You volunteer to outline the concepts that should be addressed and to prepare several activities related to each. The teacher agrees to locate needed materials and to plan student groupings and instructional schedules for

PERSPECTIVES ON DIVERSITY 1.1

Myths That Prevent Collaboration across Cultures

- **Simply by virtue of membership in a cultural group, a person will be able to deal with others of that population in a culturally competent way. Not true.**
  If such persons have assimilated the values and communication styles of the Anglo culture as their own, they may be even less tolerant of traditional values or styles than Anglos. Equally important, they may not be trusted by their own communities if they have internalized Anglo values.

- **A member of a minority community who works in a mainstream agency is able to represent his or her community. Not true.**
  Unless they are respected leaders within their communities, they are not considered by their communities to be appropriate representatives. Respected elders often provide leadership within ethnic communities. However, the elders often have no role of visibility or authority within the Anglo culture and must be "found." In order to have an effective relationship with the ethnic community, trust and respect from the elders must be gained first.

- **A single member of "the" minority community can represent the whole. Not true.**
  For example, there really is no "Hispanic community" in most cities. There are, rather, Hispanic communi*ties*. Individuals from Puerto Rico, Mexico, Spain, and Peru, for example, would not consider themselves to be from the "same" community. We speak of the African American community, the Hispanic community, the Asian community, and the Native American community, when there really are no such communities.

- **The Anglo or dominant culture is *the* U.S. culture, not simply *a* culture. Not true.**
  This is one of the most difficult myths, not from a logical point of view, but because of invisible assumptions and expectations. For most people reared as Anglo Americans, Anglo American assumptions and expectations are presumed, unconsciously, to be "human" assumptions and expectations. If we see someone speaking with a certain pitch of voice and making certain gestures, we assume that the person is agitated or angry; we rarely conceive the thought that we might be misinterpreting their behavior because of our own cultural norms. If someone else seems indifferent to a suggestion, again, we think that we understand what we see. Our culturally based assumptions and interpretations are so completely ingrained that we experience them spontaneously—and invisibly.
  Members of all cultures tend to internalize and become consciously unaware of their own norms. For members of a dominant group in a culture this condition is exaggerated; they are usually surrounded by people and institutions based on their set of values. Thus that system is constantly

(continued)

ney have less exposure to contrasting values and behaviors
rs of minority groups.

**:ence is something we each pick up, with time, by working with
e different from ourselves. Not true.**

npetence is a skill, and perhaps an ability that requires sub-
rt to learn. Working with someone from a different ethnic tra-
s not necessarily lead to uncovering differences in expectations,
cation styles, and values. An analogy is that of a married couple
lived together 50 years or more. Even they can fail to learn each
underlying assumptions, expectations, and communication styles.
Instead of learning these invisible differences, they develop a reliable and
consistent misinterpretation, which leads to *predictability* in the relationship,
not understanding.

From Elliott, C. Adams, R. J., & Sockalingam, S. (1999). *Ten myths that prevent collaboration.* [Available
online: www.awesomelibrary.org/multiculturaltoolkit-myths.html]. Retrieved November 27, 2001.

the lessons. In this case, you and the teacher are both actively participating in accomplishing the task, even though the division of labor may not be equal.

The second component of responsibility concerns *equal* participation in the
critical decision making involved in the activity. In the example just described,
you and the teacher had different responsibilities for the task, but to be collaborative you must participate equally in deciding the appropriateness of and possible needed modifications in the material you prepare, and you are equally
responsible for deciding if the grouping and proposed schedule are workable.

Individuals Who Collaborate Share Resources

It should be a given that each individual engaged in a collaborative activity has
resources to contribute that are valuable for reaching the shared goal. The type
of resources professionals have depends on their roles and the specific activity.
Time and availability to carry out essential tasks may be the critical contribution
that one person offers. Knowledge of a specialized technique may be another's
resource. Access to other individuals or agencies that could assist in the collaborative activity may be a third person's contribution. If professionals cannot contribute a specific resource, they may be perceived as less serious about the
collaborative goal, and they may encounter difficulty establishing parity.

For a different type of situation in which resources are shared, think of working with parents. For example, sharing resources often occurs when parents and
school professionals collaboratively plan home reward programs for students.
The parent is likely to have access to rewards to which the student responds (e.g.,
video games, computer access, special meals, access to a bicycle or car). The special services providers may be able to recommend the number of positive behaviors the student should display, the frequency of rewards, and the plan for

systematically phasing out the rewards once success has been achieved. The program would not be possible without the contributions that everyone makes.

You may have found that sharing resources is sometimes the key motivator for individuals to collaborate. In fact, pooling the available—but too-often scarce—resources in schools can lead to tremendously satisfying efforts on behalf of students; at the same time, it enhances the sense of ownership among the professionals. Unfortunately, the reverse may also occur: A scarcity of resources sometimes causes people to hoard the ones they control. Collaboration becomes unlikely when that happens. Ultimately, when resources are limited, the choice becomes this: Fall together through collaboration and make the best of what is available, or fall apart as individuals compete to obtain resources that may even be inconsequential in terms of value.

Individuals Who Collaborate Share Accountability for Outcomes

Whether the results of collaboration are positive or negative, all the participating individuals are accountable for the outcome. Suppose you and several colleagues plan a parent information meeting. One person arranges for a room, another orders coffee, and a third reserves a video and projector for the presentation. Shortly before the meeting is to begin, you realize that no one has remembered to pick up the video. In a collaborative effort, all the professionals share the resulting need to change the program at the last minute or to arrange to have someone dash to retrieve the video. Similarly, if a school leadership team is meeting to discuss the results of the evaluation data collected but one member has not finished compiling the results, the team is accountable for re-setting the meeting date or for assisting the member aggregating the information.

Emergent Characteristics

Several characteristics of collaboration can have multiple functions—they are mentioned both as prerequisites for as well as outcomes of collaboration. We refer to these as **emergent characteristics** (Cook & Friend, 1990a). These characteristics must be present to some discernible degree at the outset of collaborative activity, but they typically grow and flourish from successful experience with collaboration.

Individuals Who Collaborate Value This Interpersonal Style

Collaboration is difficult but rewarding. Professionals who anticipate collaborating must believe that the results of their collaboration are likely to be more powerful and significant than the results of their individual efforts, or else they are unlikely to persevere. Typically, success in collaboration leads to increased commitment to future collaboration, and so beliefs and attitudes become increasingly positive. As a former graduate student once reported, "I used to work in a school where there was no collaboration. I worked very hard, but it was like beating my head against a wall. Now I work in a place where collaboration is the

PUTTING IDEAS INTO PRACTICE 1.1

Creating a Collaborative Culture

To what extent does your school have a collaborative culture? That is, to what extent are teachers encouraged to work collegially—by grade levels, instructional teams, teaching teams, and so on? Does collaboration extend to all school staff members, including related services providers, bilingual educators, and paraprofessionals? If you are trying to enhance the collaborative culture of your school, these activities could help to build a strong foundation for it:

1. Work with your administrator or school leadership to periodically schedule social activities for school staff. Friday morning treats that everyone gathers to share in the teachers' lounge, quarterly pitch-in lunches, or even occasional evening or weekend gatherings at someone's home or another location are examples of social events that encourage individuals to get to know each other better, thus laying the foundation for professional collaboration.

2. Try having professionals trade jobs for short periods of time so that everyone builds their understanding of each other's roles and responsibilities. For example, a special educator might teach the eighth-grade English class while that teacher co-teaches the science class in which the special educator normally would be. This strategy often leads staff members to comment to one another, "Gee, you really work hard!" The increase in respect contributes to strong collaboration.

3. Suggest to your administrator or school leadership team that optional study groups be formed at school. Perhaps one group could address the general topic of collaboration while others find reading material on and discuss co-teaching, teaming, communication, and other pertinent topics. These groups could meet at lunch or before or after school, with the goal of clarifying ideas and looking for new strategies. The groups could then update other staff members by sending brief summary e-mail messages to the entire staff.

norm. I work even harder than I used to, but now it's fun." Individuals who collaborate truly believe that two heads are better than one.

Professionals Who Collaborate Trust One Another

Even if you firmly believe in the beneficial outcomes of collaboration, you cannot suddenly introduce it, fully developed, into your professional interactions. If you recall your experiences as a new employee of a school district or agency, you probably remember experiencing a phase in which you learned about your colleagues, the norms of the school setting, and the manner in which to approach the other professionals with whom you worked most closely. And even though you interacted with other professionals during that time, the extent to which you could collaborate was limited. Only after a period of time in which trust, and subsequently respect, are established can school professionals feel relatively secure in fully exploring collaborative relationships. Once begun, however, those relationships may be strengthened until trust of colleagues becomes one of the most important benefits of collaboration. This scenario describes the emergence of trust: At the outset, enough trust must be present for professionals to be willing to begin the activity, but with successful experiences the trust grows. Conversely, trust is most fragile when a collaborative relationship is relatively new. If a colleague violates a shared confidence, fails to contribute to the activity, or communicates inaccurately, trust is likely to be damaged.

A Sense of Community Evolves from Collaboration

In collaboration, participants know that their strengths can be maximized, their weaknesses can be minimized, and the result will be better for all. The concept of community is receiving significant attention in contemporary professional literature (e.g., John-Steiner, 2000; Kronick, 2000; Lawson, 1999; Wineburg & Grossman, 1998). What is increasingly recognized is that the development of a sense of professional community leads to better outcomes for students and satisfaction and support for educators. Perhaps you have experienced the sense of community in a church, social, or student group. The willingness to work toward a common goal is accompanied by a decrease in concern about individual differences.

Taken together, these emergent characteristics highlight the opportunities you have and the risks you take when you begin to collaborate. You may attempt to establish trust and either succeed or be rebuffed; you may attempt to communicate an attitude supportive of collaboration and find that some but not others share your beliefs. Collaboration is certainly not easily accomplished, nor is it appropriate for every situation. More than anything, the emergent characteristics capture the powerful benefits of accepting the risks of collaboration. When collaborative efforts result in higher levels of trust and respect among colleagues, and working together results in more positive outcomes for both students and professionals, the risks seem minor compared to the rewards.

The Dilemmas of Collaboration

Exploring the definition and characteristics of collaboration can lead to the impression that collaboration is unequivocally the best way to approach today's complex educational problems. However, a number of issues arise when school professionals attempt to establish collaborative relationships. These issues pertain to school structure, professional socialization, and logistics.

School Structure

It has long been recognized that professionals in schools typically do their substantive work in isolation from others (e.g., Goodlad, 1984; Lortie, 1975; Sarason, 1982), and this recognition and concern about its implications for the teaching profession continue even today (Mitchell, 1997). This structure of

PUTTING IDEAS INTO PRACTICE 1.2

Internet Resources for Collaboration

As most professionals know, the Internet is a tremendous source of information on almost any topic. Although only a few sites specifically address the professional collaboration that occurs among school staff members, the following sites include collaboration and pertinent related topics:

www.nichcy.org

The National Information Center for Children and Youth with Disabilities website contains extensive information on many topics related to educating students with disabilities. The information, intended primarily for lay audiences, is straightforward and addresses many common questions, including those related to inclusive practices and collaboration.

www.ldonline.org/ld indepth/add adhd/tec home school collab.html

LD OnLine is a website dedicated to information about learning disabilities for parents, teachers, and students. Included on the site are many ideas for collaboration, particularly between parents and teachers as they work to meet the needs of students with learning disability.

www.air.org/cecp

The Center for Effective Collaboration and Practice exists for the purpose of improving services to children and youth with emotional disabilities. It received federal funding, and the website contains links to many other organization and agency websites that provide valuable information. The site also includes interactive discussion forums.

http://teachnet.edb.utexas.edu/~lynda_abbot/teacher2teacher.html

Teacher-to-Teacher Collaboration is a website sponsored by the University of Texas. It includes links to sites that focus on assisting teachers to connect with and interact with one another. It also includes information about professional development and relevant site links for that topic.

Other suggestions: As you seek information related to collaboration and related topics, don't forget to check your own state department of education's website. Many have information that is practical and directly related to state policies and also have links to other local sites.

physical isolation is contrary to the concept of collaboration, and its drawbacks are becoming clearer even as the pressure to create schools with a collaborative culture mounts. Within this physical isolation from other adults, each school professional sets about working with students. How do they accomplish this? Essentially, they take charge. In their classrooms or offices, they are the experts who hold authority and power over students, and so they typically use a directive style to promote student learning, which is appropriate. However, constant use of this style with students may interfere with professionals' ability to switch to a collaborative style for interactions with colleagues and parents.

Professional Socialization

Physical isolation and the use of a directive style with students are part of what contributes to the wide variation in emphasis in schools on collegial relationships. However, a norm of isolation sometimes is still fostered through professional socialization. First, in some teacher and other professional preparation programs, you might discover that as you are successfully completing your student teaching, practicum, or internship experiences, your supervisor leaves you alone to work with students. In other words, your professional training itself might encourage a belief that working in isolation is the role of the professional.

Second, this socialization of isolation may continue as you enter your profession and gain experience. Even for some teachers who participated in collaborative preparation programs, school cultures of independence or self-reliance are so strong that what evolves is a belief that you should handle your professional problems yourself. If you seek help, it is often only after you have decided that whatever is occurring is no longer your problem; your goal becomes seeking another to take ownership of it.

This discussion of structural isolation and individual characteristics of professionals in schools may leave the impression that collaboration is seldom likely in school settings. That certainly is not always the case. In fact, we find that school collaboration is gradually increasing. We mention the issue of structural isolation only to raise your awareness of the difficulties in collaborating and to stress that even if you have learned about the importance of collaboration and embrace its value, you may work with colleagues who do not. We also want to convey some of the resulting challenges that you will undoubtedly experience as you attempt to collaborate. These challenges are not unique to your specific school setting or professional relationships; they result from many factors that are part of all school professionals' experiences. Ultimately, these dilemmas provide the rationale for exploring the skills described later in the text because it is those skills that can enable school professionals to complement their other professional skills with collaborative ones.

Pragmatic Issues

When we described the defining characteristics of collaboration, we noted that resource sharing is essential, and we mentioned resources such as time, space, and materials. We consider the topic of pragmatic issues further in Chapter 13 with the extensive attention they merit; we mention the topic here just to acknowledge that pragmatic issues are another type of dilemma facing those who collaborate.

This discussion of the dilemmas that school structure, professional socialization, and pragmatic issues present for collaboration could have a somewhat sobering effect on your enthusiasm for it. In part, we hope this is so. Collaboration can be a powerful vehicle for accomplishing professionals' goals of educating students, but we believe it can also be overused and misused. Collaborative efforts should be implemented only with a realistic understanding of their complexities and difficulties, because such understanding will lead to careful consideration of the extent to which collaborative efforts are feasible and recommended.

COLLABORATION IN A CONTEMPORARY CONTEXT

How has collaboration come to be so important in special education that it is the subject of entire books and courses in professional preparation programs? What is fostering the development of so many collaborative structures in schools? Why is so much attention now devoted to the quality of the working relationships among professionals, paraprofessionals, and parents/families? What is occurring for students with special needs is simply a reflection of the direction of many endeavors in our society and their application in education (Cook & Friend, 1991). By examining the larger context for collaboration, you can better understand its prevasiveness in today's world and its necessity for today's schools.

Societal Trends

Consider the world in which we now live. A valuable starting point is the arena of work: The vast majority of jobs available at the beginning of the twenty-first century are in service industries in which individuals interact with clients or customers to meet their needs (e.g., retail sales, telecommunications). This is a sharp contrast to preceding eras in which many workers toiled in isolation on assembly lines. Contemporary life also is characterized by an accelerated flow of information: People are inundated with it, whether through the Internet, the deluge of advertising that arrives each day, the seemingly endless array of television talk shows, or the stacks of publications that pile up, usually unread, in many homes, offices, and classrooms. Few individuals can hope to keep up with even the most crucial events occurring in their communities and their professions, much less throughout the world. Headline news programs and online summaries often have to suffice.

One response to the pressures of contemporary society's changing labor needs and its information explosion is an increasing reliance on collaboration (Nelson, 2001). For example, business managers, much more so now than in the past, are involving employees in decision making as a strategy for improving organizational effectiveness. Furthermore, employees report they find their jobs more satisfying if they participate in reaching decisions. Researchers agree that a sense of ownership and commitment appears to evolve through participation in such activity, and cutting-edge employers target team approaches that foster shared decision making as a major training topic for employees at many levels

Collaboration has become common in most fields, including business, health care, and social services.

(Bassi & Van Buren, 1999; Medved, 2001). All of these ideas, coming not from education but from business and industry, are directly related to collaboration.

Business is not the only domain in which collaboration is essential. In fact, collaboration seems to have become a standard for all that is worthwhile in contemporary professional culture. For example, Bennis and Biederman (1997), in their examination of the most significant innovations of the twentieth century, including the personal computer, aviation technology, and feature-length animated films, concluded that none of them would have been possible if not for a high degree of collaboration among very talented people. Huxham (1996) contends that collaboration is becoming an expected approach for professional interactions throughout the world, whether undertaken voluntarily by parties in a multinational business deal or mandated by political leaders. A cursory look at collaboration on the Internet raises the topic for fields as diverse as meteorology, interior design, physics, and business management.

Collaboration also has become increasingly important in the human services. For example, it is viewed as a means through which welfare, mental health, and other services can be more effectively provided to children and their families (Briggs, 1999; Marans, Berkowitz, & Cohen, 1998) as well as to the elderly (Simmons, Ivry, & Seltzer, 1985). In health care, collaboration is a means for bringing together medical and health care providers to integrate the delivery of services (Sullivan, 1998), a means of increasing the community's health (Institute of Medicine, 1996), a means of improving public health agency performance (Lovelace, 2000), a means of improving services in intensive care (Baggs, Ryan, Phelps, Richeson, & Johnson, 1992), and a means of working with families (Widrick et al., 1991).

School Collaboration

If we begin with the premise that schools are a reflection of larger society, the current trend toward collaboration in our nation and around the world makes it quickly apparent why collaboration is such a significant trend in schools. Many examples of the trend are evident. For example, teachers are being asked to team with each other and with other school professionals, including media specialists, science consultants, and speech/language therapists (Bishop & Larimer, 1999; Gentry & Ferriss, 1999; Hadley, Simmerman, Long, & Luna, 2000; Kew, 2000). In all these efforts, the goal is to provide enhanced instruction to improve student learning, particularly in urban and rural areas. Middle-school approaches are an especially interesting application of teacher-teacher collaboration (e.g., Park, 1999; Sparapani & Norwood, 1997) because they are premised on strong collaboration among teaching teams in core academic areas. Teachers in middle schools have regularly scheduled shared planning time so that they can integrate curricula, coordinate assignments and other major activities such as field trips, and discuss issues related to their shared students.

A second type of collaboration emphasized in the general school literature concerns school-university partnerships, often under the guise of school reform (Kersh & Masztal, 1998). One common example of partnership for preprofessional preparation is a professional development school (PDS) model (Johnston et al., 2000; Walker, 1999) in which university faculty members work in school settings and school professionals serve as instructors in a highly collaborative manner to prepare future teachers. However, other partnerships also have formed, including the use of distance education in science instruction (Trentin & Gibelli,

Collaboration occurs both formally and informally among school professionals.

1998), the creation of high school–community college dual enrollment programs (Gomez, 2001), and the development of specialized programs to meet the needs of at-risk learners (DiSibio & Gamble, 1997).

A third type of general school collaboration receiving renewed attention is peer collaboration. Researchers are finding that when students work with partners on various instructional tasks, they generally learn more than if they had worked alone (e.g., Samaha & DeLisi, 2000). Further, professionals have come to value peer interactions as a means of preparing students for their likely roles in the world of work (e.g., Van Meter & Stevens, 2000).

Finally, collaboration has not been ignored by school administrators. Principals are forming school leadership teams, collegial work groups to share decision making on critical school issues (Wesson & Kudlacz, 2000). They also are working collaboratively with teachers to help them set professional goals for each year and to make judgments about the quality of their performance (Sparks, 1997). They are emphasizing that teachers work with each other to solve problems about students experiencing difficulty, to establish and assess academic standards, and to create positive working relationships with parents. School as a collaborative community of learners is now a consistent theme for administrators (Lehr, 1999; Niebuhr & Niebuhr 1999; Sergiovanni, 1994).

Special Education Collaboration

Although special education collaboration might be considered a subset of school collaboration, it has become so much a part of policy and practice that it merits separate attention. In fact, IDEA has, in essence, made collaboration a required part of special education services. As shown in Figure 1.2, collaboration is either specifically mandated or strongly implied in the entire process of identifying students who receive special services, in delivering of their instruction, and in interacting with parents.

Unfortunately, considerable confusion has accompanied the evolution of collaboration in special education, especially since the increasing adoption of inclusive practices. For example, in some schools the terms *collaboration* and *inclusion* are used interchangeably. In others, collaboration is considered a way to deliver services, often confused with co-teaching, a service delivery approach that is discussed in detail in Chapter 8. Figure 1.2 outlines several terms associated with current special education practice and their appropriate applications.

A discussion of special education collaboration would not be complete without mention of early childhood programs, where collaboration is generally integral. For example, early intervention services are based on the beliefs that parents or other caregivers are the primary teachers of young children and that professionals can foster their participation through collaboration. Further, early intervention programs are mandated to coordinate services among all providers (e.g., educators, social service agencies, medical professionals), and this mandate exists within a context of collaboration (Dinnebeil, Hale, & Rule, 1999; Fowler, Donegan, Lueke, Hadden, & Phillips, 2000). Although you will learn more about collaboration in early childhood special education in Chapter 12,

---

Figure 1.2   Collaboration Expectations within IDEA

◆ **General education teachers**

At least one general education teacher must participate on the IEP team if the student has any general education involvement. This provision makes general education teachers integral to the team of professionals who design and implement special services.

◆ **Least restrictive environment**

The law presumes that students should receive education in a general education setting, and it requires justification for any placement that is not general education. This presumption strongly suggests that classroom teachers and special educators will need to work together on behalf of students

◆ **Assessment process**

Parent roles in the assessment process have been clarified; initial parent permission for assessment does not constitute permission for possible special education placement. This process requires ongoing communication between school professionals and parents. Even more communication responsibility occurs when students are reevaluated: Since a decision may be made in some cases to omit standardized testing, parent involvement in decision making is even more critical.

◆ **Transition**

Because transition must be addressed for students beginning at age 14, strong collaboration is necessary and should involve students as well as parents. Further, transition plans often require the involvement of professionals from other agencies, and so interprofessional collaboration may be required.

◆ **Discipline and behavior support plans**

For any student with behavior problems, a functional assessment and behavior support plan is required. The process of gathering data, identifying the problem, designing alternative interventions, implementing them, and evaluating the outcomes typically will include participation by several professionals, paraprofessionals, and parents/family members.

◆ **Paraprofessionals**

Paraprofessionals, teaching assistants, and other individuals in similar roles should receive appropriate training for their jobs and supervision of their work. Although not all interactions with paraprofessionals may be collaborative, the specific expectation for teacher-paraprofessional interactions can foster collaboration.

◆ **Mediation**

Unless declined by parents, states must make no-cost mediation available to parents as a strategy for resolving disagreements concerning their children with special needs. The implication is that a strong bias exists toward all parties, working together on behalf of students, to design the most appropriate education rather than escalating conflicts.

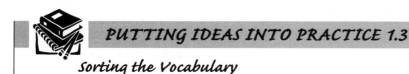

PUTTING IDEAS INTO PRACTICE 1.3

Sorting the Vocabulary

The number of terms associated with the field of special education can be overwhelming. When terms are used inconsistently, or even interchangeably, confusion can easily result, and services for students can suffer. You may encounter the following three groups of terms in your collaborative work. Are there other terms you would add to the list? Where would you place them?

Program Beliefs	Service Delivery Options	Instructional Strategies
Least restrictive environment	Intervention assistance teams	Peer tutoring
Integration	Co-teaching	Adaptive instruction
Mainstreaming	Consultation	Modified curriculum
Inclusion		

for now you should realize that many professionals point to this area when seeking exemplary practices in school collaboration.

A FRAMEWORK FOR LEARNING ABOUT COLLABORATION

The importance of collaboration in society, schools, and special education forms a rationale for focusing on the study of it. The complexity and subtlety of collaboration (Friend, 2000) suggest that in order to learn to form effective partnerships with others, you should strive for as complete an understanding of collaboration as possible. To accomplish this purpose, we offer a framework for learning about collaboration (Figure 1.3) that presents the components of collaboration and their relationships to one another. It is this framework that shapes the material presented in this textbook as well as its organization.

The first component of the study of collaboration concerns your *personal commitment* to collaboration as a tool for carrying out the responsibilities of your job, including your beliefs about the benefits of working closely with colleagues and parents/families and the added value of learning from others' perspectives. Although it is difficult to offer specific skills training related to this commitment and no chapter is devoted solely to this component of collaboration, you will find that throughout this textbook you will be asked to reflect on the importance of and merit in collaborating with others.

The second component of collaboration comprises *communication skills,* the basic building blocks of collaborative interactions. Although most educators

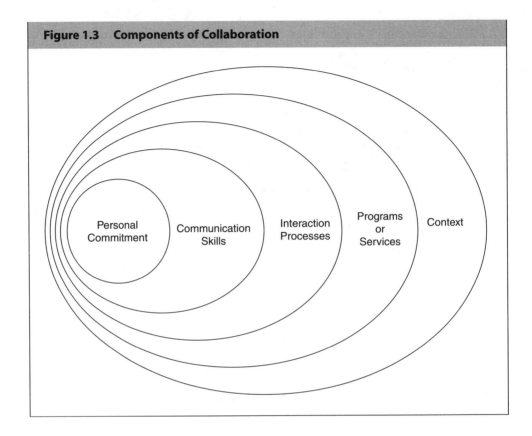

Figure 1.3   Components of Collaboration

Personal Commitment · Communication Skills · Interaction Processes · Programs or Services · Context

have relatively strong communication skills in order to be in their professions, the skills needed for collaboration are somewhat more technical and are best learned with extended practice. For this reason, Chapters 2, 3, and 4 outline those skills, provide many examples of their uses (and misuses), and offer opportunity to practice them. The assumption is that you will continue to refine these skills as other topics are explored in later chapters.

The third component of collaboration includes *interaction processes,* that is, the steps that take an interaction from beginning to end. The most common interaction process is problem solving, and that topic is addressed in Chapter 5. Other processes include responding to conflict and resistance, topics addressed in Chapter 11. For all interaction processes, strong communication skills are essential.

The fourth component of collaboration is the set of *programs* or *services* in which collaborative activities occur. For this textbook, the services emphasized include teaming (Chapter 6), consultation (Chapter 7), and co-teaching (Chapter 8). It is within these services that interaction processes to design and deliver student services occur.

The final component of collaboration is *context*. Context refers to the overall environment in which collaboration occurs. Because people are so often critical in determining the climate for collaboration, special attention is given in this book to parents, paraprofessionals, and others (e.g., related services personnel and administrators) in Chapters 9, 10, and 11. Pragmatic issues (Chapter 13) and issues related to collaboration (Chapter 12) complete this part of the framework.

As with any textbook, some topics cannot be adequately addressed. For example, although mention is made of peer collaboration, the emphasis here is on adult–adult interactions, and so student partnerships are not prioritized. Likewise, even though professionals often collaborate around designing and implementing academic and behavior interventions for students, those topics merit separate attention; we believe that attempting to address collaboration as well as instructional strategies in one textbook does a disservice to both.

SUMMARY

Collaboration is an interpersonal style that professionals often use in their interactions with colleagues, parents, and others. It can only exist voluntarily in situations in which individuals with parity have identified a mutual goal and are willing to share responsibilities, resources, and accountability. Several characteristics of collaboration both contribute to its development and are potentially its outcomes: attitudes and beliefs supportive of a collaborative approach, mutual trust, and a sense of community. However, individuals who collaborate may also find that dilemmas occur related to the structural and professional isolation of schools, professional socialization, and practical matters concerning resources such as time. Collaboration in the realm of special services is critical as a reflection of societal trends that are, in turn, being mirrored in schools through reform efforts and special education trends such as inclusion. Studying collaboration includes understanding your personal commitment, learning communication skills and interaction processes, creating programs and services in which collaborative approaches can be used, and recognizing context factors that foster or constrain collaboration.

ACTIVITIES AND ASSIGNMENTS

1. Peruse recent issues of popular news magazines. What examples of societal collaboration are addressed? What universal themes can you identify related to the advantages and disadvantages of collaboration from these materials?

2. How is collaboration being addressed in other university coursework you are taking? What collaborative activities (e.g., teaming, consultation) are most emphasized? If you have a colleague in a business program, compare your

experiences, courses, and learning requirements on topics related to collaboration. How are they similar? How are they different?

3. In your professional setting, identify two different situations in which you work with one or more other professionals to provide services to a student with special needs. Select one in which you believe collaboration is possible and one in which collaboration is unlikely. Complete an analysis of the extent to which the defining characteristics of collaboration are present or could be established in each situation. Which characteristics can most easily be met? Which may pose significant barriers to developing effective collaborative relationships?

4. Discuss the following question with colleagues: How should a professional respond when all the individuals on a team are attempting to collaborate, but one individual undermines their attempts?

5. Discuss the issue of parity with a group of classroom teachers. To what extent do they perceive that they have equal status with special services providers? How could issues related to parity be addressed? Repeat your discussion of parity with others who have roles similar to yours. How do their views about teachers' and special services providers' parity compare to those of the classroom teachers?

6. Suppose you are a new special education teacher in a school in which collaboration occurs informally among some teachers, but is not a highly valued part of the school's culture. Further, imagine that the school has received a mandate to move strongly toward inclusive practices. As a special educator, what do you believe your role is in accomplishing the dual goals of collaboration and inclusive practices? How might you use Figure 1.3 to analyze the steps that should be taken and to discuss them with your administrator?

7. If you have worked in a setting in which collaboration was valued and encouraged, write a summary of your experience. Use this as the basis for a discussion with others to generate specific examples of the characteristics of collaboration.

8. Complete an analysis of your preparation for school collaboration. On one sheet of paper, list courses, experiences, and activities you have had that have contributed to your professional socialization *for* working collaboratively. On another sheet, list the courses, experiences, and activities you have had that could *interfere* with a positive belief about collaboration. Write a reflective essay in which you assess your readiness for this crucial dimension of your professional responsibilities.

FOR FURTHER READING

Adkins, A., Awsumb, C., Noblit, G. W., & Richards, P. L. (1999). *Working together? Grounded perspectives on interagency collaboration.* Cresskill, NJ: Hampton Press.

Bennis, W., & Biederman, P. W. (1997). *Organizing genius: The secrets of creative collaboration.* Reading, MA: Addison Wesley.

Burrello, L. C., Lashley, C., & Beatty, E. E. (2001). *Educating all students together: How school leaders create unified systems.* Thousand Oaks, CA: Corwin Press.

Fishbaugh, M. S. E. (2000). *The collaboration guide for early career educators.* Baltimore: Brookes.

Friend, M., & Bursuck, W. (2002). *Including students with special needs: A practical guide for classroom teachers* (3rd ed.). Boston: Allyn & Bacon.

Johnston, M., Brosnan, P., Cramer, D., & Dove, T. (Eds.). (2000). *Collaborative reform and other improbable dreams.* Albany: State University of New York Press.

Kronick, R. F. (2000). *Human services and the full service school: The need for collaboration.* Springfield, IL: Thomas.

2

Interpersonal Communication

Connections

Regardless of the setting or structure, collaboration depends on effective interaction among those involved. Chapter 2 begins a discussion of communication skills necessary for effective interaction and provides a framework for the specific skills presented in Chapters 3 and 4. Together, these three chapters provide the foundation for engaging in interpersonal problem solving as described in Chapter 5 and its use in consultation, teaming, and co-teaching. This chapter examines how interpersonal communication occurs. We identify skills that are prerequisite to effective interactions, consider factors that affect listening, examine the impact of nonverbal communication, and outline principles for effective communication.

Learner Objectives

After reading this chapter you will be able to:

1. Identify the attributes and concepts common to most models of interpersonal communication.
2. Define *frame of reference* and apply it in listening to others.
3. Define *listening* as a skill and describe strategies to enhance listening.
4. Identify and give examples of four types of nonverbal cues and describe how they affect communication.
5. Describe the principles of effective verbal and nonverbal communication.

INTRODUCTION

Effective communication is essential to nearly all aspects of your professional success. The skills of effective communication are critical in the performance of your instructional, administrative, planning, or other intervention responsibilities, as well as in your collaboration with colleagues and parents. To that end, many professional preparation programs and performance reviews include an assessment of communication skills, and increasingly, certification and licensure in education and allied professions require similar evidence of strong ability to communicate.

MODELS OF COMMUNICATION

Human communication has been conceptualized in a variety of ways. However, because no single communication model is universally accepted, we will consider some conceptual elements that are common to most and clarify the interactional model and definition of communication relied upon in this textbook.

Common Attributes of Communication Models

In the most general sense, human communication can be thought of as the means by which information is transmitted from one person to another. This description suggests elements that are common to all models. Communication is a *process* of exchanging information between the *sender* and the *receiver*. The information, or content of the communicative act, is the *message* (Trenholm, 2001). It is the totality of what is communicated—the words, noises, facial expressions, and stance of the communicator are all part of the message. Verbal messages are composed of printed or spoken words; nonverbal messages are conveyed by behaviors other than words (e.g., facial expressions, vocal noise, and gestures). Everything a sender or receiver says or does is potentially part of the message, as long as someone receives and interprets the communication.

Channel refers to the medium through which messages are transmitted. Because nearly all messages in human communication are either seen or heard, the most frequently used channels are visual and auditory. However, all human senses may be involved in sending and receiving messages. The cologne someone wears or the firmness of a person's handshake also sends messages through olfactory or tactile channels.

Another element for consideration in this approach to understanding communication is *noise*. It is anything that interferes with or distorts the ability of communicators to send or receive messages. You are familiar with distracting sounds that often interfere with communication, such as public address system announcements, sirens, or loud talking in the hall. In addition, conditions such as physical discomfort, a hot room, an unpleasant odor, an inappropriate choice of words, a person's tendency to frown, or a person's physical appearance are other kinds of "noise" that interfere with the transmission of a message.

Two additional concepts frequently are identified as key to any model of human communication. The concept of *continuous feedback* specifies that while sending a message, the sender is simultaneously receiving information related to that message or the environment. For example, when you speak you can hear yourself and judge if you are saying what you intended. If you decide that you have not been understood, you may elaborate or restate your message to clarify it. Simultaneous with your expressive communication, you are obtaining from the receiver of your message information that lets you know how your message is being received. A confused look, a frown, or a question may cause you to restate your message, whereas a smile, nod, or interested look may encourage you to continue speaking or to go on to a new topic.

The second concept is that messages are *multichannel*. At any given point during interpersonal communication, several messages probably are being transmitted simultaneously over different channels. Sending a single message over multiple channels can strengthen or emphasize the message. You do this when you smile, nod, and touch someone's shoulder while giving her a compliment. Alternatively, simultaneously sending discrepant messages through different channels complicates the communication. You do this when you smile while expressing disagreement with another's opinion.

Rogers and Steinfatt (1999) have proposed a model that includes all of the foregoing elements and adds an emphasis on communication as a process that occurs over time. This model is presented in Figure 2.1.

Communication Types

Although communication can be understood using many approaches, an interesting categorization system presented by Schmuck and Runkel (1994) is especially valuable in understanding the types of communication that you are most accustomed to using in educational settings. This system classifies communication as unilateral, directive, and transactional.

Unilateral communication is one-way—a speaker provides information to a listener. No face-to-face interaction occurs; the listener has no opportunity to query the speaker at the time the message is transmitted, nor can the speaker clarify or revise the original message. Examples of unilateral communication include educational film or television, written memos, audiotaped lectures, and announcements over the school's public address system.

Some individuals prefer to give or receive messages unilaterally through mediated channels. Indeed there is evidence that different mediated channels such as e-mail, fax, and voice mail have greater or lesser value depending upon the communication intention and goal (Westmyer, DiCioccio, & Rubin, 1998). Under certain circumstances, such as a speaker's nervousness or a listener's hostility and inability to listen well, clear and unambiguous information without the opportunity for immediate discussion can be advantageous in managing one's presentation of self-relevant information. Combined with the asynchronous dimension that can be introduced with a number of these approaches, mediated unilateral communication can be an important impression management tool (O'Sullivan,

---

Figure 2.1   A Communication Model

This model illustrates the communication process between two participants who create and share information with one another in order to reach a mutual understanding. Each exchange between the participants is a communication act that may occur at a certain point in time. This act often builds upon previous communication exchanges and is followed by others in the future, thus creating a communication process over time.

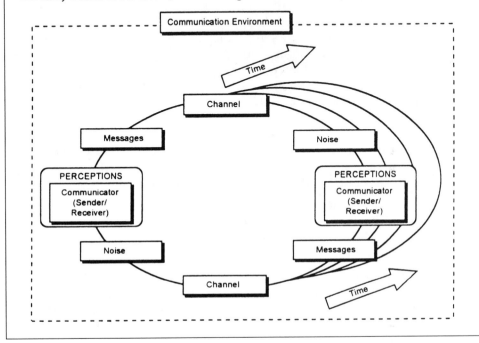

Based on Rogers & others (1998, p. 15). Rogers, E. M., & Steinfatt, T. M. (1999). Intercultural communication. Prospect Heights, IL: Waveland Press (p. 115).

2000). Through these channels, one might achieve her self-presentation goals better than face-to-face or other interactive modes.

Directive communication characterizes much of what occurs in schools. It occurs face-to-face when the speaker (usually the adult) sends a message to a listener (generally the student), who indicates receipt and comprehension of the message. This is a frequent mode of communication as school professionals direct, explain, or lecture and students comply, understand, and listen. This type of communication is complete when the students let the adult know (or when the adult concludes) that the information has been received and understood. Because many adult–student interactions in schools consist largely of directive communication, instructional and special services professionals are likely to be quite accomplished at this type of communication and provide clear, meaningful directions, explanations, and lectures. Other professional situations in which you may experience directive communication are staff meetings and professional development activities conducted in lecture format.

Despite the prevalence of directive communication in schools, it is in many ways incompatible with the effective interpersonal communication needed for collaborative interactions. Instead, *transactional communication* is a two-way, reciprocal interaction in which each participant simultaneously sends and receives messages while alternately assuming the role of speaker or listener. In this process, participants exchange information: The receiver tries to discern the sender's view and help the sender to know whether the intended meaning was communicated by informing the sender of the perceived message and of his or her reactions to it. The sender may then modify, restate, or reinforce the original message in order to clarify the communication. Participants in this complex, reciprocal process mutually influence each other to create shared meanings. Contemporary models of interpersonal communication stress that participants both send and receive information throughout their interactions. In these models each participant may be labeled a *sender-receiver* to emphasize the duality of roles.

Interpersonal communication, the primary concern in this chapter, relies on a transactional approach. By adding this concept to those already presented we can now offer a more elaborated definition of communication:

> Interpersonal communication is a complex, reciprocal process through which participants create shared meanings as messages are transmitted continuously from one sender-receiver to another via multiple communication channels.

This concept of transactional communication grounds our thinking about effective interpersonal communication. Its attributes include the primary elements discussed earlier (e.g., process, channel, and message) as well as extensions of them (e.g., sender-receiver, multichannel, and continuous feedback).

PREREQUISITES TO EFFECTIVE INTERACTIONS

Collaborative relationships require much more than just initiating interactions and hoping that the characteristics described in Chapter 1 fall into place. Effective interpersonal communication is essential for almost any kind of cooperation or collaboration (Trenholm, 2001), and there are some fundamental prerequisites to the needed communication skills. So, how do you assure your personal readiness to begin collaborating with a colleague? Several important prerequisites to effective collaborative interactions involve your self-awareness and your ability to understand others.

Frame of Reference

Every individual enters each life experience with a unique perspective. Your past experiences, acquired attitudes and beliefs, personal qualities, past and present feelings, and expectations for others affect what and how you observe and perceive, and ultimately how you respond and act. What you bring to a situation, independent of the situation itself, is called your *frame of reference.* It is your predisposition to respond in some particular manner to a particular situation.

Frame of Reference and Your Role

Your general professional socialization, discussed in Chapter 1, contributes to your frame of reference. At the same time, however, the specific discipline into which you were socialized (e.g., special education, school psychology, math, literacy) and through which you prepared for a particular professional role (e.g., classroom teacher, occupational therapist, speech and language specialist, school psychologist) also contributes elements to your frame of reference. This latter component may be considerably different from that of colleagues in other disciplines.

For example, general education teachers and special services providers may have pronounced differences in their perceived levels of responsibility for facilitating student learning. Consistent with their disciplinary preparation in general education, classroom teachers are likely to view their primary responsibilities as facilitating the progress of a group of students through a prescribed curriculum to meet established grade-level standards. Their professional studies emphasized curriculum, its scope and sequence, instructional methodology, techniques for group management, and strategies for delivering specific subject matter content. Group instructional tasks, curriculum "coverage," and standards are prominent in their frames of reference.

On the other hand, the professional preparation and socialization you experienced as a special services provider probably emphasized individual variations in human development and learning, assessment of individual differences and learning needs, and intervention strategies to respond to unique needs of individual students. Not surprisingly, you probably believe your primary responsibilities are to identify a student's current level of functioning and learning needs, then to design and deliver services tailored to meet those needs. Your professional background, a major component of your frame of reference, leads you to focus on unique needs of *individual* students.

These differences in classroom teachers' and special services providers' frames of reference may have a profound impact on how they interact with one another. For you to successfully undertake collaborative activities, you will no doubt find that awareness of these variations and sensitivity to their influences are essential.

Substantial differences also can characterize the frames of reference held by the various disciplines that provide special services. Some of these differences reflect the diverse philosophical and theoretical orientations within these fields (e.g., a preference for psychoeducational versus behavioral approaches), some reflect variations in the nature of the special services provided (e.g., specialized instruction, therapy, or diagnostic evaluation), and still others relate to the specific knowledge bases of the disciplines. It is easy to understand how a speech and language specialist with responsibility for a student's articulation therapy might have a very different frame of reference from the adaptive physical education specialist. The former works individually with students, diagnosing the speech disability, designing interventions to remediate it, and perhaps delivering services in a one-on-one situation. However, the adaptive physical education specialist may focus on assessing a student's general physical status and then design a program to maximize the strengths and reduce the deficits of the student. This specialist often will deliver individualized services for the particular student within the group of students served. Similarly, reading specialists are likely to have frames of reference that differ in significant ways from those of occupational and physical therapists, administrators who differ from special education teachers, and so on.

Frame of Reference in Multicultural Settings

Of equal or greater importance to your frame of reference is your cultural identity. It significantly contributes to the unique perspective, or worldview, you bring to every interaction. Culture is readily observable. It includes the artifacts, achievements, and symbols of a people. Culture also refers to many different elements that influence your sense of identity including race, ethnicity, gender, age, occupation, geographic location, and religion (Banks & McGee-Banks, 1999; Kalyanpur & Harry, 1999).

Cultural identity is reflected in one's cultural orientation and worldview. Highly diverse cultural orientations have been identified across disciplines and cultures. For example, Braithwaite (1997) has described orientations emanating from Navajo philosophy as focus on a sense of place, duality in life and cultural identity. McCroskey and colleagues (1996) have examined the degree to which cultural norms demonstrate a value for high or low immediacy in Australia, Finland, Puerto Rico, and the United States and how teacher immediacy relates to student achievement in those cultures. Others have posited that cultural orientations manifest themselves in such patterns as courtesy, respect, and tolerance for ambiguity (Cui, Van den Berg, & Jiang, 1998). Culturally based value orientations are often described in terms of an individualism/collectivism. This is a continuum which represents the emphasis a culture places on individual goals, achievement, and fulfillment versus interdependence and emphasis on the well-being of the group as a whole (Lynch, 1998; Trumbull, Rothstein-Fisch, & Greenfield, 2001a; Watkins Eatman, 2001). Generally the dominant culture of the United States is thought to reflect an individualistic orientation in which the uniqueness, self-realization, and self-expression of individuals are highly valued. About 70% of the world's cultures can be viewed as collectivistic (Triandis, Brislin, & Hui, 1988; Trumbull et al., 2001). Collectivist cultures, such as most American immigrant groups as well as African American, Native American and Alaskan Native cultures place value on meeting the needs of the group and are likely to be oriented toward the extended family and kinship-help patterns. No ethnic or other cultural group is clearly individualistic or collectivistic in its orientation, and not all members of a cultural group share the same values. These orientations are used to describe a continuum of values that may help to distinguish key beliefs and patterns of groups and individuals. The differences in these orientations will be examined in Chapter 13. Here we use the individualism/collectivism continuum as a framework for considering characteristics of cultural styles and patterns that are evident in cross-cultural communication.

In the following Perspectives on Diversity feature, communication styles associated with both extremes of the continuum are outlined.

Understanding one's own value orientations is a critical first step. Next it is important to consider how these orientations influence communication. Then it is helpful to examine how these match the orientations of others in the school and community. It is likely that you will find you are more aligned with certain individuals than others—this is one indication of cultural similarities and differences. These are probably the same people with whom you believe you can work collaboratively. Your efforts to achieve cultural self-awareness will help you begin to develop culturally and competent and effective communication skills that will enhance your collaborative interactions with colleagues and parents.

In our culturally pluralistic and self-conscious society, there is a temptation to try to avert the complexity of cultural differences by ascribing specific cultural values to groups of people who are of the same ethnicity, gender, or age. Although members of these groups share similarities, considerable diversity exists within each of the groups, too.

We hope that these examples of variation in frames of reference help you to focus on how your frame of reference—unique because of your personal, professional, and cultural history—is both similar to and different from those of others

PERSPECTIVES ON DIVERSITY 2.1

Individualistic and Collectivistic Influences in Cross-Cultural Communication

Individualistic	Collectivistic
Low-context: communication is explicit and direct; one "gets to the point."	**High-context:** communication relies on context, past experience, and indirect cues.
Talk: self-assertion is achieved through talk; talk is used to achieve comfort in groups.	**Silence:** comfort may be derived from silence; silence is used communicatively and is valued.
Directness: individuality, uniqueness are asserted, opinions expressed to disagree, persuade, and avoid ambiguity.	**Indirectness:** hints and subtle cues are used to maintain harmony and ambiguity is tolerated to maintain harmony.
Uneven turn-taking: One party may dominate; both parties may introduce topics and speak at length about them.	**Balanced turn-taking:** turns are distributed evenly; each party takes short turns and does not randomly shift topics.

Based on Watkins, R., & Eatman, J. (2001). *An Introduction to cross-cultural communication.* (Technical Report #14; chapter 2) [electronic version]. Champaign-Urbana, IL: Culturally and Linguistically Appropriate Services for Early Childhood Research (CLAS) Institute.

with whom you may want to collaborate. What is most important to understand is that no two people experience a single interaction in exactly the same way.

Selective Perception

How often do you discuss a shared experience with a friend or colleague only to find later that you have quite different opinions about what transpired? Your understandings of what occurred may be so different that you even question if you were actually at the same meeting or if you participated in the same interaction. This is not uncommon. It is impossible for people to process and internalize everything that occurs around them. In any instance there is an infinite number of sounds, sights, smells, feelings, and tastes that compete for your attention. So you have to select which stimuli you will attend to or experience in the situation. This is an illustration of *perception,* a process for selecting, organizing, and interpreting all of the information available in a given situation. To be effective, these perceptual processes must be highly selective.

Everyone uses selective perception. They choose, either consciously or unconsciously, to focus on some pieces of information while largely ignoring others. This is often necessary in professional interactions because such communication is quite complex (Lustig & Koester, 1999). When more information is transmitted than can be assimilated, your frame of reference guides your selective perception, filtering out or obscuring some information and focusing your attention on other information. Generally, the biases in your frame of reference can enhance or inhibit your perception and thus your understanding of another's situation.

Consider the following exchange at a team meeting:

◆ Mr. Swanson, the 10th-grade English teacher, has come to a meeting of a child study team to discuss Lucia, a student in his class who has a learning disability. He reports: "Lucia is having an extremely hard time with our writing program. She can *tell* me all of her ideas in a very organized fashion, but she can't *write* them because her spelling is seriously deficient. Her written work is simply unacceptable. I'm an English teacher, not a spelling teacher! There's no way Lucia can succeed in my class. She really should be in a special education class. I tried your peer-tutoring suggestion, and her papers are good, but it's probably because her tutor spells so well. Lucia just dictates her compositions. I have very high standards, and it wouldn't be fair to lower them for one student."

One team member at the meeting thinks: "Here we go again! It's another version of 'I can't stand having this kid in my class, and I won't adapt the assignment. Just get the kid out of my class.' I can't let this guy push Lucia out of his class. I'll have to stand firm on this."

Another team member says to herself: "It's always difficult for secondary teachers when they first start to include kids with learning disabilities. He's completed both his B.A. and M.A. in English literature and wants to teach English, not spelling. I could discuss differential standards with him. Maybe he'd see that Lucia is benefiting from the writing program and, as a result, she is making progress toward meeting her IEP goals.

PERSPECTIVES ON DIVERSITY 2.2

A Cultural Self-Awareness Journey

Step 1: Your Cultural Roots and Heritage

1. When you think about your roots, what country(ies) other than the United States do you identify as a place of origin for you or your family?

2. Have you ever heard any stories about how your family or your ancestors came to the United States? Briefly, what was the story?

3. Are there any foods that you or someone else prepares that are traditional for your country(ies) of origin? What are they?

4. Are there any celebrations, ceremonies, rituals, holidays that your family continues to celebrate that reflect your country(ies) of origin? What are they? How are they celebrated?

5. Do you or anyone in your family speak a language other than English because of your origins? If so, what language?

6. Can you think of one piece of advice that has been handed through your family that reflects the values held by your ancestors in the country(ies) of origin? What was it?

Step 2: Your Cultural Values, Biases, and Behaviors

1. Have you ever heard anyone make a negative comment about your country(ies) of origin? If so, what was it?

2. As you were growing up, do you remember discovering that your family did anything differently from other families to which you were exposed because of your culture, religion, or ethnicity? Name something that you remember that was different.

3. Have you ever been with someone in a work situation who did something because of his or her culture, religion, or ethnicity that seemed unusual to you? What was it? Why did it seem unusual?

4. Have you ever felt shocked, upset, or appalled by something that you saw when you were traveling in another part of the world? If so, what was it? How did it make you feel? Pick some descriptive words to explain your feelings. In retrospect, how do you wish you would have reacted?

5. Have you ever done anything that you think was culturally inappropriate when you have been in another country or with someone from a different culture? In other words, have you ever done something that you think might have been upsetting or embarrassing to another person? What was it? What did you do to try to improve the situation?

6. If you could be from another culture or ethnic group, what culture would it be? Why?

(continued)

7. What is one value from that culture or ethnic group that attracts you to it?

8. Is there anything about that culture or ethnic group that concerns or frightens you? What is it?

9. Name one concrete way in which you think your life would be different if you were from that culture or ethnic group.

From Lynch, E. W. (1998). Developing cross-cultural competence. In E. W. Lynch & M. J. Hanson (Eds.), *Developing cross-cultural competence: A guide for working with young children and their families* (2nd ed.) (pp. 87–89) Baltimore: Brookes.

She's learning to structure her ideas and present them in a logical fashion. She's demonstrating strong composition skills that should be evaluated independent of her spelling."

In the example, both professionals picked up on information presented by Mr. Swanson, but they attended to different aspects of his report based on their individual roles and previous experiences. You can understand easily the thoughts of the two team members if you are aware of the different, strongly held biases of each: The first team member believes that classroom teachers do not care about students with disabilities and that they want to minimize their work. The second team member believes that all teachers want to teach well and feel that their teaching benefits their students. Both professionals identified and selectively perceived something in Mr. Swanson's statements that corresponded with critical elements in their own frames of reference.

The message for professionals who engage in collaborative activities is clear: Your own frame of reference may prevent you from understanding someone else's communication. You can become more aware of how you perceive others' communications and learn to consider multiple frames of reference by constantly challenging yourself to develop alternative explanations for others' statements. For example, what might a classroom teacher mean who says, "I'm not sure this student will *ever* learn how to divide!"? The teacher might be conveying general frustration at the student's difficulties, a statement of fact that the rest of the class is ready to learn a new skill while the student in question has not mastered the concept of division, or doubts about his or her own teaching abilities. Continuing to remind yourself to think divergently and consider alternative meanings will help you to suspend judgment of others, critically examine your own perceptions, avoid making premature decisions or conclusions, and more accurately comprehend multiple elements of complex situations.

COMMUNICATION SKILLS

Although the multiple dimensions of interpersonal communication processes are complex and occur simultaneously, our experiences have demonstrated the need to identify discrete skill categories and examine them individually. Precisely because of the complexity of interpersonal communication, effective skill acquisition requires the isolation and practice of distinct skills in much the same way that learning to speak a foreign language requires practice in vocabulary development, pronunciation, and phrase acquisition. Similarly, improving one's gold swing requires learning certain elements of the skill in isolation (e.g., addressing the ball, gauging the backswing, orienting the club face, and calibrating the follow-through). As with language learning or athletic development, effective communication skill development is enhanced by acquiring and practicing discrete communication behaviors and then blending them into a smooth and effective process.

After you acquire discrete communication behaviors, you can practice using them in ways suggested in this textbook. As you gain comfort with them, you will begin to integrate and use them together with other skills to facilitate the more complex interaction processes such as problem solving or conflict resolution.

Communication skills and strategies can be classified in many different ways (e.g., Constantinides, 2001; Peterson & Nisenholz, 1998). In this text, we treat verbal and nonverbal communication separately and organize our discussion of selected verbal strategies around the use of statements (Chapter 3) and the use of questions (Chapter 4). We use the remainder of this chapter to examine listening skills, provide an overview of nonverbal communication factors, and consider principles and suggestions for effective communication.

Listening

Listening is so critical an element of communication that we choose to present it separately rather than as part of a particular category of skills. It involves multiple skills, some of which are prerequisite to the development of other skills and some of which result from skill development in other areas. Further, effective listening involves the simultaneous use of many skills—both verbal and nonverbal.

Listening is essential in all aspects of life. People listen for pleasure at concerts and movies, for learning in courses and meetings, and for understanding in day-to-day interactions with families and friends. You may best understand the importance of listening if you recall experiences of *not* being listened to—whether at a party, in a work setting, or at home. In all these settings, you may have participated in parallel conversations, much like the parallel play of children, in which individuals, either simultaneously or alternately, talk about the topic that most interests them without much regard for others. The speakers appear to have agreed to take turns speaking and acting as an audience for each other without responding in any meaningful way to what the other person says. If you have been part of such adult parallel play, you surely realize that dissatisfaction and feelings of being dismissed usually result.

Listening is the foundation for all relationships. In collaboration, listening is especially critical. It is a complex, difficult-to-measure process for attending to and accurately comprehending what another person is saying and then demonstrating that this has occurred (Brammer & MacDonald, 1999). It is a primary means for gaining information, but it is also a means of conveying interest in the messages of others.

Rationale for Listening

A primary benefit of listening is that it helps establish rapport (Petress, 1999). This occurs in two ways: First, when you listen you show concern and a desire to understand the other person and the situation. By listening you communicate both concern for the speaker as an individual and also the intent to understand what that person has to say. Second, listening helps build rapport when it allows you to demonstrate accurate understanding. Attention, willingness to listen, and desire to understand are important elements in establishing rapport, but accurate understanding is required to build and maintain a relationship. When you demonstrate precise understanding of what the person has said, you are perceived as being both competent and a worthy collaborator.

Another major benefit of effective listening is that you obtain sufficient and accurate information necessary for participating in a collaborative activity. Too frequently, professionals assume they understand an inadequately articulated comment and begin acting on it as they perceive it. This is a dangerous practice for several reasons. First, it is quite improbable that anyone can accurately understand a situation that is not clearly described. Without accurate understanding, appropriate actions are rare. Second, a knee-jerk response may give others the impression that they are not competent. Have you ever had the following happen? People listened haphazardly as you described a problem, responded quickly, and left you thinking, "If it was so easy, why couldn't I think of an answer? I'm embarrassed to have thought it was such a problem!" This kind of situation does nothing to establish parity or rapport. Finally, and perhaps most threatening to the collaborative relationship, a rapid and inaccurate response to a person's comments suggests little concern for his or her perception of the issue and even less concern for the person as a significant individual.

Factors That Interfere with Effective Listening

Have you ever found that despite good intentions to listen carefully to what a colleague was describing, by the time the other person finished giving a clear and precise description, you were not at all sure what had been said? This experience is common, and it illustrates how difficult it is to listen. In fact, it is estimated that although we spend about 50 percent of our communication time "listening" to others, our listening effectiveness is only about 25 percent (Boyd, 2001). Think back to those times when you recognized that you were not listening to someone else. Can you identify what interfered with your listening? DeVito (2001) describes several obstacles to effective listening that may be the culprits.

Rehearsing a Response

Perhaps while your colleague is talking you catch the drift of what is being said and proceed to work on framing what you will say when you have the opportunity to speak. Similarly, at a team meeting perhaps you anticipate that it will soon be your turn to report, and so you review your notes and miss what someone else is saying.

Daydreaming

When you listen, you are engaged in an inefficient process. You are capable of receiving information more rapidly through listening than an average speaker can convey, even a speaker who talks at an unusually high rate of speed. The result is that you have some spare time to think even while you listen. Unfortunately, you may use this time to mentally prepare a shopping list, plan a week's vacation, or think about a new instructional unit. You may find yourself suddenly daydreaming and discover that you have lost track of the speaker's message.

Stumbling on "Hot" Words

To what words do you respond strongly? **Inclusion?** High-stakes testing? Accountability? Sometimes when a speaker to whom you are listening uses a "hot" word, you may begin to think about the meaning of the word and its implications for you. This special category of daydreaming has the same impact: You temporarily halt effective listening while you cognitively address other matters.

Filtering Messages

Occasionally you may simply not want to listen to a particular message. For example, think about times you have attended a staff meeting on a topic about which you were already knowledgeable. Did you listen while the topic was announced and then "tune out"? If so, you were filtering the message. You might have done the same thing if the information had little relevance to your situation. Finally, your frame of reference may cause you to filter messages. As we noted earlier, your frame of reference may cause you to selectively attend to specific parts of a message and ignore others, thereby causing you to perceive the message inaccurately.

Being Distracted by Extraneous Details

Most people at one time or another find listening difficult because their attention is drawn to a detail that is extraneous to the message being conveyed. For example, have you ever spent so much time wondering where a colleague or parent got such an unusual haircut that you could not attend to what was being said? Perhaps you interacted with someone who had a minor speech impairment and you discovered it was especially difficult to attend to the words instead of the impediment. Any distractions—physical, verbal, gestural, environmental—may distract you and interfere with effective listening.

Suggestions for Improving Your Listening Skills

Because listening has a powerful metacognitive component, refining your listening skills requires addressing your ability to sustain attention and monitor your comprehension of the verbal message. And although there are no simple solutions for becoming a more effective listener, you can improve your skills by trying the strategies presented in Putting Ideas into Practice. The key to success, however, lies in deliberately monitoring your listening behavior and systematically using such strategies.

Nonverbal Communication

Much valuable information is transmitted without words. Skillful use of nonverbal behaviors is essential in communicating attitudes necessary for establishing and maintaining positive relationships (e.g., interest, acceptance, warmth) and powerful as a tool in clarifying, emphasizing, or obfuscating the meaning of verbal messages (Egan, 2001).

Everyone is aware that "body language" and voice can influence communication, but the impact of nonverbal behaviors is greater than you may have suspected. In fact, the words used in your communication may convey far less information than do the nonverbal components. Mehrabian (1971) reported that the full impact of an individual's spoken message may be broken down as follows: 7 percent verbal components, 38 percent vocal (volume, pitch, rhythm) components, and 55 percent facial expression.

Nonverbal Cues

People communicate nonverbally in several ways. Three primary classes of nonverbal cues are (1) body movements, such as facial expression, eye contact, posture, and gestures; (2) vocal cues, such as quality of voice and the pacing or flow of speech; and (3) spatial relations, which include the physical distance between the participants. Minimal encouragers form a fourth class of nonverbal cues, even though they contain verbal components. Each of these categories of cues affects the nature of the communication between people.

Nonverbal behaviors can be effective means of demonstrating that people care about what another person is saying and that they are listening with empathy.

Suggestions for Improving Listening Skills

Good communicators are good listeners. Here are a few suggestions for improving your listening.

Mentally prepare for listening:

- Deliberately shut out competing thoughts and issues.
- Direct your attention to the speaker and resist engaging in distractions such as e-mail or paperwork.

Mentally rehearse the information:

- Identify main themes or key words.
- Practice mentally repeating these themes as the speaker shares more.

Categorize the information:

- Develop a schema that helps to "map" the ideas (e.g., classify case information according to behavior, academics, family).

Make notes of informational details:

- Use notes when a large amount of information is being shared.
- Explain the reason for note taking.
- Jot down only important concepts and details.

Use a signal as a cue to remember ideas:

- Use signals when you have a thought or concern that you want to share (e.g., bend and hold your little finger down; turn your ring around).

Seek to make connections between inferences, facts, and opinions.
Attend to nonverbal behavior and tone of voice.
Listen to what is *not* being said.

Two additional vocal behavior—interruptions and the use of silence—also influence communication and are discussed at the end of this section.

Spatial Relations

Spatial relations refer to the physical distance you keep between yourself and other in an interaction. Hall (1981, 1966) has described four spatial zones that people seem to use in their interactions with others: (1) intimate distance, (2) personal distance, (3) social distance, and (4) public distance. These zones can be schematically represented by four concentric circles of personally defined space around each person. The smallest circle represents the intimate distance and the largest, outermost circle represents public distance. Typically, the greater the distance between people in an interaction the less their intimacy. Perhaps you have had experiences where you felt uncomfortable because the person with whom you were speaking stood too close to you. During interaction between colleagues who do not know each other well, the amount of space between them should be great enough to avoid inappropriate intimacy.

Body Movements

The phrase "one picture is worth a thousand words" shows recognition of the full impact of nonverbal communication. Without even using words, you can communicate a wide range of attitudes and feelings through *body movements*— gestures and facial expressions. Consider the influence of nonverbal communication in these examples:

- ◆ "I'm really interested in what's going on with Kim and Amir," the counselor said as she set her papers aside and sat down facing the teacher. She looked at the teacher and, leaning forward slightly in her chair, she said, "Do you have any insights that would help me understand their situation?" Without pause, she said, "Please let me know what you think about their progress." She then sat quietly looking at the teacher, waiting for a response.
- ◆ "I'm really interested in what's going on with Kim and Amir" the counselor said as she entered the room. She glanced at the teacher, then at the papers she was carrying, and sat down at her computer as she said, "Do you have any insights that would help me understand their situation?" Then, without pause, she glanced first at her watch, then at the teacher, and began reading and responding to e-mail as she said, "Please let me know what you think about their progress."

Engaging in a competing task while attempting to listen indicates lack of interest in the speaker and is likely to interfere with the relationship.

What did the counselor's body movements communicate to you? In the first example they probably suggested that she was interested in the other person's information and ideas. In the second example, her nonverbal message probably contradicted her verbal message. What was the likely impact of her discrepant verbal and nonverbal communication on the teacher?

In these examples, only a few movements and gestures were described. In the actual situation one would observe many more nonverbal cues that contribute to the message. Eye contact, facial expression, and gestures such as reaching out or touching someone's shoulder also affect the meaning communicated.

Vocal Cues

Paralanguage—the vocal, rather than verbal, component of language—also communicates a great deal of information separate from the verbal content of the message. Paralanguage includes voice tone, pitch, and volume, speech rhythm, and pacing or tempo, as well as the use and timing of silence.

Many of the elements of paralanguage may reach extremes when the speaker is experiencing intense emotions. For example, pitch results from the tightness of one's vocal cords. When you are calm, depressed, or tired, your vocal cords are relaxed and your pitch is lower, whereas excitement or anxiety tends to make your pitch higher. The pace of speech may also indicate emotion; rapid speech can signal excitement and enthusiasm or nervousness and insecurity. Thus, you may observe that someone who is anxious or uncertain about a situation may speak very rapidly at a high pitch while someone more confident and relaxed is likely to speak slowly at a lower pitch.

Another way of making judgments about appropriate personal space during interactions is the topic of conversation. Generally, when two colleagues discuss a problem that is very disturbing to one of them, the listener should be near enough to the speaker to indicate concern but not so close as to seem threatening or intrusive. On the other hand, if the speaker is distressed or sad, physical closeness and a touch on the shoulder might be exactly what the speaker needs.

Minimal Encouragers

A category of skill that involves both nonverbal and verbal messages is called *minimal encouragers*. It includes words, phrases, silence, and other nonverbal cues designed to indicate that you are listening and understand what someone is expressing and to encourage the person to continue communicating. Common minimal encouragers include silence, head nods, quizzical facial expressions, hand gestures, other indications to keep talking, and spoken cues such as "Uh-huh," "Hmmm," "And . . . ," "So . . . ," and "Okay."

You use minimal encouragers to invite the person with whom you are interacting to continue sharing information with you. One of the most effective, but seriously underused, minimal encouragers is silence. As you become comfortable with allowing a few seconds of silence, you may find that it gives others time to gather their thoughts and then convey them to you. When you use silence, or when you nod or use one of the other encouragers, you are also allowing yourself time to phrase your next question or statement.

DEVELOPING EFFECTIVE COMMUNICATION SKILLS

As you learned in the preface, this text includes a number of features designed to assist readers to develop the communication skills needed for effective interactions in collaborative relationships. In later chapters you will read definitions and descriptions of skills, examine examples or models of the skills and processes, and have opportunities to practice them by completing activities and exercises. At this point we stress the importance of understanding basic principles and the development of attitudes that facilitate the refinement of communication skills. These skills can be learned with knowledge and practice (Trenholm, 2001).

Principles for Effective Interpersonal Communication

This and other texts offer numerous examples, rules, and suggestions for improving interpersonal communication. In order to apply those suggestions or "tips" at the appropriate time and in the most effective manner, it is necessary to understand the principles that guide their use. Here are several essential universal principles for nonverbal and verbal communication.

Nonverbal Communication Principles

The foregoing examples demonstrated the highly subjective nature of nonverbal communication. We noted that rapid speech may indicate enthusiasm or anxiety, but these are two distinctly different feelings. The physical distance between two individuals should be "near enough to . . ." but "not so close as to . . ."; what is appropriate for any particular interaction may be inappropriate for another. There are no specific prescriptions for "correct" body language. Instead, two critical concepts—*congruence* and *individualism*—may help you understand the meaning of your own nonverbal communication and that of others.

Congruence

Communication is not simply a series of verbal or nonverbal behaviors. It is composed of clusters of both verbal and nonverbal behaviors or cues that occur concurrently. When talking, an individual is simultaneously communicating something through gestures, movements, facial expressions, posture, paralanguage, and words. As Rogers (1951) noted more than 50 years ago, believable behavior generally occurs in congruent clusters; that is, several behaviors occur simultaneously that have the same or highly similar meanings. Rogers attributed the characteristics of genuineness to congruence. Incongruence may unintentionally reveal feelings or attitudes one is hoping to conceal (e.g., the principal who chuckles while telling a staff member, "This is serious!"). This is illustrated in the following case description:

- ♦ The community liaison talked quietly with several parents while others freshened their coffee. When everyone returned to the seating area, he smiled and said, "If we're ready to continue I'd like to describe the role of the Community Liaison Office." He paused and, smiling slightly, looked around the room as people took their seats in the semicircle of chairs. "We are here to talk things over with you. Whenever you have questions or want more information about your child's program, we will be here to discuss your concerns and try to answer your questions." He paused, smiled slightly, and looked slowly around the room again. When he made eye contact with a group member, he maintained it long enough to give the member the opportunity to raise a question or offer a comment. "As parents we all have concerns," he continued, moving a chair into the semicircle to sit between Diane Long and Jerome Jackson. Putting his hand on the arm of Diane's chair and looking at her, he interrupted himself. "Diane, do you remember when my son started talking about getting a job and I ran checks on the business through the employee relations department at your office?" Smiling shyly and laughing, Diane said, "I surely do! That was one long week in our neighborhood." The community liaison laughed while still looking at Diane, then he leaned forward in his chair, put his elbows on his knees, and let his clasped hands fall between them. He glanced down for a silent second. Then, looking up, he said slowly, "Yes, as parents we all have concerns about the decisions our children make and the challenges they must face. We know that we have to let go if we want our kids to grow into independent, productive adult living. But it's hard—especially because we know their special needs." Quickening his pace slightly, he looked directly at each group member and said decidedly, "That's where the Community Liaison Office comes in. We have information about community opportunities, hazards, and supports; and we know your sons and daughters. Maybe most important," he continued while sitting up and smiling broadly, "we want to understand what you're experiencing. We've been there!"

This speaker's nonverbal cues strengthened his verbal message. His body movements or gestures (e.g., eye contact, touching Diane's chair, and smiling) and his vocal cues (e.g., speaking softly or decidedly, laughing, and changing verbal pace) were congruent with his verbal message. Together, his verbal and nonverbal strategies communicated sincere understanding and genuine interest in parents' concerns.

The speaker's use of space was also congruent with his verbal message. By physically joining the group and sitting among group members, he strengthened his verbal message that he was one of them. By leaning into the group while sharing his own feelings, he suggested that the group is a safe place to express intimate and personal feelings.

Individualism

The concept of individualism emphasizes the subjectivity involved in interpreting nonverbal communication. The meaning of a single nonverbal cue depends not only on the context in which it occurs but also on its specific meaning to the individual demonstrating the behavior and to the person observing it. For example, you may strive to maintain constant eye contact with a colleague to demonstrate your interest and attention. Your colleague, on the other hand, may feel uncomfortable and find your "interested" eye contact to be a penetrating stare that creates a feeling of being exposed or scrutinized too intensely. Similarly, you may observe a colleague sitting with his arms crossed and worry that he is not "open" to your ideas. In fact, he may be cold or searching for a comfortable position while seated in an armless chair!

To develop effective nonverbal skills you should identify your own patterns of nonverbal behavior that affect communication positively or negatively and learn to anticipate individual differences in how others react to your nonverbal behaviors. Activities at the end of the chapter should assist in developing this understanding.

Verbal Communication Principles

In discussing the mutual influence that characterizes interpersonal communication, we stressed that the verbal and nonverbal messages you send greatly affect the types of responses you receive. In Chapters 3 and 4, we consider two primary verbal strategies—statements and questions—and examine how their use affects interpersonal communication. In this section of the chapter we take a look at two aspects of verbal communication that have significant impact on interaction—concreteness and neutrality. We then conclude with suggestions for enhancing the effectiveness of verbal communication.

Concreteness

You are more likely to understand verbal interactions if they involve the exchange of concrete, specific information. Such verbal expressions communicate more clearly than the vague or general phrases and expressions commonly heard in personal as well as professional conversations.

Imprecise language is the cause of much miscommunication. Vague language may significantly obscure the message so that it may not be possible to determine what the sender intended. For example, if a teacher says he "handled" the problem, is it possible to determine what the teacher's actions were? If a colleague asks you for assistance with a student's disruptive behavior, do you know if the colleague wants you to help select strategies for her to use in class or if she wants you to intervene with the student? Do you even know the nature and extent of the student's "disruptive behavior" that is the source of her concern? The answer to each of these questions is "Of course not." In each of these examples the language was far too vague to communicate effectively. The examples below illustrate how a vague statement or question may be made more concrete. The very different meanings conveyed in the concrete examples underscore the level of misunderstanding that occurs when communication is vague.

Statement: I was concerned about her reaction.
Alternative A: I felt somewhat angry and very rejected when she asked to have her son transferred to another class.

Alternative B: I thought that she might turn her anger on her son when she got home.

Question: Has Corretta improved in your class?
Alternative A: Has Corretta's off task behavior decreased in your science class?
Alternative B: Has Corretta's participation and understanding improved in her literature assignments, now that we've provided her with books on tape to listen to prior to the class discussions?

From these examples, you can easily see how important concrete language is. Yet, listen to yourself and to your colleagues as you discuss students and school-related issues, and see how routinely your conversations proceed around vaguely described topics. As you listen you probably will recognize that concreteness exists on a continuum from quite vague to very specific. As you practice and develop proficiency in communicating clearly you will learn to judge situationally the amount of concreteness needed for successful interactions.

Neutrality

Neutrality promotes the development of interpersonal trust because it conveys a nonjudgmental and accepting attitude. Although you often will be required to judge situations and evaluate ideas as you work collaboratively, you will want to avoid judging the people with whom you work. Successful collaborators are people who communicate that they are nonjudgmental and nonevaluative about others.

Consider the following alternatives:

Say: I've noticed that you walk around the room while giving directions.
Rather than: You pace around the room too much.
Or: You shouldn't walk around the room so much.

Say: I'm not sure I understand the selection of that activity for this lesson. Would you take a minute to help me see the connection?
Rather than: Why would you have selected that activity? You couldn't have thought it would be effective with these students, could you?

Each example demonstrates how information can be communicated with or without neutrality. Notice, too, that positive evaluations and judgments can have undesirable effects on relationships similar to those with negative evaluations. If a colleague generally praises you and expresses positive evaluations of you as a person when discussing a shared project, you may come to expect it and feel criticized or uncertain when these evaluations are not offered. Evaluations of people can be avoided by focusing your comments on the activity rather than the person. Using concrete, specific language also helps to clarify the focus.

Say: Your calm, quiet voice helped me to slow down and think about what I was saying.
Rather than: You're wonderful! Just your voice helps me to think things through.

Suggestions for Improving Your Communication Skills

In addition to the communication principles given throughout this chapter, we offer several suggestions you may find helpful as you attempt to refine your own verbal and nonverbal skills.

Become a Student of Communication

Because communication is the smallest unit of concern in interactions and comprises the most basic set of skills needed in collaborative activities, you will want to learn more and become more skillful with communication skills as you participate in collaborative interactions. A note of caution is warranted, however. Like most people, you may conclude that you already have a high degree of communication skill, since you communicate regularly in your professional and personal life. As you read about the skills in this chapter and in Chapters 3 and 4, you may believe you have "had that course" or acquired the skills elsewhere. Keep these two points in mind: First, understanding or being aware of communication skills alone does not improve your communication. Only through self-reflection and continuing practice can you improve your skills. Our students repeatedly share with us that focusing on and rehearsing skills is somewhat humbling; implementing the skills is much more difficult than simply recognizing them! Second, regardless of your knowledge or proficiency level after much practice, you will never fully master communication, since each new person, interaction, and situation will require you to practice and refine your skills further. We are reminded of this lesson regularly as we teach and learn from others.

Nurture and Communicate Openness

Perhaps the most pronounced theme that runs through our work on collaboration, and specifically this text, is the absolutely essential requirement for openness. *Openness* refers to your ability to suspend or eliminate judgment and evaluation of information and situations until you have explored adequately the various potential meanings and explanations. For example, when we discussed emergent characteristics of collaboration in Chapter 1, we noted that in order to collaborate, individuals should value joint decision making or at least be willing to experiment with it. In Chapter 5, we will emphasize the importance of fully exploring problems to avoid formulating hasty and inaccurate problem statements. Hopefully, the importance of an attitude of openness became even more explicit earlier in this chapter, where we discussed the need to be aware of your frame of reference and those of others to minimize misunderstandings in communication and remove blocks to listening. Openness, in the context of verbal communication, is similar to the sense of acceptance associated with the neutrality principle, but the focus in that discussion was on eliminating judgments about people rather than deferring judgments about situations. In this context we are encouraging you to set aside your biases and explore various aspects of a situation before attempting to decipher the message.

PUTTING IDEAS INTO PRACTICE 2.2

Listening Strategies to Try

Becoming a proficient communicator requires practice. As you think about becoming a student of communication, you might try some deliberate practice activities. For example, during a team meeting or planning period with a colleague, do the following:

◆ Set a listening goal. Identify ahead of time what information you are going to try to gain from your interaction.

◆ Identify at least three listening strategies that you will use during your interaction in order to accomplish your listening goal.

◆ Make mental notes about the speaker's body language and other nonverbal behaviors. Consider what these behaviors may be communicating. Are they consistent with the words your colleague is using? Do they suggest a stronger or weaker interest than the words convey?

◆ While listening, identify the main themes or points your colleague is sharing.

◆ After the interaction, assess your success in attaining your listening goal. Write a summary of your colleague's primary points and concerns. Summarize your listening behaviors and decide which were most and least useful in accomplishing your listening goal.

Keep Communication Meaningful

You will invest more in communication when you believe the information shared will be meaningful to you. It is unlikely that you will invest significantly in communication around topics or information that you have not sought or that you do not see as important. Specifically, unrequested suggestions and advice, although frequently shared, often have little meaning and may have an unintended negative impact. How meaningful and effective would it be if, with no request from you, a colleague said to you over lunch, "I've watched you with José, and I think you might have more success if you used a concrete model of the task performance." The notion of providing a concrete model for this student may have great value, but such unsolicited advice is likely to be unwanted and seem intrusive. It may well make you feel defensive and hesitant to discuss the matter.

A second aspect that influences the meaningfulness of communication is the *amount* of information being communicated. Too much or too little information is not meaningful. Have you had the experience of asking a colleague or co-worker a simple question, such as "How is the new student adjusting?" and you get a diatribe with more information than you ever wanted to know about the situation? You may have asked the question in passing or out of general interest and started a verbal landslide. You probably know a number of people who tend to give such lengthy responses. Do you try to avoid giving them an opening to speak?

This, or simply "tuning out", is a common response to such highly talkative people. Conversely, have you ever found yourself providing too much information to others? As you begin observing your own communication, you may find that you sometimes obscure the meaning of what you are trying to communicate by doing this.

Alternatively, everyone experiences exchanges in which too little information is shared. You may have had experiences trying to communicate with someone who seems to expect you to be a mind reader. If so, you know how difficult it can be to ensure clear understanding when others withhold needed information.

As you work toward effective interpersonal communication, you should ensure that communication is meaningful by judging the amounts of information wanted by the people with whom you are interacting. When you are relying on information from others, you may find that when they give you too much or too little, your task is either to work to obtain more information or to focus and narrow the information they are supplying.

Use Silence Effectively

We noted earlier that silence and pauses are important nonverbal behaviors that are related to speech flow and pace or may be used as minimal encouragers. However, beyond these uses, silence is an extremely powerful communication tool in its own right. You are undoubtedly familiar with the "deadly silence" parents and teachers use to communicate disapproval or anger to children. You may have even used it or experienced it yourself in adult relationships. Surely silence can be awkward or seem punishing in conversations, but very few people seem to understand how powerful it is in communicating interest, concern, and empathy, as well as respect to others. It also has another advantage and can be a very helpful strategy because it allows others to pause and think through what they are trying to communicate; this very often enhances the quality and meaning of their messages.

The definition of silence for our purposes is the absence of verbal noise or talk. But how long must there be no talk before a space in the talk can be considered silence? Goodman (1978, 1984) has offered several concepts that help to clarify this. He suggests that the length of time between two speakers' verbal expressions varies within each conversation, and the amount of silent time that qualifies as a "silence response" is relative to each conversation's tempo and patterns of speech, two topics addressed earlier. For example, if two people exchange several comments and pause for about one and a half seconds after each speaker completes a thought and before another starts, then a pause of two or three seconds may be required for a silence response. On the other hand, if two people are talking but only allowing about a quarter of a second of verbal space between taking turns to talk, one second may constitute a silence response.

Silence and its impact are more easily understood when you consider the alternatives: interruptions, overtalk, and reduced verbal spacing. *Interruptions* occur when one speaker disrupts another's message in order to deliver his or her own. Interruptions may occur while the speaker is still talking or during a brief pause in speech. When someone is speaking and another interrupts, there is a period of *overtalk* in which both speakers are talking simultaneously until one relinquishes the conversation to the other. The final alternative, *reduced verbal spacing*, is related to silence and pauses but also distinct from them. It refers to the pace of the turn taking in verbal interaction. It occurs when a new speaker begins talking during what is meant to be a brief pause in someone else's speech. In its most exaggerated form, one speaker appears to clip off the last word or two of the previous speaker's talk.

All of these alternatives to silence (interruptions, overtalk, and reduced verbal spacing) have similarities. They may occur because the person using them has a need to control the situation, to demonstrate knowledge, to try to reduce the speaker's rambling talk, or simply to be center stage. Whatever the reason, these responses are likely to have a negative impact on the conversation and relationship. They say, "Listen to *me*," "It's *my* turn," "What *I* have to say has more value than what you're saying." These responses certainly suggest to the other person that he or she is less competent, important, or interesting than the person taking control of the conversation. They are likely to produce frustration and sometimes anger as the person who is verbally "crowded" feels less and less understood and valued.

In your conversations, interviews, and professional discussions, try to develop a habit of protecting verbal space. It will give the other person the opportunity to finish talking and give you the opportunity to consider what the other has said and how you want to respond. In addition to avoiding verbal crowding, this silence response or verbal space conveys that you are interested in the other's comments and are taking the time to comprehend the message before responding.

A final point to consider is that the amount of silent space that creates the positive impact you desire varies with each conversational pair. Analogous to inadequate silence, unnaturally long periods of silence can convey disinterest or other negative messages. There are no inviolable rules about verbal spacing. Sometimes, in a fast-paced discussion, three seconds is a significant silence. At other times, particularly if the topic is emotional and one or more speakers are describing personal feelings, silences of several seconds or more than a minute may be appropriate nonverbal cues. Through experimentation you can learn to determine the desirable amounts of silence in each relationship and conversation within that relationship.

Adapt Your Communication to Match the Task and the Relationship

Professionals who are effective communicators tend to adapt their communication according to the task, the relationship, and the characteristics of the individuals involved. This includes choosing language that is clear and efficient, identifying the information content that is needed, and using verbal communication strategies that will best elicit the preferred responses. If you think about the individuals with whom you interact, you will probably include colleagues, administrators, parents, paraprofessionals, and professionals from other agencies. Furthermore, you may differentiate ongoing and regular collegial relationships from more temporary and infrequent interactions, such as annual review meetings. The nature of the relationship and its level of development should influence your choice of the appropriate communication style. As you collaborate in established or developing relationships, one of your responsibilities is to use communication strategies that will best facilitate the collaborative activity. Because there are no simple rules or strategies for adapting your verbal communication, your ability to understand the principles and learn to use many of the skills included in this text can help you to do this.

SUMMARY

Effective communication is critical in all areas of life, and it is particularly essential to your success as a school professional. Three primary types of communication include unilateral, directive, and transactional. Unlike the first two, transactional communication emphasizes that participants in the communication process engage in continuous and simultaneous communication across multiple channels. This model is characterized by mutual influence as participants strive to develop shared meanings. Attributes common to this and most communication models include channel, message, sender-receiver, and noise. It is also characterized by the concepts of multichannel communication and continuous feedback.

In preparing for collaborative interactions, you should come to understand your own and others' frames of reference and how these have been shaped by past experiences, your professional preparation, and cultural identity. Furthermore, you should remain vigilant in monitoring the possible effect your own frame of reference or that of others may have on your interactions.

Listening and nonverbal communication are fundamental to interpersonal communication. Listening is a complex process that can be impeded by various internal and external events. However, it can be improved by using metacognitive and other strategies. Nonverbal cues are powerful communication mechanisms that include body movements, vocal cues, spatial relations, and minimal encouragers. Principles of nonverbal and verbal communication provide guidance for successful interactions. Two significant concepts for understanding nonverbal communication are individualism and congruence. Principles of verbal communication emphasize concreteness and neutrality. Effective communication is characterized by openness, meaningfulness, effective use of silence, and an ability to adapt communication to meet the needs of the task and the relationship.

ACTIVITIES AND ASSIGNMENTS

1. To open yourself to considering alternative meanings and frames of reference, try to generate four distinctly different possible meanings for the statements below. Get additional practice by doing the same for statements made by others in the course of conversations during the next few days.

Practice statements:

a. Teacher: I really don't know what to do to help her. I desperately need your help.

b. Parent: He's been in special education for three years now. Isn't he caught up yet?

c. Speech and language specialist: If I'm going to work in classrooms with students, shouldn't I take courses in how to be a teacher?

2. Use the four types of nonverbal cues as if they were a checklist and observe interpersonal interactions to see if you can identify examples of each class. See if you can describe the ways in which nonverbal cues influence (strengthen or detract from) the messages being conveyed. Does the degree of congruence between the verbal and nonverbal messages affect the communication?

3. Read the following vague statements or questions and imagine a situation in your professional setting where each could apply. Then write four alternative, more specific and concrete statements or questions for each.

a. How is he doing at school?

b. She's lazy and insubordinate.

c. That parent is always involved.

4. Tape-record (with permission) an interaction with a client or colleague. This may be at a meeting or in casual conversation. Listen to the tape later and identify any verbalizations that communicated bias or evaluation. Try to construct alternative responses that are neutral.

5. Challenge yourself to allow increasingly greater verbal space in some conversations. Lengthen, ever so slightly, the verbal space that follows someone else's turn to talk and precedes yours. As you do this in different interactions, observe how it affects the pace and comfort of the conversation.

FOR FURTHER READING

Banbury, M. M., & Hebert, C. R. (1992). Do you see what I mean? Body language in classroom interactions. *Teaching Exceptional Children, 24*(2), 34–38.

Burley-Allen, M. (1995). *Listening: The forgotten skill: A self-teaching guide* (2nd ed.). New York: Wiley.

DeVito, J. A. (2001). *The interpersonal communication book* (9th ed.). New York: Longman.

Griffith, D. A., & Harvey, M. G. (2001). Executive insights: An intercultural communication model for use in global organizational networks. *Journal of International Marketing, 9* (3), 87–104.

McKay, M., Davis, M., & Fanning, P. (1995). *Messages: The communication skills book* (2nd ed.). Oakland, CA: New Harbinger.

Wolvin, A., & Coakley, C. G. (1995). *Listening* (5th ed.). Dubuque, IA: Brown & Benchmark.

3

Using Statements

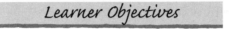

Connections

Using the discussion of collaboration prerequisites and the basic structure for communication detailed in Chapter 2, Chapter 3 outlines principles for making appropriate statements during interactions. Throughout this chapter these principles are applied, using situations for providing feedback as specific illustrations.

Learner Objectives

After reading this chapter you will be able to:

1. Identify the types of statements used to provide, seek, and clarify information.
2. Generate examples of the types of statements used for each communication purpose.
3. Define *interpersonal feedback* and list criteria for effective feedback.
4. Describe guidelines for effective interpersonal feedback.

INTRODUCTION

Statements are central elements of communication. Consider the message that each of these statements conveys:

- ◆ Emil scored at the 4.6 grade level on reading comprehension.
- ◆ You should ask José's parents to have his medication level checked.
- ◆ You said that you're experiencing difficulty in accomplishing the therapy goals in the classroom.
- ◆ I heard that nearly all of the students with learning disabilities will take the proficiency tests.
- ◆ Veda seems overwhelmed by the academic demands.
- ◆ When Roger began to slip sideways after he was sitting on the floor with the other students, you reached down to reposition him. But Jacob gently pushed him back into the proper position and you sat back.
- ◆ I wonder what you're thinking about the situation.

You use statements for many purposes: to provide information, to clarify information, and occasionally, to seek information. The material in this chapter will demonstrate that the way you structure, word, and deliver statements has a significant impact on the verbal responses you receive from others and on your relationship with the individuals with whom you are interacting. Certainly you use both questions and statements together in your interactions. But, as we noted in Chapter 2, our approach is to first assist you in developing discrete skills. This requires treating statements and questions as though they occur separately so that later you can blend them into effective interactions.

PURPOSES OF STATEMENTS

Statements That Provide Information

The most common function of statements is to provide information to others. You use statements when your primary purpose is to tell others something you think they want or need to know or what you want them to know. You may tell someone about a newly developed intervention strategy, you may explain how the changing composition of an interagency council will influence your program, or you may describe direct observations you made of a classroom or of a particular student's performance. You may also tell others about a situation or experience you have had, or you may give them advice about their own situations. We identify two primary types of statements whose overall purpose is to provide information—*descriptive statements* that outline events or experiences and *guiding statements* that subtly or explicitly direct actions by evaluating or advising.

Descriptive Statements

Often, you use statements to provide a verbal account of a situation, behavior, opinion, or feeling. When such a verbal account is offered without evaluation or advice, it is descriptive. Descriptive statements can be used to relate both overt and covert content. The most straightforward form of descriptive statement is that which provides a verbal account of an *overt* event, situation, or behavior. This requires identifying observable behaviors or permanent products such as written work and describing them without making judgments about them. You probably already have skill in this area because providing precise and objective descriptions of behavior is a basic component in the preprofessional training of most special services providers, although practice in this skill is usually aimed at describing student behavior.

Because the definition we have given for descriptive statements specifically excludes evaluating or advising, examples of evaluative and advisory statements are given to illustrate what descriptive statements are *not*. The following examples are provided solely to help you discriminate among descriptive, evaluative, and advisory statements. They are not meant to model effective means of delivering advice or evaluation, two topics addressed later in this chapter. Contrast the ways in which the same event can be described in the following statements:

> *Descriptive:* When Maryanne left the room during the discussion, several team members looked at each other. You stopped speaking and asked the group, "Should I wait for Maryanne to return?"
>
> *Evaluative:* You shouldn't have let Maryanne leave like that. It upset the team, and you didn't know whether you should continue.
>
> *Advisory:* You need to get everyone to agree on ground rules for participation before you have that team try group problem solving again.

The first of the foregoing examples meets the criteria for descriptive statements and stresses overt events—the observable behaviors of Mary-anne, the group leader (you), and the other group members. Those behaviors are described without evaluation or advice in the first examples. The next statements do not meet the criteria for descriptive statements. The second is evaluative ("You shouldn't have" conveys judgment about another's behavior). Notice, too, that in addition to being evaluative, this statement contains several *inferences* ("upset the team"; "You didn't know") based on behaviors that were specifically described in the first statement. The third statement is advisory ("You need to" suggests action).

Another frequent and important use of descriptive statements is for detailing *covert* events, attitudes, perceptions, and feelings. Because covert material is not directly observable, descriptions of such events will involve some inference, but the inference should not be so great as to constitute an *interpretation*. For example, "I thought the team meeting was efficient, and it seemed like everyone was satisfied with the decision" reflects inferences that, if examined, could probably be traced back to specific behavioral indicators. On the other hand, a statement such as "I thought the team meeting was efficient, and it was clearly effective in getting people to make the right decision" describes the speaker's opinion of the team meeting, but it also makes a large inferential leap and interprets the information. It suggests that the speaker is equating effectiveness and efficiency with his sense that a correct decision was made.

Distinctions among descriptive, evaluative, and advisory statements of covert material also are illustrated in the following examples:

Descriptive: I became so anxious when it was my turn to speak at the in-service workshop that my hands and the papers I held shook. I perspired, my mouth was terribly dry, and I felt all tongue-tied. I felt like the floor would fall out from under me.

Evaluative: I'm such a disaster as a speaker. I'm really not a good spokesperson. I *look* nervous and nobody can follow what I'm saying.

Advisory: I must avoid getting into situations where I'll have to talk in front of other people because they are so upsetting to me. I should have Carlos represent us at meetings.

The topic in these examples is the speaker's feelings (covert) about public speaking. The descriptive statement includes neither evaluation nor advice, as it describes feelings ("anxious," "tongue-tied"). This statement goes further in providing a concrete description of the feelings through describing observable behaviors (shaking hands, perspiration, dry mouth). The second statement is not descriptive because it contains evaluation ("I'm such a disaster"; "I'm really not . . . good"). Similarly, the third statement offers advice ("I must avoid"; "I should have") rather than description.

Although these illustrative statements were designed to provide clear examples of the descriptive, evaluative, and advisory concepts, in your day-to-day interactions you are not likely to find such clear-cut examples. Instead, you generally will encounter statements similar to the two below. They each contain descriptive and nondescriptive components. Consider each carefully and see if you can identify their evaluative, advising, and descriptive elements. Consider, too, the levels of inference they imply.

- I observed Timothy in his occupational therapy group and I was amazed! He has such a low self-concept that when he made a mistake he marked all over his project in black marker and tore it up. He threw it at the wastebasket and put his head on the table. His behavior was pathetic.
- I observed your group, and you shouldn't feel so bad about your lesson. You're a really good therapist and you do a great job with some very challenging students! Your presentation took only one minute, and you demonstrated all of the three movements we talked about.

The first example contains some descriptive phrases ("observed," "marked all over," "tore it," "threw it," "put his head on the table"). It also contains an evaluative phrase ("behavior was pathetic") and highly inferential reference ("low self-concept"). It does not contain any advisory phrases. Similarly, the second example also includes descriptive and nondescriptive elements ("I observed," "Your presentation," "the three movements we talked about"). An evaluative phrase ("You're a really good therapist") and an advisory one ("You shouldn't feel so bad") also are present. The statement does not make inferences, but it includes nonspecific terms and would be improved by more concrete language.

As you begin to attend more closely to the statements you and others make during your interactions, you undoubtedly will find that purely descriptive statements are rare. And although it is often difficult to describe something without evaluating or advising, you can improve your skills in this area by monitoring your own statements. As you will see later in this chapter and in the next, skill in using descriptive statements contributes greatly to effective interactions. By conveying information without judging or advising, purely descriptive statements minimize the likelihood of offending the receiver. Such statements promote clear and honest communication without causing listeners to become defensive.

Guiding Statements

Some statements provide information in order to guide action—to urge others to act, feel, or think in a certain way. Two categories of guiding statements are those that explain and those that advise.

Statements that provide information in an instructive way and rely on reasoning, an understanding of cause-and-effect relationships, or logic are *explanations*. They translate ideas and interpret information. Use of these statements nearly always means that the person offering the explanation has greater expertise or knowledge than the one receiving it. Explanations can be appreciated, particularly when someone requests them—such as when you ask a colleague to explain a new service delivery policy to you or when you ask another specialist to help you interpret student performance data. You will find that this type of statement is particularly valuable when you are asked to share your knowledge to clarify a point, elaborate an idea, or answer a question. The use of explanations is also an effective strategy for developing the shared meanings that are so important in effective communication.

Although the ability to give clear explanations is considered an essential competency for teachers, it generally is classified as an instructional rather than interpersonal skill (Johnson & Roellke, 1999; McCaleb, 1987). As an instructional skill, explaining typically includes emphasis on clearly presenting material and using examples. Some frameworks also include using advance organizers, demonstrations, paraphrasing, or review of salient points as components of effective explaining. The skills of defining concepts, answering questions, and giving corrective feedback also are considered part of explaining in instruction.

As a school professional, you are familiar with explanations and aware of their value in your professional interactions. Our caution here, however, is that because you are likely to be proficient in giving explanations, you may tend to overuse them. We suggest that you strive to employ them infrequently with colleagues because they represent directive communication, not the two-way transactional communication described in Chapter 2. Explanations are most appropriate when they provide others with information they have explicitly requested. When they are uninvited, explanations may have all of the undesirable effects of unsolicited advice, which is addressed as part of our next topic.

Advice is a category of information-providing statements intended to guide action by suggesting, hinting, or even commanding that someone take specific actions or accept certain beliefs. *Suggestions* are statements of "gentle advice" offered as possibilities for consideration; they communicate clearly that they are tentative

PUTTING IDEAS INTO PRACTICE 3.1

Tips for Sharing Information

Knowledge or information is power. When you provide others with accurate, objective, and useful information, you are empowering them. Once empowered with information and the knowledge and skills to use it, people are increasingly able to take control over their professional and personal lives and to take action to get what they want and need to succeed (Man, 1999; Turnbull & Turnbull, 2001). As teachers and service providers, your tendency may be to explain regularly and provide copious information that may not be received as useful or relevant to colleagues or parents. Here are some tips to help you practice useful strategies and avoid others.

◆ Determine what information is needed or requested.
◆ Offer objective, accurate descriptions or explanations.
◆ Identify and focus on main points.
◆ Ensure that the information is relevant to the person receiving it.
◆ Avoid the use of "jargon" and clarify those terms that cannot be avoided.
◆ Minimize the use of evaluation and advice unless it is requested.
◆ Do not offer interpretations or try to read minds.

and subject to the evaluation of their recipient. For example, when a colleague suggests to you, "One option might be to consider some of the new materials we just received," he or she is giving you a hint or a tip. Your colleague is simply offering one of potentially many sets of information for your evaluation and is acknowledging that in your role as decision maker you may accept or reject it.

Advice may be offered also as a direct *command* that insists on compliance or cooperation. In many interactions, commands may seem overly directive, such as when someone says, "You will certainly have to change that" or "You must get some hands-on training." Commands are often received badly. They may remind their recipients of someone's inappropriate exercise of authority over them or of years of parental directives. They often imply the sender's superiority over the receiver. When any of these things happen, commands are likely to cause resistance and become less effective than other efforts to guide behavior.

However, commands are not always negative, and they do not necessarily imply that the recipient is inferior to the speaker. Sometimes they are time-savers when the participants agree that one party has greater expertise in a given area. When such agreement is present it can eliminate the air of arrogance that some people perceive is associated with commands. This situation is illustrated in the following statement made by a physical education teacher, who is telling a special education teacher how to adapt a classroom game so a particular student can participate. In this example, a series of commands may well be the most efficient approach to guiding the action of a colleague.

Although service providers are likely to be proficient at giving explanations, overuse of this skill, especially when they have not been asked for information, can interfere with communication and hamper collaboration.

◆ First, point to the target and say, "Throw it there." Then wait ten seconds to see if Victor responds. If not, physically prompt him to throw the beanbag.

Like explanations, whether offered as a suggestion or a command, advice is unlikely to be helpful and may well be detrimental to relationships if given to someone who has not requested it. Unfortunately, advice is a frequently overused response when people are trying to assist others in problem solving. This should not be difficult to understand in the context of the professional socialization factors we discussed in the first chapter. School professionals are likely to be competent, independent problem solvers, and they may quickly jump to designing and presenting solutions as advice when they begin working with others. However, unsolicited advice is likely to be perceived as intrusive and even arrogant. Recipients of this unrequested information are likely to feel defensive and misunderstood. For these reasons we encourage professionals in collaborative situations to wait until asked before giving advice to other adults.

Statements That Seek Information

A second function of the statements you use is to seek or solicit information from others. This function may be accomplished through the use of *inflection, commands,* and *indirect questions.* To illustrate the use of inflection, imagine this statement spoken with a querying tone of voice that may sound almost like a question: "The books are no longer available. If only I knew what that meant!" Commands also may be used to request information in conversation. Statements like those below request information without using direct questions. You may notice that the tone changes across these examples, with the first (a command) sounding demanding and the second and third (indirect questions) being more invitational.

- Give us the results of the assessment.
- I wonder what was going on in the group when he began singing.
- I'd really like to know more about that.

Using statements to seek information is an appealing alternative to excessive question asking, as discussed in the next chapter. You can alternate or integrate information-seeking statements with questions to avoid creating an atmosphere of interrogation. Using general statements similar to those above is particularly valuable when initially exploring an issue.

While information-seeking statements offer a viable alternative to serial questions, they cannot substitute entirely for questions. Indirect questions and inflection express one's interest and invite others to continue talking, but they often are vague and lead to unfocused responses. They seem to be most effective in initiating discussions. As discussions progress and require greater focus, you may find yourself using commands (e.g., Tell me which boy was late.) to obtain specific information. As previously noted, commands can sound demanding and using a series of such statements may interfere with the relationship. If, after you have used inflection, commands, and indirect questions to initiate discussions and invite others to share their thoughts and ideas, you find that you still need specific information, carefully worded questions may be the preferable strategy.

Statements That Confirm or Clarify Information

Statements often are used to confirm or clarify information that has already been shared. When used in this way, they may be addressing simultaneously the combined purposes of providing information and seeking information. Frequently, statements designed to confirm or clarify are restatements of already available information offered to ensure that participants are developing the common meanings and shared understanding essential for effective communication. Typical ways of clarifying statements are through *paraphrasing, reflecting, summarizing,* and *checking.*

Paraphrasing

In paraphrasing, you restate in your own words what you think another person has just said. Paraphrasing focuses on relatively small units of information that were discussed by just one other individual, and it involves little or no inference. Consider the following example.

A teacher and principal are discussing how to handle a problematic situation that includes the parents of a student with disabilities.

Teacher: I'm not sure I should meet alone with his parents. We seem to be in conflict all the time.

Principal: You have ongoing conflict with these parents (inflection indicates the tentative nature of this response and suggests a querying attitude).

Teacher: Well, not "ongoing." Actually, it was just once—at our meeting last month. They were furious at me when I told them his grades at our conference. The father got red in the face, hit the table a couple of times, and left really angry. He won't return any of my phone calls.

Principal: It was only one event, but it's still unresolved and you think they—especially the father—are still angry with you.

Teacher: Yes, but I did get to talk to the mother on the phone. She apologized and explained that her husband's been working two shifts, is really tired, and has been getting angry easily. He also feels guilty because he can't help with homework while he works so much. The mother says he wants to meet with me to see how we can help their son—I'm just not sure.

Principal: Even though the parents seem to have gotten over their anger and want to respond constructively, you're still not certain you should meet with them.

Teacher: Yes. It may be calm now, but I've given two tests since our last meeting. He failed both of them. His father's having problems with his temper.

Principal: His father may get angry again if you tell him about the test grades.

The foregoing example provides an opportunity to examine how paraphrasing functions to influence the relationship. By accurately restating the main points in the teacher's statements, the principal demonstrated attention to and accurate understanding of what the teacher was relating and thus conveyed interest in the problem as well as in the teacher as a person.

PUTTING IDEAS INTO PRACTICE 3.2

Clarifying and Confirming Information Using Statements

Sometimes we use statements to confirm or clarify information. When used this way, statements help to demonstrate that we are listening to others and want to understand them.

- Paraphrasing—restate what another has said, using many of the same words.
- Reflecting—restate what another has said but use additional descriptive words to try to capture the affective message as well.
- Summarizing—restate concisely several main points from a preceding or ongoing discussion.
- Checking—restate and often ask for confirmation that the restatement is accurate and that the persons involved have similar perceptions of what has occurred.

The principal's paraphrasing also helped to clarify the information provided. If any of the principal's restatements had been incorrect, the teacher would have been able to rephrase or modify them. Because the principal's paraphrases were succinct and captured the essence of the teacher's comments, they also helped to focus the discussion and encourage the teacher to examine the situation more closely. This strategy maintained the teacher as the central figure and helped the principal and the teacher establish a shared understanding of the situation. These effects on relationship may become clearer if you contrast that example with this alternative:

Teacher: I'm not sure I should meet alone with his parents. We had a falling-out last month.

Principal: I agree. We don't need conflict between parents and staff. Let's have the counselor meet with them instead.

The principal may appear to be supporting the teacher, but such a quick response reveals the principal's tendency to solve problems independently and suggests both lack of concern for the teacher and her perception of the problem as well as lack of respect for the teacher's own resources. Perhaps more important, by contrasting the two examples and their resolutions, you can see how the principal's quick solution or advice in the second example neither solved the problem nor demonstrated respect for the teacher as an independent professional capable of solving a problem with some support.

Reflecting

Reflection, a clarifying statement more complex than paraphrasing, was popularized by the psychologist Carl Rogers (1951) more than 50 years ago. It focuses on circumscribed information provided by a single individual, but it also includes references on the part of the speaker. In reflection, you describe what another person has said and try to capture the affective meaning of the message. Because you cannot observe another's feelings, you examine the verbal and nonverbal information provided in both the overt and covert aspects of the communication and infer what this information communicates about the emotional meaning. Reflection is a way of making explicit the information that is being conveyed implicitly during interaction. It demonstrates that you understand another's feelings, as the following vignette illustrates. Imagine that the previous example of the teacher and principal discussing an angry father ends like this:

Teacher: Yes. I may be calm now, but I've given two tests since our last meeting [*heavy sigh*]. He failed both of them [*laughs and looks away*]. His father's having problems with his temper.

Principal: His father may get angry again if you tell him about the test grades. The way you laughed makes me think you're anxious about this.

Teacher: Yes, I met another angry father alone last year, and he was really a bully and physically pushed me. I know he was *trying* to scare me, and he was successful. I'm afraid to meet alone with people like that. Can you meet with us?

Principal: His father may get angry again and possibly even pose a physical threat. You'll feel safer if someone could meet with you and the parents. I'm quite sure I'm available, but if not, can we reschedule the meeting?

In this excerpt, the principal restated the teacher's messages in her own words and reflected the teacher's feelings and thus conveyed his understanding of the situation from the teacher's point of view. This response is often integral in building relationships and in promoting a sense of trust, since it conveys that the speaker's ideas and feelings are valued.

These illustrations of reflection are presented out of context and can only suggest how reflection functions. In fact, our examples may unintentionally suggest that reflection is a simple type of verbal statement. Although the wording may be simple, accurately perceiving and reflecting someone's verbal and nonverbal messages is an extremely complex endeavor.

When you reflect accurately, you convey understanding of another person's thoughts, feelings, and experiences; in other words, you *empathize*. Understanding accompanied by congruent nonverbal behavior is referred to as *empathic listening* (Gamble & Gamble, 1999; Rogers, 1972). When you convey empathy through reflection and supportive nonverbal behaviors, you help to establish trust in your relationship with others. Reflection has other advantages as well. When you hear your own messages reflected it may give you the opportunity to consider complex thoughts a little longer and may allow you to have a better understanding of your own experiences.

However, it is important to recognize that reflection does not go very far beyond the speaker's overt messages. Its intention is not to explain anything new to the speaker. Reflection is thus distinguished from interpretation, which does go beyond the information the speaker has presented. Interpretation attempts to explain the speaker's experience in terms of a theory or a level of understanding beyond what the speaker knows. As Goodman (1978) points out, interpretation is usually an attempt to show an understanding of the speaker that is better than the speaker's self-understanding. Consider this alternative response to the teacher's concern about meeting with an angry parent:

Principal: You're afraid the father will be angry and violent. This is a lot like your conflict with many of the male teachers. You seem to be easily threatened by men.

This example is exaggerated to emphasize the potentially intrusive nature of this type of response and to support our contention that interpretation should be used very little, if at all, between school professionals in work settings. Interpretation may be very appropriate in more help-oriented or therapist–client relationships, but interpretation as described here goes beyond the scope of what is appropriate between colleagues.

Summarizing

Summarizing consists of one or more statements that restate, in concise form, several preceding statements made by the individuals involved in the interaction. It is a means of ensuring that all involved individuals understand what has

Summarizing is an important strategy for confirming information and ensuring that all share the same understanding.

been said, and it functions in much the same way as a summary section at the end of a lengthy piece of expository text. Summarizing differs from paraphrasing in at least two significant ways. When you paraphrase, you are simply restating what one other person has just said. Paraphrasing is relatively immediate and it is a response to a discrete, self-contained piece of information. On the other hand, summarizing is not as immediate and it is a response to several pieces of information, often presented by more than one participant. The following examples of summarizing heard at team meetings illustrate this point:

- *Example 1:* Let's see if we agree on the major points. Mrs. Cardenas, you've said you're concerned about Tom's disruptive and off-task behavior in your math class; Mr. O'Reilly said Tom's behavior is appropriate but wants him to have an extra period of art since he does so well in that class. And, Tom, you said you want to drop the math class until next semester because you feel like you're too far behind to ever catch up. Does anyone want to correct anything or add comments?
- *Example 2:* It seems we've considered all the main issues. Cathy, you've described your efforts to implement peer tutoring, self-instructional materials, and computer-based activities in the classroom. Despite all the planning you and the grade-level team have done, Yanina still requires too much assistance to work independently in your classroom. And Hank, you've seen Yanina work semi-independently with the computer when you sit near her, and you'd like to try to provide some in-class assistance. Have I missed anything?

Checking

Checking—the clarifying or confirming function of communication—is sometimes referred to as *perception checking* or *checking for accuracy.* All of these referents have the same purpose as we have described for clarifying. We mention this here and again in Chapter 4 because this function is so frequently addressed through combining a statement and a question. In fact, if paraphrasing, reflecting, and summarizing are to be maximally effective, they themselves will be checked, or followed up with a question to ensure agreement and accuracy. The final questions in the preceding illustrations of summarizing are examples of checking.

GIVING VERBAL FEEDBACK

In Chapter 2 we discussed the concept of continuous feedback and noted that communicators simultaneously send and receive messages as they interact, and so it is not possible to communicate without feedback. In the strictest sense, all transactional communication, whether verbal statements, questions, or nonverbal messages, is feedback. This kind of feedback is often not intentional, but it provides important information and often leads to changes in behaviors of the participants. In this chapter our focus is on intentional verbal feedback as a skill that should be purposefully developed and used by school professionals.

Although you will use statements throughout your interactions, one specific situation in which they will be relied upon extensively is when you provide verbal feedback to others. And since effectively giving feedback is an essential but often poorly applied communication skill, the ideas in this section should provide opportunities to practice both your general skill for making statements and their specific application in giving feedback. Most simply, feedback is providing others with information about their behaviors or performance. It can be given for many different purposes, including the following:

1. Providing objective information about observed behaviors of others or observed conditions.
2. Providing information about the impressions or feelings that these behaviors or conditions cause.
3. Clarifying what the observed behaviors or conditions may mean or signify to the individual involved.

Characteristics of Effective Interpersonal Feedback

To collaborate successfully with others, you will need to be adept at giving effective feedback. You also will want to learn to solicit and accept feedback from others as a means of securing valuable information about your own communication behaviors and about your collaborative relationships. This is true whether your collaboration is aimed at helping each other develop and refine the skills presented in this text or targeted at work-related activities.

Feedback has a clear set of characteristics. It should be (1) descriptive, (2) specific, (3) directed toward changeable behaviors and situations, (4) concise, and (5) checked for clarity. Any effective feedback statement includes all of these characteristics.

Feedback is Descriptive Rather than Evaluative or Advisory

An individual is more likely to listen when someone simply describes what has been observed. As noted earlier, descriptive information is nonthreatening and nonjudgmental. The implication of this for feedback is depicted in the following examples:

> **Say:** I noticed that you raised your voice.
>
> **Rather than:** You talk too loud all the time.
>
> **Or:** You shouldn't yell.
>
> **Or:** Have you tried keeping a calm voice?

When you describe a personal observation, the other individual is free to use the information or not as he or she sees fit. On the other hand, evaluative or advisory feedback conveys that the other person should take action or change. This is likely to cause the person to feel defensive and criticized rather than willing to make a change.

As you may have surmised, avoiding judgmental statements requires the elimination of both negative and positive comments. The following statements easily might be seen as evaluative and are likely to be threatening to the person hearing them:

- ◆ You didn't do that very well.
- ◆ Your system doesn't make any sense.

Equally important, however, is the fact that positive comments also convey a judgment. For example:

- ◆ You did good work when you . . .
- ◆ You do such a good job with . . .

Individuals who make positive judgments are likely also to make negative ones. The person receiving the feedback is justified in assuming that those who give praise or compliments also make critical evaluations, whether they are stated openly or not.

Feedback is Specific Rather than General

Descriptions of specific behaviors are more easily understood than are general comments. "You sounded angry" communicates much less than "I noticed that every time you spoke you frowned and raised your voice." As emphasized in Chapter 2, specific and concrete language helps to ensure clear communication.

Feedback is Directed toward Behavior or a Situation That the Individual Can Change

In order for feedback to be useful, it needs to be directed at something the receiver can control or do something about. Feedback directed toward an attribute or situation the receiver cannot control is generally pointless and likely to interfere with effective communication. Physical traits such as height, age, or sex and situational aspects such as the size of the room or the administrator's leadership style are not behaviors that an individual can change. Telling someone that his age and physical appearance make it hard to talk to him could be more detrimental than helpful. On the other hand, information such as "You were busy filing papers when I was talking to you" or "I notice that you usually look at the desk when I'm talking" is information that may be acted upon if one chooses. You only increase others' frustration when you remind them of some attribute that cannot be changed.

Feedback is Concise

Concise feedback is easier to understand than feedback that contains extraneous detail or information. When first learning to give feedback, you may feel obligated to give very detailed information or to make many statements. When giving feedback, more is not necessarily better; too much information or too much verbiage, irrelevant information, and redundancy detracts from the main message. For example, compare the following two feedback statements. Which is more likely to help a teacher understand the colleague's confusion?

- Example 1: In terms of your language, I mean the words you used, you used complex and technical words that I didn't understand. The vocabulary you used was too specialized for me to understand. I didn't know what all your vocabulary meant so I didn't understand your main points. Everything has to be explained well or I get really disturbed and close out everything you say.
- Example 2: When you used technical terms I got lost. It would help me if you would define your terms and make your point again.

Feedback is Checked to Ensure Clear Communication

Perceptions of any event usually vary among individuals. Several people may participate in the same situation and yet experience it differently. Similarly, when you give feedback, the receiver may not receive the information the way it was intended. Although most of our examples of characteristics of effective feedback have focused on statements, questions are often needed to check for accuracy. An effective method for checking others' understanding of the feedback you have given is to ask them to paraphrase your feedback to see if it corresponds to what you intended. For example, you might say,

> I'm really concerned about whether I'm communicating clearly. Would you summarize what you've understood me to say?

Frequently when receiving feedback, the person will spontaneously confirm or appear to understand the feedback with a general comment, such as "Yes, I did do that" or "That's right." In this situation it may still be advisable to check for understanding. This checking might be done by re-phrasing or questioning as shown here:

Rephrasing: So it is correct to say that you . . .

Questioning: You said, "That's right." Which particular observations were correct?

PERSPECTIVES ON DIVERSITY 3.1

Cultural Considerations in Giving Feedback

In Chapter 2 cultural influences on communication were outlined. Collectivistic cultures were described as highly contextual, comfortable with silence, often indirect, and characteristically balanced in turn taking. Here are some suggestions that may make giving and receiving feedback more comfortable in cross cultural situations.

♦ Begin a session or conversation with salutations and inquiries about the individual's well-being.

♦ Use many contextual examples and descriptions.

♦ Use pauses and short periods of silence to allow the other to speak, clarify or question.

♦ Consider using reflection to provide the other with feedback about subtle cues and behaviors observed.

♦ Ensure the other has time and a welcoming environment for summarizing and responding to the feedback.

You also may want to check the accuracy of your observations that are the subject of your feedback, particularly if you are uncertain about what you observed. In checking for accuracy you might ask if the receiver agrees with your description of the observation. Two examples follow:

♦ It seemed to me that you were asking James questions more frequently than you were the others. Would you agree with that?

♦ Does it seem accurate to you that you asked James more questions than you were the others?

Suggestions for Giving Effective Feedback

Three suggestions for providing feedback are extremely important. Feedback should be (1) solicited, (2) direct, and (3) well-timed.

Feedback Should Be Solicited Rather than Imposed

Feedback, like advice and explanations, is most effective when someone has requested it. An individual who requests feedback is more likely to use it than one on whom feedback is imposed. Unsolicited feedback may make the receiver feel defensive and assume a "Who asked you?" attitude. When you first attempt to work collaboratively with a colleague, you should not assume that your colleague actually wants feedback. One way to avoid ineffective interaction is to wait for your colleague to provide an opportunity for you to give feedback. Then you need merely to confirm the request. The most direct way of ensuring that your colleague wants the feedback you believe he has requested is to respond to his apparent request with a question, such as "Are you asking for my feedback?" or "Do you want to know about that?" The following excerpt illustrates this:

Statement: I don't know why Jimmy doesn't follow directions. Do you think I'm not giving them clearly? How can I be more successful with him?

Response: It sounds like you'd like to examine how you give directions. Would it be helpful if I shared my observations on that?

Most frequently your colleague will not ask for feedback and you will face the prerequisite task of finding a way to be invited to provide it. Depending on the openness and attitude of your colleague, you may emphasize different aspects of the situation and use different communication skills to set the stage for giving feedback.

Feedback Should Be Direct Rather Than Indirect

Feedback is most effective when it is given directly to the person who can use it by the person who has made some observation. For example, instead of asking the principal to tell your co-teacher about ineffective teaching behavior, generally you should tell him or her personally. Similarly, although many school professionals write notes to communicate with other adults, notes may also decrease the effectiveness of feedback. Indirect feedback is more easily misinterpreted than is feedback given directly to the person involved. This is due in part to the lack of transactional communication in notes. The giver cannot check the feedback for accuracy, and the receiver cannot adequately clarify it.

Feedback Should Be Well-Timed

The immediacy of feedback is a subject of considerable attention in the research on learning, particularly in reference to learning new skills. Corrective feedback is most beneficial to learners when it is given immediately following the relevant event or behavior. This is not always possible or appropriate for interpersonal feedback, partly because it is not necessarily meant to be corrective or instructional in nature. But several guidelines can help you to determine the appropriate timing for feedback.

You should always ask yourself, "Is now the best time to give feedback?" If your colleague is extremely busy or rushed, the feedback may seem like an irritating intrusion. Or if some event has left your colleague upset and confused, immediate feedback may be seen as unduly demanding or even critical. Our recommendation is to provide feedback as soon as appropriate, not only so that it is recent but also so that it demonstrates your sensitivity to your colleague's receptiveness.

When you find you must delay giving feedback, you should use recent examples in your feedback statement. Your colleague who receives the feedback is more likely to understand and benefit from recent examples than from those that are more distant and possibly forgotten. The more time that passes between the event and the feedback, the less vivid the event will be in her memory.

In general, when giving feedback to others, ask yourself these questions:

◆ Will this person understand me?
◆ Will this person be able to accept my feedback?
◆ Will this person be able to use the information?

The most significant consideration is that feedback be constructive to the recipient. What you are about to say should be helpful and appreciated by this person. These considerations, along with use of the other characteristics and strategies we have presented, should maximize the effectiveness of the feedback you give to others.

SUMMARY

Statements are the primary verbal means of providing information to others. Statements that describe events or experiences and those that attempt to guide action are the most frequent forms of statements that provide information. A second purpose of statements is to seek information, often through commands or indirect questions. Confirming or clarifying information is the final purpose of statements and frequently is achieved through paraphrasing, reflecting, summarizing, or checking.

A communication skill that relies largely on statements—giving interpersonal feedback—illustrates several principles of communication. Characteristics of effective feedback include that it is descriptive, specific, directed toward changeable behaviors and situations, concise, and checked for clarity. In addition, for feedback to be maximally effective, it should be solicited, direct, and well-timed.

ACTIVITIES AND ASSIGNMENTS

1. Think of a problem with a student one of your colleagues has mentioned. Imagine an interaction in which you try to assist your colleague to solve the problem. Write down eight to ten statements you would probably make, then classify the purpose and format of each. Do you use certain types of statements more than others? What is the primary purpose of most of the statements you wrote? Is this what you believe is the best approach to helping someone solve a problem? If you find you are not using an appropriate range, review your responses to the above questions and construct different types of statements.

2. Explain to a colleague or a parent that you are trying to improve your verbal communication skills, and ask permission to tape-record an interaction with him or her. Review your tape and classify each statement according to its purpose and format. Consider which statements could be improved and write improved versions. Discuss your tape and written responses with a classmate or colleague.

3. Videotape a drama or soap opera on television and practice paraphrasing, reflecting, and summarizing the conversations. Invite a classmate to join you, and compare notes. You also can use this same tape to practice giving feedback.

4. Think of a student a colleague has recently talked about. Imagine that your colleague has asked you for help with the student. Make a list of all the questions you would ask the colleague about the student. Try to rephrase each of these queries as an indirect question.

5. Study and critique the text material on interpersonal feedback. Write an original example for each of the five characteristics described in the text. Write a separate statement to illustrate each characteristic even though one good example may include several of the key characteristics. Review your work with a classmate or colleague.

6. Critique each of the examples below to determine if they include the characteristics for effective feedback. Revise statements as necessary to include all characteristics.

   a. After you smiled and said, "Okay," Juan looked very relieved. Then when you nodded for him to join the group, a big smile covered his face. Is that what you observed too?

   b. The way you handled Jimmy seemed better today. He has made a lot of progress in his spelling, and your patience with his bad behavior has improved tremendously.

   c. You've really managed to get Sandy to behave in class. You should be very proud of yourself for what you've accomplished!

7. Observe someone interacting with one or more individuals (e.g., a parent and a child in the community, colleagues in a meeting, a friend at a party). Then write feedback statements describing what you observed. Evaluate your feedback statements against each of the five characteristics of effective feedback.

FOR FURTHER READING

Alessandra, T., & Hunsaker, P. (1993). *Communicating at work.* New York: Fireside.

Brammer, L. M., & MacDonald, G. (1999). *The helping relationship: Process and skills* (7th ed.). Boston: Allyn & Bacon.

Egan, G. (2001). *Skilled helper: A problem-management and opportunity-development approach to helping* (7th ed.). Belmont, CA: Wadsworth.

Okun, B. (2002). *Effective helping: Interviewing and counseling techniques* (6th ed.). Pacific Grove, CA: Brooks/Cole.

Verderber, R. F., & Verderber, S. K. (2002). *Communicate* (10th ed.). Belmont, CA: Wadsworth.

4

Asking Questions

Connections

Chapter 4 is in many ways analogous to Chapter 3. It focuses on a specific type of verbal communication skill—asking questions—and draws on communication information presented in earlier chapters. Strategies for enhancing your skill in asking questions are presented, and interviewing is outlined as a common situation in which question-asking skills are used.

Learner Objectives

After reading this chapter you will be able to:

1. Describe the major purposes of questions.
2. Analyze the characteristics of questions to determine their format and degree of concreteness.
3. Describe strategies that can facilitate effective question asking.
4. Delineate the purpose of interviews.
5. Outline activities that maximize interview effectiveness.

INTRODUCTION

Questions are a primary means of verbally soliciting information during interactions, including collaborative ones. They are crucial at the outset of interpersonal problem solving to elicit pertinent information, and they continue to be essential throughout the process for clarifying interactions and sharing ideas and understandings. Skillful use of questions can mean the difference between an interaction that is successful and one fraught with misperceptions and parallel communication.

Because questions are used in casual conversation and informal collaborative interactions as well as in more formal situations such as meetings and interviews, mastering the skill of asking well-phrased, appropriate questions should be a priority. This is especially true for teachers who may have to learn to modify existing behaviors because many of the question-asking techniques they learned during their professional preparation are focused on querying students for instructional purposes, a communication situation tremendously different from interacting collaboratively with other professionals and parents.

As with any verbal communication, the way you phrase a question will greatly affect the quality of response you receive. Therefore, prior to asking a question, you should decide what type of response you are seeking and what type of question would best elicit that information; then you can phrase your questions accordingly. At the same time, you should strive to clarify your questions and also embed them within interviews, one common question-asking context.

PURPOSES OF QUESTIONS

As you learned in Chapter 2, virtually all of your communication with others both provides information to them and enables you to gather information from them. When you look more closely at how questions are used in interactions, you will find that they can be categorized as having one of three primary intentions or purposes: (1) to seek information, (2) to provide information, and (3) to clarify or confirm information. These intentions parallel those for statements addressed in Chapter 3. Because the topic has been previously addressed, it is treated here only briefly. Refer again to Chapter 3 to review these concepts.

Questions That Seek Information

The most straightforward function of questions is to query others for information. You often ask querying questions when your primary purpose is to seek information about a topic on which you do not have sufficient experience or knowledge. You might ask whether a student's program is effective, what steps need to be taken to arrange a new service for a student, or when the next team meeting will be. All of these questions have information seeking as their foundation, as do these examples:

- What are your professional development goals for this school year?
- Which instructional strategies have you used with her?
- What led the parents to involve an independent evaluator?
- What kinds of feelings underlie her response?

Questions That Provide Information

Another function of some of the questions you ask may be to provide information to the persons with whom you are interacting. As with statements, this usually is accomplished by making evaluations or by attempting to guide the action of others by giving suggestions or advice. Evaluative questions, although seemingly constructed to query and spoken with a questioning inflection, typically convey far more information than they elicit. For example, think about the impact of these questions:

- What about the resistance her parents are likely to have toward your model of inclusion?
- What would make you think that rehabilitative services would be aware of the problem?
- What do you think would happen if you asked Maria's parents to take her for an ophthalmological exam?
- You still haven't talked to the physical therapist, have you?
- Why would you want even to attempt that type of intervention?

Questions that evaluate have limited value in interactions. Did you find yourself feeling defensive in response to some of the questions just presented? If so, your reaction is a common one to questions that imply you should "do more."

Some of the questions you ask may convey an even stronger message than those just illustrated. Such questions are actually direct commands or advice with a querying format attached as an apparent afterthought. Like statements that are meant to guide others, these questions are used to direct or advise a person to take an action or to respond to a situation in a prescribed manner. For example, consider these questions:

- You'll call Tom's parents, won't you?
- Why don't you try giving him only one task at a time?

Like questions that evaluate, you should rarely use questions that advise. They, too, may be perceived as negative by respondents. For one thing, advisory questions are sometimes seen as dishonest. If the speaker has advice to give, why disguise it as a question? The exception to this situation is when a question format is used to convey a tentative suggestion or gentle piece of advice, such as "Would parent conferencing or a meeting with the school counselor help in any way?" Furthermore, an advisory question tends to make others feel as if they are being "put on the spot" because it usually implies that there is only one right answer to give—and that right answer has been predetermined by the person asking the question. Generally, if your purpose is to convey information, you should do so with statements, not with questions.

Questions That Clarify or Confirm Information

Sometimes you ask clarifying questions to confirm information that you already have obtained but may not fully understand. For example:

- Did you say that Mohammed has missed three classes this week?
- Are you saying that you favor the tutoring option over the afterschool program?
- What did you mean when you said his parents are aware of the problem?

As you strive to develop the shared meaning that is so critical in interpersonal communication, questions that clarify information through confirmation constitute an extremely important strategy. They allow you to check your perception of the information being shared with your colleague's perception of that same information. Clarifying questions may serve the same purpose as paraphrasing or reflecting. In fact, they often are used in conjunction with these types of statements. After paraphrasing information provided by a colleague, you may check your mutual understanding with brief confirming questions such as, "Did I describe your situation correctly?" or "Have I understood what you were saying?"

CHARACTERISTICS OF QUESTIONS

In addition to understanding the purposes of questions, your skill in using questions relies on your ability to recognize and manipulate their various characteristics. By considering aspects of format and the degree of concreteness, you can phrase your questions effectively and efficiently.

Question Format

An essential characteristic of questions is their format, the way in which words are used and sequenced to create the question. Although format is not usually a critical dimension of the statements we make during interactions, it is very important for the information-seeking purpose of questions. You may receive widely varying responses to questions simply on the basis of how you word them (Brammer & MacDonald, 1999).

Open/Closed

An *open question* is defined as one for which an infinite range of responses is possible (Bloor, Frankland, Thomas, & Robson, 2001). For example, if you ask a colleague, "What did John do in your class today?" you cannot predict the nature of the response you will receive. Other examples of open questions are as follows:

- What would you view as satisfactory performance for Yolanda?
- In what specific ways could I assist you with Mario?

Sometimes you want to encourage others to continue speaking or to obtain their perception of an event or situation without imposing any limits to their responses. In such instances an open question is the best choice.

In contrast, a *closed question* is one in which the range of responses is limited either explicitly or implicitly (Gamble & Gamble, 2001). First, you may explicitly limit the range by specifying the response options in the questions, as in the following examples:

- Would you prefer that we meet before school, during lunch, or after school?
- Is Carey older or younger than the others in his group?
- Does Jennifer have no friends, just one friend, or several friends?

A second way in which you may limit response options is implicit, that is, by inferring them in the wording of the question. Analyze these examples:

- Can you meet during lunch today?
- How old is Carey?
- How many friends does Jennifer have on the team?

In the first example, the inferred limit on the response is yes/no. In the second, the limit is set because there is only one correct answer. In the third, the limit is established by the inference that a finite number of students with whom Jennifer may have friendships are on the team.

One basis for deciding whether to use open or closed questions should be whether you are seeking an elaborated response or a simple one. Closed questions may be used to limit the scope of the conversation or confirm information. However, sometimes you will find that even though you ask a closed question, you receive an elaborated response, such as when the question "Has Lupita's time management improved?" launches a five-minute description of her latest rash of missed classes and incomplete work. Conversely, even an open question such as "What does Paul say about school when he's at home?" may only elicit the very narrow answer "Nothing." Your choice of open or closed question format nevertheless establishes general parameters for the type of response you hope to receive.

Another consideration in selecting between open and closed formats is the nature of your relationship with the person from whom you are seeking information. Sometimes your concern about building a relationship will be as great as or greater than your need for specific information. In these cases, you may decide to ask open questions that allow your colleague to offer freely any information he or she wishes to share. When open questions are used, the person is less likely to infer that there are correct answers or that precise responses are needed. Questioning only with closed questions may cause the person being queried to feel that he or she is being tested since the range of appropriate responses is limited. Such a situation may cause the person to become defensive and less forthcoming.

Direct/Indirect

Most of the questions you ask use a *direct* format. That is, the question is phrased as an interrogative and, if written, would end in a question mark. All of the examples in the previous section were direct questions.

An alternative question-asking format is the *indirect* question. In this format, it is not completely clear that anyone is being queried, since the question is

PUTTING IDEAS INTO PRACTICE 4.1

Two Approaches to Sequencing Questions

The sequence of the questions one asks may be as important to the quality of the communication as the specific question format. If you are trying to decide between using closed or open questions to obtain information from a colleague or parent, you will no doubt weigh the advantages and disadvantages of each. But consider, too, the advantages of two different approaches to how you sequence them.

As the name suggests, the *funnel* approach to questioning begins with broad, open questions and proceeds to the more narrow and limiting closed questions. This often is useful when the topic is sensitive, the person being questioned is uneasy or insecure about the questions, or the person is highly invested in the topic and has much to share before focusing on specifics. This may be particularly useful when you are questioning a teacher or a parent about a situation that person has brought to you for your assistance. Often the problem, or the person's perception of it, is so complex that it should be explored broadly before it can be accurately focused and identified.

An *inverted funnel* approach begins with closed questions and proceeds to more open ones. The objective is to use very focused questions in the beginning to get the respondent to recall issues and facts about the topic of concern. This may help the respondent to consider elements of the situation that he might not otherwise. It may raise his consciousness and get him "into the right mind-set." Proponents of this approach report that it motivates the person gradually to speak more freely about a topic than other approaches do. Both ways of sequencing questions are useful. You will learn the advantages of each as you practice.

phrased as a statement, not as a question (Snow, Zurcher, & Sjoberg, 1982). This topic was discussed in Chapter 3 (see "Statements That Seek Information"). Perhaps you have used indirect questions similar to these. Compare them to the direct questions that follow them.

Indirect: It would be interesting to know what would happen if we included Jorge in the community-based training program.

Direct: What would happen if we included Jorge in the community-based training program?

Indirect: I was thinking about the possibility of asking Jason's parents to talk to the other parents about accessing support groups.

Direct: What do you think about the possibility of asking Jason's parents to talk to the other parents about accessing support groups?

Asking indirect questions may be appropriate when you are unsure whether a direct question would offend another person. Notice that by using the first-

Poorly planned and badly phrased questions result in the need for more questions. A barrage of questions may seem like a police interrogation.

person singular pronoun ("I wonder"; "I would like to know"), the implied responsibility for the idea contained in the question stays with the question asker; the person answering the question need not assume ownership for the idea expressed. In contrast, when you ask direct questions, you turn responsibility for the response to the other person. Thus, in awkward or uncomfortable situations, or in other cases in which you want to be certain you are not imposing a potentially unwanted idea, an indirect format may be preferable.

An indirect question format also carries a risk, however. Your question could be perceived by the other person as rhetorical; if this occurs you may not receive a response. You should then rephrase the question to be direct if you judge that a response is required.

Single/Multiple

Another element of how you format your questions concerns the number of questions you ask at one time (Hargie, Saunders, & Dickson, 1994; Ivey & Ivey, 1999). In general, *single* questions are preferable to *multiple* questions. Which of these question-asking examples is likely to result in the most constructive interchange?

- ◆ When you think about the changes we've been making for Erminia over the past couple of weeks, which ones seem most responsible for the improvement in her behavior?
- ◆ What do you think of the changes we've made for Erminia over the past couple of weeks? Do you agree that they're really improving her behavior? Which one do you think has been most effective?

In the first example, one well-phrased question is asked and the other person has the option of sharing ideas and perceptions. In the second example, three questions are asked and the respondent is left wondering which one to answer.

Multiple questions occur for several reasons. First, you may have the habit of beginning to talk even while you are still mentally identifying your question. This may cause you to need several tries to arrive finally at the question you intended. Another cause of multiple questions relates to specificity. You may first ask a vague question, then realize that it will not elicit the specific information you intended, and so you then try again and perhaps again. A third reason multiple questions occur is that individuals may conversationally rush past the person with whom they are speaking. That is, they may ask at one time an entire series of questions they wish to have answered. Examples of these types of multiple questions follow.

- *Thinking and Talking at the Same Time:* Is Shiva mastering her math facts? How about her problem solving? Is she turning in her math homework? Overall, how successful is Shiva in her math class?
- *Moving from Vague to Focused Questions:* How is Changnam doing? How has he adjusted to his vocational program? What issues are still coming up in having Changnam work with his job coach?
- *Asking a Series of Related Questions at One Time:* What are the highest needs the parents listed on the community services questionnaire? What resources do we have available for meeting their needs? When can we meet to begin planning the partnership program for next year?

Regardless of the reason for multiple questions, when you use them you leave your interaction partner wondering how to respond. That person may wonder which question you really meant to have addressed. Or the person may simply answer the single question that was best remembered, often the first or last question asked. Alternatively, you may put him or her in the position of being suspicious or defensive, since multiple questions sometimes convey the impression that you are "fishing" for information.

Our simple and firm recommendation is to avoid asking multiple questions. If you have several questions, carefully phrase each one, ask the questions in a logical sequence, and permit the other person time to respond after each one. If you find that you tend to ask multiple questions on a regular basis, monitor this behavior and learn to pause for a few seconds before asking a question in order to phrase it effectively.

Degree of Concreteness

Just as statements can be phrased with varying levels of specificity or concreteness, so too can questions. At times you will want to pose very general questions, such as when you are initiating relationships or just beginning to explore situations. Most often, however, you should ask questions that elicit more specific and concrete information. We refer to the latter as *focused* questions.

A focused question delimits the topic sufficiently so that the respondent can clearly identify the specific type of information requested. With few exceptions,

PUTTING IDEAS INTO PRACTICE 4.2

Questioning Yourself

Reflection and introspection are important activities for the good communicator. Understanding your own motivations and opinions and how they influence your communication is critical for effective communication. Try questioning yourself to decide if your personal perspective or frame of reference is interfering with your communication. Consider these questions:

◆ What are my feelings about the situation?

◆ What is my opinion?

◆ Am I making assumptions about the person or situation?

Questioning yourself is also useful when you are planning the questions you will ask others.

◆ What is the goal of this interaction?

◆ How much do I really understand about the situation?

◆ What information do I need?

◆ How will the person respond to this type of message?

◆ What will I do with this information?

once you have established a relationship, you should use focused questions in your problem-solving interactions (Alessandra & Hunsaker, 1993). Surely the most convincing evidence of this comes from one type of experience most special services providers have had. Surely you remember a time when you asked a question such as "How is Katie doing?" because you specifically wanted to know about Katie's reaction to the intervention you had spent hours designing. If so, you may have found that your vague or unfocused question resulted in an accounting of Katie's overall progress, her upcoming surgery, the progress she was making in other areas, and so on. A more focused question, such as "How is Katie succeeding in the language program we designed?" would have been more likely to elicit the information you wanted.

Focused questions play a critical role in clear communication. When questions are too vague, you may have to interpret someone's response or, at the very least, ask additional questions in order to refocus attention on the information you seek. Occasionally, a vague question may lead the respondent in a direction that pulls the entire interaction off a constructive course. Focused questions, on the other hand, help to direct the course of the interaction.

Making questions more focused in order to obtain specific and concrete information can be achieved primarily in two ways. First, by considering carefully the purpose of your question, determining the type of information you wish to tap, and then selecting the most appropriate format, you greatly improve your

PUTTING IDEAS INTO PRACTICE 4.3

Sabotaging Communication with Generalities

Sometimes the words we use communicate and elicit generalities rather than the specifics we seek. Generalities communicate little. "I really value that." or "You've done great work." may communicate that someone is pleased, but it is unclear what aspects of the event are valued, great, or otherwise pleasing. To understand the message, it is necessary to examine the situation further with, "Please tell me what elements you value." Or "What aspects of the work do you think I did well?" These words and phrases are a few of those that signal generalities. They should alert you that further clarification is likely to be needed.

all	every	more	all the time
never	always	soon	worse
more or less	nearly	once in a while	they say
almost	about	better	a bit
could be	sort of like	nice	soon

ability to gather specific, concrete information. Second, particular wording or phrasing considerations can also help you further to focus your question. These focusing techniques, described in the following discussion of presupposition and prefatory statements, can be used whether the question is open, closed, single, direct, or indirect.

Presupposition

Presupposition refers to specific question content that conveys to respondents an expectation of what they should know and thus helps to focus the question. Presupposition can vary from little to great depending upon question construction. The following questions contain a high level of presupposition:

- ◆ What is your greatest concern about having Erin in your classroom?
- ◆ What behavior management system are you using with Evan?

In the first question, the presupposition is that the respondent has concerns and that these are prioritized. In the second, it is that the respondent is using a behavior management system with the student. In contrast, the following questions have little presupposition:

- ◆ Do you know whether Pat is returning?
- ◆ How did you do that?

Presupposition is a potent tool for focusing interactions. Especially when used in an open question, it is a means of embedding in the question a particular topic that you want targeted in the response. It thus enables you to query in a way that

Asking Questions across Cultures

As illustrated in Chapter 2 and Chapter 3, the individualism/collectivism continuum is a useful framework for observing and responding to communication patterns in cross cultural contexts. By the very nature of their work, busy educational professionals who operate on tight schedules are likely to adopt communication patterns that are characteristic of individualistic cultures. This may result in communication challenges with families holding more collectivistic orientations. Here are some suggestions for bridging these cultural differences by using high context strategies when asking questions:

◆ Employ a conversational tone, using "small talk" when appropriate.

◆ Ask permission: "May I ask you a question?"

◆ Use indirect questions and accept ambiguity in initial responses.

◆ Encourage the discussion of past and current experience.

◆ When seeking to increase focus, use prefatory statements and presupposition.

◆ Be patient and attend to the relationship at least as carefully as the need for information.

maximizes the likelihood you will receive elaborated, accurate information that is concrete and specific. For example, consider the following versions of the same basic question that you might ask parents about their satisfaction with their child's current educational program:

◆ Are you satisfied with your child's program this year?

◆ Are you satisfied with the progress your child has made in her program this year?

◆ What aspects of your child's program have you been most satisfied with this year? [after parents' response] What aspects have caused you the most concern?

Little presupposition is contained in the first version of the question. If you use this question format, the parents probably will give a yes or no answer and they might not explain their specific reactions to the program. The second variation includes a greater degree of presupposition by making the assumption that the student has made progress, but since the question is closed, you may receive a response similar to what you received with the first question. The third set of questions contains a high level of presupposition. They assume that the parents have identified program strengths and weaknesses and that some of these are more important than others. Further, since their format is open, highly presuppositional questions are likely to enable the parents to discuss in more detail their response to the program.

There is another benefit to presupposition that you may detect in the preceding examples. Presupposition often conveys that you value another person's perception of and interest in a situation. Communicating such valuing may help to strengthen your relationship.

Prefatory Statements

Well-phrased questions are the heart of effective question asking, but sometimes asking a well-phrased question requires that you precede the question with a carefully structured statement to establish the context (Wolf, 1979). Several types of statements you might use during an interaction to respond to others (e.g., those that describe or guide) were presented in Chapter 3. Here we are concerned with statements you may use when you want to ask a question and must first "set it up." You are establishing parameters for the question and the response, sometimes by raising possible answers, sometimes by reminding the other person of previously discussed issues, sometimes by cueing your interaction partner that you are going to change the subject. The statements you use to accomplish this are called *prefatory statements.*

Each of the following questions is preceded by a prefatory statement. What purpose does each accomplish?

- ◆ We've considered an immediate program change for Harbajan as well as several interventions that might eliminate the need for the change. At this point, what strategy do you think would be best for him?
- ◆ Yesterday you mentioned that the adaptation to Maria's communication board was not working. I wanted to get back to you about that. What seems to be the problem?
- ◆ We've been talking about finding ways for teachers to be released to attend team meetings. I am also concerned about the scheduling difficulties of arranging for the occupational therapist to be here. What are our options for adjusting the OT's schedule to match the rest of the team's?

In the first two examples the prefatory statement focuses the respondent's attention on specific aspects of the topic the person asking the question wants addressed. In the final example, it also signals the person about a change in topic ("I am also concerned"). The results in all these cases is that the respondent may be more prepared to participate in the interaction.

In addition to these general prefatory statements, there are two specific types that may sometimes be appropriate during your interactions—the exemplar and the continuum. In an *exemplar,* you phrase a prefatory statement that provides examples of the types of answers that you might be seeking. For example, in the following segment of the interaction, an administrator set up options in her prefatory statement:

- ◆ We've agreed that we'd like to have a series of meetings with teachers to clarify how the general education setting could be more supportive of students with special needs. There are quite a few options for doing this. We could use the upcoming institute day or ask the superintendent for an extra day at the beginning of the next school year. Another option would be to discuss this at the staff meeting. I'm sure there are others. What ways do you think would be best for holding these meetings?

The examples of alternatives for conducting the meetings help the others to think about options. And yet the phrasing of the question clearly conveys that the administrator has not already selected any of the options named.

The other type of prefatory statement, the *continuum,* is similar to the exemplar but is used when feasible responses tend to fall along a range. For example, you might use a continuum prefatory statement to raise options for reward or punishment systems to employ with a student, to describe potential levels of staff involvement in decision making on a special services team, or to raise programming options that are progressively more restrictive. The following interaction segment illustrates a continuum prefatory statement:

- ◆ Through the years, Juan's teachers have used a wide variety of behavior management techniques with him. Some have preferred to rely almost totally on a system of rewards, others have used a combination of rewards and punishers, and still others have found that punishers alone are most effective. What type of behavior management system have you found most appropriate for Juan?

In general, the statements with which you preface your questions become integral to them. You can use prefatory statements to raise issues you believe should be noted but that are not being discussed. You may also implicitly give the person you are interacting with permission to address a sensitive or awkward topic by mentioning it.

SUGGESTIONS FOR EFFECTIVELY ASKING QUESTIONS

In addition to the principles for constructing effective questions given throughout this chapter, several techniques suggested here may help you to further refine your question-asking skills.

Use Pauses Effectively

A key to effective question asking is pausing (Brammer & MacDonald, 1999). Two particular uses of pauses can improve the effectiveness of your question asking. The first involves the pauses you make for a moment before you ask a question. You use these to ensure that your question is phrased to convey exactly the message you intend. Second, you might pause after asking a question to allow the person you are questioning time to think about, phrase, and deliver a reply.

We meet many special services providers who find that pausing is an initially frustrating technique, but once they master it they find it very powerful. Perhaps you know that you have a tendency to keep talking if someone does not respond immediately to a question you have asked. Do you follow it with another question? Do you propose a response for the person? Both these habits seriously interfere with one of the primary purposes of asking questions—to obtain information. Adding pauses to your repertoire of communication skills can only increase your effectiveness.

Monitor Question-Asking Interactions

Another strategy for becoming a successful question asker is to monitor your understanding of the relationship between how a question is asked and the type of response obtained. If you begin consciously to observe others ask questions, you will increase your own skill in discriminating appropriate from inappropriate questions. Another variation of this strategy, of course, is monitoring your own question-asking skill. How often do you use a closed question when your intent is to obtain an open response? In what situations do you tend to resort to vague instead of focused questions?

You may sometimes have successful interactions in your collaborative activities even though the quality of your questions is mediocre. However, this may create other problems. For example, some people want to interact and tend to respond in great detail even to closed questions. They may do so by taking their cue about the type of response desired from the way a question is asked. Thus, in some situations you may need to be especially careful that your questions are accurate and well phrased. Otherwise, the information you receive may be simply a reflection of what you unintentionally conveyed that you wished to hear!

Make Questions Meaningful

Too many or too few questions during an interaction can seriously limit communication clarity (Stewart & Cush, 2000). Have you ever participated in a question-asking situation that sounded like this?

Counselor: Did you try that strategy we discussed?

Teacher: Yes.

Counselor: Did it work?

Teacher: Yes.

Counselor: Are you satisfied with how things are going now?

Teacher: Not really.

Counselor: Why? Is it still her behavior?

Teacher: Yes.

In this exchange you may get the sense that a verbal Ping-Pong match is occurring. Often, combining prefatory statements and different question formats will improve this type of interaction. Before reading further, take a few minutes to try to rephrase the counselor's questions using these strategies.

At the other end of the continuum, asking too few questions is just as inappropriate. Consider this exchange:

Psychologist: Tell me what you're concerned about with Miguel.

Teacher: He has a poor attitude toward school.

Psychologist: Clarify that, please.

Teacher: He is often late, he seldom completes assignments, and he doesn't respond to rewards.

Psychologist: And you've tried the contract system we discussed.

Teacher: Yes. It was effective for a while, but then Miguel lost interest.

Psychologist: Tell me what you think happened.

With no questions but many commands and other statements, the interaction becomes directive and its sense of parity and mutual participation are seriously undermined. Furthermore, you can see that emergent characteristics in a collaborative relationship, trust and respect, are not nurtured using this approach to interactions.

By paying careful attention to the information you need and carefully constructing questions to elicit that information, you are most likely to ask meaningful questions that accomplish their communication purpose and contribute to your collaborative relationship.

CONDUCTING INTERVIEWS

When we discuss the topic of question asking with students and fieldbased professionals, they frequently assume that questions are used primarily as an interviewing technique. Although we hope that this chapter has illustrated the tremendous range of uses for questions, interviewing does provide an opportunity for you to focus your attention on your question-asking skills. We stress interviewing, therefore, as an application for illustrating the use of question asking.

An *interview* is an interactive process with multiple purposes. In school-based professional interactions, a primary purpose is for one party to obtain information from the other. Interviews can be thought of as occurring in steps or stages (Gamble & Gamble, 2001). First, you prepare for an interview by generating appropriate questions and arranging the setting so that it is as comfortable as possible. Second, you introduce the interview by stating its purpose and ensuring that the persons being interviewed are comfortable. Next, you ask the substantive questions of concern, and then you close the interview by reviewing the information collected, checking its accuracy, and stating the actions, if any, to be taken later. Finally, after the interview, you carry out those responsibilities you agreed to during the interview. The success of an interview requires knowledge about the context and process of interviews and skillful use of various verbal statements, as well as skillful question asking. To use interviews effectively as a specialized process in your collaborative activities, you should consider these suggestions.

Prior to the Interview

Have you ever attempted to interview a teacher about a student's progress while standing in the classroom doorway so that the teacher can "keep an eye on" his class? Perhaps the teacher was repeatedly distracted by student misbehavior. You were probably interrupted several times as students sought the teacher's assistance. And both you and the teacher may have been uncomfortable because you did not have a place to put your notes and materials. If so, it is likely that neither of you was particularly satisfied with the outcomes of such an interview.

The goal of your activities prior to an interview should be to create an interaction situation conducive to effective communication. To accomplish this, you should arrange an appropriate setting for the interview, prepare yourself for the interview, and assist the interviewee to prepare.

Arranging the Setting

The physical characteristics of the interview setting can have a significant impact on the psychological comfort of the person being interviewed and thus on the quality of the information that is shared. Figure 4.1 summarizes a wide range of factors to consider if the setting is to be optimum. The items collectively address privacy, comfort, and equality of status. Although you may not be able to produce all of the listed conditions in your school setting, you should strive to maximize these three overall setting characteristics.

Preparing Yourself

You will obtain more information in a more efficient manner if you prepare yourself carefully for the interview (Ivey & Ivey, 1999). This requires two distinct tasks.

Figure 4.1   Checklist for Interview Settings

_____ The location for the interview is isolated enough to convey a sense of privacy.

_____ The furniture available is designed for adults, not children.

_____ A table instead of a desk is available as workspace.

_____ The chairs are arranged around the table so that they are at right angles to each other.

_____ The interview area is free of distracting materials (e.g., clutter, confidential papers, the popular magazine you purchased on the way to school).

_____ A clock or watch is visible.

_____ The lighting is adequate.

_____ The temperature is comfortable.

_____ The setting is quiet.

_____ Appropriate amenities are available if needed (e.g., tissues, papers and pencils, coffee).

_____ The setting is neutral (e.g., conference room, the learning center, media center).

First, prepare the questions you plan to ask. For an informal interview, this may be a matter of jotting a few notes or simply gathering your thoughts prior to the interview. For more formal interviews, you may choose to write out the questions to be used and the order in which they will be asked. Second, anticipate how your interviewee may react to the questions. Consider the topic from that person's perspective. Is it sensitive or emotion laden? Might the person be confused by your questions? What areas might need clarification? How will you respond to the interviewee's reactions?

Assisting Others to Prepare

Too often, interviews are unsuccessful because the person being interviewed was surprised by certain questions and became suspicious of the interviewer's motives, or the interviewee was simply unprepared to address the topic the interviewer has planned. When you function in the role of interviewer, you can avoid these problems by sharing information in advance with the person you will interview. Specifically, you should let the person know ahead of time that you need to conduct an interview. This seems like an obvious and necessary courtesy when considering parents or perhaps administrators, but it is frequently overlooked when the person is a colleague with an office or classroom down the hall. In addition, you should clarify with the other person the topic for the interview. With a close colleague, a general comment about the topic may be sufficient. With parents, others outside the immediate school setting, and sometimes with colleagues, it may be beneficial to provide a specific set of questions you plan to ask as well as a list of the topics or a summary of the information that may be discussed.

Interviews are more successful when they are planned and everyone knows the schedule and topics.

During the Interview

Once you are seated face-to-face with the person you are interviewing, what should you do to ensure that the interview accomplishes your goals? Answering that question involves separately examining each of the three phases of an interview: (1) the introduction, (2) the body, and (3) the close.

The Introduction

The purpose of the introduction to any interview is to establish the ground rules for it and to put both the interviewee and yourself at ease. The introduction includes completing these tasks:

1. Spend a short period of time chatting to establish a relaxed atmosphere.
2. State the purpose of the interview.
3. Indicate how much time should be needed for the interview. This assists you and the other person to keep to a schedule as needed.
4. Thank the other person for her time and effort.
5. If you plan to take notes or record the interview, explain what you plan to do and, particularly with recording, obtain permission. You may find that in most cases, notes are a more expedient recording option since tapes have to be reviewed—a time-consuming task. However, you may also have to learn to be comfortable with the additional time it takes to jot notes while interacting with another person.

The Body

The substantive part of the interview commences once the introduction has been completed. During this stage, you will rely heavily on the skills discussed in this chapter and Chapter 3 for seeking and gathering information. In addition, these interviewing suggestions (Brinkley, 1989) may be helpful:

1. Carefully order your questions and statements. Usually, ordering means focusing on low-inference information that is overt early in the interview and minimizing or leaving until later the high-inference observations and discussion of content that is covert. For example, you probably should ask a colleague early during the interview about events that have happened in the classroom setting, delaying discussion about the affective components until later.
2. Cluster your questions and statements by topic. Clustering assists the logical flow of information during the interview. For example, you may find it best to group together all discussion pertaining to a student's academic functioning and likewise to cluster discussion about social skills.
3. Use silence and minimal encouragers. The more you talk during an interview, the less likely it is that you will achieve the purpose of the interview.
4. Monitor time. Once time limits have been established, try to adhere to them, even if it means scheduling an additional interview session. This

is a matter of courtesy. Colleagues, parents, and others have other obligations, and you should be sensitive to their needs to finish an interview within the established time frame.

The Close

Closing an interview should provide an opportunity to summarize what has occurred during the rest of the interview and to conclude the interview in a manner that leaves a sense of closure for all participants. These are suggestions for closing your interviews:

1. Review the major topics. Highlight all perspectives discussed. Your summary should be an accurate description of the interview.

2. Outline any plans made during the interview. This is an opportunity to clarify who has agreed to do what after the interview is concluded. You may find that it is useful to write this information so that no confusion occurs later.

3. Set a time to follow up on any actions taken. Follow-up can occur in subsequent face-to-face interactions, by telephone, or through correspondence.

4. Ask whether any additional topics should be addressed. If the other person introduces a new topic and time is becoming an issue, you may decide to schedule an additional interview. You should clearly convey to the interviewee that the only reason for delaying discussion is the time factor. If you are perceived as avoiding the topic, you will sabotage the quality of the interview's atmosphere.

5. Indicate what you will do with the information obtained. If you have taken notes, you might offer to duplicate them for the other person. Clarify whether the information should be shared with others.

6. Express appreciation for the person's time and effort.

After the Interview

How much follow-up occurs after an interview depends on the purpose for the interview. Of course, if you agreed to provide materials, complete a task, or contact another resource person during the interview, you will fulfill these responsibilities. If you suggested sharing the notes or audiotape of the interview with the other person, you should do so as soon as possible.

The single most critical element for you to consider after an interview is confidentiality. Unless you have clarified with the interviewee that the information conveyed during the interview will be shared with others, you should make every effort to protect the confidentiality of the information, even if it seems innocuous. For example, sometimes special services providers share with other teachers the success that a particular teacher is having with an instructional technique. Although that seems harmless and perhaps flattering, it could cause problems. The teacher who has been used as an example may wonder why the other techniques she is using are not being praised, she may be annoyed at being used as an example, and other teachers may feel some resentment because of the attention to the teacher. The point is this: Assume that information shared during an interview is confidential. If you are not sure about the information, check with the other person before repeating it so that you do not violate a confidence and thus damage the quality of your work relationship.

Final Thoughts on Interviewing

Our discussion of techniques for interviewing describes the process as it should occur in ideal conditions. Admittedly, you may find that you have to interview parents or colleagues when insufficient time is allocated, no private space is available, or your respondent is uncooperative or uncommunicative. In such situations, our advice is to assess the situation and adjust two factors: (1) your expectations for what you will be able to accomplish during the interaction and (2) the extent to which you attempt to follow all the recommendations we have offered. For example, if you are interviewing a parent who becomes angry, it may be nonproductive to summarize points and propose follow-up strategies. An alternative would be to telephone the parent at a later time and, using the interaction skills you have been learning, propose the follow-up you prefer. Similarly, if only 10 minutes is available for an interview, you probably should make the judgment to dispense with introductory visiting and comments (except purpose). Being able to assess situations such as interviews and adapt the skills and techniques you possess is an indicator of a high degree of interactive competence.

SUMMARY

Asking questions is the primary means through which you seek information during collaborative activities. Three key characteristics of questions are purpose (to seek, clarify, or provide information), format (open/closed, single/multiple, direct/indirect), and concreteness. Questions often are surrounded by statements or words that are not directly part of the question but serve to clarify or facilitate them. One type of such supportive words is the prefatory statement, including the exemplar and the continuum. Questions often are used within the process of interviewing. Care should be taken prior to, during, and after interviews to ensure that appropriate information is sought, clarified, and acted upon.

ACTIVITIES AND ASSIGNMENTS

1. To practice recognizing the characteristics of questions, set up a game of question tag. One person begins by asking a question and then calls the name of a classmate. That person must make the question more specific by varying one (and only one) characteristic. If correct, that person stays in the game

and calls on another to respond to the question, again changing it by one characteristic. If incorrect, he or she is "out." To make the game more difficult, expand the number of characteristics each person must change, or specify the changing characteristic.

2. Listen to a professional interviewer on radio or television. Analyze the questions the person asks according to the information outlined in this chapter. How would you rate the quality of the interviewer's question-asking skill? How is the situation in which an interviewer asks questions different from the situations in which you ask questions? What impact might this have on the answers respondents give? (The value of this exercise derives from studying the interviewer, not the interviewee, because of the differences in responses likely to occur between interviews in media and those in day-to-day situations.)

3. Question asking is a sophisticated skill that requires attention and considerable practice, but attending to all its characteristics simultaneously can lead to frustration and a sense of being tongue-tied. An alternative is this: Select one or two of the characteristics of questions, based on a self-assessment of your skill needs. Then practice asking questions that focus on those characteristics. Once you master those, select another, and then another until attending to the way in which you phrase questions becomes an automatic part of your communication. Ask a classmate to assist you in assessing your question-asking skill.

4. Set up an informal role-play with your classmates. Work in triads, with one person facilitating the interaction by asking questions, one person responding to the questions, and one person functioning as the observer. Choose a topic of conversation that is of concern or interest to your group. Role-play for five minutes. Then stop for feedback from the observer regarding the different characteristics of questions used by the speaker as well as the level of specificity in the questions. As time allows, rotate roles. Simplify the exercise at first by agreeing to focus on one or two characteristics and adding more later.

5. Tape-record yourself during a collaborative activity in your school setting. Write down each question that was asked, highlighting those that you asked. Classify each of your questions for purpose and characteristics as well as classifying those of the others. A variation of this activity is to ask the other participants to listen to the tape with you and then discuss your questions and explain why they elicited particular responses. Afterward, exchange tapes with a classmate and repeat the analysis. Compare your results and resolve any discrepancies.

6. What could you do to remind yourself during an interaction to use appropriate question-asking skills? Develop a plan for improving your skills. If possible, involve a colleague who might be able to provide feedback.

7. Recall an interview in which you were present but were not the facilitator. To what extent were the tasks and activities for interviewing carried out? What recommendations would you now make to the person who facilitated that interview?

8. Observe a colleague or one of your own instructors and listen for the use of "yes"–"no" questions, such as: "Does that make sense?", "Do you understand?" For every time they ask such a question, construct a question of your own that would better assess the understanding of the individual or class. Compile a list of the closed, dichotomous questions and the alternatives that you constructed and discuss the list with a classmate.

FOR FURTHER READING

Anderson, R. (1999). *Interviewing: Speaking, listening, and learning for professional life.* New York: McGraw-Hill.

Buchanan, S. (1994). How to beat the conference blues. *Teaching K–8, August–September,* 104–105.

Cormier, B., Cormier, L. S., & Cormier, W. H. (1998). *Interviewing strategies for helpers: Fundamental skills and cognitive behavioral interventions* (4th ed.). Monterey, CA: Brooks/Cole.

Leeds, D. (2000). *The 7 powers of questions: Secrets to successful communication in life and at work.* New York: Berkley.

McGough, D. J. (1997). The perspective interview: Facilitating meaning-making in one-to-one conversations. *Journal of Experiential Education, 20*(2), 75–79.

Merriam, S. B. (1997). *Qualitative research and case study applications in education.* San Francisco: Jossey-Bass.

Okun, B. (2002). *Effective helping: Interviewing and counseling techniques* (6th ed.). Pacific Grove, CA: Brooks/Cole.

Stewart, C. J., & Cash, W. B. (1997). *Interviewing principles and practices.* New York: McGraw-Hill.

Stewart, D. J., & Shamdasani, P. N. (1990). *Focus groups: Theory and practice.* Newbury Park, CA: Sage.

Taylor, S. J., & Bogdan, R. (1998). *Introduction to qualitative research methods: A guidebook and resource.* New York: Wiley.

Wolf, D. P. (1987). The art of questioning. *The Council of State Governments, 60*(2), 81–91.

5

Interpersonal Problem Solving

Connections

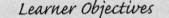

Chapter 5 presents interpersonal problem solving as the most commonly used interaction process through which professionals collaborate. It forms a bridge between Chapters 2, 3, and 4 on communication skills and Chapters 6, 7, and 8 on teaming, consultation, and co-teaching. To effectively problem solve, you must use strong communication skills; to successfully create and maintain collaborative services, problem solving is essential.

Learner Objectives

After reading this chapter you will be able to:

1. Identify three types of problems you may encounter in your professional roles that would be appropriate for interpersonal problem solving.
2. Distinguish between reactive and proactive approaches to problem solving.
3. Balance the potential value of interpersonal problem solving in terms of improved solutions with the possible costs of time personnel resources.
4. Assess whether a professional problem you face is appropriately addressed through interpersonal problem solving.
5. State and carry out the steps in a systematic interpersonal problem-solving sequence.
6. Identify at least two strategies for facilitating each problem-solving step.

INTRODUCTION

Nearly all of the professional tasks and activities for which you are responsible can be conceptualized as some type of challenge or problem to be solved. Many, many times each day you act essentially alone to solve problems or make decisions. You may do this when you decide which intervention, therapeutic technique, or equipment would be best used with particular students. You also independently problem solve when you reallocate time in order to accommodate a disruption in your day's plan, when you design (and redesign) your schedule, and when you set priorities for supplies you need for the next school year.

Increasingly in school settings, you share responsibility for problem solving with others. This is referred to as **interpersonal problem solving.** Examples of interpersonal problem solving in special services are many: The team meetings you attend to determine the appropriate placement for students are interpersonal problem-solving activities, as are your conferences with colleagues to describe how to adapt instruction to meet students' needs. These examples represent two very different contexts for interpersonal problem solving, one fairly broad and involving many people, the other quite specific and involving only two people. Even the other processes in which you are likely to engage with colleagues or parents (e.g., meeting as a committee, interviewing, planning) often are specialized applications of interpersonal problem solving. A single set of principles applies to the entire range of problem-solving activities you undertake with others.

We consider interpersonal problem solving perhaps the most fundamental component of successful interactions. In fact, we are convinced that it is virtually impossible to collaborate with colleagues and parents without systematically and effectively employing an interpersonal problem-solving process.

A CONTEXT FOR INTERPERSONAL PROBLEM SOLVING

Before turning to the steps in the interpersonal problem-solving process, it is important to examine concepts related to understanding problem characteristics in order to set the problem-solving context. Analyze these three interactions:

Speech/language therapist: At our last meeting we had discussed whether we should start working with Jason on using voice recognition software. Jason and his parents agree that this would help him immensely with his school assignments. Jason is eager to get started.

Inclusion facilitator: Do we have the most current version of that software and a computer that Jason can have access to all day?

Teacher: What do I need to learn if Jason is going to be using this software?

Principal: Maybe we should make a list of what needs to be done and questions that we have.

Teacher 1: I don't know how I'm going to get a schedule made up. Too many people want me to be too many places at the same time.

Teacher 2: I know what you mean. The flexible services for kids are great, but I'm not sure I can handle what it does to *my* life!

Teacher 1: Let's start with the "givens." We've got to have one of us available to cover the English classes during first and second hour since there are so many students with IEPs in those classes.

Teacher 2: And we promised that at least one of us would be free to meet with teachers during fourth-hour lunch.

Teacher 1: Let's block these things out on a master schedule. . . .

Psychologist: We've all agreed that we've taken positive steps toward ensuring that our students are educated with their peers in general education classes whenever possible, but we've also decided that we're encountering some dilemmas and that we should make some refinements for next year.

General Education Teacher: For one thing, we really need to look at how much support classroom teachers are receiving. Some of the students have very challenging behaviors. Teachers would appreciate more opportunities to brainstorm ideas about supporting students without disrupting instruction.

Special Education Teacher: From the special education perspective, I'd like to see us discuss how to set priorities. Sometimes I feel like I'm being pulled in so many directions that I'm not accomplishing what is really necessary to support the students.

Principal: I'm also wondering how we could make better use of paraprofessionals and grandparent volunteers to provide more support in classrooms.

Although we will address in detail the topic of problem identification in the next section, it is clear that the situation addressed in the first interaction illustrates a straightforward, **well-defined problem:** identifying specific actions to take to help a student use assistive technology. The primary task is to list the actions and then ensure that they are initiated. Well-defined problems are usually fairly easily identified and understood. Difficulties in solving them are often the result of overlooking necessary solutions or encountering obstacles in implementing the solutions (e.g., the carpenters fail to appear).

In the second interaction, the problem is somewhat more complex. The teachers have identified the problem situation as arranging their schedules, but there is no clear-cut single solution. Instead, they are working within a set of factors that have to be accommodated (e.g., the need to "cover" English classes and to have someone available during lunch). This is a **partially-defined problem,** in which the goal is clear and some guidelines exist for addressing the goal but the specific means for reaching it are varied. The problem could have multiple solutions, but the range is constrained by a set of external factors. Partially-defined problems typically are not difficult to identify. Solving them depends on the potential for successfully implementing any of several possible solutions.

In today's schools, professionals increasingly rely on each other to find solutions for student and instructional problems they encounter.

The third interaction is the most complex. The problem is identified as a need to refine the inclusive programs of students in the school. What types of refinements are necessary to improve student learning? What are reasonable expectations for teachers and other staff for support? What resources are necessary to take the programs and services to the next level? How should decisions be made regarding the distribution of resources? The options for specifying and accomplishing the broad goal of increased integration are nearly infinite. This is an illustration of an **ill-defined problem.** It does not have clear parameters, nor is it easily resolved.

While you undoubtedly address all three types of problems in your role as a special services professional, ill-defined problems probably occupy a significant portion of your time. Much of the complexity of collaborating to provide services to students is related to the number of ill-defined problems that must be addressed. The steps for problem solving outlined in the next section are valid for the first two types of problems, but they are especially critical for addressing ill-defined ones.

Reactive and Proactive Problem Solving

Another dimension on which problem solving may vary is the urgency of the problem-solving activity. In **reactive problem solving,** you are faced with responding to a crisis or dilemma. Some event occurs that focuses your attention on a matter to be resolved. Examples of this might include the interactions you have with a parent concerning a sudden change in student behavior, a meeting between you and a teacher to adapt classroom materials to be more appropriate for a given student, and a conference among all the members of an intervention assistance team to generate strategies to enable a student with a significant disability to succeed in class. Much interpersonal problem solving in schools is reactive.

Conversely, problem solving can be **proactive** when an anticipated situation focuses attention and triggers the problem-solving process before a crisis occurs. For example, in the first interaction described on previous pages, proactive problem solving is illustrated: Members of a team are anticipating challenging areas for integrating a student *before* dilemmas occur. Other illustrations of practice problem solving include planning a student's program, arranging support services before they are needed, and deciding how best to use staff time, given anticipated student enrollment for the next school year.

Using a systematic approach for problem solving is beneficial in addressing both proactive and reactive problems. In fact, one benefit of following specific steps in problem solving is that less time may eventually be required for resolving reactive problems, so more proactive problem solving is possible.

Deciding Whether to Problem Solve

In addition to understanding the type of problem to be solved collaboratively and knowing whether the process will be reactive or proactive, you are faced with a crucial question prior to beginning problem solving: Is this a problem we should solve?

Your immediate answer to this question might be "Of course—it's my job!" But that thinking is why special services personnel sometimes repeatedly discuss the same problem without progress. It is also one of the reasons why time is at such a premium for special services providers. The belief that any ill-defined problem, proactive or reactive, *must* be solved if it pertains to a student with special needs undoubtedly arises out of the professional socialization factors discussed in Chapter 1. While laudable, it should be balanced by an analysis of the realities of the situation.

Before even considering whether you should undertake problem solving with a colleague or group of colleagues, you should first consider the situation from the point of view of your own involvement. For example, you can reflect on whether the problem is one that you should even be involved in solving. If a student with a Section 504 plan is experiencing difficulties in class, you might provide limited assistance to the teacher. However, you might need to clarify that you do not have time for a lengthy problem-solving process, given the needs of the other students you are responsible for serving. Another consideration is whether a *collaborative* approach to problem solving is indicated. If you are an occupational therapist meeting with a group of teachers to develop fine motor activities for students in inclusive classrooms, you are likely to provide technical assistance and use a somewhat directive style. This is more efficient and effective than collaboratively problem solving.

After you consider your own role in the problem-solving situation, you can turn your attention to factors that affect problem solving with colleagues. These are questions to ask yourself as you encounter a problem that you and others are being asked to resolve:

1. Are the persons who have responsibility and resources for addressing the problem committed to resolving it?
2. What might happen if nothing is done to resolve the problem?
3. Are adequate time and resources available to resolve the problem?
4. Does the problem warrant the effort and resources required to make significant change?

Combined, the answers to these questions can help you to decide whether undertaking collaborative problem solving is warranted. In some cases, the information will lead you to an affirmative decision: Perhaps you are not familiar enough with the situation to make judgments about the impact of not addressing the problem. Or perhaps the individuals involved have expressed a strong commitment to tackle the problem. On the other hand, sometimes the answers to these questions lead you to a negative decision: Perhaps the people who would be key in addressing the problem do not have adequate time to devote to it. Or perhaps the problem—although affecting a student, a program, or some other aspect of the school setting—is beyond the control of the people interested in addressing it and therefore not a constructive use of staff time.

In addition to enabling you to assess the feasibility of problem solving, these preliminary questions also help you assess the possibility of collaborating to problem solve. The questions can alert you to participants' beliefs that there are probably many "right" solutions for this or any problem and that group problem solving and decision making are the preferred approaches for this situation. These are applications of the emergent characteristics of collaboration described in Chapter 1.

Because your judgment about whether to problem solve is based on preliminary information, throughout problem solving you should continually reassess the appropriateness of your decision. At any point in the process you may find that someone has lost commitment to solving the problem, that the problem is no longer within the control of the persons addressing it, or that the problem is no longer significant. If any of these situations occurs, you may want to reconsider your initial decision to address it.

STEPS IN INTERPERSONAL PROBLEM SOLVING

Once you and your colleagues have determined that you can and should address a given problem and that necessary conditions are in place for successful collaborative problem solving, you are ready to begin the problem-solving process. The steps for interpersonal problem solving have been described by many authors (e.g., Conoley & Conoley, 1992; Fishbaugh, 2000; Pugach & Johnson, 2002; Snell & Janney, 2000), and while the steps seem straightforward, their complexity lies in skillful implementation (Harris, 1995). The steps and critical questions

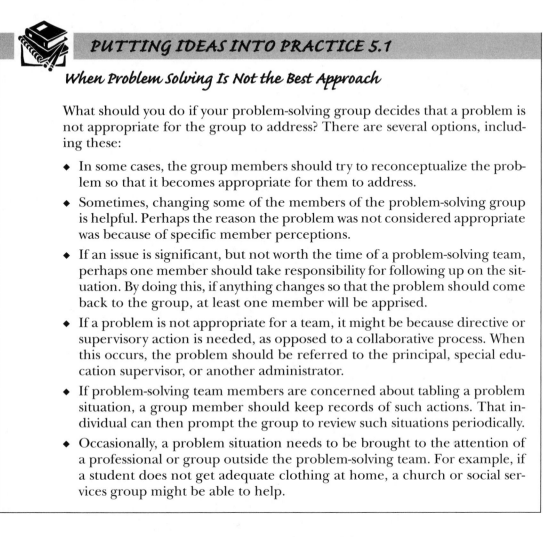

PUTTING IDEAS INTO PRACTICE 5.1

When Problem Solving Is Not the Best Approach

What should you do if your problem-solving group decides that a problem is not appropriate for the group to address? There are several options, including these:

◆ In some cases, the group members should try to reconceptualize the problem so that it becomes appropriate for them to address.

◆ Sometimes, changing some of the members of the problem-solving group is helpful. Perhaps the reason the problem was not considered appropriate was because of specific member perceptions.

◆ If an issue is significant, but not worth the time of a problem-solving team, perhaps one member should take responsibility for following up on the situation. By doing this, if anything changes so that the problem should come back to the group, at least one member will be apprised.

◆ If a problem is not appropriate for a team, it might be because directive or supervisory action is needed, as opposed to a collaborative process. When this occurs, the problem should be referred to the principal, special education supervisor, or another administrator.

◆ If problem-solving team members are concerned about tabling a problem situation, a group member should keep records of such actions. That individual can then prompt the group to review such situations periodically.

◆ Occasionally, a problem situation needs to be brought to the attention of a professional or group outside the problem-solving team. For example, if a student does not get adequate clothing at home, a church or social services group might be able to help.

associated with each are outlined in Figure 5.1. We explain them in greater detail throughout the remainder of this chapter.

Identifying the Problem

When we ask special services providers to list the steps for interpersonal problem solving, they nearly always correctly specify at least one of the first ones: identifying the problem. However, in working with school professionals, we have learned that this step is far more easily recognized than implemented. Problem identification is difficult to accomplish and often is made even more so when the problem is ill-defined or the number of participants in interpersonal problem solving increases.

Not surprisingly, research supports the fact that problem identification is the most critical step in problem solving (Jayanthi & Friend, 1992; Nezu &

Figure 5.1   Model for Interpersonal Problem Solving

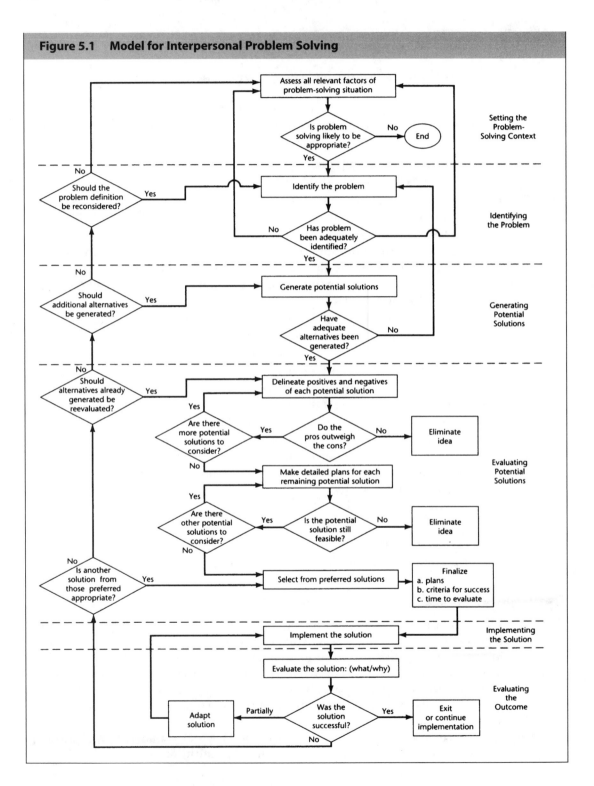

D'Zurilla, 1981; Welch & Tulbert, 2000) and that the rest of the process can be successful only if the problem is accurately delineated (Bergan & Tombari, 1975). We also find that phrasing problems as questions is a successful means of encouraging constructive problem identification. Phrasing problems as questions conveys to participants that "answers" are possible and lends a constructive tone to collaborative problem solving. Problems worded as statements are more likely to be seen as insurmountable. This question-working approach to stating problems is followed throughout this chapter.

Characteristics of Well-Identified Problems

When you identify problems, the issue may be as specific as addressing a student behavior problem (e.g., What strategies could be implemented to increase Jeff's appropriate play with other students on the playground?) or as broad as designing approaches for integrating students with disabilities (e.g., In what ways might we make our school more inclusive for all students, those with disabilities as well as those without?). Regardless of the scope of the problem, it should have the following set of characteristics.

An Identifiable Discrepancy Exists between Current and Desired Situations

In interpersonal problem solving, you should state the problem clearly enough so that the discrepancy between the current situation and the desired situation is apparent. For example, in a situation concerning a student's inappropriate classroom behavior, a description of the current conditions might focus on how often, for how long, and at what intensity the behavior is occurring. The desired situation might be the specification of appropriate behavior expectations for the classroom, using the same types of detail. In problem solving concerning a team's intent to plan a staff development program, the current situation might include information about the staff's knowledge about a topic of concern; the desired situation might be a description of the knowledge required for proficiency to be demonstrated.

Participants Share the Perception That the Problem Exists

For interpersonal problem solving to occur, all participants need to share recognition of a specific problem (Welch, 1999). This is directly related to the concept of a mutual goal that was presented as a defining characteristic of collaboration in Chapter 1. If a special education teacher is dissatisfied with the progress a student is making in a general education class but the teacher in that class believes progress is adequate, the shared recognition of a discrepancy between the actual and the ideal is missing. Likewise, if a school social worker expresses concern about a student's self-concept, but the student's parents do not perceive a problem, the parents and social worker are unlikely to engage in interpersonal problem solving. Note that in both examples, a different problem might be mutually identified if the participants discuss further their initial perceptions. But unless this occurs, the problem-solving process should be terminated or the problem redefined to everyone's satisfaction.

Participants Agree on the Factors That Indicate the Discrepancy

Efforts to clarify what factors define the gap between what is and what should be facilitate clear communication in problem solving. For example, analyze the problem of successfully including a student with a physical disability in a general education class. What is success? Without specifying how to define the current status of the student and the status after some intervention selected on the basis of interpersonal problem solving, there is no way to determine whether successful integration has been accomplished. In this example, success could be indicated by the student's improved attitude toward school, parents' and teachers' perceptions of student attitude, the extent to which other students interact with the student with a disability, or any number of additional measures. (Note that you will read about the importance of specifically measuring the factors defining the gap in the later section on finalizing plans.)

Problem Statements Invite Many Kinds of Solutions

The objective of problem identification is to describe in the clearest terms possible the discrepancy between the current and the ideal situations so participants can look for alternative strategies to move from the former to the latter. There-

---

PERSPECTIVES ON DIVERSITY 5.1

Enriching Problem Solving with Diverse Participants

Have you ever considered how the diversity of a problem-solving group can enrich the problem-solving process? Whether member diversity exists because of race or ethnicity, religion, gender, age, or any other factor, the different perspectives that participants bring can lead to better understanding of problems, more options for solving them, and more insights into implementing and evaluating solutions. Here are some examples:

◆ The differences among participants may lead to some tensions. These can result in spirited discussions and the need to clarify terms being used and strategies being suggested. For example, one teacher believes strongly that the student should either be expected to behave or sent to the office for classroom infractions. Another sees that the behavior is the result of being overwhelmed by classroom demands and that providing structure and clarity is the true problem.

◆ Individuals with different backgrounds may think very differently about how to solve a problem. The result can be a longer list of potential solutions and a greater variety of ideas. Some individuals may see that family involvement is essential for success, others may stress focusing on what can be accomplished at school with or without parent involvement, and yet others might see intervention as needing either a strong behavioral or humanistic focus.

fore, you should avoid unnecessarily narrowing the problem statement (Hobbs & Westling, 1998; Martinez, 1998). To clarify this point, analyze this initial problem statement: "How can we assist this student with learning disabilities to succeed in his math class?" Although the problem is as yet incomplete, since the gap has not been specified and the factors defining the gap have not been outlined, it is appropriate because it does not attempt to suggest a single strategy that is needed to ensure success. But what if the problem had been stated in this way: "How can we assist this student to learn his basic multiplication facts?" The latter problem statement includes the assumption that success in math will occur if math facts are learned. If the goal of problem solving is to help a student succeed, it might be appropriate to provide a calculator and work on real-life problem-solving applications. The second problem statement might preclude this possibility from being discussed; the first problem statement is more likely to leave this option available, along with many other strategies that include the student, his peers, his teacher, other professionals, his family, and so on. The range of potential solutions is broadened because the problem statement is free of preferred strategies.

Suggestions for Identifying the Problem

The following strategies can help you and your colleagues better identify problems in your interpersonal problem-solving efforts.

Think of Problem Identification as Having Both Divergent and Convergent Elements

Too often in schools, problem identification is thought of as primarily a convergent process, that is, one that focuses on rapidly narrowing the problem description. While this may appear expedient, it is usually neither efficient nor constructive. Instead, we encourage you to think of the early phase of problem identification as divergent, that is, as a phase in which the goal is to explore all possible problem definitions so that none is overlooked.

One means of keeping early problem identification divergent is to challenge the assumptions that underlie initial problem statements. For example, this is a problem statement that you might encounter:

- ◆ How can we get Josh's parents, Mr. and Mrs. Keller, to participate in the behavior management program that Josh needs?

It has a number of assumptions, including the fact that Josh's parents should be involved in a behavior management program, that Josh truly needs the program, and that "we" should take responsibility for involving Mr. and Mrs. Keller. What would happen if you negated one or several of these assumptions? Perhaps the problem would be reconceptualized as one of these:

1. How can we get Josh's behavior management program to work at school?
2. How can we improve Josh's behavior at school?
3. How could Josh be helped to be more involved in controlling his behavior?

Once underlying assumptions have been challenged and alternative conceptualizations of the problem have been explored, participants in problem solving are more likely to be able to identify the problem's most essential characteristics and use them to formulate a revised problem statement. This reformulation of the problem is convergent. It emphasizes that all participants need to reach agreement on the problem prior to generating solutions for it. However, it is also important to recognize that challenging assumptions may or may not lead to a redefinition of a problem; the point is that it is a strategy for making problem identification deliberate for all participants in the problem-solving process.

Describe the Problem Precisely

The need for using concrete and specific language in verbal communication will be addressed in detail in Chapters 8, 9, and 10. Its importance in problem solving, especially during problem identification, cannot be overstated. For example, in problem solving about a student, you should strive to describe the observable behaviors or performance indicators that characterize the student's academic or social performance. Some teachers might call a student unmotivated. Your task during problem identification is to clarify what is meant by "unmotivated." Does this mean that the student is absent? Does it mean that assigned work is not returned to school? Does it imply that the student sleeps during lectures? Only by specifying the exact behaviors or performance indicators that comprise the meaning of "unmotivated" can the problem be identified clearly.

In addition to using concrete and specific language, when identifying a problem you will want to confirm that all participants share the same understanding of the particular words used. An example of a word that is often perceived differently by professionals is **inclusion.** For some special services providers, inclusion refers to integrating students with disabilities into general education classes primarily for social purposes. For others, it means having students attend classes in which they can complete the academic work. For yet others it means integrating students physically, instructionally, and socially, regardless of the disability. Imagine the difficulties that might result if a group of individuals were problem solving on this topic without establishing a shared meaning for the word!

Confirm Problems with Multiple Sources of Information

One of the dangers in interpersonal problem solving is that participants will rely on a single source of information to identify a problem. An important strategy for ensuring successful problem identification is the use of multiple sources. In problems related to students, this might entail completing an observation of the target student in several different school settings, reviewing student records, and interviewing parents and teachers. In problems related to programs, teams, or services, this might include confirming district policies, reviewing available data (e.g., needs assessment or a staff development activity evaluation), and interviewing key people to ascertain their perceptions.

Problems can be confirmed in many ways. Sometimes data already exist in the form of student records, district surveys, or state guidelines. In other cases, some type of data collection may be needed, whether formal or informal, quantitative or qualitative. The important point is to be certain that the problem identified is an accurate description of what is actually occurring.

Allow Adequate Time for Problem Identification

All of the strategies for accurately identifying problems require time. Successful problem identification relies on high-quality interactions between the participants in interpersonal problem solving and opportunities for reflection and analysis. Unfortunately, in many school settings the problem-solving context conveys the message that the problem identification step should be completed as quickly as possible so that the more important task of resolving the problem can begin. Such thinking overlooks one key point: Without adequate time, accurate problem identification is unlikely and problem resolution is improbable. In Chapter 13, you will learn more about prioritizing time use and making the best possible use of time for collaboration.

Our recommendation is to begin systematically to increase the amount of time spent identifying problems. In many situations, multiple sessions are preferred for this, especially when additional data need to be gathered. Although this approach may seem awkward and time-consuming at first, the long-term benefit is far more efficient problem solving. One strategy for ensuring that adequate time is allowed for problem identification is to use a checklist for exploring various aspects of a problem. The checklist could include medical factors, instructional items, social areas, family or community factors, and so on.

Monitor the Problem-Solving Context

At the beginning of this chapter, we noted the importance of monitoring the problem-solving context. This is particularly critical during problem identification. The participants may not have had enough information initially to determine whether interpersonal problem solving was appropriate for a given situation; such information may emerge during this problem-solving step and lead to a different decision about the appropriateness of problem solving. Likewise, you should monitor to ensure that other participants remain committed to solving the problem once its parameters are set.

Generating Potential Solutions

Once you have clearly identified the problem, you are faced with the sometimes daunting task of proposing alternative means for resolving it. The purpose of the second major step of problem solving is to stimulate the creation of the maximum number of potential solutions by the widest range of participants. This problem-solving step relies heavily on divergent thinking (Dettmer, Dyck, & Thurston, 1999; Salisbury, Evans, & Palombaro, 1997).

Suggestions for Generating Potential Solutions

Studies of both creative processes and critical problem solving have contributed greatly to our knowledge about how to generate potential solutions in interpersonal problem solving. The following are some solution-generating techniques designed to encourage divergent thinking.

Brainstorming

The most familiar strategy for generating potential solutions is *brainstorming*. In brainstorming, the participants in the problem-solving process call out solutions as they think of them, facilitating their own thinking by listening to the ideas generated by others. The rules typically given for brainstorming during interpersonal problem solving include these:

1. Accept all ideas that are offered without evaluating them.
2. Propose ideas freely, even if they seem infeasible.
3. Have someone write down the ideas being generated.
4. "Play" with the ideas to generate even more ideas.

In addition, you may find it helpful to set a time limit for generating solutions; this focuses attention on the process but also acknowledges the time constraints of school-based problem solving.

Brainstorming is one effective strategy for generating solutions during interpersonal problem solving.

The following example is an illustration of brainstorming in order to resolve a student problem:

♦ A special education teacher described a dilemma to colleagues at a problem-solving meeting. He was responsible for supporting Jorge, a student with a mild learning disability but with significant problems with peer and adult social interactions. The student's behaviors included pushing other students, teasing and bullying, refusing to respond to requests by teachers and others, and often saying that any problem was someone else's fault. The special education teacher was concerned that other students were beginning to say they didn't like Jorge and they didn't want him in their group. After the problem was identified as how to improve the student's social interactions in the classroom, the special education teacher and his colleagues generated these potential solutions:

1. Begin a formal social skills training program.

2. Teach the other students tolerance.

3. Involve the family in designing an intervention.

4. Videotape the student so he can see his behaviors.

5. Videotape the teacher to see whether her responses to the behaviors might be maintaining them.

6. Videotape the entire class to watch the students' interactions.

7. Transfer the student so he can get a "fresh start."

8. Transfer the teacher so he can get a "fresh start."

9. Ask the counselor to schedule several sessions with the class on respectful interactions and understanding diversity.

10. Ask the principal to visit the class to convey to the students the seriousness of the matter.

11. Check the media center for a videotape on social interactions to use with the class.

12. Set up a classwide system that rewards respectful interactions.

13. Give bonuses to Jorge for appropriate social interactions.

14. Design some nonthreatening activities and arrange small student groups that include Jorge in order to help him practice social skills.

15. Have a class meeting to discuss the problem.

16. Hire a paraprofessional for the classroom.

17. Ask the district to provide an external consultant to observe the student and classroom and make recommendations.

18. Ask the district special education coordinator to observe the class.

19. Ask the district special education coordinator to teach the class for several days while the teachers work on a solution.

20. Look for a pattern based on the observations: Is the student experiencing more problems after weekend or holiday? Late in the day? During particular subjects (e.g., math) or activities (e.g., independent work time)?

This example demonstrates why brainstorming can be such a powerful technique in problem solving. First, notice that playfulness was an integral part of the brainstorming. For example, no one seriously expects the student or teacher to transfer for a fresh start (ideas 7 and 8), and yet letting those ideas surface led to the idea of asking the counselor to come to the class to work with students, in essence a fresh start for the entire class.

Another brainstorming concept illustrated in this example is **chaining,** that is, linking a series of ideas through a concept or other stimulus. Items 4, 5, and 6 form a chain about using videotaping to understand the teacher–student and student–student dynamics in the classroom. Items 17, 18, and 20 comprise a chain about classroom observation. In fact, the value of chaining in generating potential solutions is a primary reason why all ideas are accepted without evaluation: Each time you stop brainstorming to evaluate an idea, you decrease the likelihood that any participant will chain with the idea just presented.

Brainstorming is the preferred strategy for generating potential solutions in many problem-solving situations. You will probably find it helpful when you and the other participants know each other reasonably well and have comparable knowledge about the problem context. It is especially productive when the size of the problem-solving group is relatively small, and it is often used when the problem is not particularly emotion-laden.

Brainwriting

Another strategy for generating potential solutions is *brainwriting*. In brainwriting, participants individually write three or four potential solutions on a blank sheet of paper. They then place their lists in a pile on the table, from which they select someone else's list. The ideas on that list are the stimuli for them to generate additional solutions. This exchange of ideas continues until no new ideas are forthcoming. The complete set of ideas is then presented to the group with duplications eliminated. Figure 5.2 is an example of how brainwriting sheets might look.

Brainwriting is a productive option when discussion of ideas may not be fruitful. For example, if you are problem solving about an emotionally charged issue, more ideas may be generated through this written process than through

Figure 5.2   Sample Brainwriting Sheets

	Problem: What steps could we take to involve parents more in school instructional activities?	**Problem:** What steps could we take to involve parents more in school instructional activities?
First writer	1. Set up a school parent volunteer program.	1. Ask parents how they'd like to be involved. 2. Have parents help before and after school. 3. Open school on Saturday.
Second writer	1. Ask our parent organization for suggestions. 2. Involve grandparents as well as parents. 3. Contact the senior citizens center to check on their interest and availability. 4. Make a list of all types of ways parents *could* get more involved.	1. Ask students how they'd like their parents involved. 2. Ask staff at other schools how they involve parents. 3. Ask a state-level consultant to help us create parental involvement.
Third writer	1. Have current volunteers recruit others. 2. Pay parents to work in school. 3. Ask for help before and after school.	1. Get the state's materials on parental involvement programs.

one involving verbal exchange. The same principle holds for topics that might be considered sensitive. Another reason for choosing brainwriting is simply to change the procedure for generating alternative solutions to encourage a fresh perspective. Finally, brainwriting sometimes is preferred when the problem-solving group is so large that not everyone may have ample opportunity to speak if brainstorming is used.

Nominal Group Technique

A third strategy you may use to generate potential solutions combines aspects of brainstorming and brainwriting. In nominal group technique (NGT) (Delbecq, Van de Ven, & Gustafson, 1986; Fleming, 2000; Okhuysen, 2001) participants individually generate and write down as many potential solutions as they can. Then the ideas are shared by having one person state one idea, writing it so that all can see the idea. Then the next individual shares one idea. This process of persons sharing single ideas from their lists continues until all alternatives are presented. Individuals may "pass" at any time they are asked to share an idea and they do not have a new option to offer. The total list of ideas is then discussed by participants to identify the most important potential solutions and to begin the process of data reduction or idea combination. Each participant writes each prioritized solution on a separate card (as many as ten ideas) and then rates each on a scale from very important (a ranking of 5) to unimportant (1). The facilitator gathers these cards and records all participants' votes for the ideas. If a clear pattern of preference for particular ideas emerges, the procedure is complete; if not, additional discussion is held and a second vote is taken.

NGT is valuable when many people need to participate in generating potential solutions and some means is needed to ensure their equal opportunity for participation. This might occur when participants traditionally have had unequal status or when some individuals tend to dominate the group.

Whether you choose to use brainstorming, brainwriting, nominal group technique, or other approaches for generating potential solutions, you should adhere to the rules outlined as part of brainstorming. Sometimes it is tempting to stop to evaluate each idea as it is expressed. But this derails the entire purpose of generating potential solutions; we have seen many problem-solving sessions in which participants never returned to this critical step once they began prematurely discussing an idea that had been offered. Worse, participants often seem to be ignorant of the fact that they have derailed and unaware of how this is limiting their problem-solving process. Remember, generating as many solutions as possible is the point of this problem-solving step.

Evaluating Potential Solutions

The list of potential solutions you generate serves as the raw material for making the specific decision about which solution to implement. In order to make an informed decision, each of the potential solutions should be evaluated. This involves two problem-solving steps: (1) delineating the positives and negatives of each potential solution and (2) outlining the tasks required to implement each.

Delineating the Positives and Negatives of Each Potential Solution

In this evaluative step, your task is to examine each potential solution from a balanced perspective. This entails listing the positive and negative aspects of each intervention or strategy. For example, in the brainstormed list of options for the student experiencing social interaction problems, one idea was to videotape the student. Positive aspects of that solution might include these:

1. The very presence of the video equipment might improve the student's interactions because of his concern about being captured on tape acting in an inappropriate manner.

2. A videotape would provide objective evidence of the seriousness of the problem.

3. A videotape would enable teachers and others to demonstrate to the parents the nature of the problem, hopefully enlisting their support for a planned intervention.

Negative aspects of the intervention might include these:

1. Jorge, the student of concern, as well as other students might be distracted in their schoolwork by the video equipment.

2. Student behavior might deteriorate as they "perform" for the camera.

3. District policies might prohibit the videotaping of any student without explicit parental permission. Obtaining permission for all the students might make the entire project too difficult to implement.

On the basis of these positive and negative aspects of videotaping, would you retain it as a potential solution? If your response is no, then you would eliminate it from the list. If your response is yes, then you would leave it on your list of options for further discussion later.

This step of weighing the advantages and drawbacks should be completed for all the items on the list of potential solutions, although for some the task will be brief. For example, another idea for addressing the student's problem was for the consultant to teach the class for several days. This was a preposterous idea that emerged from the playful part of brainstorming and then led to the generation of other possible solutions. Obviously, this unrealistic potential solution and others similar to it should be quickly discarded.

Outlining Tasks for the Potential Solutions

By eliminating some of the potential solutions on the basis of their positive and negative aspects, you shorten considerably the list of potential interventions or strategies. But you probably still have several options, all of which seem possible. The second evaluation step, outlining the tasks that would be required to implement each of the remaining potential solutions, is the means through which these possibilities are further analyzed and narrowed.

Consider another idea from the brainstormed list. One of the potential solutions is to set up a classwide reward system for appropriate social interactions.

Busy professionals should clarify how solutions generated during problem solving will be carried out and when they will check on the success of the solution.

What are the tasks that would have to be completed for this option to be implemented? You and your colleagues would have to discuss with the general education teacher what type of system might be consistent with classroom expectations already in place. You would also need to specify what "appropriate social interactions" are and how they would be observed. You would also need to specify what the rewards would be and when they would be given. You might want to discuss alerting parents/families that a system was being implemented, and so a letter of explanation might have to be generated. What other tasks would be required?

After considering the tasks associated with each of the possible solutions, you should decide whether each still seems like a feasible option. If not, you would discard the idea. If so, you would retain it as a likely solution, and you might select it for implementation.

Selecting the Solution

Following all of the steps described thus far should have led you to a list of several clearly articulated, carefully outlined potential solutions, all appropriate for resolving the problem. Now the task is to select one of these.

This selection can be based on several factors. One consideration may be intrusiveness. If an intervention or strategy will disrupt classroom routine or require changes in staff assignments, it may become the second choice after one that fits into existing routines and staff responsibilities.

PUTTING IDEAS INTO PRACTICE 5.2

Problem-Solving Practice

Problem solving in groups is often more easily discussed than implemented. Here are a few dilemmas that might occur and some suggestions for addressing them. If you have time, you could set up each of these dilemmas as a role-play:

◆ At the very beginning of a problem-solving meeting, one teacher says, "We know what the problem is. Let's spend our time finding a way to solve it."

  Among harried educators, this type of comment is not unusual. However, it can undermine problem-solving success. You might respond using strong communication skills, stating that you are not completely clear on everyone's perspective and that you would prefer that the group clarify the problem first.

◆ As ideas are being generated, one participant makes a negative comment about each idea, pulling the conversation into arguments about the merit of each potential solution.

  Creativity and chaining are unlikely to occur when brainstorming is interrupted by such discussion. If the problem is chronic, the problem-solving group might want to review its operating rules prior to the start of a meeting. Brainwriting could also be used as an alternative. A last-resort strategy is to say to the individual, "When we discuss each idea instead of getting a lot of ideas out together, it interferes with my thinking. I'd like to get a long list of ideas and *then* discuss whether each has value for this situation.

◆ It is time to stop the meeting, but no one has agreed to take on responsibility for implementing the planned student intervention. People are packing up their belongings and moving toward the door.

  Time problems can be especially acute for group problem solving. If a situation is complex, participants could plan to devote two sessions to the conversation. They might also use e-mail to complete the assignment of responsibilities after the meeting. However, if the issue is that everyone seemed reluctant to take on the responsibility of the selected intervention, they might need to assess why that is occurring. If the solution is too time-consuming to be realistic or too complex to be easily put into place, perhaps another idea should be selected.

Feasibility is another factor that influences selection of solutions. A simple solution that requires no new resources typically is preferable to one that involves separate budget items. Similarly, a solution that necessitates coordinating multiple activities and people may be less feasible in a busy school setting than one that minimizes the number of implementers.

A third—and admittedly not very systematic—means for selecting among the potential solutions is individual preference. Although all the solutions may be feasible and none particularly intrusive, the people who have the most responsibility for implementing them may simply be more comfortable with one over the others. This consideration should not be ignored; the likelihood of a successful outcome is dependent to some extent on the commitment and attitude of those directly involved in implementation.

As you and your colleagues select a solution, try to identify the basis on which this decision will be made. There are no "correct" criteria for making this judgment, but the criteria used should be clear to all participants.

Implementing the Solution

Now you have selected the solution to be implemented. Because you have done a great deal of planning throughout the problem-solving process, many details of implementation plans have already been identified. However, one more planning phase is required before actual implementation of the intervention or strategy.

Finalizing Implementation Plans

In preparation for implementation, your responsibility is to review with other participants the plans that were made during the evaluation step of problem solving. Finalizing these plans typically includes (1) reviewing and refining detailed plans for implementing the solutions, (2) determining the criteria by which success will be determined, and (3) scheduling a time to evaluate the outcome(s) of the applied solution.

Detailed Arrangements

The selected solution is more likely to be successful if you and your colleagues specify all necessary arrangements and assign all responsibilities. Some special services professionals find listing responsibilities helpful in accomplishing this. In the sample chart in Figure 5.3, the first column includes the task to be done, the second shows the person responsible, the third includes the target completion date, the fourth addresses the outcomes expected, and the fifth and final column contains space for writing comments.

Criteria for Success

Yet another issue to clarify in the final planning for implementation is the selection of specific variables and criteria that will be used to determine whether the intervention or strategy has been successful. This is consonant with the definition of the desired situation discussed as part of problem identification. In interventions related to students, this could include specific levels of achievement on designated assessment instruments or a quantifiable improvement in attendance. In strategies that address staff problems, this may require the development of a needs assessment questionnaire or survey and clarification of what outcomes will signal success. The form presented in Figure 5.3 includes space for specifying criteria.

Figure 5.3   Problem-Solving Responsibility Chart

Problem: _____   Date: _____

Solution to be attempted: _____   Evaluation Date: _____

Results: _____

Action/Task	Person(s) Responsible	Target Completion Date	Expected Outcomes	Comments

Scheduled Time for Evaluation of Outcomes

A final topic to address prior to implementation is a specific time for assessing the success of the solution (or the outcomes). Inattention to this issue is a mistake we repeatedly observe in interpersonal problem solving in schools. Well-intentioned interventions or strategies are abandoned because of failure to assess systematically whether or not they are having the desired impact, and the first step of assessment is arranging for a time to jointly discuss the solution and its effectiveness.

Carrying Out the Solution

After completing all of these steps, you are ready to implement the intervention or strategy. Quite simply, you *do* whatever it is you have planned—whether it is a student intervention concerning academic or social behavior, a staff development plan, a co-teaching unit, or an adaptation to the curriculum. The "what" of implementation is as varied as the problem situations you encounter. During implementation you rely on the commitment and expertise of those in your problem-solving setting.

Evaluating the Outcome

The evaluation time scheduled during final planning functions as "no-fault insurance" for interpersonal problem solving. During this step of the process, you should determine whether the established goal has been reached. You also determine whether those involved in the problem-solving process are satisfied with the impact of the intervention or strategy.

Depending on what you learn during this problem-solving step, you will plan different courses of action. If the intervention or strategy is meeting with success, it becomes an opportunity for congratulating each other on that success. In such a case, the decision to be made is whether to continue the intervention or strategy for another defined period of time, or if the problem has been resolved, to terminate it. A schoolwide behavior management system is an example of a "solution" that might be continued over a long period of time; a student reward system for completing assignments is one that you might choose to phase out.

If the implemented solution is only partially successful, your decisions focus on extending or adapting it. You and the other participants in the problem-solving process would analyze whether elements of the solution are unsatisfactory and should be modified or the current intervention needs to be continued for another period of time. In either of these situations, another date for feedback would be scheduled so that you can continue to monitor progress.

An unsuccessful outcome is a third possibility in interpersonal problem solving. Although this is much less likely if the steps in the process have been systematically followed, we recognize that you may need a set of strategies for addressing this frustrating situation.

The first action you and your colleagues should take when faced with an unsuccessful outcome is to analyze the reasons for the lack of success. You might examine the intervention or strategy itself to ascertain whether it was flawed, and consider whether the solution was implemented with integrity. You might also consider whether other ideas might have been more effective in solving the problem, whether the problem was accurately identified, and whether the problem-solving context was inappropriate. For example, perhaps you lacked certain information that was important for the success of the solution, or perhaps new information emerged during the problem-solving process that is affecting implementation.

Additional possibilities might also account for the lack of success. In fact, your analysis should include a reexamination of each phase of the problem-solving process in a search for information that would explain what prevented the intervention or strategy from being successful. A list of questions to guide your analysis and the sequence you should follow for doing this are included in the model of the problem-solving process in Figure 5.1, beginning with the negative response to the question, Was the solution successful?

Once you and your colleagues have identified the source of the problem, the next task is to return to the point of the interpersonal problem-solving process at which the difficulty occurred and complete the steps again, correcting it. This may be as simple as selecting another solution that was previously proposed and evaluated, or it may be as complex as returning to the very beginning of the problem-solving process to reanalyze the context and the presenting problem.

SUMMARY

Interpersonal problem solving is the central process used in collaborative activities, whether you are addressing well-defined, partially-defined, or ill-defined problems. Prior to undertaking interpersonal problem solving, you should assess the problem-solving context. If interpersonal problem solving seems to be appropriate, then these steps are followed: Identify the problem; generate potential solutions; evaluate the potential solutions by outlining the pros and cons of each and then specifying the tasks that would have to be completed to accomplish each; select a solution from those preferred and finalize implementation plans; implement the solution; and evaluate the outcome of the intervention or strategy. On the basis of the outcome, you may decide to continue with the implementation, make adaptations, or if the outcome is unsuccessful, assess at which point the process may have broken down and return to that step in the interpersonal problem-solving process.

ACTIVITIES AND ASSIGNMENTS

1. How do individual and interpersonal problem solving differ? How might the barriers to collaboration that come from professional socialization (see Chapter 1) affect interpersonal problem solving?

2. Identify three professional problems you currently are addressing for which interpersonal problem solving might be appropriate. What types of prob-

lems are they? What is your own perspective on the appropriateness of your involvement in solving them? Use the questions for analyzing the problem-solving context with these problems. How likely are your problems to be resolved? What should you do if they cannot easily be resolved?

3. Why is it important to examine underlying assumptions during problem identification?

4. Use the professional problems you identified in Activity 2 to practice techniques for generating potential solutions. Write one problem statement so that your group or class can all read it. Then select and use one of the recommended techniques to generate potential solutions. Repeat this procedure using different problem statements and different techniques.

5. Identify a problem you are addressing in your school. After generating a list of potential solutions, complete the evaluation steps. First, make a list of positive and negative aspects of each and eliminate those in which the negatives outweigh the positives. Then list the tasks that would have to be completed to implement each of the remaining options.

6. Attend a problem-solving meeting, which could be either a pair of teachers doing instructional planning or a team meeting to discuss a student issue. Observe what occurs during the meeting. How clearly can you identify team members' use of the problem-solving steps? How often do members backtrack? Why? If you were asked to give participants feedback, what would you say?

7. In this chapter, feasibility and cost were included as criteria to consider in selecting a possible solution for a problem. What other criteria might participants in interpersonal problem solving apply in judging the potential of the solutions they have generated?

8. Audiotape yourself engaged in problem solving with a colleague. As you review your tape, analyze how you ensure that you are proceeding from one step to the next. Have a classmate review your tape for the same purpose. Compare your analyses.

9. What if your plan for an interpersonal problem-solving meeting does not go as planned? With a partner or small group, sketch out how such a situation could arise (e.g., a general education teacher is dissatisfied with every solution, a special education teacher does not think she can find time to work in the classroom, a parent states that his child's behavior is not a problem at home). Then role-play how to respond in such an interaction. What communication skills do you need in order to keep the problem on track?

FOR FURTHER READING

Gable, R. A., & Manning, M. L. (1999). Interdisciplinary teaming: Solution to instructing heterogeneous groups of students [electronic version]. *Clearinghouse, 72,* 182–185.

Hertzog, H. S. (2000, April). *When, how and who do I ask for help? Novices' perceptions of learning and assistance.* Paper presented at the annual meeting of the American Educational

Research Association, New Orleans, LA. (ERIC Document Reproduction Service No. 446087)

Jayanthi, M., & Friend, M. (1992). Interpersonal problem solving: A selected literature review to guide practice. *Journal of Educational and Psychological Consultation, 3,* 147–152.

Snell, M. E., & Janney, R. E. (2000). Teachers' problem-solving about children with moderate and severe disabilities in elementary classrooms. *Exceptional Children, 66,* 472–490.

Stambaugh, B. (2001). *Team troubleshooter: How to find and fix team problems.* Palo Alto, CA: Davies-Black.

VanGundy, A. B. (1988). *Techniques of structured problem solving* (2nd ed.). New York: Van Nostrand Reinhold.

Welch, M. (1997). The MATS form: A collaborative decision-making tool for instructional adaptations. *Intervention in School and Clinic, 32,* 142–147.

Teams

6

Connections

Collaboration is critical to the success of a number of structures and applications in schools. Chapter 6 examines school teams as the first of several school activities and services that rely on collaboration. In Chapters 7, 8, and 13 we offer similar discussions of consultation, co-teaching, and staff development—additional activities that depend, in part, on collaboration for their success. In this chapter we explore teams and their many features, including their definitions, essential characteristics, and developmental stages. We consider different models of school teams and reflect on characteristics that contribute to team effectiveness. Strategies for conducting effective meetings are presented.

Learner Objectives

After reading this chapter you will be able to:

1. Define teams and describe their characteristics.
2. Discuss the stages of team development.
3. Compare and contrast multidisciplinary, interdisciplinary, and trans-disciplinary teams.
4. Describe three different purposes of student-centered teams and delineate their importance for special services providers.
5. Describe the relationship between teams and collaboration.
6. List strategies for promoting team effectiveness.
7. Discuss activities that contribute to the success of meetings.

INTRODUCTION

You were born into a social group—your family—and you have become increasingly involved in a wider and wider range of groups as you have become an adult and a professional. For example, you still are a member of a family group, and you may belong to a neighborhood or community group, staff group, sports group, recreational or fitness club, professional association, political party, or civic group. If you conduct an inventory of the groups to which you belong, you might be surprised to discover that your participation in these groups accounts for nearly all of your social activities. Although social scientists describe many different types of groups, they identify the three most important types relative to daily interaction as family, friendship, and work groups (Argyle, 1999; Pillari & Newsome, 1997). The focus of this chapter is on just one type of social group, that is, work groups or teams.

Team approaches have long been a valued part of the special services professions and have become increasingly popular structures for addressing a wide range of school matters. Enthusiasm for school reorganization emerged from the wave of reports and studies of educational reform in the 1980s. These reports frequently recommended restructuring schools to allow for greater teacher empowerment through shared decision making. Teaming is the most frequently advocated structure for making these changes, as illustrated by continuing attention to site-based management teams, interdisciplinary and grade-level teaching teams, planning teams, professional development teams, school improvement teams, and so on. Different approaches to schoolwide decision making have been established by an array of groups, including legislation, professional associations, teacher unions, parent and community groups, and creative educational leaders.

The activities in which school teams engage and the decisions they make are myriad. They address issues such as curriculum, school image, governance, professional development, and resource management (Fullan, 1994; Maeroff, 1993). Changes have been made in school schedules, curriculum structure, budgeting priorities, staff development designs, and personnel roles and responsibilities through such teams (Darling-Hammond, 1999; Olson, Murphy, & Olson, 1998). The skills and processes discussed in this text are appropriate for the full range of school teams, including those that are the focus of this chapter—collaborative teaming activities that directly benefit students.

School-based special services providers may find the current fervor about teams puzzling. First, team approaches are integral to designing effective intervention programs for students. Teaming is quite familiar to most special educators and may not seem worthy of much attention. Second, although considerable attention has been given to teams as a feature of school restructuring and reform, the role of special educators in this restructuring often has been ignored (Clark & Astuto, 1994; Pugach, 1988). This conspicuous oversight in the literature on reform of general education may make it difficult to understand how some team structures will affect special services and special services providers.

It is not our purpose to try to sort out the numerous reform proposals or to examine how proposed organizational structures may influence particular services. Instead, we want to acknowledge these as viable examples of teams and offer a framework for discussing teams in various school contexts. This framework addresses the development of teams in special services, reviews the types of teams in which special services providers typically participate, examines the elements that influence team effectiveness, and considers the relationship of team structures to collaborative relationships.

TEAM CONCEPTS

Team approaches were centerpieces in special education and related services for many years before federal and state laws mentioned them. Mental health teams served the needs of students with emotional disorders long before the schools were obligated to educate them (Elliott & Sheridan, 1992; Menninger, 1950). Similarly, a rich tradition exists of professional teams meeting to discuss and plan for students with mild to moderate disabilities (Armer & Thomas, 1978) and for students with moderate to severe disabilities (Gallivan-Fenlon, 1994; Hutchinson, 1978; Orelove & Sobsey, 1987). A team approach to assessment and decision making for students with disabilities has been mandated by federal law since the 1975 passage of P.L. 94-142, the Education for all Handicapped Children Act (now Individuals with Disabilities Act, IDEA).

A profusion of definitions for teams has been offered by authors in the various disciplines that rely on team structures. Pfeiffer (1980) described a team as a group of individuals from different disciplines who contribute their unique skills in pursuit of their common goal of cooperative problem solving. Abelson and Woodman (1983) stressed that "a team is two or more interdependent individuals who work and communicate directly in a coordinated manner in order to reach an agreed upon goal(s)" (p. 126). Hersey (1984) added the dimension of relationships by suggesting that relationships among team members must be in place for teams to exist. These and other authors stress shared goals, direct communication, interdependence, coordination, and clear procedures as essential features of teams.

Additional conceptualizations of teams that emphasize service delivery have emerged in the literature that addresses education and services for children with special needs. For example, interactive teaming is advanced by Thomas, Correa, and Morsink (2001) as a mutual or reciprocal effort made by groups to provide a student with the best educational program possible. A strength of interactive teaming is its emphasis on effective, comprehensive, and cohesive services derived from the collaborative work, rather than individual efforts, of team members. Howard, Williams, Port, and Lepper (1997) described a collaborative education team as "an instructional arrangement of two or more people in schools and communities who share cooperative planning, instructional responsibilities, and evaluation responsibilities for the same students on a regular basis for an extended period of time" (p. 414). Essential components of these definitions are the clear emphases on services to students and the interaction among team members with unique and specialized skills. Some definitions specify that the purpose of teams is to make decisions about programs for children (Ormsbee, 2001); others also have decision making as their purpose but expand their work to include the direct delivery of services (Ogletree, Bull, Drew, & Lunnen, 2001). Examples of teams that operate for these complementary purposes are offered in a subsequent section of this chapter and throughout the text. Our goal here is to call attention to the range of definitions and purposes that exist and to offer the definition below that allows for either or both purposes.

> An educational team is a set of interdependent individuals with unique skills and perspectives who interact directly to achieve their mutual goal of providing students with effective educational programs and services.

Characteristics of Teams

The definition and discussion above provide a foundation for understanding teams. This understanding can be clarified further by examining the characteristics integral to teams. Based on social sciences literature, the essential characteristics are awareness of team membership, regulation of interactions by shared norms, and interdependence of team members. For our purposes we add the further characteristics of unique skills and perspectives of team members and the goal of shared service delivery.

Awareness of Team Membership

Individuals cannot be part of a team unless they perceive themselves to be. Extending this notion, team members must also be perceived by others as forming a team (Feldman, 1985). Although this characteristic of teams may seem almost too fundamental to mention, it is an issue in many schools. For example, a group of professionals in diverse roles will be assigned to a staff development team to prepare their colleagues for increased inclusive practice. They function effectively in their initial planning meetings, but then express surprise that they are supposed to coordinate their efforts and otherwise function as a clearly delineated work group, and their actions reflect this confusion. Thus, just knowing one is a team member and that others are too is a critical first step of teaming.

This is not as straightforward as it may at first appear for teams involved with making program decisions and delivering services to students. Changes and lack of clarity regarding membership sometimes make awareness of team membership a complex matter. For example, the role of a paraprofessional may be extremely important to a team and that individual may be considered to be a member of a specific team. Yet schedule conflicts and limited work schedules may make it impossible for the paraprofessional to be an active and full member of the team, especially in meetings and decision making. In such event it will be difficult to determine if the paraprofessional is an actual team member. Another particular challenge—transiency—occurs as the case loads or school assignments of professionals change or as students are transferred to new programs or classes. The dynamic nature of school teams requires members to take special care in monitoring team membership and clarifying changes to it (Downing, 1999).

Regulation of Interactions by Shared Norms

A team is an organized system of individuals whose behavior is regulated by a common set of norms or values (Johnson & Johnson, 2000; Sherif & Sherif, 1956). For example, teams may have both formal as well as unspoken but clear expectations for members about arriving on time, using lay language when parents are present, articulating and resolving conflict among members, and so on. Regular and direct interaction among team members is central to the concept of a team (Salend, 2001; Thomas, Correa, & Morsink, 2001). Shared norms regarding how interactions occur, and many other agreed-upon norms, facilitate effective team functioning (Abelson & Woodman, 1983; Thousand & Villa, 2000).

When teams are first established, they need to devote considerable time to establishing norms. This is sometimes a deliberate effort that results in written "ground rules." Oftentimes it is less formal, although it also may be quite deliberate. In these cases team members establish and "learn" norms through their successful and unsuccessful interactions with one another. Dynamic team membership, which is characteristic of many school teams, poses challenges for maintaining team norms (Downing, 1999; 2002). As team membership changes, team norms may change and all members will need to review and recommit to them.

Interdependence of Team Members

Members of teams are highly interdependent because their organizational roles are functionally interrelated (Cavallaro & Haney, 1999; Johnson & Johnson, 2002); that is, an event that affects one member is likely to affect the rest of the team, and team actions will affect each individual member (Fiedler, 1967; Lewin, 1951). For example, if one team member is called suddenly into a conference that conflicts with a team meeting, the remaining members may not be able to make important decisions because of that person's absence. Interdependence extends to the delivery of services as well. Consider a situation in which a team develops an integrated service plan that calls for one person to supply a communication device and teach a student to use it. A second team member is to design class discussions in which the student can use the communication device to develop better language skills. If the first person is unable to secure the needed device, it will be most difficult for the second team member to proceed with the planned language instruction. The effectiveness of one team member has direct impact on the effectiveness of another, and perhaps of the entire team.

Team Members' Unique Skills and Perspectives

Concepts and definitions of teams as components of service delivery emphasize the unique and diverse skills and abilities of team members as central characteristics. Idol, Nevin, and Paolucci-Whitcomb (1994) describe a collaborative team process as "teams of people with diverse expertise to generate creative solutions to mutually defined problems" (p. 1). They submit that the interaction and the diverse expertise of team members result in better solutions than an individual team member could devise independently. Regardless of the purpose or

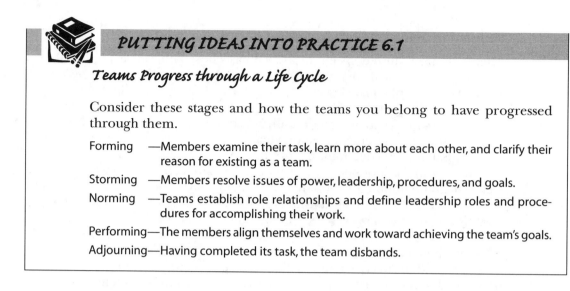

PUTTING IDEAS INTO PRACTICE 6.1

Teams Progress through a Life Cycle

Consider these stages and how the teams you belong to have progressed through them.

Forming   —Members examine their task, learn more about each other, and clarify their reason for existing as a team.

Storming   —Members resolve issues of power, leadership, procedures, and goals.

Norming   —Teams establish role relationships and define leadership roles and procedures for accomplishing their work.

Performing—The members align themselves and work toward achieving the team's goals.

Adjourning—Having completed its task, the team disbands.

size of a team, the unique skills, expertise or perspectives of team members provide alternative perspectives and a rich context for creating programs and services (Cook & Friend, 1995; Dettmer, Dyck, & Thurston, 2002; Pfeiffer, 1980).

Shared Goal of Effective Service Delivery

Having a mutual goal is an essential element of every team definition across the various disciplines. Contemporary concepts of teams in education and related services specify their service delivery focus as the overall goal shared by all members of the team. Whether the team's specific purpose is to study and plan a child's program or to deliver specific services or interventions directly, service delivery is fundamental. From this perspective, teams include those groups (often comprised of some members who will not be working with a student) that make decisions about a student's eligibility for services, as well as co-teaching teams or teacher–parent teams working to implement home and school behavior intervention programs. Maintaining the team's focus on the delivery of services is an important team function. This is particularly true when disagreements occur or when one or more team members is distracted from the central task.

Developmental Stages for Teams

There is widespread agreement that teams progress through developmental stages in their formation and operation (Friend & Cook, 1997; Palmer, 1988; Thomas et al., 2001). Teams have life cycles that progress from infancy to mature stages regardless of their purposes or the tasks they must perform. Five stages in the development of a team were described by Tuckman and Jensen (1977) as "forming, storming, norming, performing, and adjourning." These stages are outlined in the box above.

Understanding the stages through which teams progress will help you to appreciate how teams function. When a team initially comes together its members do not fully understand their task and they are not clear about how they will relate to each other and to the team leader. During the initial stage, *forming,* members tend to want clear instructions from others and they are polite in their efforts to learn about each other and their purpose for becoming a team. The *storming* stage demonstrates that a group can become a team by resolving issues of leadership, procedures, and purpose. During the storming stage members are more comfortable with one another and they communicate freely. They may challenge the team's leadership and disagree with one another as they strive to gain a shared understanding of their task and how to approach it. Having weathered the storm, a team enters the *norming* stage, in which members begin to build trust as they redefine and establish role relationships and procedures for accomplishing their work and handling conflicts. Norming is necessary for teams to establish their patterns of functioning, which might have to do with record keeping, seating arrangements, communication patterns, and so on. What is most important at this stage is that a team culture develops and gives the team its unique identity. The *performing* stage occurs when a team's development levels off and the team can devote its primary efforts to accomplishing its goals. Finally, a team progresses to *adjourning* when its tasks are complete.

Rationale for and Benefits of Teams

The primary rationale for a team approach to decision making and service delivery lies in its efficiency and potential for high-quality outcomes. If we accept the premise that educating students with special needs requires the participation of professionals with diverse and specialized skills, the challenge of coordinating the information and intervention efforts of the individual members of the group becomes clear. Having all of the professionals meet to plan and discuss implementation of programs is far more time effective than any kind of individual reporting could be. Moreover, the process of group communication may lead to different decisions and changes in perspectives that would not be possible in one-to-one communication. Implementing a coordinated and coherent program is more efficient and, happily, more effective when all of the professionals involved are in communication with each other.

Given that teams are an application of collaboration, all of the benefits and outcomes to be realized through collaboration (see Chapter 1) also are possible through teamwork. Specifically, all of the emergent characteristics of collaboration could become outcomes of effective teamwork. Team members can be expected to develop a high level of interpersonal trust and, thus, more respect for one another. As the trust grows so, too, does the sense of community among team members.

TEAM MODELS

Many models for effective teaming have been articulated (Howard et al., 2001; Thomas et al., 2002; Thousand & Villa, 2000). In this section we consider several models for student-centered teams that can be distinguished along two dimensions. The first distinguishing dimension is the team's configuration, or disciplinary working relationship, which can be identified as multidisciplinary, interdisciplinary, or transdisciplinary. The second dimension is the team's purpose or function. Three types of student-centered teams are considered along this dimension: (1) special education teams that make decisions about students' referral to, assessment for, and determination of eligibility for programs in special education; (2) student-centered problem-solving teams that address issues related to students experiencing academic, social, or emotional problems at school; and (3) service delivery teams of persons involved in the coordinated design, implementation, and evaluation of students' programs. Any given team may be classified on both dimensions simultaneously. For example, a service delivery team may be multidisciplinary, interdisciplinary, or transdisciplinary in its approach. A special education team or a problem-solving team could be similarly classified.

Disciplinary Relationships

The composition of student-centered teams varies according to the team's purposes and the student's needs (Downing, 1999; Salend, 2001). Team members may be direct service providers or support staff (Haring & McCormick, 1990). Direct service providers are parents and staff who work directly with children on a regular basis. Support staff are generally professionals who provide indirect services such as teacher consultation, technical assistance, or staff development on a less regular basis. They may sometimes work directly with children or their families, but this is usually on a restricted or limited basis. Support staff may be psychologists, occupational therapists, augmentative communication specialists, or other specialists whose services are not required on an intensive basis.

The nature of the working relationships among team members of different disciplines is one dimension that may be used to distinguish different team models. Three models have evolved over the years that occur along a continuum from little to great collaboration. These are (a) multidisciplinary, (b) interdisciplinary, and (c) transdisciplinary teams. The order in which these approaches developed in the field parallels their order on a collaboration continuum.

Multidisciplinary Teams

Although case-centered teams have a long history in special education and related fields, the passage of P.L. 94-142 in 1975 established as a federal requirement that multidisciplinary teams, including school professionals, parents, and sometimes the student, implement evaluation and placement procedures for students with disabilities. With this mandate and its reiteration in the current IDEA (Individuals with Disabilities Education Act), multidisciplinary assessment and group decision making regarding classification, placement, and the development of an Individualized Education Program (IEP) became formal elements of special education procedures. The term *multidisciplinary* was applied to such teams to convey that a number of perspectives and disciplines were represented within them.

The rationale for multidisciplinary special education teams is that a group decision provides safeguards against individual errors in judgment and ensures greater adherence to the law's due process requirements (Pfeiffer, 1980). As Reynolds, Gutkin, Elliott, and Witt (1984) have noted:

> Multidisciplinary teams have been expected to provide a number of functional benefits beyond those provided by any single individual. These benefits include: greater accuracy in assessment, classification, and placement decisions; a forum for sharing different views; provision for specialized consultative services to school personnel, parents, and community agencies; and the resources for developing and evaluating individualized educational programs for exceptional students. (p. 63)

Research in behavioral sciences supports this use of teams to improve decision-making effectiveness and quality. Abelson and Woodman (1983) summarize several widely accepted reasons for this: (1) a group offers a greater amount of knowledge and experience; (2) a greater number of possible approaches to a problem exist within a group; (3) participation in decision making increases acceptance of the decision; and (4) problem solving in a group involves greater communication and understanding of the decision.

Multidisciplinary teams that make decisions about eligibility and programs may well realize the benefits described above, but they operate under some limitations as well. The professionals from different disciplines who make up the team maintain independence from one another as they perform their related duties. Representatives of each discipline contribute unique information and perspective, but their efforts are not deliberately coordinated or integrated (Foley, 1990; Jordan, Gallagher, Hutinger, & Karnes, 1988). For example, members of multidisciplinary teams individually provide specialized and discrete services directly to students whose complex needs require intervention from professionals representing different disciplines. In this model the professionals function independently, work toward their individual treatment goals, and do not consistently share or coordinate information. They communicate simply to exchange information about their independent work, and their model might best be viewed as a patchwork quilt in which different—sometimes contrasting—pieces (of information) are placed together, but not necessarily with a blended, unified result. As this description illustrates, the collaboration in this model often is minimal, if it occurs at all.

Interdisciplinary Teams

Coordination of information and services is the primary goal shared by members of interdisciplinary teams (Carpenter, King-Sears, & Keys, 1998). In this model, as in the multidisciplinary model, professionals from different disciplines perform related, specialized functions independent of each other. However, they communicate more regularly than do members of multidisciplinary teams. Their ongoing sharing of information is instrumental in their efforts to develop and work toward a collective goal of service coordination. By doing this, they are more likely to develop and pursue interventions that support and complement one another. This helps to ensure that the services they provide students are not duplicated and that gaps do not occur. The coordination of services is such a central feature of

Three Models of Team Interaction

Different team models may be distinguished by the nature of the working relationship among persons from different disciplines. This relationship varies in terms of communication of information, service goals, and the role relationships of the individuals.

Component	Multidisciplinary	Interdisciplinary	Transdisciplinary
Philosophy of Team Interaction	Members acknowledge importance of contributions from several disciplines; services remain independent.	Members share responsibility for services among disciplines; individual are primarily responsible for specific disciplines.	Members commit to teach, learn, and work across disciplines in planning and providing integrated services.
Role of the Family	Families typically meet with team members separately by discipline.	Families may meet with the team or with representatives; individual team members report by discipline.	Families are members of the team and determine their own team roles.
Lines of Communication	Members exchange information about independent work, may not see themselves as part of a team.	Teams meet regularly for case conferences and consultations.	Teams meet regularly for information sharing, learning across disciplines, consultation, and team building.
Assessment Process	Members conduct assessments by disciplines and in separate environments.	Members conduct assessments by discipline and share results.	Members participate in collaborative assessment, observing and recording across disciplines.
Service Plan Development	Members develop separate plans for intervention within their disciplines.	Goals are developed by discipline and shared with the team to form a single service plan.	Staff and family develop a plan together based on family concerns, resources, and priorities.
Service Plan Implementation	Members implement their plans separately by discipline.	Members implement the parts of the plan for which their discipline is responsible; coordinated services are.	Members share responsibility and accountability for how the plan is implemented by the team.

Adapted from Woodruff, G., & Hanson, C. (1987). Project KAI, 77B Warren Street, Brighton, MA 02135.

interdisciplinary models that a specific role for managing such a team (sometimes called a service coordinator) may be established (Howard et al., 2001).

Transdisciplinary Teams

Transdisciplinary approaches to teaming are the most recent to have evolved in special education and related services. They also are the most collaborative of all of the team models. In these teams, professionals perform their related tasks interactively and individual team members may actually share or blend their roles (Jordan et al., 1988). In a process known as *role release,* professional roles are combined, at least in part, and one or two team members may be responsible for delivering all interventions to a student. Other team members remain available to assist and advise the primary interventionists through consultation, training, and feedback. Members with different disciplinary expertise share their skills and engage in mutual training and staff development in order to make this possible.

Often early intervention and preschool programs for young children are implemented by transdisciplinary teams. This is considered to be a holistic approach in which primary interventionists implement strategies common to their own disciplines as well as some that are derived from other disciplines. For example, a preschool teacher may implement specific language development interventions designed and modeled by the speech and language specialist on the team. After receiving some training and technical assistance from the physical therapist, the teacher also may implement certain positioning routines. It is not uncommon for the teacher, who is a generalist in this situation, to feel insecure about her or his skills in the specialized language and physical therapy areas. The in-depth knowledge of the specialists is essential for designing interventions and assisting primary interventionists to implement them. However, it is the generalist orientation of the teacher that may be best suited to providing services for the whole child.

Types of Student-Centered Teams

The second dimension in which teams can vary is their purpose or function. We refer to those teams that exist on behalf of students as student-centered teams, and they are the focus of this discussion. Three types of student-centered teams that differ in their primary purpose, their basis in law, and their accountability are described and illustrated here.

Special Education Teams

A special education team exists to make decisions about a student's referral, assessment, and eligibility for special education. This team may be referred to as a child study team, school assessment team, placement team, planning team, or multidisciplinary team. The specific composition, structure, and procedures of this type of team vary across states, but they are consistent with the requirements put forth in IDEA and highlighted in the box on the following page. Usually members of these teams include a parent, a representative of the school district

Ensuring that students have a voice in planning their educational programs is an important key to success.

who is knowledgeable about special and general education services, a general education teacher, a special education teacher, a psychologist, and other specialists whose expertise may be needed to evaluate the student and plan programs to meet the unique needs of the student. Whenever appropriate the student with the disability should also be included. These teams gather and review information about referred students and determine if an individual assessment is needed. If an assessment is completed, the team reviews the results and determines whether the student has a disability that interferes with his or her ability to progress in the general curriculum, whether the student requires special education and related services, what goals and objectives should be set to address the student's unique needs, and the setting in which the student's education should occur. If problems arise in implementing the student's program, the team reconvenes to consider strategies for resolving them.

The rationale for special education teams, including the presumed superiority of decisions made by these teams, was the subject of an earlier discussion. Even though multidisciplinary special education teams were envisioned as having the potential to enhance school-based services to students with disabilities, early research demonstrated many problems with such teams. For example, team functioning was adversely affected by (1) use of nonsystematic approaches to collecting and analyzing diagnostic information, (2) minimal participation by parents or regular educators on the teams, (3) use of a loosely construed decision-making/planning process, (4) lack of interdisciplinary collaboration and trust, (5) territoriality, (6) ambiguous role definition and accountability, and (7) lack of experience and training for professionals to work together (Fenton, Yoshida, Maxwell, & Kaufman, 1979; Kaiser & Woodman, 1985; Pfeiffer, 1981).

PUTTING IDEAS INTO PRACTICE 6.3

IDEA Provides Guidelines for IEP Team Composition

IDEA provides guidelines for the composition of multidisciplinary teams. The term *individualized education program team* or *IEP team* means a group of individuals composed of—

(i) the parents of a child with a disability;

(ii) at least one regular education teacher of such child (if the child is, or may be, participating in the regular education environment);

(iii) at least one special educator, or where appropriate, at least one special education provider of such child;

(iv) a representative of the local education agency who—

    a. is qualified to provide, or supervise the provision of, specially designed instruction to meet the unique needs of children with disabilities;

    b. is knowledgeable about the general curriculum; and

    c. is knowledgeable about the availability of resources of the local education agency;

(v) an individual who can interpret the instructional implications of evaluation results;

(vi) at the discretion of the parent or agency, other individuals who have knowledge or special expertise regarding the child, including related services personnel as appropriate; and

(vii) whenever appropriate, the child with a disability.

As the field recognized the shortcomings of the multidisciplinary team concept, various analyses of their implementation were conducted and proposals for improving team functioning were advanced. Among the problems most frequently addressed was the lack of preparation in effective collaboration and team participation skills (Ormsbee & Haring, 2000; Schamber, 1999). Fortunately, professional preparation programs, materials such as this textbook, and other resources listed at the end of this chapter have responded to this professional development need.

Another serious barrier to effective special education teams, as noted by Pryzwansky and Rzepski (1983), may stem from the fact that they are mandatory. Pryzwansky and Rzepski suggest that this characteristic has led to a narrow definition of the team's purpose and functioning, preventing such teams from appropriately clarifying and expanding their conceptual base. Without a clearly understood foundation, teams lack the grounding on which to build a more integrated structure. The result is that many multidisciplinary teams serve mostly as gatekeepers of special education instead of teams that provide instructional program designs and support for all of the students they consider.

Student-Centered Problem-Solving Teams

One significant response to some of the practical barriers associated with special education teams was the development of building-level, problem-solving teams to assist teachers in accommodating students with behavioral or learning difficulties in their classrooms. These teams evolved, in part, to augment the formal referral and evaluation processes in special education. Often known as prereferral teams or prereferral intervention teams, they were meant to provide prereferral screening for special education services and immediate support for teachers trying to develop appropriate in-class interventions. Over the past several years, the focus for such teams has shifted to preventive problem solving, collegial support for responding to challenging student needs, and opportunities for professionals to problem solve about students—whether or not they have IEPs (Bay, Bryan, & O'-Connor, 1994; Nelson, Smith, Taylor, Dodd, & Reavis, 1992; Westby & Ford, 1993). This shift is reflected in alternative names for prereferral teams—for example, intervention assistance teams (IATs), student support teams, and student assistance teams.

Although evidence supports the effectiveness of intervention or prevention teams, limited comparative data have established the efficacy of specific team approaches (Rock & Zigmond, 2001; Welch, Brownell, & Sheridan, 1999). Variations in structures and implementation decisions may be necessary in different school ecologies, and schools must select appropriate criteria for discriminating and selecting among program structures. Some examples of successful teams include teacher assistance teams, intervention assistance teams, prereferral intervention teams, and various models of service delivery teams.

Teacher Assistance Teams (TATs)

The TAT was one of the earliest examples of a prereferral intervention assistance model. As originally developed by Chalfant, Pysh, and Moultrie (1979), this teacher support system or peer problem-solving group consists of three elected teachers and the referring teacher. Parents are invited to become members and, when appropriate, specialists also are invited; the latter, however, are not regular members. The team provides teachers with the support needed to accommodate students with learning and behavior disorders in their classrooms. The referring teacher defines the problem, develops alternative interventions jointly with other TAT members, and then selects the preferred intervention. The TAT functions on the assumption that general education teachers have the knowledge and talent individually or jointly to resolve a great number of the problems they encounter in teaching students with learning and behavior problems. TATs reflect belief in the superiority of group decision making that underlies the multidisciplinary team structure, but they differ from these special education teams by not including specialists as team members unless a specialist's unique expertise is needed for a particular case. The TAT either provides direct assistance to the referring teacher or helps the teacher to obtain follow-up from special education personnel. This model continues to have strong advocates (e.g., Evans, 1990; Graden, 1989; Pugach & Johnson, 1995).

Intervention Assistance Teams

Another variation of a student-centered problem-solving team is the intervention assistance team (IAT). This team is premised on the belief that solving problems about students experiencing behavioral and learning problems should enlist all of the resources available at a school, including those of special education and related service staff (Burns, 1999; Whitten & Dieker, 1995). The IAT model uses procedures similar to those of the TAT approach in which the classroom teacher refers a student, team members gather additional information, and they all meet to consider the information as they engage in a team problem-solving process. The primary difference between IATs and TATs is that the IAT approach goes beyond the general education teachers and includes special education, a speech or language therapist, and often other specialists such as counselors, school psychologists, and social workers (Friend & Cook, 1997; Tarver-Behring & Spagna, 1999).

IATs have been found to be effective in meeting student needs and providing support to teachers (Burns, 1999; Whitten & Dieker, 1995), especially when administrative support for the process is strong (Kruger, Struzziero, Watts, & Vacca, 1995). Other authors report that intervention assistance teams produce successful results, but that several elements of such teams require further study (Lloyd, Crowley, Kohler, & Strain, 1988; Sindelar, Griffin, Smith, & Watanabe, 1992).

Prereferral Intervention Teams

An alternative to teacher assistance teams and intervention assistance teams, a prereferral intervention team model developed by Graden, Casey, and Bonstrom (1985) uses a multidisciplinary building-based team and combines teacher consultant and team formats in a six-stage process. The first four stages are prereferral processes and the final two are formal referral, assessment, and eligibility determination processes, as follows:

Stage 1. *Request for Consultation.* This is the referring teacher's initial contact with the system. This stage usually involves informal contact with a consultant (generally a special educator, psychologist, or social worker), although some districts may require a building-based team review and subsequent assignment to a consultant.

Stage 2. *Consultation.* The standard steps of behavioral consultation are followed.

Stage 3. *Observation.* This stage entails observation in the classroom by the consultant, feedback regarding the observation to the referring teacher, and collaborative development, implementation, and evaluation of interventions based on observations.

Stage 4. *Conference.* In this stage a child review team meets to share information and make a decision regarding the continuation, modification, or termination of the intervention.

Stages 5 and 6. The final stages encompass the formal special education referral process and program planning meetings.

This prereferral intervention method is similar to the TAT in its emphasis on teacher support and prevention. It is also similar to multidisciplinary teams in its reliance on special services providers as key players in the process. By including a consultation component, this team approach also incorporates elements of the consultative structure that was discussed in the first part of this chapter.

Service Delivery Teams

A number of team structures exist to plan and deliver education and related services to students. You may be familiar with examples such as teaching teams in middle school, grade-level teams in elementary school, and co-teaching teams at any level. These teams focus largely on planning for, implementing, and evaluating the ongoing, often daily, delivery of educational services to one or more students.

Co-Teaching Teams. In special education, co-teaching is an increasingly common service delivery arrangement in which special education teachers and general education teachers share planning and classroom instructional responsibilities in inclusive settings (Cook & Friend, 1995; Walther-Thomas, 1997). In this model the general education and special education teachers engage in team planning and in jointly delivering instruction to a diverse group of students. This educational strategy is examined in depth in Chapter 8.

Teaching Teams in Middle Schools. In a study of middle schools that enroll seventh graders, MacIver (1990) reported that about 42 percent of early adolescents in a sample of 2,400 public schools received instruction from interdisciplinary teams of teachers at some time between grades 5 and 9. In this study, the interdisciplinary teams of teachers, with each member teaching a different subject to the same group of students, produced a wide range of benefits, particularly if they had a designated leader, adequate planning time, and a commitment to the interdisciplinary team concept, demonstrated through their willingness to use planning time for team participation. Specifically, middle school teaching teams were seen to increase the effectiveness of instruction, to provide teachers with a much needed support system, to help ensure that students' problems would be recognized and solved, to improve students' work and attitudes, and to have a positive impact on the school's overall program for the middle grades.

Grade-Level Teams. A grade-level team structure is very similar to that of the middle school teaching team, even though it has not received wide attention in the professional literature. Grade-level or departmental teams are constructed around members with highly similar interests and expertise (i.e., the grade level or subject matter they teach). The nature of the decisions these groups make may focus on curriculum, division of labor for instructional preparation, schedule, budget, or other matters of group interest or concern. These teams do not exist for the purpose of case consultation or conferencing, but they may elect to discuss and jointly solve problems about student-related issues. The probability of grade-level or departmental teams focusing the resources of the decision-making team on a particular case or student increases greatly if more than one team member has contact with the same student, or if a special educator can regularly attend such meetings to facilitate discussions about student needs.

Effectiveness of Teams

The effectiveness of a team can be evaluated in terms of its goal attainment because, as noted earlier, the team's purpose for existence is to achieve this goal. Another criterion for judging team effectiveness is its output. Abelson and Woodman (1983) note that a team is effective when its productive output exceeds or meets the organization's standards of quality and quantity. In schools, teams are considered effective when their output meets the standards of their profession and the expectations of the various constituencies, including administrators, parents, and peers. The output might be the number of referrals to special education, the number of students on whose behalf problem solving occurs, or the number of intervention strategies implemented in classrooms.

A model of business team effectiveness advanced by Nadler, Hackman, and Lawler (1979) suggests that the ultimate effectiveness of a team depends on (1) the level of effort team members devote to the team's task, (2) the level of knowledge and skills within the team, and (3) the strategies the team uses to accomplish its work. Furthermore, these factors are affected by the design of the task, the composition of the team, and the appropriateness of the strategies used by the team. Additional criteria for judging team effectiveness are derived from the studies of multidisciplinary teams mentioned earlier. In combination, these factors and design elements are critical in developing effective teams, and we include them in the characteristics of effective teams described below.

The Team's Goals Are Clear

The goals of an effective team are clearly understood by all of the team's members. Mutual goals represent the team's primary purposes, but each activity the team pursues to achieve its purposes will also have goals. Members of effective teams have clear understanding of both the central goals and the activity or process goals, and their actions as a team reflect this understanding.

Members' Needs Are Met

In effective teams, the personal needs of team members are satisfied more than frustrated by the group experience. The interpersonal needs of being included, respected, and valued can be met through active participation in a team. Conversely, teams in schools are not likely to be effective in achieving their goals if the team prevents individuals from meeting these interpersonal needs or attaining their individual professional goals. Satisfying members' needs, however, does not mean that individuals always "get their way." When members' needs differ, resistance and conflict may occur. These topics are addressed in Chapter 11.

PUTTING IDEAS INTO PRACTICE 6.4

A Checklist for Effective Teamwork

Use this checklist to reflect on a number of elements that contribute to effective team functioning. Consider the teams in which you participate. Are the conditions below being met? What specific actions might you take to help your team accomplish each condition?

❑ Team members understand the team's task and the expectations and standards it is to meet.

❑ Team members consistently make contributions based on their knowledge and experience.

❑ Team members listen openly to the contributions of others.

❑ Contradictory information is shared by team members to facilitate team understanding.

❑ Team members challenge suggestions they believe are unsupported by facts or logic, but avoid arguing just to have their way.

❑ Conflicts arising from different points of view are used to improve team understanding and are resolved constructively.

❑ The team does not agree to poor solutions just for the sake of harmony.

❑ Differences of opinion are discussed and resolved.

❑ Team members strive to make the problem-solving process efficient and to facilitate rather than hinder discussion.

❑ Team members encourage and support others who may be reluctant to offer information or suggestions.

❑ Each team member understands the value of time and works to eliminate extraneous and/or repetitious discussion.

Adapted from Maddux, R. B. (1986). *Team building: An exercise in leadership* (rev. ed.). Menlo Park, CA: Crisp.

Members Have Individual Accountability

Team members should clearly understand their roles as well as those of other members. Earlier, we identified role interdependence as a defining characteristic of teams because work teams are constructed with members who have complementary and interconnected parts to play. Each member has responsibility for something the group needs in order to function. The structure of an effective team provides for individual accountability that increases the tendency of team members to devote adequate effort to meeting their team responsibilities. Individual accountability is achieved by assessing the quality and quantity of members' contributions. Conducting such assessment serves many purposes, including clearly identifying contributions, reducing duplication of effort, reinforcing and clarifying responsibilities, articulating needs for assistance, and minimizing "freeloading" by noncontributing members.

Group Processes Maintain the Team

The group processes used in effective teams serve to increase, or at least maintain, the team's capacity to work collaboratively on future endeavors. Specifically, these group processes ensure that leadership and participation are distributed throughout the team. Leadership skills, such as initiating discussion, setting standards, encouraging, summarizing, and gaining consensus, can be used by different members of the team. A team that wants to make maximum use of the diverse experience, expertise, and information of its members distributes leadership roles. Team members recognize that leadership is necessarily a shared responsibility and assume that role when necessary to support the functioning of the group (Kinlaw, 1993).

Team Members Have Leadership Skills

There is considerable literature documenting the need for effective team leadership (Johnson & Johnson, 2000). Most authorities agree that all team members need to have leadership skills even when they are not assuming the formal role of team leader. Leadership skills are those that help the group to function effectively and progress toward its goals. From that perspective it should be clear that a group member other than the designated leader may take an active role in facilitating the team's progress. By offering a summary of positions stated by others, asking clarifying questions or simply helping to ensure that all team members have the opportunity to participate in discussion and decision making, a team member demonstrates leadership and helps the team progress. Some of the elements of effective teams are presented in the box on the facing page. As you consider how you might help to ensure that these conditions are met in the teams to which you belong, you will be considering how you will contribute your leadership skills to the team. Many of the communication skills that will help you to make those contributions are presented in Chapters 2–5 and 11. For now you will be well served by reflecting on the specific effectiveness indicators.

CONDUCTING MEETINGS

When we talk about teams with students or field-based colleagues, the discussion inevitably turns first to the burdens and challenges of meetings and then to strategies for ensuring successful team meetings. In this chapter we have presented background information on teams and discussed team characteristics as well as skills and strategies for developing effective teams. Knowing the purpose of teams, acquiring communication and interaction skills, and understanding the team development process provide you with an important knowledge and skill base within which you can apply some key strategies that will assist you in making your team or other group meetings successful.

Prior to the Meeting

Decide Whether a Meeting Is Needed

Often meetings are held without a clear understanding of their need. In busy school settings, it is not uncommon for professionals to get so caught up in the details of scheduling a meeting that they become unsure of the reasons the meeting is being convened. It is generally a good idea to avoid meetings about things that can be conveyed more easily or clearly in writing or on the telephone, such as schedules of events, procedures for ordering materials, and so on. Meetings are valuable when there is a need for a group or team to discuss a matter and reach a shared understanding of its elements. They are also useful when group advice or problem solving is needed or when there is an issue to be resolved and it's not clear who is responsible for it. Clearly, meetings are needed for student-centered decision making regarding such matters as program or intervention planning.

Decide the Purpose

There are several reasons for having meetings including information sharing, data gathering, problem solving, and decision making. Information sharing is often done adequately outside of meetings by using e-mail or other written, one-way communication strategies. But many times groups need to clarify the information and thus find that meetings provide helpful opportunities to ask clarifying questions and to gain a shared understanding of the information. The purpose of a data-gathering meeting is to obtain information from group members and to solicit feedback from them. This is particularly helpful when several members have different pieces of information all of which are needed to gain a full understanding of the topic at hand. Problem-solving processes were discussed in Chapter 5 where their characteristics and strategies for their successful completion were delineated. Problem solving and decision making, particularly in regard to a student's program, require a meeting of a team of responsible persons.

Every meeting is likely to have more than one purpose, but one will be central. For example, when the primary purpose is problem solving, data gathering and information sharing will still occur and contribute to the effectiveness of the problem solving. Knowing the central purpose of a meeting helps to determine who should be invited and what procedures and processes should be followed during the meeting.

Articulate Desired Outcomes

Expectations for the outcomes of a meeting will drive the behavior of team members. The desired outcomes should be explicit so that all group members hold the same expectations and can work toward a common set of expectations. Imagine a meeting in which one member believes the purpose is to explore common interests of members from two agencies while another believes the meeting has been called to agree to resource sharing between agencies. Suspicion is likely to develop as one shows exceptional interest in the resources of all participants. Imagine that same meeting if the purpose were stated in advance: to examine the resources available within each agency for assisting Jaime's family to maintain a regular schedule of counseling and physical therapy.

Delineate a Realistic Agenda and Time Frame

It is essential that everyone attending a meeting be given advance information about what to expect. Advance preparation and distribution of an agenda lets participants know what to expect and what to do, bring, and prepare. Although all school professionals are busy and may think that preparing an agenda is an unnecessary expenditure of time, it is time very well spent. It reduces confusion and greatly increases the likelihood that participants will come prepared. Agendas are most effective when they provide an explicit statement of the desired outcomes, participants' roles, the steps that will be followed during the meeting, the person responsible for individual items on the agenda, and the anticipated time allocation for each agenda item or step. There is such widespread agreement that agendas are critical to success of a meeting that most word processing programs and computer clip art packages include standard agenda templates.

The fifth-grade team at Wilson School is composed of four classroom teachers and a resource teacher. Because there are 10 special needs students in the

Sharing a concrete agenda promotes clear communication and a shared sense of purpose.

four classes, the team is augmented by an adapted physical education teacher and a speech and language specialist when those students are being reviewed. The team meets weekly for one hour. Every other week the meetings focus on curriculum and instruction for all students and the teachers plan instructional units and strategies. On alternate weeks the team is augmented by the special services providers and the meetings focus on student progress and program planning. Once monthly the team conducts an in-depth review and program-planning session for one student. The second student-centered meeting each month regularly includes three types of items: a "quick review" of progress for up to three students; a more sustained discussion of a particular element of one student's program; and a brief period devoted to team business. In the sample agenda shown in Figure 6.1 the team is conducting quick reviews of three stu-

---

Figure 6.1   Agenda for a Team Meeting

Wilson Team Meeting
1/27
3:00 P.M. to 3:55 P.M.
Team 5 Meeting Room

Type of meeting:	Case Review	**Facilitator:**	Barb
Scribe:	Kathy	**Timekeeper:**	Bill
Attendees:	(5th grade) Bob, Susan, Paula, Bill, Kathy Resource/Guest—Aaron (Unit Psychologist)		
Outcomes:	Assignment of needed actions relative to Jaime K., James, and Enrique Identification of Gerald's educational progress and needs		
Please bring:	Calendars, notes on Jaime K., James, and Enrique Gerald's assessment plan		

—Agenda—

Quick Review—Jaime K.	Bill	10
Quick Review—James	Susan	10
Quick Review—Enrique	Susan	10
Assessment Results—Gerald Review progress since last assessment Identify current educational needs	Kathy	20
Schedule Update	All	5

dents: Jaime K., James, and Enrique. Susan, the adapted physical education teacher, will lead the discussion of two students, and Bill, a classroom teacher, will lead the review discussion of Jaime K.'s progress. Kathy will lead a more detailed discussion of Gerald's assessment results. Throughout the meeting, Barb will facilitate and keep the team on the agenda items while Bill keeps track of time and helps the team to complete tasks in a timely fashion. Bill and Barb monitor the team's activity and ensure that a few minutes at the end of the meeting can be used to coordinate schedule changes for the team. Other items to note on the agenda include the suggestion that team members bring progress notes on students, Gerald's assessment plan, and their own calendars. Kathy is the designated note taker for this meeting, and a unit psychologist will be in attendance as a resource person when Gerald's assessment results are reviewed.

Careful thought and planning should be given to ensuring that the agenda is realistic in terms of potential outcomes and the time allotted for individual items. As a general rule of thumb, recognize that everything will take longer than one expects, especially if the team has not yet developed its norms and aligned itself with clearly articulated goals. As teams become comfortable with their role and function, they become more efficient and more time effective. The fifth-grade team at Wilson School has worked together for a semester and has become accustomed to the team process and time management strategies. When they began their work in September, they could only conduct two or three quick reviews or one more in-depth matter and discuss business. After six months of team meetings, they are able to address several students in one session as is indicated in the sample agenda.

Arrange the Setting

There are elements of room arrangement and atmosphere that will contribute to the success of your meetings. These factors will influence the psychological and physical comfort level of the participants. The location and physical characteristics of the meeting room should afford privacy and limited distractions. Other factors to consider are also consistent with those discussed in relation to interview settings in Chapter 4 and include seating arrangements, temperature, and light and noise levels.

During the Meeting
Review Agenda and Timelines

After team members assemble, the facilitator should review the agenda and get team concurrence that the proposed sequence, time allocation, and member roles are appropriate. Of special importance is the statement of an ending time. If a team member has to depart early, it should be noted at the beginning of the meeting and the agenda order adjusted if needed. Other adjustments may be called for when the team examines the agenda. Teams should resist the desire to talk about schedule or team business early in the meeting. Because time is such a tremendously scarce commodity in schools, it is often the paramount concern as teams begin their meetings. Yet, if scheduling becomes the first order of business it tends to become the primary topic of the meeting.

Participate Effectively

Different roles are significant to a team's success, and team members often rotate through the roles of facilitator, recorder, and group member. For meetings to progress smoothly, members must know their roles and how to perform them. When teams are first forming, it is often useful to spend time learning the roles and the skills each entails.

The facilitator generally leads the meeting and takes responsibility for premeeting preparation and coordinating postmeeting follow-up. The designation of a group member to serve as timekeeper who signals the facilitator when scheduled time periods are ending is a useful support for the facilitator, who can then concentrate on the quality and focus of the group work. The facilitator guides the team through its agenda by focusing energy on a common task, encouraging members to participate, remaining neutral, and suggesting alternative methods for reaching agreement or making a decision. Specific strategies that assist the facilitator include clearly defining the role, obtaining agreement on the purpose and process to be followed in the meeting, listening, supporting the recorder, and asking clarifying questions.

The recorder, sometimes called a scribe, is the keeper of the group memory. Like the facilitator, the recorder remains neutral. The recorder captures the ideas and suggestions of group members without interpreting or evaluating them. When group members have trouble expressing themselves, it is tempting for the recorder to put words in their mouths, but effective recorders never do that. Skills that are helpful in this role include the ability to listen for key words or concepts and record them verbatim. One cannot record all that is said, so identifying the most salient points is critical. It is especially helpful if the recorder can prepare summary notes that the members may have following the meeting. One strategy for doing this is to have an established note-taking format and use it to record main points. An example of the notes taken by the Wilson School fifth-grade team during the quick review of Jaime K.'s progress is provided in Figure 6.2. These notes are very brief and serve only as a summary of the material covered during the meeting, but they also include the decisions made regarding follow-up responsibilities for team members. In this case, Susan will collect data to quantify the amount of time Jaime K. stays on-task during reading class. The method of data collection is not specified, presumably because the team members are comfortable with an established process and it does not require description in the notes.

Group members are as important to team functioning as are the facilitator and recorder. Good group members monitor and support the facilitator and recorder. They observe the facilitator to ensure that he or she remains neutral and does not try to influence the group. If the facilitator begins expressing opinions or disagreeing with the group members, it is incumbent upon the team members to call attention to it. A member of the Wilson School team might say, "Barb, I think that you may be steering the group toward a decision that James should

Figure 6.2	Team Meeting Notes

Wilson Team Meeting
1/27
3:00 P.M. to 3:55 P.M.
Team 5 Meeting Room

Type of meeting:	Quick Review	**Facilitator:**	Barb
Scribe:	Kathy	**Timekeeper:**	Bill

Attendees: Bob, Susan, Paula, Bill, Kathy
Guest: Aaron (Unit Psychologist)

Outcomes: Assignment of needed actions relative to Jaime K., James, and Enrique

Please bring: Notes on Jaime K.

—Agenda—

Quick Review—Jaime K.	**Bill**	**10**

Summary observations: Math (Bill)—behavior plan implemented as scheduled; record indicates reduction in off-task behavior; Reading (Bill)— parents report that he is bringing his book home and reading aloud with Mom nightly; APE (Susan)—has begun to volunteer for volleyball; endurance increased to 15 minutes of play; continues to complain about pain in shoulder

Questions: Is time on-task increasing during reading period?

Is his grip weaker—right hand?

Conclusions: behavior plan in math successful at this time; parent reading effort—positive results

Action items:	Person responsible:	Deadline:
Collect on-task data in reading	Bill	2/10
Measure grip strength—right hand	Susan	1/29

have more time in the resource room." Similarly, a good group member monitors the recorder's writing. If the recorder misinterprets what a speaker has said, an effective group member catches it and suggests a change. Group members also need to employ effective interaction skills, listen to others, avoid being negative or defensive, and participate in the group discussion and decision making.

After the Meeting

Regardless of your role, you are likely to have follow-up responsibilities after the meeting. The group notes will indicate if you have a specific task or work assignment and the date at which it should be completed. All team members have responsibility for continuing their implementation of the educational plan, recording data, as well as supporting and coordinating with other members.

COLLABORATION AND TEAMS

In the first part of this chapter we examined variations in school teams. We distinguished among many models for teaming by examining the level of collaboration among members from different disciplines or perspectives. In that discussion we noted that team members' levels of collaboration may be seen as existing along a continuum, with multidisciplinary teams having the least collaboration, interdisciplinary teams functioning with greater collaborative relationships, and transdisciplinary teams having the most collaborative relationships of the three. In the discussion of disciplinary working relationships it became clear that this is not the only dimension that can be used to distinguish types of teams. We now consider teams in their broadest sense and reflect on the ways in which team concepts blend with concepts of collaboration.

The distinctions between the elements of a collaborative style and those of a team structure are not always completely clear, nor do they necessarily need to be. This is partly because the defining characteristics of a team are those that define the relationship among team members, just as the defining characteristics of collaboration are those that define the relationship among participants in a collaborative activity. Moreover, the defining characteristics of a team are very similar to those of collaboration because it is these elements of collaboration that distinguish a team from a loosely constructed group or a committee.

Effective teams are characterized by collaborative relationships among members. Team members share parity, have a common goal, share responsibility for decision making, and share accountability for outcomes. Teams have common norms and shared beliefs and values, and team members trust one another. Collaboration's emergent characteristic of interdependence is a critical defining characteristic of a team. The relationship between teams and collaboration is simple: An effective team is a collaborative work group. However, when some members dominate interactions or insist on pursuing only their own agenda, or when members defer to someone perceived as having the greatest power, a group referred to as a "team" is not functioning in a collaborative way, regardless of its label.

SUMMARY

An educational team is a group of interdependent individuals with unique skills and perspectives who interact directly to achieve their mutual goal of providing students with effective educational programs and services. The defining characteristics of educational teams include awareness of team membership, shared norms, members with diverse skills and perspectives, a shared goal of effective service delivery, and interdependence. Teams have life cycles and progress through stages as they mature. Models for teaming in schools can be distinguished along two dimensions. The first dimension is the working relationship among people from different disciplines, including multidisciplinary, interdisciplinary, and transdisciplinary team models. The second distinguishing dimension is the purpose of the team. In this chapter three types of student-centered teams were presented and illustrated: (1) teams that make decisions about student referral, assessment, and eligibility for special education services; (2) problem-solving teams concerned with issues affecting students' academic, social, or emotional problems at school; and (3) service delivery teams that provide direct services to students. Features of effective teams include clear goals, individual accountability, shared responsibility, functional group processes, and leadership. Care should be taken and careful attention given to planning and conducting team meetings. Teams, by definition, share many characteristics with collaboration. In fact, effective teams may be described as collaborative work groups.

ACTIVITIES AND ASSIGNMENTS

1. List the teams of which you are a member. Consider which teams are most effective. What are the characteristics of the effective and ineffective teams you have experienced?

2. Think about the organization and dynamics in your school or other professional setting. What are the common types of concerns and issues that arise? What team structures would be most effective in assisting you and your colleagues to meet the educational needs of all students?

3. Preparation for a team meeting is important to the team's success. Outline the steps you would take to prepare to lead a student-centered problem-solving team.

4. The dynamics of a team meeting facilitate or impede its progress. Attend a team meeting and observe the behaviors and comments of team members. Prepare a description of member behaviors that were helpful to the team's functioning and those that were not. Discuss these with classmates or colleagues.

5. Identify a team experience that you have had or observed that was not as successful as you would have liked it to be. Using the characteristics of collaboration presented in Chapter 1 and the issues raised in this chapter, analyze the situation and describe how these factors may have contributed to the problems.

6. Review the suggestions for conducting a team meeting. Compare these with the suggestions for conducting interviews (Chapter 4). Make a list of those things you will do to create the appropriate expectations and atmosphere at the beginning and during the next team meeting you facilitate.

FOR FURTHER READING

Cavallaro, C. C., & Haney, M. (1999). *Preschool inclusion.* Baltimore: Brookes.

Dettmer, P., Thurston, L. P., & Dyck, N. (2002). *Consultation, collaboration, and teamwork for students with special needs.* (4th ed.). Boston: Allyn & Bacon.

Doyle, M., & Straus, D. (1993). *How to make meetings work!* New York: Berkeley.

Friend, M., & Cook, L. (1997). Student-centered teams in schools: Still in search of an identity. *Journal of Educational and Psychological Consultation, 8*(1), 3–20.

Johnson, D. W., & Johnson, F. P. (2000). *Joining together: Group theory and group skills* (7th ed.). Boston: Allyn & Bacon.

Maddux, R. B. (1986). *Team building: An exercise in leadership* (revised ed). Menlo Park, CA: Crisp.

Ogletree, B. T., Bull, J., Drew, R., & Lunnen, K. (2001). Team-based service delivery for students with disabilities: Practice options and guidelines for success. *Intervention in School and Clinic, 36,* 138–145.

Thomas, C. C., Correa, V. I., & Morsink, C. V. (2001). *Interactive teaming: Consultation and collaboration in special programs* (3rd ed.). Upper Saddle River, NJ: Prentice Hall.

Thousand, J. S., & Villa, R. A. (2000). Collaborative teaming: A powerful tool in school re-structuring. In R. A. Villa and J. S. Thousand (Eds.), *Restructuring for caring and effective education: Piecing the puzzle together* (2nd ed.). Baltimore: Brookes.

7

Consultation

Connections

In Chapter 7, yet another service delivery approach that emphasizes collaboration is explored. Similarly to Chapter 6 on teaming and Chapter 8 on co-teaching, Chapter 7 uses the foundational information about collaboration contained in Chapter 1 to examine the definition and characteristics of consulting, approaches for implementing it in schools, and its relationship to collaboration. It also provides additional opportunities to apply the communication skills you learned in Chapters 2, 3, and 4. Consultation is appropriately used when students can be successful with indirect service, and it is often employed in work with parents and families, the topic for Chapter 10.

Learner Objectives

After reading this chapter you will be able to:

1. Define *consultation* and outline the characteristics of consulting relationships among professional educators and between educators and parents.
2. Articulate a rationale for the use of consultation in schools with diverse groups of learners.
3. Identify models of consultation educators sometimes use, describe examples of each, and indicate when each might be instructionally appropriate.
4. Explain the relationship between consultation and collaboration.
5. Describe how collaboration can effectively serve consultants as an interpersonal style.
6. Outline several issues that currently affect consultation as a collaborative service delivery option in schools.
7. Recognize how consultation can be affected by the cultural perspectives of consultants and consultees.

INTRODUCTION

Professionals who work with students with special needs in schools have for many years recognized that one way to support them is indirectly, through consultation with their teachers. For example, in the 1960s school psychologists acknowledged that there were too few professionals to directly meet with all the students who should access their services. Instead, they began shifting their role responsibilities to consult with general education teachers, who then implemented in their classrooms the ideas that were generated during a structured problem-solving process (Tractman, 1961). As the idea of mainstreaming grew in the late 1960s and early 1970s, special education teachers, too, sometimes assumed consulting roles (McKenzie, 1972). Their purpose was to provide assistance to general education teachers whose class groups included students with disabilities. They seldom worked directly with the students, except to demonstrate a technique or strategy. They met with teachers to problem solve about needed classroom interventions and to troubleshoot with teachers when challenges arose.

With the emphasis in today's schools on inclusive practices and accountability for all students learning, consultation continues to be a service delivery option used by special education teachers, school psychologists, speech/language therapists, occupational therapists, early childhood educators, and other special services providers (Bergin & Bergin, 2000; Palsha & Wesley, 1998; Mattison, 2000; Vargo, 1998). For many of these professionals, consultation is just one type of support they are expected to provide; for others consultation is their primary job responsibility.

CONSULTATION CONCEPTS

Because consultation has been used in schools for several decades, much has been written about it and many definitions have been offered for it. For example, Parker (1975) defined consultation as a "process for the delivery of services to pupils through teachers and other school personnel [in which] professional[s] give their expertise to classroom teachers to enable them to resolve the social, emotional, and learning problems of children who need help" (p. 1). Caplan (1970) offered that consultation is a "process of interaction between two professional persons—the consultant, who is a specialist, and the consultee, who invokes the consultant's help in regard to a current work problem with which he is having some difficulty and which he has decided is within the other's area of specialized competence" (p. 19). More recently, Conoley and Conoley (1992) call consultation a "voluntary, non-supervisory relationship between professionals from differing fields established to aid one in his or her professional functioning" (p. 3). Brown, Pryzwansky, and Schulte (1995) define consultation as a "voluntary problem solving process that can be initiated and terminated by either the consultant or consultee" (p. 8).

From our perspective, key elements of these definitions as well as those proposed by many others (e.g., Dettmer, Dyck, & Thurston, 1999; Erchul & Martens,

1997; Rosenfield & Gravois, 1996) contribute to a contemporary meaning for consultation. The definition of **consultation** can be summarized as follows:

> School consultation is a voluntary process in which one professional assists another to address a problem concerning a third party.

Further, the extensive research exploration of consultation documented in the professional literature demonstrates that this service delivery option has been clearly articulated, widely implemented, and carefully examined for its benefits and drawbacks.

Characteristics of Consultation

Of course, knowing a definition of consultation is only a beginning. In order to use consultation effectively, it also is essential to know more about its nature. The characteristics of school consultation have been extensively described in the literature for school psychology, counseling psychology, special education, and other special services (e.g., Heron & Harris, 2001; Kampwirth, 1999). Generally, the characteristics seen as most essential are the following:

Triadic and Indirect Relationship

Although consultation in other disciplines (e.g., law, business, and medicine) may occur between two individuals and not relate to a third party, in schools it is typically triadic, involving three parties and with an indirect relationship between the consultant and the client. The consultant (special services provider) and the consultee (whether an individual teacher, parent, or administrator, or a group of professionals or parents) together design services that the consultee provides to the client (most often a student). The client is not a direct participant in the interaction but is the beneficiary of the process. For example, a psychologist who acts as a consultant may meet with a teacher to plan classroom-based interventions for students, but since the psychologist does not interact with the students, his or her relationship with the students is indirect. Similarly, a consultant supporting students through the use of assistive technology might meet with a special education teacher, a general education teacher, and a parent to discuss the types of devices that might enhance student participation in the classroom and the software that could be used to help them acquire critical academic skills. With the exception of observing and possibly modeling how to use a new piece of equipment, the consultant's interactions are entirely with the adults, but they occur for the benefit of the student.

Voluntariness

A consultee may be puzzled by a situation and seek the assistance of a consultant, or a consultant may notice some difficulty and offer insight to a consultee for remedying the problem. In each case, both the consultant and the consultee have the prerogative of entering or terminating the relationship at any time. This characteristic of voluntariness establishes the principle that consultation cannot be a coerced process (Burdette & Crockett, 1999; Noell & Witt, 1999; Wilczynski, Mandal, Fusilier, 2000). Both professionals agree to participate, and they each can withdraw when they choose. For example, Ms. Chang might ask Ms. Goldstein, the school's nurse, to meet with her because she has concerns about a student's personal hygiene. Ms. Goldstein agrees to meet to problem solve about the issue, and she also follows up two weeks later to see whether the strategies they planned were effective. Conversely, Ms. Goldstein might have noticed this problem and approached Ms. Chang about it, who welcomed the conversation and was relieved to discuss and address the problem. It is important to note, however, that the nature of consultation may change when the consultant rather than the consultee initiates the process (e.g., Harris & Cancelli, 1991); this form of consultation sometimes might feel to the consultee as though it is not truly voluntary.

Expert and Directional Relationship

Most scholars of consultation emphasize that consultants and consultees mutually influence each other and that consultants do not have authority over consultees. They also recommend that consultants be facilitative, empathic, and collegial (e.g., Graham, 1998; Knoff, Sullivan, & Liu, 1995; White & Mullis, 1998). Regardless of its egalitarian nature, however, the consulting relationship exists only because it is perceived that the consultee, not the consultant, has a work-related problem. Thus, the primary reason for the interaction is the consultee's perception of a problem that cannot be solved without another's expertise. In fact, it is difficult to imagine why consultees would participate in consultation un-

Consultation can be an efficient and effective means for some students to receive special services.

less they were relatively certain a consultant had expert knowledge and could provide insight on the matters they had been unable to alleviate themselves. Even when both the consultant and the consultee have a significant interest in the student, the assumption for consultation is still that the classroom teacher has primary daily teaching responsibility for the student and thus is the direct beneficiary of consulting assistance.

Problem-Solving Process with Steps or Stages

The number of steps in the consultation process varies according to the author outlining them, but they typically include (1) *entry,* the physical and psychological beginning of a series of interactions and the establishment of trust and respect; (2) *problem identification,* the establishment of a goal for the interaction; (3) *planning,* the decisions about how to reach the intended goal; (4) *intervention,* carrying out the planned interventions; (5) *evaluation,* the determination of intervention success; and (6) *exit,* the termination of the consulting relationship. Some evidence suggests that consultants do not follow these steps in a rigid manner; the specific sequence followed depends on the situation (Erchul & Martens, 1997). Thus, knowing the precise steps or stages is not as critical as recognizing that consultation is a process comprised of such steps.

The process of consulting might look like this: A school psychologist meets with a middle school team to discuss Ernie, an eighth grader who is often absent, who is refusing to attempt assignments, and who is becoming disruptive in class. At that first meeting, the psychologist asks a few questions (e.g., In what areas does Ernie excel? How have Ernie's behaviors and patterns of learning changed since the beginning of the year?) but mostly listens to the teachers discuss their frustrations. The group also jokes about their need for sweets and arranges for someone to stop at the local doughnut shop prior to the next session. At the second meeting, the psychologist and the teachers more specifically identify the problem they will address, and they generate alternative solutions for it, weighing the pros and cons of each. The teachers agree to try several interventions for the next two weeks. After that time, the entire group meets (again with doughnuts) to evaluate the effectiveness of the interventions. Some changes are made, and the psychologist clarifies that his role is essentially finished, but that he will check back with the group in a couple of weeks. The process, from entry to exit, has been carried out. If Ernie is a student receiving special education services through consultation, a series of problem-solving cycles would occur during the course of the school year.

Shared but Differentiated Responsibilities and Accountability

Consultants and consultees do not share the same responsibility and accountability. If you are a consultant, your primary responsibility and areas of accountability are to ensure that the consulting process is appropriately followed and to offer specific and feasible assistance responsive to the consultee's needs (Rosenfield & Gravois, 1996; Smith 1996). Because consultants do not control consultees' decisions about whether to accept and implement specific strategies, ultimately they cannot be accountable for the success or failure of the consultation outcomes if they have appropriately carried out their part of the process. On the other hand, if you are a consultee, you have the responsibility to participate in good faith in the consultation process and to seriously consider the assistance being offered (Heron & Harris, 2001). If you agree to use a strategy, you are responsible for doing so appropriately. This concept of *treatment integrity*—that is, the systematic implementation of strategies developed during the consultation process and carried out by a consultee—is essential (Kratochwill & Stoiber, 2000). If consultees do not implement agreed-upon interventions, the effectiveness of consultation cannot be assessed. Finally, a consultee's accountability includes gathering data and making judgments about whether or not the problem has been resolved, or whether another intervention is needed and desired.

Rationale for and Benefits of Consultation

As with the other service delivery options discussed in this text, consultation is, first, a viable option for successfully educating students with disabilities or other special needs. Thus when consultation is implemented, it should be designed to benefit students who have IEPs. For example, some students with IEPs are entitled to supports, but they do not need the amount or intensity of service offered through co-teaching or instruction in a separate setting, or they need it only in certain domains (Elliott & McKenney, 1998). In such cases, consultation may be an appropriate service, or part of a package of services. Consultation might also represent a transition strategy: If a student has made tremendous progress during elementary school, so much so that the student's eligibility for special services is marginal at best, the team might decide to send the student to middle school with consultative services instead of direct services. The consultation is provided as a means of helping the student move from elementary to middle school. In this case, it might also be a strategy for assisting the student and family to transition out of special education programs and services. Taking these various applications of consultation together, then, you can see that the overall rationale for consultation is that it comprises a low-intensity service that can be used to support students in the least restrictive environment.

Consultation, however, has many other benefits. For example, it can be a low-cost and efficient means by which students with special needs who do not have IEPs (e.g., at-risk learners) can receive focused attention by professional staff. That is, a special education teacher may have time to arrange three brief meetings with a classroom teacher concerned about a student, even though the special educator could not justify spending several class periods working with that student or being in that classroom.

In addition to providing a limited type of service to students at risk, consultation often also plays a prevention role for some learners. If a general education teacher can work with a psychologist to assist a student with serious behavior issues, as a team they may be able to prevent the problems from becoming so serious that consideration for special education is needed. Likewise, a speech/language therapist might assist a first-grade teacher to design language devel-

PUTTING IDEAS INTO PRACTICE 7.1

Consultant Myths

Much has been written to help consultants refine their practice. One author, Allen Menlo, took the perspective that some of the beliefs that often guide professionals' practice might instead interfere with effective consultation. He suggests that we challenge and reverse our thinking on beliefs such as these:

◆ *People tell the truth about themselves.* In fact, most people wish to present themselves in the best light, and so they may give a selective description of themselves or their actions. Consultants should keep in mind that when a consultee's recall of a situation does not match that of others it is not necessarily dishonest; it is most likely the consultee's actual perception, filtered by a need to appear skilled.

◆ *The best way to get a favor is to give a favor.* In fact, most people are glad to do a favor for others, but they dislike having to ask for one. Think of a time when a friend had car trouble. You were probably pleased to be able to offer assistance in the form of a ride to work. But also think about a time when you had car trouble; you may have hesitated to ask for a ride because you did not want to inconvenience anyone. For consultants, the lesson is this: Sometimes it is better to enlist someone's participation by asking them to do so as a favor to you instead of offering them the favor of your expertise.

◆ *Each person's thoughts and feelings are unique.* In fact, educators are likely to share similar perspectives on many matters pertaining to working with students with disabilities, instructional strategies, and so on. If consultants want to establish a strong working relationship with a teacher or another consultee, sometimes it is beneficial to tap their own deepest thoughts about the situation. Those thoughts just may resonate with the consultee.

Adapted from Menlo, A. (1986). Consultant beliefs which make a significant difference in consultation. In C. L. Warger & L. Aldinger (Eds.), *Preparing special educators for teacher consultation.* Toledo, OH: Preservice Consultation Project, College of Education and Allied Professions, University of Toledo.

opment lessons to help several of the students, thus eliminating the need for them to be referred for formal services. Students who are entitled to special education services should receive them, but consultation can prevent some students from ever needing such a high level of support.

Yet another benefit of consultation concerns professional development. When teachers seek assistance from consultants, one incidental outcome often is an increase in their knowledge and skills. For example, when Mr. James asks Ms. Jarrod to work with him to create a strategy for a student who does not complete or return homework, Mr. James learns about giving students choices in their homework assignments. He then decides that he might try that approach with other students who seem to need additional motivation. This professional development aspect of consultation can be enhanced when consultants point out to consultees how to apply their specific work to other students and situations.

When the benefits of consultation are considered along with its rationale, you can view consultation not only as a service delivery option for students with disabilities, but also as an alternative for meeting student needs and enhancing the strategies in consultees' repertoires by efficiently deploying the professional resources in a school. In fact, as mentioned in the opening to this chapter, one of the early justifications for using consultation occurred during the 1960s, when mental health services came to schools but there were not enough counselors and psychologists to serve all the students identified for assistance. Those professionals began working with teachers, who in turn provided services to students. This indirect approach was recommended again as behavioral approaches became popular in schools at the end of that decade (Tharp & Wetzel, 1969). Now, with students with IEPs in general education settings and many students who are at risk for failure commanding educators' attention, it is not surprising that the same strategy is frequently used. For example, notice how the psychologist described above was meeting with the middle school team. By doing this, all the teachers benefit from his expertise and they coordinate their intervention efforts. The psychologist's time investment is fairly limited, but the positive impact can be significant.

CONSULTATION MODELS

Knowing the definition and characteristics of consultation along with the rationale for making it part of your school's service delivery options lets us proceed to the next level of specificity—exploring models through which consultation may be practiced. Although there is little variation in the general consultation process, the practice of consultation is based on theoretical perspectives that have led to the development of several distinct consultation models (Behring, Cabello, Kushida, & Murguia, 2000; Kampwirth, 1999). These models prescribe consultants' orientation and the assumptions that undergird their interactions with consultees. They also dictate the types of interventions consultants are likely to use. Two models—behavioral consultation and clinical consultation—are particularly applicable to schools and are explored in detail in the following sections. Several other models exists, and these are summarized in Figure 7.1.

Behavioral Consultation

Tharp and Wetzel's (1969) text on using applied behavior analysis in naturalistic settings established **behavioral consultation** as a distinct model to guide the consulting process. These authors proposed that consultation was an efficient means of implementing behavioral interventions with large numbers of individuals. Educators took that message to heart, and since that time, the model has

---

Figure 7.1   Alternative Models of Consultation

In addition to behavioral and clinical consultation, models commonly implemented in schools, the following consultation models have been described:

◆ **Mental Health**
Based on Caplan's (1970) work, this consultation model addresses social and emotional problems, acknowledging that some issues are based in the client, come in the consultee's reaction to the client, some in the structure of a program, and some in the program's administration. Typical practitioners of this model are counselors or psychologists who have had specialized training in it.

◆ **Organizational**
Sometimes the appropriate level for intervention in consultation is the organization. In this model, it is assumed that the leaders of an organization are the consultees (e.g., the principals in a school district) and that the clients are the employees (e.g., the teachers). Through needs assessment, self-analysis, and professional development, consultants using this model assist organizations to function more effectively and efficiently, often focusing on staff morale.

◆ **Program**
Consultation may be an appropriate strategy through which to evaluate program effectiveness. In such cases, program consultation may be implemented. In this model, the consultant gathers data about the targeted program (e.g., the inclusive services in a school) using multiple sources, analyzes the data, and presents the results along with suggestions for program improvement.

◆ **Education and Training**
Although not always thought of as such, professional development can be considered a model for consultation. Using large-group, small-group, demonstration, and other approaches, a consultant implementing this model would have as a goal improving the knowledge and skills of consultees (e.g., teachers) so that interventions for clients (e.g., students) will improve.

---

become the most frequently used type of consultation in schools (Sheridan, Welch, & Orme, 1996), employed by special education teachers, school psychologists, occupational therapists, inclusion facilitators, and others.

Behavioral consultants rely on several assumptions to guide their practice: First, they themselves must have a thorough understanding of behavioral principles and practices and be able to apply them to their consultees. They also must ensure that consultees either have similar understanding or enough understanding of those principles to carry out behavioral interventions in a systematic way. Second, behavioral consultants presume that the consultee controls reinforcers that will be effective with the client or student, that is, that teachers have rewards or consequences that will affect student actions. Third, consultants using this model believe that data collection is not only important but also crucial, and they stress data-based decision making.

Procedures

Of all the consultation models described in the professional literature, behavioral consultation has the most clearly defined steps or stages. They comprise a highly refined problem-solving process that mirrors the general consultation process presented earlier in this chapter. The first step is problem identification. This involves obtaining a description of the problem and determining how to gather information to confirm its existence and character. The second step, problem analysis, is closely related to the first. The consultant directs the consultee on how to gather detailed and objective information about the problem. Based on the results obtained, the consultant and consultee move to the third step, intervention. They plan a behavioral strategy to address the problem and positively affect the client, and they clarify each professional's responsibilities related to the intervention. The consultee carries out the plan with input as needed from the consultant. Eventually, the final step, evaluation, is reached. The consultant and consultee use the data the consultee has been collecting to determine whether the strategy has had the desired impact. Based on what they find, they either conclude the consultation, make changes in the strategy and continue, or begin again (Kampwirth, 1999; Heron & Harris, 2001; Idol, Nevin, & Paolucci-Whitcomb, 2000).

You will find that the fundamental problem-solving steps of behavioral consultation are very similar to the generic problem-solving steps that professionals carry out in team meetings, co-teaching planning, and informal interactions with colleagues. Their uniqueness lies in their reliance on the principles of behaviorism—for example, description of problems in observable terms, the use of specific reinforcers applied to both the consultee and the client, the use of data to monitor progress, and a highly analytic approach to the entire process. Those steps and the entire problem-solving process were discussed in greater detail in Chapter 5.

Analysis of the Behavioral Model

The popularity of behavioral consultation for schools is undoubtedly due to its reliance on well-researched strategies that often result in successful outcomes. Since behavioral consultants emphasize data collection, documentation of consultation's effectiveness can often be made. However, several issues and concerns may arise when behavioral consultation is used. For example, some consultees, including parents and classroom teachers, may object to seemingly coercive behavioral principles and may resist the use of this approach. Alternatively, they may lack the understanding of behavioral principles necessary to systematically carry out proposed interventions. For example, a parent might forget to consistently reward his child for completing homework, and if this happens, the plan for helping the student is unlikely to succeed.

In addition, behavioral consultants always must be aware of the ethical dilemma of using behavioral technology to change students' behavior to accommodate the preferences of teachers and parents, rather than assisting students in making self-identified changes that directly benefit them. That is, behavioral consultants need to stress building positive student behaviors such as asking for assistance when stumped on assignments or monitoring their own on-task behavior, rather than emphasizing compliance behavior such as sitting quietly in class.

To address some of the issues in traditional behavioral consultation, over the past several years a new variation of the model has emerged. In *conjoint behavioral consultation,* specialists, classroom teachers, and parents/families work closely together to design, implement, and evaluate interventions to improve student learning and behavior (Sheridan, Kratochwill, & Bergan, 1996). By doing this, the key adults in a child's life can coordinate their efforts to assist the child. Research suggests that this model is perceived as being acceptable and effective by teachers and parents, and it is particularly valuable for increasing parent involvement in their child's education and building positive school–home relationships (Elksnin & Elksnin, 2000; Freer & Watson, 1999).

Clinical Consultation

Clinical consultation is a diagnostic model that traditionally has been used by school and counseling psychologists, diagnosticians, speech and language specialists, and, to a lesser degree, by social workers and occupational and physical therapists. In addition, as educators work closely together to address the needs of at-risk students in inclusive schools (LeCapitaine, 2000), special education teachers who provide services to students with IEPs in general education settings are using this model more and more. In this model, the consultant is concerned with accurately identifying or diagnosing a client's problem and prescribing strategies for resolving it (Bell & Nadler, 1985; Erchul & Martens, 1997; Kampwirth, 1999). Clinical consultants' first consideration is that the source of the problem is in the client, not the consultee. For example, if a teacher asked a special education teacher to help her decide how to respond to a student whose attention-getting behavior in the classroom was becoming a serious matter, the special educator would tend to assume that an intervention was needed for the student, not that the teacher's interactions with the student were rewarding the behavior. The consultant would try to help the classroom teacher see the problem clearly (perhaps the student behavior was a means of avoiding difficult assignments) and to design a strategy to change the student's behavior (perhaps by giving the student only a small part of the assignment at one time). If this approach was not successful, the consultant might look at the environment, the teacher's actions in the classroom, and so on.

However, in this model the consultant is not actually involved in the ongoing implementation of the intervention or the monitoring of it. The consultant presumes that the dilemma for the consultee is the identification of the specific problem, not the implementation of strategies to resolve it. In the previous example, the special educator who is the consultant would make suggestions about the intervention, but would not stay involved in the situation unless the teacher asked for a follow-up.

Procedure

The steps for clinical consultation are not as clearly prescribed as they are for behavioral consultation. Clinical consultants typically would meet with a consultee, either a parent or a teacher, to learn about a student's apparent problem, and they would assess the specific problem. In this model, that assessment might include observing the student, interviewing the student, or even directly administering some type of diagnostic instrument. Clinical consultants would then analyze the problem the teacher reported by considering the diagnostic information they had gathered, including the student's strengths and needs. Next, they would suggest interventions for the consultee to try. Although clinical consultants would not implement the intervention, at a later date they might follow up to determine whether the outcome was successful.

Analysis of the Clinical Model

Because consultant involvement generally is confined to the diagnostic and recommendation stages, clinical consultation may be preferred when consultants have limited time in which to offer assistance to consultees or when a complex problem needs clarification that can be offered by an expert diagnostician. The former situation might occur when a special educator is preparing to offer a general education teacher suggestions for interventions for a student who is at risk for failure. The latter might occur when a student who has an IEP has a sudden increase in disruptive or aggressive behavior or experiences unanticipated difficulties in meeting IEP goals and objectives (Ray, Skinner, & Watson, 1999). However, because this consultation model generally assumes that the problem exists primarily in the client, it is not particularly useful if the problem is one that involves the student, the teacher, the environment, and other factors in combination. Also, this model is premised on the consultee having the professional skills to act on the consultant's recommendations. If the consultee does not understand the consultant's conceptualization of the problem or does not have the skills to implement and monitor the intervention, the model has limited utility.

Choosing and Using Consultation Models

As you were reading about behavioral and clinical consultation, you might have wondered whether consultation actually occurs in the clear described steps and following the theoretical perspective outlined, or whether you should just take ideas from these models as well as others and blend them into your own style. As with many concepts and procedures related to your profession, the answer is probably to use both approaches, thinking about consultation models but adapting them to your own experiences and job setting.

Gallessich (1982) has been a key proponent of teaching consultants about multiple models and creating the expectation that they make deliberate choices about how to work with other professionals. Her point is well-taken: She maintains that much of the consultation that occurs, and this is especially true in schools, is atheoretical; that is, it is not clearly guided by any model. She contends that if consultants are deliberate in selecting their approach, they have other the-

In some situations, the consultant may directly observe the student in a classroom setting prior to making recommendations to the teacher.

ory-based alternatives from which to choose if the original approach does not seem effective. Without a theoretical grounding of models, often consultants do not have a strategy for changing tactics when the situation calls for such an action.

At the same time, consultation is seldom as "pure" as the models described in the preceding sections. All consultants tend to put their own signatures on their work by incorporating their own personal styles, adapting procedures to fit contextual variables, and relating their consulting to their other role responsibilities, whether direct service to students, staff development, co-teaching, or others. This individualization of consultation models is certainly expected. The only caution to raise is that individualizing should not have the effect of altering the major assumptions and procedures of the various models. If it does, it will undoubtedly compromise the likely effectiveness of the process.

Thus, a third option is emerging to guide consultants' practice. Some authors (e.g., Erchul & Martens, 1997; Kampwirth, 1999) are proposing integrated models of consultation that draw from multiple theoretical perspectives. The advantage of this approach is that the best features of each of the traditional models can be tapped, while at the same time the specific opportunities and constraints for consultative services that exist in school environments can be taken into account.

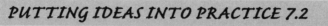

PUTTING IDEAS INTO PRACTICE 7.2

Ethical Issues in Consultation

The practice of consultation often includes a number of ethical issues. Which of the following might affect you as you serve in a consulting capacity?

1. Issues for consultants
   ♦ Breadth and depth of professional knowledge and skill for addressing the situation described by the consultee
   ♦ Understanding of when to seek help from another source instead of continuing to try to work with the consultee
   ♦ Belief in an eclectic approach to consultation so that intervention plans are not confined to a single theoretical perspective

2. Issues related to consultees
   ♦ Preservation of confidentiality regarding the consultee (and the client), and understanding of when to breach confidentiality and the potential impact of doing so
   ♦ Education of consultees regarding the importance of their active participation in consultation
   ♦ Respect for a consultee who, with valid reason, chooses not to follow the recommendations of the consultant

3. Issues related to clients
   ♦ Development of interventions that are based on contemporary educational practice and solid research evidence
   ♦ Development of interventions that encourage positive client behavior and lifelong independence
   ♦ Development of interventions that are respectful of family preferences and beliefs
   ♦ Development of interventions that follow legal guidelines for the education of students with disabilities

Adapted from Heron, T. E., Martz, S. A., & Margolis, H. (1996). Ethical and legal issues in consultation. *Remedial and Special Education, 17,* 377–385, 392.

CONSULTATION AND COLLABORATION

The emphasis on relating collaboration and consultation in special education can be traced to the early 1970s, particularly in the fields of school and counseling psychology (e.g., Kurpius & Brubaker, 1976; Pryzwansky, 1974). The viewpoint was expressed that consultative interactions were more likely to be successful if they were facilitative and supportive rather than prescriptive (e.g., Parker, 1975). By the end of the 1970s, it was clear that for psychologists and counselors in schools, a collaborative or facilitative approach to consultation was generally recommended over other approaches.

Consultation as a role responsibility for special education teachers was rapidly evolving during the same time period (Friend, 1988). The Vermont Consulting Teacher Program (Christie, McKenzie, & Burdett, 1972), begun in the late 1960s, was setting a precedent for the systematic use of teacher consultation. It was implemented by highly trained consulting teachers who held specialist degrees and adjunct faculty appointments at the University of Vermont. As these consultants worked with, trained, and offered course credit to classroom teachers, their status as trainers and university faculty reinforced the notion of consultant as expert. Later, an additional issue arose in this model: Although in the original Vermont model the consultative relationship was voluntary, as this approach spread to other geographic areas the participation of teachers became less voluntary—students with disabilities were mainstreamed and special education teachers or other special services providers were assigned to consult with general education teachers, often without any preparation for the consultant role.

The backlash that occurred should not have been surprising. Critics made it clear that it was inappropriate for special education to try to "fix" general education; general educators did not need special educators to serve as experts to tell them what to do with the students in their classrooms (Friend, 1988). Nor was it likely, in many instances, that special educators knew what to do in a general education classroom, since at that point in time most of them worked primarily in separate special education classrooms or resource rooms, with students coming to them and no in-class services provided.

By the early 1980s, the special education teacher consultation literature was countering the criticism of special educators as questionable experts for general education settings by renewing an emphasis on collegial relationships (Evans, 1980; Friend, 1984). Collaborative approaches to consultation began to be advocated at this time (Idol, Nevin, & Paolucci-Whitcomb, 1994). This trend has continued and is also reflected in school and counseling psychology (Kampwirth, 1999; Vargo, 1998; Witt, 1990), although some professionals believe that many teachers actually prefer a directive rather than a collaborative style to the consulting process (Witt et al., 1991).

The debate about the role of collaboration in the consultation process has become more intense in recent years. Some authors contend that collaboration is not a well-enough understood concept to even consider its application to consultation (e.g., Erchul, 1999). They argue that interpersonal influence must be studied in order to understand the style consultants use in working with consultees. Other authors (e.g., Gutkin, 1999) propose that the process of consultation can be implemented with variations along two dimensions: (a) coercive–collaborative and (b) directive–nondirective. Unlike most current thinking in the field and the perspective taken in this textbook, they suggest that directiveness is not the opposite of collaboration, and they offer that research is needed to examine consultation in light of this reconceptualization of the interpersonal aspect of it. For you as a practitioner of consultation, what is important to understand is that inquiry into the relationship between collaboration and consultation is far from complete and knowledge about how it affects consultant practice is likely to continue to emerge.

It should be noted that today, with the increased enrollment of students with disabilities in general education classrooms, the concept of collaboration and the notion of consultation sometimes are framed as a discussion of voluntariness. In some instances, a special services provider as well as a classroom teacher have responsibility for a student's education. This situation increases the likelihood that the teacher will initiate some consultation, but that the special educator may initiate even more. For example, if a student with autism is included in an intermediate classroom, an inclusion facilitator might request a weekly meeting to determine the student's progress and design interventions. The teacher may benefit from these meetings, but at the same time may feel unwanted pressure to participate in them, particularly during busy times of the school year. The teacher may not believe that the meetings are truly voluntary.

Despite these historical and contemporary issues related to collaboration in consultation, by using our definitions the distinction between these two terms can be clearly articulated so that special services providers can base their practice on an understanding of each. Because collaboration is a style or an approach to interaction, it can be attached to the consultation process, just as it can be attached to problem solving, assessing, and co-teaching. Moreover, a consultant may choose to use a collaborative approach at some consultation stages and not others, just as the consultant may choose to use it with some consultees and not with others.

However, ascribing collaboration to the consultation process does not make it a unique model (Conoley & Conoley, 1988) in the sense of the models presented earlier. *Any* model of consultation can be implemented collaboratively. For example, behavioral consultation has clear, theoretically based principles that prescribe its practice. Whether or not behavioral consultation is carried out collaboratively is an issue that is distinct from the model itself. Behavioral consultation can be conducted collaboratively within a relationship characterized by parity, mutual goals, shared decision making, and all the additional characteristics of collaboration. However, behavioral consultation also may be conducted by someone who, using a directive style, retains much of the decision-making responsibility, prescribes interventions, and offers expert advice and explanations to consultees. This same analogy could be made for each model of consultation: Each could be implemented by a consultant who may or may not emphasize the use of a collaborative style of interaction.

The Consulting Relationship

As you observe and participate in consultative interactions you will notice that effective consultants deliberately select a style of interaction to suit the circumstances. Sometimes the nature of the consultation situation or the needs of the consultee require the consultant to use a directive style. For example, you may receive an isolated request from a colleague seeking assistance in interpreting a student's assessment results. Your caseload, available time, and knowledge of your colleague's other sources of professional support, among other considerations, may lead you simply to offer your expert opinion of the assessment results. Similarly, you may occasionally find in a collaborative, ongoing consultation relationship that a specific topic is more appropriately addressed directively.

Consider a consultation situation in which you and your colleague, Jane, have been working together collaboratively for several weeks to design and evaluate a systematic reward system for use with Henry, a student in her class. Increasing district demands, the inclusion of many students with disabilities, and a number of other events have created significant and competing demands for Jane. Henry, the student whom you share, is no longer responding satisfactorily to your jointly planned intervention and has begun to display again his problematic and disruptive behaviors. You and Jane both recognize that you have a problem that must be addressed, but Jane does not currently have the emotional, physical, or logistical resources to participate in any significant way in a collaborative problem-solving effort. Consequently, you may need to solve this pressing problem independently (e.g., by making an immediate adjustment in the implementation of the intervention with Henry). Alternatively, depending on the situation and your assessment of it, you may decide that neither a directive nor a collaborative approach is appropriate. If Henry's lack of progress appears to be only temporary and Jane's stress seems to be the most salient issue, you may determine that a nondirective, supportive, or empathic style is most appropriate.

If you develop an understanding of how collaboration and consultation can be distinguished from one another and how they work in tandem, it will guide you in your own practice and help you to communicate clearly with your colleagues and others. This is particularly important since much of what has been written about consultation has been written for school and counseling psychologists, not for special education teachers or other special services providers. It is additionally significant since considerable confusion about essential concepts continues to flourish in the consultation literature (e.g., Coben, Thomas, Sattler, & Morsink, 1997; Dettmer et al., 1999; Idol et al., 2000).

Consultants have the responsibility to work effectively with professionals and parents/family members who are from other cultures.

Issues in Consultation as Collaborative Service Delivery

The field of consultation has a rich history, and as it continues to evolve rapidly in the twenty-first century, it faces a number of significant issues. In addition to the various issues presented throughout this chapter and those summarized in Figure 7.2, the following are particular areas of concern for consultants.

Understanding of Consulting Relationships

Consultation is effective only if both parties are active participants. Consultants must strive to avoid being seen as academic and behavioral magicians; general education teachers must contribute significant information about their classrooms and students for consultants to offer meaningful assistance. A dilemma occurs in some schools, however. Some consultants feel pressure to have solutions ready to dispense to consultees. In others, classroom teachers expect consultants to have answers and are disappointed when such on-the-spot advice does not improve the problem that led to the consultation in the first place. The challenge for schools using consulting is to educate all participants about their roles in the process and to discourage professionals from making inaccurate assumptions about others' roles and responsibilities (Friend & Cook, 1988). For example, consultants should resist the urge to offer advice without an adequate understanding of the classroom environment and teacher expectations. How-

---

Figure 7.2   Current Issues in School Consultation

The field of school consultation is facing a wide variety of issues that will shape its future. In addition to the issues discussed in the text, the following represent other concerns for the field. Which ones might affect your practice? Which might be concerns among your school colleagues?

◆ The differences in consultation between professionals such as teachers and psychologists and consultation between professionals and parents/families

◆ The appropriate variations in practice for consultation when carried out by special education teachers versus specialists such as psychologists and counselors

◆ *Treatment integrity,* or the extent to which teachers receiving consultation assistance actually systematically carry out the agreed-upon interventions

◆ The impact of special education teacher consultation on student achievement and behavior as compared to more direct interventions

◆ Accountability in consultation for both consultants and consultees

◆ The relative merits of the various models of consultation used in schools, and the potential to create integrated models that pull together the best aspects of each of the traditional models

◆ Parent/family involvement in and response to school-based consultation services, particularly for those from nondominant cultures

ever, classroom teachers must reciprocate with patience, recognizing that high-quality results are only likely with considerable effort.

Time Allocation for Consultation

For special education teachers, psychologists, and others who have both consulting as well as direct service responsibilities, a dilemma often arises regarding the time available to consult. Understandably, time working directly with students is arranged first, and too often consulting becomes an informal, sometimes unstructured, and occasionally unsystematic add-on to professional schedules. Educators who consult should have time allocated in their schedules to do so. If consultation is seen as a luxury instead of as a necessity, the demands of direct instruction, testing, report preparation, and meetings may preclude its careful use. More information about the quandry of time in relationship to collaborative interactions is presented in Chapter 13.

Multiculturalism

Over the past several years, increased attention has been paid in consultation to issues that arise when a consultant is from one culture and the consultee, whether a teacher or the family, is from another culture (Henning-Stout & Meyers, 2000; Lopez, 2000; Nastasi, Varjas, Bernstein, & Tayasena, 2000). Concerns relate to language differences and the communication issues that may arise, as well as to consultants' appreciation of how their own culture may influence their practice. In addition, consultants should ensure that they acquire and use appropriate cultural sensitivity in the development of the interpersonal relationships, in the consultant's awareness of the consultee's receptivity to various interaction styles, and in the appropriateness of various strategies and interventions consultants may suggest to consultees (e.g., Rogers, 2000). More detail on these and related competencies is presented in the Perspectives on Diversity feature.

Confidentiality

When consultants build trusting relationships with consultees and problem solve with them, it is likely that information will be shared that should be held in confidence. For example, a teacher might mention that she is so frustrated with the acting-out behavior of a student that she finds herself negatively responding to nearly everything he does. This honest admission should not be shared with other colleagues. And although that might seem obvious, in the press of completing many professional responsibilities and with the pressure that now comes with working in schools, many consultants need to be reminded that they are obligated to keep confidences, even relatively small ones, in order to preserve the benefits of this service delivery option and in order to convey respect for consultees. Ultimately, confidentiality is an ethical issue, one that merits serious and continued attention in schools.

When considered as a whole, consultation has an important niche in the array of services to students in schools. However, for it to be effective, consultants

PERSPECTIVES ON DIVERSITY 7.1

Cross-Cultural Consultation Competencies

To effectively interact with professionals or parents/families from other cultures, the following competencies are recommended for consultants:

◆ **Understanding of One's Own and Others' Culture**
Consultants must become sensitive to the biases they have because of their own culture and background. In addition, they must work to overcome these biases as they interact with individuals from other cultures. Most important, they should set as a goal to understand others' perspectives from the context of their culture.

◆ **Communication and Interpersonal Skills**
Consultants are obligated to learn about the communication patterns of other cultures and to be respectful of those patterns. In addition, they should recognize that communication that occurs through the use of an interpreter might be distorted.

◆ **Consultation Process as Culturally Embedded**
Each stage in the consulting process should be examined for its "fit" with the culture of the consultee and client. In addition, consultants should analyze whether, given cultural factors, the entire notion of consultation is an appropriate means for intervening with some professionals and parents/families.

◆ **Evaluation of Consultation Effectiveness**
Consultants may need to become familiar with and use qualitative strategies for measuring the effectiveness of their work. The use of stories, ethnography, and other qualitative data sometimes can more accurately capture the successes and problems of consultation in a multicultural context.

◆ **Knowledge of Specific Cultures**
Depending on the situation in which consultants work, they may need knowledge about bilingual education, the process of acculturation, immigration, and available services. They may also need to be aware of cultural implications related to mental health, disability, assessment, and other matters pertaining to education.

◆ **Use of Interpreters**
Consultants should have knowledge about working with interpreters, including recognizing the limitations of interactions conducted through an interpreter. Directly related to this topic are the issues of distinguishing between learning and behavior problems and the challenges of learning a second language.

Adapted from Rogers, M. R. (2000). Examining the cultural context on consultation. *School Psychology Review, 29,* 414–418.

must select an approach carefully, monitor the impact of their suggestions on the student and consultee, and constantly evaluate the quality of their practice. Some consultants, such as psychologists, may find consultation a responsibility easily integrated into their jobs. For others, such as special education teachers, consultation may have to be mindfully nurtured to reach its potential.

SUMMARY

Consultation is one of the activities that special services providers often associate with collaboration in schools. It is a voluntary process in which one professional assists another to address a problem concerning a third party, typically a student. The characteristics of consultation are that it is triadic and indirect, and voluntary. It is also an expert and directional relationship, a problem-solving process, and a process that involves shared but differentiated responsibilities for decisions and accountability for outcomes. Consultation can have several different theoretical orientations including behavioral and clinical models. Each model is based on specific assumptions, uses similar procedures explicated in varying degrees, and includes both advantages and disadvantages. Although consultants seldom use "pure" versions of consultation models, they provide a framework and alternatives for practice. Collaboration may be used within the consultation process, but consultation may be conducted with little collaboration as well. The matter of consultees' preferences for collaboration versus directiveness in consultation is not settled and usually depends on the specific consultee and situation. For consultation to be successful, a number of issues should be addressed: participants' understanding of the process and their roles and responsibilities in it; time allocations for consultation; participants' awareness of and responses to their cultural differences; and confidentiality.

ACTIVITIES AND ASSIGNMENTS

1. Think about the position titles and descriptions that special services providers have in your school or in a school you are familiar with. Do those who might be described as consultants have responsibilities consonant with the description of consultation provided in this chapter? How would you write a position description to maximize a consultant's effectiveness?

2. Consultation has the characteristic of being voluntary. However, some special services providers have consultation as an expected role responsibility with teachers who instruct students with special needs. How can you reconcile these seemingly contradictory notions?

3. What does it mean to say that consultation is expert and directional? What is the implication of this concept for working with general education teachers? What opportunities might it create? What barriers might it create in collegial relationships?

4. If you were offered a position that emphasized behavioral consultation, how prepared would you be for it? What specific skills of behaviorism do you perceive would be most important to have? How would these apply to your work with consultees? What advantages and disadvantages do you see for this consulting model?

5. If someone asked you to distinguish collaboration from consultation and define *collaborative consultation,* how would you respond? Why is collaborative consultation usually not considered a unique model of consultation?

6. Identify one consultation experience that you have had or observed that was not as successful as you would have liked it to be. Using the characteristics of collaboration presented in Chapter 1 and the issues raised in this chapter, analyze each situation and describe how these factors may have contributed to the problems encountered in the consultation and/or on the team.

7. As you have observed consultants working in schools, what have you noticed related to the issues mentioned in the chapter? To what extent do consultants seem sensitive to educating others about consulting relationships, time, multiculturalism, and confidentiality? Interview a teacher who recently has worked with a consultant. What was that professional's perceptions of the experience?

8. Teaming and consulting are both service delivery arrangements for students with disabilities or other special needs. Both are most successfully implemented when collaboration is a priority. In what ways might collaboration issues in these arrangements *differ* from one another?

FOR FURTHER READING

Burdette, P. J., & Crockett, J. B. (1999). An exploration of consultation approaches and implementation in heterogeneous classrooms. *Education and Training in Mental Retardation and Developmental Disabilities, 34,* 432–452.

Erchul, W. P., & Martens, B. K. (1997). *School consultation: Conceptual and empirical bases of practice.* New York: Plenum.

Henning-Stout, M., & Meyers, J. (2000). Consultation and human diversity: First things first. *School Psychology Review, 29,* 419–420.

Kampwirth, R. J. (1999). *Collaborative consultation in the schools: Effective practices for students with learning and behavior problems.* Upper Saddle River, NJ: Merrill.

Noel, G. H., & Witt, J. C. (1999). When does consultation lead to intervention implementation? Critical issues for research and practice. *Journal of Special Education, 33,* 29–35.

Sheridan, S., Kratochwill, T., & Bergan, J. (1996). *Conjoint behavioral consultation: A procedural manual.* New York: Plenum.

Soo-Hoo, T. (1998). Applying frame of reference and reframing techniques to improve school consultation in multicultural settings. *Journal of Educational and Psychological Consultation, 9,* 325–345.

Truesdell, L. A., & Lopez, E. (1995). Series: Consultation models revisited [Series of articles, one per journal issue]. *Journal of Educational and Psychological Consultation, 6.*

8

Co-Teaching

In Chapters 6 and 7 you learned about teaming and consultation school activities in which collaboration is valued. In Chapter 8, we add another collaborative activity—co-teaching. Co-teaching is a special form of teaming that is a unique blend of direct and indirect services in which a general educator and a special educator jointly instruct pupils in a single classroom. As inclusive practices have become more prevalent, so has co-teaching. To introduce you to co-teaching, we outline basic concepts related to it, describe several specific ways for co-teachers to use this service delivery option while taking advantage of both professionals' expertise, raise topics that co-teachers should discuss, and present some administrative and logistic issues that can affect the effectiveness of co-teaching for meeting students needs. As with teaming in Chapter 6, we also clarify the relation of co-teaching to concepts of collaboration.

Learner Objectives

After reading this chapter you will be able to:

1. Define *co-teaching* and distinguish it from related vocabulary (for example, inclusion, teaming).
2. Articulate a rationale for the use of co-teaching in schools with diverse groups of learners.
3. Identify six approaches to co-teaching, describe examples of each, and indicate when each might be instructionally appropriate.
4. Explain the relationship between co-teaching and collaboration.
5. Describe relationship issues that may affect the implementation of co-teaching.
6. Outline several administrative and logistic factors that can foster or constrain co-teaching.
7. Demonstrate a commitment to co-teaching by explaining its appropriate use in public school settings and planning lessons that incorporate it.

INTRODUCTION

A shift in philosophies about the educational needs of students with disabilities, evolving school reform and restructuring movements, and changing legislative priorities for appropriately educating students have increased pressures for more use of inclusive practices in schools (Friend & Bursuck, 2002; Huefner, 2000). Students who just several years ago might have spent the majority of the school day in a self-contained special education classroom often now are educated in general education settings with supports and services coming to them there (Elliott & McKenney, 1998; Fisher & Frey, 2001). Students with mild disabilities who used to spend an hour or a class period in a resource room sometimes now receive similar supports, but within their general education classrooms (Walther-Thomas, Korinek, McLaughlin, & Williams, 1999). One result of this inclusive trend has been that general education teachers, special education teachers, speech/language specialists, and other service providers have had to create ways to offer students specialized instruction while helping them to remain part of the classroom community. This has led to the development of alternative service delivery options. Co-teaching is one such option for delivering special education and related services to students with disabilities (Cook & Friend, 1995; Hourcade & Bauwens, 2001), students who are deaf or hard of hearing (Kluwin, 1999; Luckner, 1999), and other students with special needs such as those whose native language is not English (Bahamonde & Friend, 1999).

CO-TEACHING CONCEPTS

Although co-teaching is an increasingly popular strategy and one of the fastest growing inclusive school practices, the quality of what occurs in co-taught classes and the benefits for students—both those with and those without disabilities—vary considerably (Welch, 2000). This may be a result of confusion about what co-teaching is and how it differs from other in-class services, as well as unevenness in its implementation. **Co-teaching,** as we discuss it here, is one of several approaches to providing special education or related services to students with disabilities or other special needs while they remain in their general education classes. Co-teaching occurs when

> two or more professionals jointly deliver substantive instruction to a diverse, or blended, group of students in a single physical space. (Cook & Friend, 1995, p. 1)

Defining Characteristics of Co-Teaching

Teacher teams have used various structures for joint instructional efforts for many years, and at elementary, middle school, and high school levels (e.g., Crespin, 1971; Trump, 1966; Warwick, 1971). Most of those teams, however, consisted of two classroom teachers who pooled their class groups and their instructional efforts. Only for the past decade has the use of co-teaching been seen as a mechanism for providing services to students with disabilities in their general education classrooms (Friend, Reising, & Cook, 1993). The professional literature on co-teaching is growing rapidly, including descriptions of the variations occurring in co-teaching practice, the challenges that accompanying co-teaching, and the efficacy of it (e.g., Austin, 2001; Tichenor, Heins, & Piechura-Couture, 2000). To truly understand co-teaching, however, an appropriate starting point is its defining characteristics since these underscore co-teaching's uniqueness as a service delivery option.

Two or More Professionals

Co-teaching involves at least two appropriately credentialed professionals—two teachers (e.g., a general education teacher and a special education teacher); a teacher and a related services professional (e.g., a teacher and a speech/language therapist); or a teacher and another specialist (e.g., a teacher and a reading specialist). The importance of this defining characteristic comes from the notion that co-teachers are peers—they have equivalent credentials and employment status and thus can truly be partners in their instructional endeavors on behalf of students.

An appropriately prepared and credentialed paraprofessional, such as a certified occupational therapy assistant (COTA), might occasionally be considered a co-teacher. In general, however, classroom volunteers and paraprofessionals who serve as instructional assistants provide support in classrooms rather than fill co-teaching roles; they typically have not had the professional preparation to co-teach nor is the instructional partnership of co-teaching an appropriate role expectation for them (French, 2001). (See Chapter 9 for a discussion of these relationships and other issues related to collaboration with paraprofessionals.) To underscore this, classrooms in some school districts in which paraprofessionals are delivering services are called *supported* or *assisted classrooms,* not co-taught classrooms. This distinction helps everyone involved to remember that paraprofessionals should not be asked to carry out the responsibilities of licensed or certificated staff, and it clarifies for general education teachers the nature of the support being provided. It is important to note that saying paraprofessionals generally should not co-teach does not mean they do not have crucial classroom roles. They still work with individual students and groups, but under the direction of teachers or other specialists and to reinforce instruction, not to routinely introduce it.

Joint Delivery of Instruction

In schools across the country, we have found a disturbing number of educators who call their arrangement "co-teaching" simply because it involves two adults in a classroom at the same time. In these situations the classroom teacher typically conducts the same type of instruction as he or she would if teaching alone. That teacher may even express gratefulness for having in the classroom "an extra set of hands." The second teacher, usually a special educator or specialist, has the *de facto* role of instructional assistant for students with disabilities and possibly for some others with special needs. This individual hovers at the fringes of the class until the core instruction is delivered and then helps those who need it, or this educator pulls individual students or a small group aside to deliver instruction completely separate from that being provided to the rest of the class. While such arrangements may occur occasionally in co-taught classes, particularly if one or more students in the class have significant disabilities, if these practices are routine the arrangement should not be referred to as co-teaching. Instead, this situation is an inappropriate underuse of a qualified professional. It is a practice likely to stigmatize students at least as much as pullout strategies and to frustrate special services providers. It is also a situation in which any benefits derived from separate instruction are diminished by the increased noise and activity in the classroom. These considerations give rise to questions about why professionals consistently would use this arrangement for any length of time.

As a far more successful alternative, in true co-teaching both professionals coordinate and deliver substantive instruction. This does not mean that they always work with students in large groups, but it does mean that they share decision making about instruction and ensure that both have active roles in teaching (Austin, 2001; Gately & Gately, 2001). Specifically, they plan and use unique and high-involvement instructional strategies to engage all students in ways that are not possible when only one teacher is present. By doing so, they frequently can integrate specialized instruction into the general teaching/learning environment. The general education curriculum provides the instructional framework for the class, yet that curriculum may be modified for students with disabilities and for others who require such accommodation (Fennick, 2001). It is important to keep in mind that two qualified teachers or other professionals can arrange instruction in a number of creative ways to enhance learning options for all students, not just for those with disabilities. With two teachers delivering instruction and increasing the instructional options for students, all students can have more opportunities to participate actively in their learning. Co-teachers should review their practices to ensure that their instructional strategies do indeed lead to more engaged time and participation for all students in co-taught classes while meeting the individualized needs of students with identified disabilities.

Diverse Group of Students

Co-teachers provide instruction to a diverse, or blended, group of students that includes students with disabilities and others who are not so identified (Hourcade & Bauwens, 2001). In fact, this dimension is one of the major advantages of co-teaching. Teachers initially may resist the perceived increase in student diversity that accompanies co-teaching, but as they implement more effective instructional interventions through co-teaching, they learn to value the arrangement. Co-teaching allows teachers to respond effectively to the diverse needs of their students, lowers the teacher–student ratio, and expands the professional expertise that can be directed to student needs. The inclusion of one or more students who have IEPs sometimes increases the range of diversity in a classroom, but that change is accompanied by the addition of another teacher part of the time.

High school co-teachers often have to discuss the special educator's knowledge of the curricular content.

Co-teachers need to ensure that the diversity in the classroom does not inadvertently result in an inappropriate seating arrangement in the classroom. For example, some co-teachers try to seat students with special needs together in one part of the classroom, presumably so that they can more easily be helped with schoolwork. Other teachers seat students with disabilities on the fringes of the classroom so that when they are receiving assistance, other students are not distracted. Although both these strategies are well-intentioned, they may have the result of socially isolating students, often the very students who are most likely to need encouragement and instruction on social skills.

Shared Classroom Space

The definition of co-teaching notes that co-teachers operate in a single physical space or classroom. This is contrasted with earlier variations of teaching teams that commonly planned together, grouped students, but then taught them in separate classrooms (Trump, 1966; Geen, 1985). Although one teacher may occasionally take a small, heterogeneous group of students to a separate location for a specific instructional purpose and for a limited time period, co-teaching should generally be considered an instructional approach that occurs in a single physical environment. This definitional element helps to distinguish co-teaching from the practice of regrouping students for different kinds of pullout programs. It also points out that the teacher relationship issues, discussed later in this chapter, are far more significant when a physical location is shared than when this does not occur.

Rationale for Co-Teaching

Understanding the rationale for co-teaching provides a foundation upon which professionals can ground the definition and consider co-teaching designs and structures for implementation in their schools. Co-teaching is first and foremost an approach for meeting the educational needs of students with diverse learning abilities (Cook & Friend, 1995; Welch, 2000). Thus, the driving force for creating co-teaching programs between general education teachers and special educators is the needs of students who have IEPs, and co-teaching should result in direct instructional and social benefits for these students. However, other students often will also benefit significantly from this service approach, and this is a reasonable expectation for a co-teaching program (Trent, 1998). For example, students who are academically gifted may have more opportunities in a co-taught class to complete alternative assignments and participate in enrichment activities (Gerber & Popp, 2000). Average students should receive more adult attention in co-taught classrooms and benefit from more teacher-led, small-group activities. Students at risk for learning failure often receive the extra instructional boost they need to make better academic progress.

A second part of the rationale for co-teaching concerns instruction (Cook & Friend, 1995; Fisher & Frey, 2001). We have stressed that the goal of co-teaching is to bring intense and individualized instruction to students in a general education setting while working as much as possible within the framework of the curriculum used there. As such, co-teaching should lead to a less fragmented and more contextualized curriculum for students with disabilities as well as to greater instructional intensity and engaged time. For example, in elementary schools co-teaching may eliminate the need for students to leave their classrooms, often during crucial instruction, to go to a special education setting for developmental or remedial work (Johnston, Tulbert, Sebastian, Devries, & Gompert, 2000). In middle schools and high schools, co-teaching often enables students to learn curricular content from teachers who are specialists in those subjects while at the same time receiving the individualized support they need. Of course, an overriding consideration in co-teaching is that the students with disabilities who are to participate in the co-taught classroom should be those whose unique educational needs *can* be met through the general education curriculum with appropriate modifications and supports (Cook & Friend, 1995).

In addition to instructional benefits for diverse groups of students, co-teaching may have other positive effects. For example, in elementary schools it often reduces the stigma associated with students leaving their general education classrooms and going to a separate place to receive special instruction. In secondary settings, it increases the opportunities students have to take electives and consider themselves truly part of their class groups, since they do not have class periods allocated for special education services. Teachers also can use co-teaching as a vehicle for creating opportunities for positive social interactions between students with disabilities or other special needs and their nondisabled peers. Finally, co-teachers often report that this service approach provides them with a sense of collegial support. While the professionals do not have as a goal master-

PUTTING IDEAS INTO PRACTICE 8.1

Suggestions for New Co-Teaching Programs

Are you just beginning to implement co-teaching as part of your school's service delivery system? Here are a few suggestions for getting new programs off to the right start.

1. Co-teachers should enlist the assistance of their principal or another administrator to introduce the concept of co-teaching to the school staff. The message that should be conveyed is that although not everyone will co-teach every year and not everyone is expected to embrace co-teaching when it is a new option, as part of an inclusive service delivery system, most general education teachers at some point will participate.

2. When paraprofessionals as well as professional staff members are going to go into classrooms, everyone involved should review the parameters of the paraprofessionals' roles and responsibilities. Further, the professional staff should communicate with each other and with paraprofessionals to clarify who has day-to-day responsibility for directing their work.

3. If general education teachers are a bit reluctant to co-teach, special education professionals might try unit-based co-teaching. That is, they might arrange to co-teach for a week or two weeks for a particular unit of instruction. By using this strategy, all the educators involved can begin to get a sense of what is involved in co-teaching without being expected to make a long-term commitment to implementing it.

4. Co-teachers should be sure to develop the habit of using "we" language —"our students," "our classroom," "the lessons we planned." The words used convey to both adults and students the belief that co-teaching is truly about partnership and parity in the instructional process.

ing each other's expertise, they learn from each other, and thus both become more effective with students. They also receive emotional support from someone with whom they share both classroom successes and challenges.

CO-TEACHING APPROACHES

The instructional potential of co-teaching makes it incumbent on those involved to collaborate effectively in designing and delivering instructional interventions that will best meet the unique learning needs of the students. Co-teachers consider a large number of factors when deciding how to structure and deliver their instruction. Based on such issues as student needs, ecology of the class, demands of the curriculum, the teachers' comfort level, and their skills for teaching and co-teaching, co-teachers select or design ways to work together to meet diverse needs in a single classroom.

The following six co-teaching approaches—(1) one teaching, one observing, (2) one teaching, one drifting, (3) station teaching, (4) parallel teaching, (5) alternative teaching, and (6) team teaching—represent some of the options used most frequently in schools. To keep co-teaching relationships and instructional arrangements fresh and effective, teachers should consider trying several of the approaches, regularly changing their co-teaching methods, and experimenting with variations on the basic information provided here.

One Teaching, One Observing

Co-teachers often find that they have options that other teachers do not to carefully observe their students in order to gain very sophisticated understanding of their academic and social functioning. When one professional teaches and the other observes, one teacher has primary responsibility for designing and delivering specific instruction to the entire group, whether that is a large-group lesson, individual assignments that the teacher is monitoring, or any other teaching/ learning arrangement. The second educator has as a goal observing a single student, a small group of students, or the entire class for behaviors the professionals have previously agreed should be noted. For example, in the English class that Mr. St. James and Mrs. Goud co-teach, several students seem to be having difficulty getting started on individual assignments. The teachers agree to observe Michael, Jose, Alfred, and Susann to find out if the problem is comprehension (the students do not begin the task and are looking around to see what others are doing), or a matter of delay (by the time the students find their pens and get headings on their papers, they forget the instructions and ask to have them repeated).

One teaching, one observing requires little joint planning and, if scheduled well, provides an opportunity for special services professionals to learn the general education curriculum design, classroom routines, and methods for large-group instruction. They may need this information before they can use approaches that require more planning. This approach has a further advantage for teachers who are new to collaborative arrangements—it does not require them to have a well-developed trust and knowledge of each other in order to begin co-teaching.

The one teaching, one observing approach has a serious drawback, however. If it is used indiscriminately or exclusively, it can result in one teacher, most typically the special educator, being relegated to the role of assistant. For this approach to be beneficial, the teachers should exchange roles periodically. This strategy has two positive effects: First, it ensures that general education teachers have the opportunity to step back from the intensity of being the classroom manager to truly and systematically see what is occurring with students. Second, it clarifies for students that there are two teachers with equivalent responsibility and authority.

To make observations most useful, co-teachers should jointly decide on specific students and specific behaviors to analyze. For example, two co-teachers may agree that they have serious concerns about Gary, a student who does not seem to be making much progress in reading and who seems to be expressing his frustration by refusing to work and occasionally bothering other students, taking their papers or pencils or calling them names. They decide to observe him more closely in preparation for a meeting they have scheduled with the intervention assistance team.

In addition to making decisions about who to observe and for what purpose, co-teachers also should use a systematic method for recording their observations, whether they do so on class lists, seating charts, or more formal behavioral data forms such as those most special educators would have in their files. They should be sure that both professionals have a copy of the information. When co-teachers meet, they can then discuss the observations and make instructional decisions based on what they have learned.

One Teaching, One Drifting

Another relatively simple approach for co-teaching is to have one teacher teaching while the other supports the classroom in a relatively passive manner. That is, one teacher maintains the primary role for managing the classroom and leading instruction while the other walks around the room to assist students who need support or who have questions about their schoolwork. For example, as Ms. Ramirez explains to students the process for long division, Mrs. Yee monitors all the students to be sure that they are writing on their papers exactly the information they should. The teachers' goal is to be sure that all students, including the three who have learning disabilities, are on the same step at the same time.

Like one teaching, one observing, this approach to co-teaching requires little joint planning, and so it makes co-teaching possible even when shared planning time is not. It also gives a role to special services providers in situations in which they may not feel competent to lead instruction (for example, a special education teacher with an elementary education background and a K–12 special education license co-teaching in a high school geometry class for the first time).

However, one teaching, one drifting also is fraught with problems and should be used only occasionally. First, particularly when planning time is not available, it is likely that this approach will become the sole or primary co-teaching approach. The classroom teacher probably will have the lead role, and the special services provider will be the "drifter." Not only does this deny an active teaching role to the special educator, it also undermines that person's credibility, especially with older students. Second, a classroom with a drifter also can be distracting to students. When professionals are walking around they can be a visual distraction, and when they whisper to individual students they may be an auditory distraction. Third, and most seriously, this co-teaching approach includes the risk of encouraging students to become dependent learners. When one teacher is always available to help on student demand, students who crave adult attention but who should be capable of doing assigned work may develop a habit of saying "I can't" in order to get extra attention and assistance. Co-teachers need to be very alert to this possible problem. If they have students needing adult attention, they should give it—but not at the cost of a student's independent learning skills.

Educators can take advantage of the positive aspects of one teaching, one drifting and avoid the negative aspects by limiting their use of this approach and by ensuring that when it is used, each teacher leads instruction and each teacher takes the drifter role. Further, co-teachers should use this approach only when it will not distract students from their learning and when no other co-teaching approach seems appropriate for the instructional situation.

Station Teaching

Station teaching is a co-teaching approach that actively involves both educators in the classroom. It involves a clear division of labor. The co-teachers divide the instructional content and each takes responsibility for planning and teaching part of it. In a classroom where station teaching is used, students move from one station to another according to a predetermined schedule. A third station may be used for students to complete independent work assignments, to participate in peer tutoring, or to work under supervision if a student teacher or another adult is available in the classroom. For example, in a third-grade classroom, one group of students is reviewing the concept of cause and effect with one of the teachers. Another group is working with the other teacher on comprehension activities related to a story read the previous day. In the third group, students are working with partners to edit their writing assignments. During the 50-minute period of time for this instruction, each student participates in each of the groups.

Although this approach requires that the teachers share responsibility for planning sufficiently to divide the instructional content, it has the advantage that each professional has separate responsibility for delivering instruction, and so it can be effective even when teachers have significantly different teaching styles or do not know each other well. In addition, students benefit from the lower teacher–pupil ratio, and students with disabilities may be integrated into each group rather than singled out. Further, because in this approach each teacher instructs all of the students, albeit in different groups, the equal status of both the students and the teachers can be maximized.

Two of the most common problems in using station teaching are the amount of noise and movement in the classroom. Some teachers may be bothered by having two teachers talking at the same time, particularly if one of the educators has a loud or distinctive voice. Co-teachers may also find that having students move around the room seems disruptive. Co-teachers also may need to think carefully about how to divide instruction so that the order in which curriculum is presented does not affect students' understanding. Material that is hierarchical cannot be presented using this approach. For example, in a social studies class, it would not work to have students in one group reading the chapter, students in a second group discussing the information, and students in the third group answering questions from the text; the group writing answers first, before reading or discussing, would be at a disadvantage!

To effectively implement station teaching, co-teachers can take several actions. With elementary and middle school students, they can make sound-muffling

PERSPECTIVES ON DIVERSITY 8.1

Who Is My Co-Teaching Partner?

Most professionals believe that neither ethnicity, gender, nor age should affect the composition of teaching teams (e.g., Bess, 2000). However, the same stereotypes that can undermine teacher–student and teacher–parent/family interactions can also affect co-teachers. Here are a few suggestions for co-teachers who are trying to understand and respect their similarities and differences (Snell & Janney, 2000):

- When co-teachers are from different cultures, they should spend some time prior to teaching discussing their cultures—language, holidays, favorite or traditional foods, and so on. By learning about each other, they can grow in their understanding of each other's perspectives.

- Co-teachers from the dominant culture should take care not to overgeneralize regarding a partner's heritage. For example, a Hispanic co-teacher may have Mexican, Cuban, Spanish, or South American roots.

- Co-teachers may find it helpful to relate their religious beliefs to their practice. For example, in some religions disability is accepted as a challenge given by God. In others, it can be considered a punishment. Further, in some cultures the goal of typical American education for students with special needs to foster independence may not have the same high priority. All these factors may affect how teachers interact with students and families and thus may also affect co-teaching.

- Another topic that co-teachers from different cultures may wish to discuss is time. In some cultures time is a fluid concept and the dominant American cultural value on punctuality may be perceived as excessive. This can affect perceptions about the importance of beginning and ending co-teaching in elementary classrooms at specific times, punctuality in arriving for planning meetings, and the sense of urgency (or lack of such a sense) to address curriculum goals.

headphones available for students to use in the independent group when an individual assignment is given. They also can provide desk carrels to help reduce visual distractions. If a student tends to have attention problems, that student might best be seated next to the teacher. If transitions are time-consuming, instead of having students move from station to station, perhaps the teachers could move. Of course, teachers also should monitor their own voice levels and ask for feedback from their teaching partners on this matter. Finally, co-teachers should also watch their time so that groups are prepared to move to the next station as scheduled.

Parallel Teaching

The primary purpose of parallel teaching is to lower the teacher–student ratio. In this type of co-teaching, the teachers jointly plan the instruction, but each delivers it to a heterogeneous group comprised of half of the students in the class. The teachers do not exchange groups as in station teaching. This approach requires both that the teachers coordinate their efforts so that all students receive essentially the same instruction and that grouping decisions are based on maintaining diversity within each group. For example, in Mr. Harris's and Ms. Brisky's history class, students are preparing for a unit exam. Mr. Harris has half of the students, including two students with learning disabilities. Ms. Brisky has the other half of the group, which includes a student with mild autism. The teachers are discussing key concepts that they highlighted during their planning period, and they are helping students to go through a study guide. Their intent was to arrange the students so that each one had several opportunities to participate in discussion and to ask questions.

Parallel teaching often is appropriate for drill-and-practice activities, test reviews, or projects needing close teacher supervision. It enables all students to participate more in instructional conversations, and gives especially shy students a smaller audience. Parallel teaching can even be used for more creative teaching activities: Each co-teacher might take a particular point of view in presenting a topic or issue, orient students to that viewpoint, and then bring the students together later for large-group discussion. For example, as part of the history class, the co-teachers address current events. One time, Mr. Harris took the position

Co-teachers in elementary classrooms can provide more intensive instruction and thus better meet diverse student needs.

that the United States was making a mistake in its actions in eastern Europe and discussed this with half the students. Ms. Brisky adopted the opposite point of view with her group. When the students came together for large-group follow-up, the teachers were able to integrate information about understanding fact and opinion, the influence of the media on people's beliefs, and other related topics, as well as debate the issue at hand.

Note that this approach cannot be used for initial instruction unless both professionals are proficient in their ability to teach the material. Although seldom a serious concern in the primary grades, this can be a significant matter in secondary schools. In terms of pragmatic issues, noise and activity levels may need to be monitored as with station teaching, and teachers need to pace instruction similarly.

To co-teach using parallel teaching, teachers should begin by checking that they are both familiar with the content and comfortable teaching it. Especially in new co-teaching partnerships, teachers might want to use outlines, study guides, or notes to stay aware of the teaching expectations. Remember that if one group of students has significantly different instruction from the other, it will be difficult to make judgments about student mastery. Students also may complain that the disparity leads to unfairness during assessments. To address the issues of noise and distraction, elementary and middle school teachers may find that it works well to have the two student groups on the floor in opposite corners of the class with desks or tables used as a sight and sound barrier.

Alternative Teaching

In nearly every classroom, there are times when it is appropriate for co-teachers to select a small group of students to receive instruction that is somehow different from that in which the large group is participating. For example, some students with special learning needs require adaptations in the form of preteaching. Students who benefit from preteaching might include those with attention problems, those who need reassurance about their knowledge or skills, and those for whom repetition is beneficial. Reteaching the instructional content is appropriate for students who did not understand the concepts taught, or for students who missed the instruction because of absence. Sometimes an alternative group is useful for doing an activity for the purpose of an authentic assessment. Thus, in alternative teaching, one teacher works with a small group of students while the other instructs the large group in some content or activity that the small group can afford to miss.

Alternative teaching is a strategy for providing highly intensive instruction within the general education classroom. Further, this approach can also be used to ensure that all students in a class receive opportunities to interact with a teacher in a small group. If one or two students have serious behavior disorders that cause classroom disruptions, sometimes having them work in a small group, one that includes positive class models, can help them and possibly alleviate classroom disruption.

The greatest risk in alternative teaching is that students with disabilities may be stigmatized by being grouped repeatedly for preteaching or reteaching, even if other students are rotated through the small instructional group. A variation of this approach, in which one teacher is located at a table and announces that students seeking assistance may come to the table, can cause problems similar to those found when one teaches and one drifts. Particularly with older groups, the student most likely to come to work with the teacher is the one who is capable of doing the task but who craves adult attention or seeks reassurance. The student who possibly would not join the teacher is the student with a disability who clearly needs assistance, but is embarrassed to seek it in front of peers.

When co-teachers use alternative teaching, they first should be sure that each teacher sometimes takes responsibility for the small group. For example, sometimes reteaching is best accomplished by the general education teacher, not the special educator. In addition, co-teachers might keep a record of student attendance in the small groups so that they ensure all students participate. Of course, the group composition and group membership should be fluid, with both factors varying.

Team Teaching

In team teaching, both teachers are responsible for planning. They also share the instruction of all students, whether that occurs in a large group, in monitoring students working independently, or in facilitating groups of students working on shared projects. For example, the teachers may alternate their roles in leading a discussion, or they may take on the roles of characters in a story as they act out a scene. One co-teacher may explain while the other demonstrates a concept; one may speak while the other models note taking on an overhead projector, and so on. Both teachers may circulate around the room as students work on dioramas that illustrate a piece of poetry, asking questions to stimulate student discussion or to check comprehension. Teachers may role-play, debate, simulate conflict, and model appropriate question asking or summarizing.

Co-teachers who team teach frequently report that it results in a synergy that enhances student participation and invigorates them, sometimes even prompting them to try innovative techniques and activities that each professional would not have tried alone. They discuss how well it works when the teachers "click" and are able to have instructional conversations with each other and students. Some co-teachers consider team teaching the most rewarding approach. This co-teaching approach also clearly communicates to students that both educators are truly teachers of equal status.

However, of the six co-teaching approaches, team teaching requires the greatest level of mutual trust and commitment. If professionals are not comfortable working together in a classroom, attempting to team teach will undoubtedly communicate that discomfort to students. Team teaching also requires that the co-teachers are able to mesh their teaching styles. If co-teachers are significantly different in their use of humor, their pacing, or their instructional format, the flow of the team teaching often is not successful. Teachers may use different styles but they should take care to complement each other.

PUTTING IDEAS INTO PRACTICE 8.2

Addressing Co-Teaching Dilemmas

Both novice and experienced co-teachers often have many questions about the best ways to deal with dilemmas that occur during co-teaching. Here are a few common concerns and ideas for addressing them:

◆ My co-teacher is responsible for students with emotional disabilities. He is frequently called away from our co-teaching to deal with a student problem. What should we do?

   In some schools, general education teachers genuinely believe that they cannot address student issues and that the special educator is the only one equipped to respond to students with emotional disabilities. Although it is prudent to call for the special educator if a student is having a crisis, it is sometimes helpful to talk with participating teachers about what constitutes a crisis and to explicitly outline how noncrisis problems should be handled (e.g., ignoring, asking for administrator help).

◆ I'm a special services provider. When I enter the classroom to co-teach, the general education teacher seems to think it is to release her for an extra preparation period. What should I do?

   If a classroom teacher repeatedly leaves the room or withdraws from instruction (e.g., grades papers) during co-teaching, the special service provider should approach that person with words like these: "I'm concerned that I've miscommunicated what co-teaching is about. It's so important for both of us to be here, actively working with students, for it to be successful." If the teacher continues to leave, the special services provider should alert the teacher that a problem-solving session is needed and then enlist the assistance of a supervisor or administrator to resolve the matter.

◆ As a special education teacher, I sometimes feel like I am being used in classrooms as a paraprofessional or helper, not a professional. How can I avoid this?

   The best way to avoid this co-teaching problem is to openly discuss the issue with your co-teacher. If expectations have been clarified before co-teaching is initiated, this issue is less likely to occur. Also, if co-teachers use the six approaches outlined in this chapter, along with the many variations of them, both teachers can and should have an active role in instruction.

Novice co-teachers should not feel obligated to attempt team teaching. Although some do and are successful, for many this approach is too fluid and relies too much on teacher compatibility for use in a new relationship. Similarly, if a special educator is co-teaching with a teacher who seems uncomfortable with a shared classroom, this approach is probably not one to emphasize. When team teaching is implemented, co-teachers should check frequently to ensure that both are satisfied with their use of it.

Understanding these six basic approaches for arranging teachers and students in a shared classroom demonstrates the importance of collaboration in co-teaching. In the next section, pragmatic and conceptual issues related to the professional relationships in co-teaching are presented to increase your readiness to implement this service delivery option.

CO-TEACHING AND COLLABORATION

We have identified co-teaching as a specific service delivery option that is based on collaboration. As you can see, however, it is not a synonym for collaboration. We again clarify that co-teaching, like consultation or team decision making, is an activity that teachers may choose to engage in while using a collaborative style of interaction. Some would argue that collaboration is more critical to co-teaching than to applications like teaming and consultation since co-teaching involves an ongoing and intense relationship between two or more professionals engaged in this professional activity. We believe that true co-teaching is optimized when a strong collaborative relationship exists, but we recognize that co-teaching can also exist, albeit in a significantly limited form, with minimal collaboration. In short, we agree with veteran co-teachers who tell us that in ideal situations, "Co-teaching is like a professional marriage."

The Co-Teaching Relationship

The most sophisticated types of co-teaching and the collaboration they require are not for everyone (Redditt, 1991). The type of co-teaching and the level of collaboration in the relationship depend on the situation, of course. But it also depends on both the personal characteristics of the co-teachers and their skills in communication and collaboration (Appl, Troha, & Rowell, 2001; Jung, 1998).

Many co-teaching issues are challenging—sometimes even threatening—to potential co-teachers. This collaborative structure requires a willingness to change teaching styles and preferences, work closely with another adult, share responsibility, and rely on another individual in order to perform tasks previously done alone. All of these factors can cause stress for the teachers. Yet what causes some teachers stress can be a source of excitement and motivation for others.

Specific skills and personal characteristics can be associated with successful co-teachers. The most essential requirement for a co-teacher is flexibility (Argüelles, Hughes, & Schumm, 2000). Commitment to co-teaching and to the co-teaching relationship is also needed (Allen-Malley & Bishop, 2000). Finally, there is general professional consensus that strong interpersonal communication skills—particularly problem-solving and decision-making skills—are essential for co-teachers (Bondy & Brownell, 1997; DeBoer & Fister, 1995; Gately & Gately, 2001).

One strategy co-teachers can use to enhance collaboration in co-teaching is to reflect on their own expectations for it and share those expectations with their co-teaching partners. The checklist in Figure 8.1 is a tool guide such a discussion.

Maintaining Collaborative Co-Teaching Relationships

Since effective co-teaching relationships rely on teaching pairs having positive, collaborative working relationships, the skills discussed throughout this text clearly are essential for co-teachers. In addition, though, numerous specific topics routinely require discussion by teaching partners. These topics are summarized on the following pages, and questions related to each are included in Figure 8.2. Using these questions as a guide for scheduled discussions, both prior to co-teaching and routinely throughout it, has proved to be useful to many co-teachers (Cook & Friend, 1995). As you review these questions, you will no doubt see that their resolution often will depend on the strength of the collaborative relationship. However, it has been our experience that working toward resolution also often helps to strengthen the relationship even further.

Philosophy and Beliefs

Understanding each other's general instructional beliefs, especially those that affect decisions about instruction, is essential to a strong co-teaching relationship. In particular, teaching partners should explore the degree to which they agree on the right of all students to learn and succeed, the teacher's role in student

---

Figure 8.1   Assessment for Co-Teaching Readiness

My co-teacher and I . . .

Agree	Unsure	Disagree	
_____	_____	_____	1. Have discussed our beliefs about effective teaching and learning.
_____	_____	_____	2. Have discussed our beliefs about student expectations.
_____	_____	_____	3. Have each shared the expectations we have for what the co-taught classroom should look like in terms of teacher roles and responsibilities and student grouping.
_____	_____	_____	4. Have conferred about our readiness to experiment with alternative teaching methods.
_____	_____	_____	5. Have discussed our perceptions on how classroom tasks can be shared.
_____	_____	_____	6. Have addressed what potential strengths and liabilities each of us brings to co-teaching.

Topic	Questions
Figure 8.2	**Questions for Creating a Collaborative Working Relationship in Co-teaching**
Topic	Questions
Philosophy and Beliefs	What are our overriding philosophies about the roles of teachers and teaching and about students and learning?
	How do our instructional beliefs affect our instructional practice?
Parity Signals	How will we convey to students and others (e.g., teachers, parents) that we are equals in the classroom?
	How can we ensure a sense of parity during instruction?
Classroom Routines	What are the instructional routines for the classroom?
	What are the organizational routines for the classroom?
Discipline	What is acceptable and unacceptable student behavior?
	Who is to intervene at what point in students' behavior?
	What are the rewards and consequences used in the classroom?
Feedback	What is the best way to give each other feedback?
	How will we ensure that both positive and negative issues are raised?
Noise	What noise level are we comfortable with in the classroom?
Pet Peeves	What aspects of teaching and classroom life does each of us feel strongly about?
	How can we identify our pet peeves so as to avoid them?

learning, and beliefs about the ability of all students to learn. However, co-teaching also requires discussion of more specific beliefs. For example, what does each teacher believe about the amount of noise and movement that is acceptable in a classroom? What instructional arrangements do the co-teachers believe are most effective—traditional lecture formats, or student-centered instruction? What types of behaviors are the co-teachers particularly bothered by? These day-to-day beliefs about classroom life are as important to discuss as the foundational beliefs each co-teacher brings to the situation.

Parity Signals

The nature of the co-teaching relationship requires that co-teachers have parity and recognize it. To that end, co-teachers find that determining in advance how they will ensure that students and others recognize their equal status helps them to build and maintain their relationship. Examples of parity signals include these: both teachers' names on the board or in the printed course schedule, both teachers' signatures on correspondence to parents, and desk or storage space for both in the classroom. It also includes participation in teaching, grading assignments, and assigning report card grades. Co-teachers should spend a few minutes generating ideas about how they can communicate to students and parents, as well as remind each other, that co-teaching is about partnership.

Classroom Routines

Experienced teachers all have preferred classroom routines. These include organizational routines (such as how students manage instructional materials and follow specific procedures at the beginning of the school day or class period) and instructional routines (such as how students are expected to seek help and follow rules about formats for papers). Teachers rarely are aware of how many routines they have. When co-teachers make this discovery, they face the task of agreeing with each other as to what routines they will employ in their co-taught classroom. It is not particularly important whose routines are adopted by the co-teachers, and in many instances the special educator defers to the preferences of the general educator, but it is important that both teachers know what the routines will be so that they can consistently communicate them to the students.

Discipline

What each teacher believes is acceptable behavior and what each views as appropriate responses to unacceptable student behavior should be discussed and, if necessary, negotiated early in the co-teaching relationship. Because teachers tend to have stronger reactions to behavioral transgressions than to academic difficulties or other failures to meet expectations, it is particularly important that co-teachers agree on how they will respond to student violations of behavioral codes. For example, how critical is it to each teacher that students keep their heads up off their desks during instruction? In an elementary school, what are the consequences for saying something disrespectful to a peer or teacher?

Feedback

Knowing your own preferred way to receive feedback from a colleague is a significant first step in determining how you and a co-teacher will give each other feedback about your activities in a shared classroom. Some teachers prefer to hear their co-teachers' reaction to a co-taught lesson immediately upon its completion. Others are more receptive if they have a break for an hour or as much as a day before debriefing with their partners. As important as *when* teachers give each other feedback is *how* they do so, as you learned in Chapter 3. Note that an assumption is made regarding this topic, namely, that co-teachers need to review and discuss their shared efforts periodically in order to maintain their professional relationship. Feedback should include not only highlighting those aspects of instruction that are especially successful and satisfying, but also planning alternatives to less successful and satisfying aspects.

Noise

Teachers differ as significantly in their tolerance for classroom noise as they do in preferences for discipline strategies or classroom routines. Noise includes teacher talk as well as student-generated noise. Since three of the six co-teaching approaches have noise levels as potential drawbacks, it is advisable for co-teachers to recognize their tolerance for noise and to talk with one another about it. As part of their feedback, they may decide either to modify the specific co-teaching approach or to develop signals to indicate that noise is approaching an unacceptable level.

Pet Peeves

All teachers have a few issues that are especially important to them, or more likely, that bother them a great deal. Pet peeves are specific triggers that could put relationships in jeopardy. For some it may be interruptions during instruction, while for others it may be the removal of supplies from their desks or failure to put materials away. Some co-teachers do not permit students to return to their lockers after they have come to class, and some are very particular in how grades are recorded in the grade book or on the computer. Pet peeves can be about student issues, classroom arrangements or materials, or adult issues. The critical element for co-teachers is to identify their own and their co-teacher's pet peeves, discuss these openly, and respect their differences.

By carefully considering what co-teaching is and how it is enhanced through collaboration, co-teachers can select approaches that enable them to begin their partnership safely and nurture it until it encompasses a wide array of shared teaching activities that optimize student learning. By initially discussing and periodically reviewing topics that can influence co-teaching success, co-teachers can strengthen their professional relationship and identify and resolve challenges or disagreements.

ADMINISTRATIVE AND LOGISTICAL SUPPORT FOR CO-TEACHING

This chapter has emphasized the key concepts related to co-teaching, the ways that co-teachers can arrange students and themselves to take full advantage of their differing expertise, and the types of topics and issues that co-teachers should discuss. However, for co-teaching to be more than an interesting option that professionals use when they like each other and when their schedules permit, strong administrative support must also be present (daCosta, Marshall, & Riordan, 1998; Lehr, 1999). If co-teaching is to be a legitimate service delivery option, it is necessary to ensure that teachers' schedules are coordinated and that teachers with particularly challenging groups of students are paired with a co-teacher. Administrators also facilitate problem solving when difficulties arise, and they reward co-teachers' efforts, even when they are not completely successful. As co-teaching programs mature, administrators clarify that it is a standard in the school that any teacher might be asked

Administrators play a critical role in addressing logistical issues related to implementing co-teaching as a service delivery option.

to co-teach, not just the individuals who initially volunteered. They also supervise situations in which one of the co-teaching participants is reluctant.

In addition to the direct support that administrators give to co-teachers, they can influence school and district policy on other matters that facilitate or hinder co-teaching efforts. These factors include the size of special educator caseload, the distribution of students with special needs in classes throughout the school, the class size typical for general education settings, the expectation for in-class versus pullout (e.g., resource) services, the diversity of student needs special educators are meeting, and special educators' assignments to one or more schools. Each of these factors is explained further in Figure 8.3.

SUMMARY

Co-teaching is an increasingly common approach to service delivery in inclusive schools, and it is one that benefits from collaboration. Co-teaching occurs when two or more teachers deliver substantive instruction to a diverse group of students in a single classroom. They do this to address diverse and specific student needs, including individualized instruction in general education settings. Successful co-teaching helps to avoid the instructional fragmentation that can occur in more traditional services and the stigmatization that may occur when students leave classrooms. In co-teaching, two teachers jointly decide how best to offer instruction, using a range of approaches such as one teaching, one observing; one teaching, one drifting; station teaching; parallel teaching; alternative teaching;

Figure 8.3   Logistical Issues That Affect Co-Teaching

ISSUE	IMPACT
♦ **Special Educator Caseload**	With a caseload of 20 or fewer students, co-teaching can be feasible. If the special educator is responsible for too many students (for example, more than 30), it may be nearly impossible to arrange co-teaching.
♦ **Caseload Distribution**	If students on the special educator's caseload are clustered in classes (but not making up more than 33 percent of the class group), delivering services is a reasonable expectation. If students are widely distributed, or the special educator is expected to co-teach in six or even more classes each day, difficulties arise.
♦ **General Education Class Size**	Co-taught classes should have approximately the same number of students as classes without this service. If several extra students are assigned because "after all, two teachers are there," the effectiveness of co-teaching is diminished.
♦ **Priority for Co-Teaching**	As a service delivery option, co-teaching occurs in lieu of other services students receive. If special educators are expected to provide resource or other pullout services to most or all of the students on their caseloads, co-teaching becomes a luxury that cannot be afforded because it is added on to those other services. In schools in which this dilemma occurs, educators often note that they cannot co-teach without additional staff being hired. Also, special educators may contend that in-class services can only be offered by paraprofessionals because teacher time must be spent delivering instruction in the special education setting.
♦ **Diversity of Student Need**	Some special educators have a single student who needs a significant amount of pullout service while all the other students could be served in co-teaching. Unless special education staff and other professionals collaborate to find a way to deliver the range of services needed by every student, co-teaching will not be feasible.
♦ **Teacher School Assignment**	In small school districts, special education teachers and other professional staff may be itinerant, serving two, three, or even more schools. In such instances, co-teaching can be only a small part of their jobs, often in a single location where it can be justified based on student numbers and needs.

and team teaching. Although co-teaching and collaboration are not synonyms, the former is greatly enhanced with the latter. To foster collaboration in co-teaching, co-teachers should discuss critical issues such as their philosophies and beliefs, parity signals, classroom routines, discipline, feedback, noise, and pet peeves. In order for co-teaching to become an integral part of the special education service delivery system, strong administrative support is needed. Without it, the use of co-teaching is likely to be limited to volunteers. Further, logistical issues related to caseloads and their distribution, class sizes, and other special educator responsibilities can foster or constrain co-teaching.

ACTIVITIES AND ASSIGNMENTS

1. Discuss co-teaching with classmates whose schools use it as a service delivery option, or talk with experienced educators about it. How does their understanding of what co-teaching is, how it should be implemented, and the issues that are part of it compare with the information presented in the text? How could you reconcile any differences? Write a reflective essay on your own perspectives of co-teaching as a role responsibility for your professional group (e.g., special education teacher or middle school math or science teacher).

2. Suppose that you are a new special educator at your school. You have been employed with the understanding that co-teaching is to be a significant part of your responsibilities. However, when you approach the first teacher on your list of teaching partners, she tells you that she was not informed of such an arrangement and is very uncomfortable with the idea. Using your knowledge of collaboration, communication skills, and understanding of co-teaching, how would you respond to the teacher? What might she say in return? What would you do if you believed the situation to be at an impasse?

3. Collaborate with a colleague to develop a series of lesson plans or a unit to be co-taught in a general education classroom. The plan should use at least three different co-teaching approaches and should specify clearly the unique needs of students and the roles of each teacher.

4. Arrange to meet with a general education teacher or teacher trainee. Using the list of topics co-teachers sometimes need to discuss as a basis (see Figure 8.2), ask that person to share his or her perceptions. Prepare a chart that includes each of the topics addressed, the other person's perceptions and beliefs, and your own. Discuss the extent of agreement or disagreement, and then reflect on how you would make this hypothetical co-teaching partnership most successful.

5. Draft a memo to describe a potential co-teaching program to the parents of all students in a particular school. The memo should describe why the program has been developed, what its expected benefits are to all students, and who will be involved. Ask a colleague to review the memo and discuss areas of confusion or disagreement with you.

6. Suppose you are co-teaching and a problem related to your collaborative relationship arises. Either you are dissatisfied with how a discipline matter is being addressed, or your partner believes that your standards for students are too flexible. What skills would you need to air the issue and work to resolve it? Role-play with a classmate how such an interaction might proceed.

7. Given what you have read about co-teaching, how would you go about deciding whether a co-teaching program was a success? What questions would you ask? To whom? How would you measure student success?

FOR FURTHER READING

Bahamonde, C., & Friend, M. (1999). Teaching English language learners: A proposal for effective service delivery through collaboration and co-teaching. *Journal of Educational and Psychological Consultation, 10,* 1–24.

Bauwens, J., & Hourcade, J. (1995). *Cooperative teaching: Rebuilding the schoolhouse for all students.* Austin, TX: Pro-Ed.

Cook, L., & Friend, M. (1995). Co-teaching guidelines for creating effective practice. *Focus on Exceptional Children, 28*(3), 1–12.

DeBoer, A., & Fister, S. (1995). *Working together: Tools for collaborative teaching.* Longmont, CO: Sopris West.

Fishbaugh, M. S. E. (Ed.). (2000). *Collaboration guide for early career educators.* Baltimore: Brookes.

Friend, M. (Co-Producer with L. Burrello & J. Burrello). (1995). *The power of two: Including students through co-teaching* [videotape]. Bloomington, IN: Elephant Rock Productions.

Friend, M. (2000). (Co-producer with Jotham Burrello and Leonard Burello). *The complexity of collaboration* [videotape]. Bloomington, IN: Forum on Education, Indiana University.

Gately, S. E., & Gately, F. J. (2001). Understanding co-teaching components. *Teaching Exceptional Children, 33*(4), 40–47.

Harris, K. C. (1998). *Collaborative elementary teaching.* Austin, TX: Pro-ed.

Walther-Thomas, C., Korinek, L., McLaughlin, V. L., & Williams, B. T. (2000). *Collaboration for inclusive education: Developing successful programs.* Boston: Allyn & Bacon.

Welch, M. (2000). Descriptive analysis of team teaching in two elementary classrooms: A formative experimental approach. *Remedial and Special Education, 21,* 366–367.

Paraeducators

Connections

In the first part of this book, you learned many skills for being an effective collaborator. You then learned in Chapters 5, 6, 7, and 8 about school programs and services that rely heavily on collaboration. Chapter 9 is the first of two chapters that address special applications of collaboration based on the people involved. In this chapter you will explore paraeducators' participation in the education of students with special needs and your working relationship with them. In Chapter 10 you will consider the special circumstances of collaboration with parents of students with special needs.

Learner Objectives

After reading this chapter you will be able to:

1. Describe the evolution of paraeducator roles in public school settings.
2. Explain instructional and noninstructional responsibilities of paraeducators, and clarify activities that should not be assigned to paraeducators.
3. Identify strategies for effectively working with paraeducators in the domains of training, planning, communication, and supervision.
4. Describe how collaboration pertains to the interactions between paraeducators and professionals.
5. Value paraeducators as individuals who contribute to the education of students with special needs while recognizing their nonprofessional status.

INTRODUCTION

Whether a novice or experienced special educator, you may find that not only do you need to interact effectively with general education teachers, administrators, other special services providers, and parents/families, but you are also assigned to work with one or more paraeducators. Consider these situations:

- As a resource teacher in a local high school, your caseload has crept from the locally recommended 25 students to 32. Given student numbers and types of needs, administrators have decided that it is not necessary to employ another special education teacher, but they have notified you that they are seeking a paraeducator to assist you with your workload.
- You work in an elementary school in a large, urban district. Your district has contracted with a private company to provide a paraeducator to support one of your students who has extraordinary needs for behavior supports. You have many questions about your role in providing information to this person, directing his work, and communicating about student progress and needs.
- As a new special educator for students with autism, you are greeted on the first workday before school by your teaching assistant who explains that you have no reason to be anxious because she knows all the routines and can let you know how everything is supposed to happen. She proceeds to explain how the room is to be arranged, which general education teachers are willing to "allow" the students to visit their classrooms, and what activities to plan for the first day with students.
- In your highly inclusive school, you are responsible as the special educator for guiding the work of three paraeducators who are assigned to work one-to-one with students with significant needs. You also share another paraeducator with the other special education teacher.

Have you encountered a situation similar to any of these? Do you know teachers who have? Collectively, they illustrate that the addition of a paraeducator to a school's special services staff can be a benefit to students and professionals, can be helpful yet somewhat problematic, or can be necessary but time-consuming. In all regards, the use of paraeducators in schools contributes to the increasing complexity of adult–adult interactions there.

PARAEDUCATORS IN PUBLIC SCHOOLS

Paraeducators are individuals who provide instructional and other services to students and who are supervised by licensed professionals who are responsible for student outcomes (French, 1999; Pickett, 1997). They may also be known as paraprofessionals, instructional assistants, classroom assistants, job coaches, therapy assistants, transition trainers, teacher aides, or teacher assistants. They may work in remedial reading, English as a Second Language, and special education programs, but they may also serve, especially in large elementary schools, in a more general capacity to assist teachers in their classrooms. Most paraeducators are women who have lived in their communities for a long time (Ashbaker & Morgan, 2001). The qualifications required of paraeducators vary widely; many states (e.g., Indiana) employ individuals with a high school diploma but no other training while a few (e.g., Kansas, Washington) mandate formal preparation for the role. Some professional organizations advocate strongly for paraeducator certification (e.g., American Federation of Teachers, 1999a).

Because no uniform system exists for tracking paraeducators employed in public schools, estimates of their number vary widely, ranging from approximately 500,000 (French, 1999; Pickett, 1996) to over 900,000 (Ashbaker & Morgan, 2001) or even more. What is clear is that the number of paraeducators is increasing and will continue to do so. In fact, recent information from the *Occupational Outlook Handbook* of the U.S. Department of Labor Statistics indicates that the job of paraeducator will be, on average, the fastest growing occupation for the next several years (Ashbaker & Morgan, 2001). Further, of all the paraeducators in schools, approximately 80 percent work with special education and related services professionals and the students for whom they are responsible (Katisyannis, Hodge, & Lanford, 2000), and they are the focus of this chapter.

Many reasons have been given for the increasing use of paraeducators for special education (Giangreco, Edelman, Broer, & Doyle, 2001). The rising emphasis on early childhood programs has undoubtedly contributed (Killoran, Templeman, Peters, & Udell, 2001), as has the growth in programs to assist students to transition from school to work or community settings. The increasing shortage of special education teachers (e.g., Daniels & McBride, 2001; Special Education News, 2000b) is also making paraeducators attractive employees to school administrators. The trend toward inclusive practices is an influence as well. When students with complex special needs are assigned to general education classrooms, their teachers see that paraeducator support is not just helpful, but essential (French & Chopra, 1999; Marks, Schrader, & Levine, 1999). However, even for students with mild needs who typically are distributed among many classrooms in inclusive schools, paraeducators have become critical in supplementing the services of special educators who cannot themselves see every student every day (Doyle & Gurney, 2000).

Historically, paraeducators were expected to assume largely clerical duties (French, 1999). They graded papers, took attendance, and collected lunch money, acting mostly to free teachers from routine tasks so they could spend more time instructing their students. Now, however, most paraeducators spend the majority of their time working with individual students or small groups of students (French, 1998). They help students to understand their assignments, listen to students read, provide physical support, and generally engage in a wide range of services that enable students to succeed, whether in inclusive classrooms or special education settings.

Until the passage of IDEA-97 (20 U.S.C. §1400 et seq.), few federal guidelines existed to inform school districts about the use of paraeducators for students with

Paraeducators are valuable staff members who assist students with instructional and noninstructional activities.

disabilities. The current federal law, although still not detailed in its consideration of paraeducators, does state this:

> Paraprofessionals and assistants who are appropriately trained and supervised [may be] used to assist in the provision of special education and related services to children with disabilities. (20 U.S.C. §1412 (a)(15)(B)(iii)

This brief statement clarifies several points: (a) that paraeducators are legitimately employed to assist in the delivery of services to students; (b) that they are not the primary service providers and must have supervision; and (c) that they are entitled to training for their duties. Each of these key areas is addressed in the following sections.

PARAEDUCATOR ROLES AND RESPONSIBILITIES

In special education and related services, paraeducators generally serve in one of two ways. First, some paraeducators are assigned as one-to-one assistants for students with extraordinary needs. These individuals typically spend most of the day with the particular student, whether in a general education or a special education classroom. Students who may need such intense support include those with autism, those with significant cognitive disabilities, or those with complex physical needs. Second, some paraeducators support special education programs but are not assigned to specific students. For example, in a high school program for students with learning disabilities, a paraeducator may be available to read tests

PERSPECTIVES ON DIVERSITY 9.1

Latino Paraeducators' Interactions with Latino Students

For all students from the minority cultures, but especially for students with special needs, learning is assisted when students can interact with adults who understand their language, culture, and communities. A recent study found that Latino paraeducators offered these positive factors for Latino students:

1. Demonstrating cariño. Paraeducators used terms of endearment, touch, and softened facial expressions, particularly when correcting student behavior or academic work.

2. Using a relaxed instructional style. Paraeducators allowed students to chat with peers while they worked and to speak spontaneously during instruction. The relaxed style enabled paraeducators to learn about students' lives outside school.

3. Accepting students' styles. Latino paraeducators were tolerant of student misbehaviors and addressed them discreetly whenever possible. They were far more likely to talk with students about behaviors than to remove privileges.

4. Incorporating student knowledge in instruction. The paraeducators used their primary language to facilitate instruction. Likewise, they related concepts being taught in students' homes and communities. These approaches seemed to foster student participation.

5. Employing wait time. The paraeducators generally waited longer for student responses than would typically be expected. This often seemed to relate to understanding the language-processing problems of students for whom English is a second language.

6. Sharing experiences. Noninstructional interactions between paraeducators and students usually occurred in Spanish. The paraeducators indicated that this approach helped them to "connect" to the students.

Although these findings pertained to students at risk, not those with identified disabilities, they offer important insights into informal contributions that paraeducators can make in the instructional process. For example, if the general education teacher or special education teacher is not Latino, a Latino paraeducator may help to serve as a cultural liaison between student and professional. Likewise, because professionals, whether Latino or not, often are balancing the needs of many students and a wide range of setting factors, the paraeducator may be more able than the professionals to build a relationship with a reticent student.

Adapted from ERIC Clearinghouse on Language and Linguistics. (2000, December). *Examining Latino paraeducators: Interactions with Latino students.* Washington, DC: Author.

to students who need such service, to assist students in organizing their assignments and materials, and to take notes for a student in his history class.

Although you might assume that the specific roles and responsibilities for paraeducators would be found in their job descriptions, you may find that most descriptions focus on the number of hours the individual is to work, the qualifications they must have for the job, and general expectations about working in schools (U.S. Department of Education, n.d.). A few school districts have clear and detailed job descriptions and may even distinguish among types of paraeducators (e.g., those addressing student behavior, those providing personal care, those assisting with instruction), but in most cases, you will not have guidelines to help you assign tasks to a paraeducator (Riggs & Mueller, 2001). A summary of the domains in which paraeducators may have responsibilities is presented in Figure 9.1, and they are explained more fully below.

Instructional Responsibilities

Whether working with an individual student or to support teachers and programs so that any number of students can be successful, the most common tasks for paraprofessionals in special education relate to instruction (Wadsworth & Knight, 1996). These tasks may include delivery of instruction, but they may also involve preparation for or follow-up to instruction.

The number of examples of instructional delivery appropriate for paraeducators is almost infinite (Downing, Ryndak, & Clark, 2000). For example, for students with mild or moderate learning problems, paraprofessionals may read individually with them, review earlier instruction to ensure their understanding, or lead them through an assignment that other students are completing independently. Paraeducators may also read tests to students, help them find appropriate resources for an assigned project or paper, and assist them in keeping books, materials, and papers organized. To minimize the possibility of stigma from being singled out in the general education classroom you might see a paraeducator working with a small group of students that includes students with disabilities and typical learners. The paraeducator might also sometimes work individually with a range of students, always keeping the needs of students with disabilities as the priority.

For students with more significant needs, paraeducators sometimes deliver an alternative curriculum within the context of the general education classroom. For example, while some students add numbers, the paraeducator works with one student to identify the numbers. A paraeducator might also facilitate student participation in a class activity by ensuring that the student is following directions, simplifying multiple-step directions, or serving as a "partner" who helps the student in the activity. This individual may have the responsibility of observing a student's behavior and providing reinforcers to the student according to a plan prepared by the special education teachers. A paraeducator working with a student with significant needs often works with other students in a classroom, but is more likely than paraeducators for students with mild disabilities to need to be near the identified student to provide necessary assistance.

Figure 9.1   Possible Domains of Paraeducator Responsibility

- **Delivery of instruction**
  Examples: Listen to a student read, carry out lessons in community settings, audiotape assignments or other materials

- **Activity preparation and follow-up**
  Examples: Operate equipment, distribute or collect student materials, adapt materials for specific student needs

- **Student supervision**
  Examples: Manage student arrival or departure (i.e., bus duty), supervise during lunch or recess, monitor students during passing periods

- **Behavior management**
  Examples: Observe and record student behavior, monitor students during time-out, help students to develop organizational or self-management skills

- **Personal care**
  Examples: Move a student from location to location, address health-related needs (e.g., suction a trach tube), help a student eat

- **Ethics**
  Examples: Maintain confidentiality regarding all student matters, preserve student dignity while taking care of personal needs, maintain composure when working with students

- **Team participation/membership**
  Examples: Attend team meetings as directed, contribute information as appropriate, engage in problem solving as needed

- **Clerical work**
  Examples: Type reports or assignments, help with paperwork to facilitate parent–teacher conferences, make copies

- **Other**
  Examples: Attend IEP meetings, complete routine communication with family (e.g., daily checklist of student behavior and academic progress), participate in parent conferences

---

Adapted from French, N. K. (1997). Management of paraeducators (pp. 91–169). In A. L. Pickett & K. Gerlach (Eds.), Supervising paraeducators in school settings: A team approach. *Austin, TX: Pro-Ed.*

Like delivery-of-instruction responsibilities, the preparation and follow-up activities of paraeducators vary greatly. They may prepare flashcards for students, use a computer program to create a rebus version of a story to be read, scan print material so that the student can "read" it using a computer, and adapt classroom materials (e.g., shorten, make larger, rearrange). After instruction, the paraeducator may grade student work, record information about student performance on particular tasks, and prepare routine correspondence for parents about a student's activities that day.

One issue should be raised regarding the instructional responsibilities of paraeducators. Despite all the anecdotal information about the instructional assistance paraeducators provide to students with special needs, virtually no literature establishes that student achievement improves as a result of interventions by paraeducators (Giangreco et al., 2001). A few isolated studies indicate that when paraeducators receive specific training to carry out interventions, students with whom they work benefit (e.g., Kotkin, 1995; Parsons & Reid, 1999). In general, though, current practices on the instructional tasks paraeducators complete, the amount of time they spend in inclusive general education classes, the intensity of their contacts with students with disabilities, and the impact of their preparation for their responsibilities are based largely on intuition and experience, not data-based knowledge. This situation should remind you of the importance of gathering your own data about paraeducators' work so that you create your own knowledge base on using them most effectively with the students for whom you are responsible.

Noninstructional Responsibilities

Even though instruction is usually a paraeducator's primary responsibility, many of them also have noninstructional responsibilities (French, 1999). These responsibilities may involve personal care, supervision, clerical work, and participation in team activities.

Some students can only receive instruction because paraeducators provide for their personal care. This may involve feeding a student, moving the student from place to place, carrying out procedures such as catheterization, changing diapers, or assisting a student to use the toilet. If a paraeducator has this type of responsibility, usually clear plans need to be in place in case the paraeducator is absent.

Many paraeducators assist educators in student supervision. Some paraeducators accompany students to recess, lunch, or assemblies to provide behavior support. Others assist in getting students off of buses and into the school building. Yet others are assigned a limited amount of lunchroom supervision, time-out monitoring, or playground duty. If a student is unable to self-ambulate, or if a student has serious behavior problems, the paraeducator may accompany such a student from class to class for safety and efficiency.

Special education, like all professions, includes a significant amount of paperwork. Paraeducators sometimes assist in getting this work completed. They may record scores on assessments onto a master record, update progress notes regarding student learning, or enter data on a behavior intervention plan. They may also assist in the day-to-day clerical work of teachers, duplicating materials for class, gathering money for field trips, or laminating materials that will be used several times. They may also draft general correspondence being sent to all parents (about upcoming conferences, for example) and assist in obtaining information from or relaying information to outside agencies.

Finally, paraeducators can function as members of the instructional team. When they work with students on a daily basis, sometimes more than any of the professionals on the team, they may have insights about student learning or be-

Professionals often have responsibility for supervising the day-to-day work of paraeducators, even though many are uncomfortable doing so.

havior that can help shape decisions being made. Similarly, they may notice small problems students are encountering that others have missed. In some cases, paraeducators may be from a background similar to that of parents, and so they may also be able to increase parents' comfort level at team meetings (Darling-Hammond, 2001; Gursky, 2000; Villegas & Clewell, 1998).

Ethical Considerations

Because the use of paraeducators is not clearly prescribed in federal law and their roles are still evolving, you may find that some of the roles described above are common for paraeducators in your locale while others are unusually or specifically prohibited. In addition, any of several ethical issues may arise concerning their work. Your responsibility is to make decisions concerning paraeducator assignments, keeping in mind local policies as well as factors such as these.

Paraeducators Supplement Instruction

Although paraeducators provide valuable instruction to students with special needs, it is clear that they are to supplement instruction that is delivered by professionals; they may not supplant it (French, 1999). Some authors even suggest that paraeducators provide an *indirect* service to students, not a *direct* service, since only professionals can offer the latter (Giangreco et al., 2001). This issue also affects accountability: Even if a paraeducator delivers a specific service to a student, the professional staff member, often the special educator, is ultimately accountable for the outcome of that service (Giangreco et al., 2001).

Paraeducators themselves have raised this issue. They report that they feel a strong sense of ownership for and commitment to the students to whom they are assigned, but that they are asked to take responsibility for making decisions they do not feel qualified to make (Marks, Schrader, & Levine, 1999; Riggs, 2001). For example, Downing and her colleagues (2000) interviewed paraeducators working with students with severe disabilities. The paraeducators reported that they were primarily responsible for making curricular adaptations and other decisions that could have a significant impact on students' education.

Giangreco and his colleagues (1997) added a sobering sociocultural perspective on this issue of paraeducators' work. They noted that in too many situations paraeducators are becoming the de facto teachers for students with significant disabilities. They raise questions about the potential negative impact on the general education teachers and typical learners' perceptions when the group of staff members generally considered least powerful in schools provides most services for the students who are likely perceived as least powerful, that is, those with disabilities.

An unpleasant but realistic sidebar to this discussion of the ethical use of paraeducators concerns the occasional administrative rationale for employing them: In some locales, paraeducators are seen as an inexpensive alternative to hiring professional staff, particularly if the intent is to get "an extra set of hands" into inclusive classrooms. This approach reflects a gross underestimation of the skills of professional staff and their purpose in inclusive classrooms, and it is a highly questionable means of delivering student services.

Ultimately, a few matters related to what paraeducators should *not* do are clear: They should not design and deliver initial instruction without teacher supervision, they should not communicate with parents regarding substantive issues, they should not write students' education plans, and they should not make critical decisions concerning student education or safety (French, 1999). Ultimately, they should not bear sole responsibility for any part of a student's education; they should assist professionals in related tasks and carry out their work with ongoing and high-quality professional involvement.

Parent Communication

When a team decides that part of a student's instruction can be provided by a paraeducator, parents/families are entitled to understand the qualifications of the individual delivering services and the scope of that person's responsibilities (Jacobson & Mulick, 2000; Mueller & Murphy, 2001; National Joint Committee on Learning Disabilities, 1999). Professionals and parents alike are faced with an ethical dilemma: How much support from a paraeducator is optimal? Is more always better? What is the rationale that should be employed for deciding on the right blend of professional and paraeducator services?

The Problem of Proximity

Paraeducators report that they believe they are crucial for helping students succeed, and educators generally report that they are highly valuable staff members (e.g., American Federation of Teachers, 1999b). Sometimes, however, these laudable characteristics can lead to a dilemma. Particularly for paraeducators assigned

PUTTING IDEAS INTO PRACTICE 9.1

Paraeducators on the Web

Are you looking for additional information about paraeducators? These websites contain a wealth of information:

www.cec.sped.org/ps/paraks.html

This Council for Exceptional Children web page contains information about the knowledge and skills standards the organization recently set for paraeducators for students with special needs.

www.wa.nea.org/PRF_DV/PARA_ED/PARA.htm

This web page of the Washington Education Association describes the characteristics of paraeducators working in schools and includes quotes from paraeducators concerning commitment to students and conditions in the workplace. A number of links to related sites are included.

www.aft.org/psrp/index.html

This web page of the American Federation of Teachers explains the types of paraeducators found in school settings. The site also includes a link to information pertaining to paraeducator certification.

www.nwrel.org/planning/paraeducator.html

On this web page of the Northwest Regional Education Laboratory, you can access a report that provides guidance for school policymakers on professional development for paraeducators. The document offers an administrative perspective on issues related to ensuring that paraeducators are adequately prepared for their jobs.

www.nrcpara.org

The National Resource Center for Paraprofessionals contains a wealth of information about paraeducators, their responsibilities, and best practices for their use in public schools. The site includes links to many other useful resources.

remc7.k12.mi.us/remc/paraeducators.htm

This website was prepared by a special education coordinator as a resource for individuals working as paraeducators. The site includes many links to information about lesson planning, classroom management, multicultural resources, paraeducator roles and responsibilities, and professional materials (e.g., journals, laws).

to a specific student in an inclusive setting, a risk exists that by remaining in close physical proximity to the student negative outcomes can occur (Hall, McClannahan, & Krantz, 1995). Among these are losing opportunities for the student to have normal social interactions with other students, inadvertently encouraging dependence, instead of independence, student behaviors, and unintentionally communicating to the general education teacher that he or she is not the primary teacher of the student. In addition, some concern also exists that assistants in close proximity may place students at greater risk for sexual abuse because they do not learn appropriate social distance (Giangreco et al., 1997).

WORKING WITH PARAEDUCATORS

The first part of this chapter has addressed the scope of a paraeducator's roles and responsibilities. The essential complement to that discussion is one about your roles and responsibilities as a professional working with pareducators (Palma, 1994). You may find that you need to be competent and feel confident to address these four areas: paraeducator training, planning with paraeducators, routine communication, and supervision.

Paraeducator Training

As noted earlier, federal law clearly states that paraeducators should be trained for the responsibilities they have in their jobs. Some school districts offer general training to paraeducators through workshops or videotapes, and a few states make training and certification a condition of employment. However, in many school districts any specific training a paraeducator receives is the result of efforts by the professional staff (Carroll, 2001). Even when paraeducators have received general training elsewhere, professionals need to provide student-specific and context-based information in order for paraeducators to do their jobs effectively. As you can see from the topics presented in the sample needs assessment in Figure 9.2, paraeducator training can include general knowledge about behavior, learning, and the law; specific knowledge about students' characteristics and needs; and knowledge and skills only indirectly related to students, such as working effectively with other adults.

You should discuss with your administrator and other special education team members how paraeducators in your school receive their training. If none is available, you might wish to use a needs assessment such as the one in Figure 9.2 to determine which topics are priorities. You might also wish to create with your colleagues a year-long plan for training all the paraeducators in your school (Lasater, Johnson, & Fitzgerald, 2000).

Planning with Paraeducators

Clearly, paraeducators are supposed to work under the direction of a special education teacher or another professional. This implies that a need exists for professionals and paraeducators to meet so that plans can be discussed, dilemmas raised and resolved, and student progress monitored. However, the limited data available suggests that such interactions are the rare exception rather than the rule. In a study of the supervisory roles that resource teachers play in working with paraeducators in inclusive settings, French (2001) found that more than 80 percent

---

Figure 9.2   Paraeducator Training Needs Assessment

Directions: The information you provide in this survey will assist in developing relevant in-service opportunities for paraprofessionals. Using the scale, rate the importance of each of the following skills in your job situation. Put a star next to those on which you would like to receive training. Also, please provide general information about your job at the bottom of the form. Thank you!

	0 = No need	3 = Some need	5 = Great need

		0	3	5
1.	Rationale of integration of students with special needs/current issues of inclusion	0	3	5
2.	Background information on specific disabilities	0	3	5
3.	Background information about the special education process	0	3	5
4.	Information gathering about individual students	0	3	5
5.	Modification of materials	0	3	5
6.	Behavior management	0	3	5
7.	Observation and recording of behavior and academic progress	0	3	5
8.	Promoting social acceptance of children with disabilities	0	3	5
9.	Legal issues	0	3	5
10.	Learning styles	0	3	5
11.	Small-group instruction	0	3	5
12.	Techniques for dealing with adults in the school system	0	3	5
13.	Assistive technology	0	3	5
14.	Working with related service providers (occupational therapy, physical therapy, speech therapy)	0	3	5
15.	Communication	0	3	5

---

* Type of assignment: inclusive class   special education   general education

* Level: preschool   elementary   middle school   high school

From Riggs, C. G. (2001). Ask the paraprofessionals. Teaching Exceptional Children, 33(3), 78–83.

of the teachers reported that they had no written plan to guide paraeducators' work and that they prefer that paraeducators be able to just "go along" with whatever is occurring in the general education classroom. This degree of flexibility has the risk of slipping into unethical practice: How can IEP implementation be documented when no records are created for the part of IEPs that paraeducators implement. This is an especially important consideration given professionals' accountability for whatever tasks paraeducators complete.

Not surprisingly, the biggest reported obstacle to professional–paraeducator planning is time to meet (French, 2001). For example, in many school districts paraeducators have the same work hours as the school day for children, and so they are not available before or after school. Similarly, paraeducators typically are not paid on teacher workdays or for preparation days prior to the start of the school year. Without an administrative commitment to professional–paraeducator planning, no simple solution to this problem exists. However, you can use some of the suggestions in Chapter 13 on finding time for collaboration to create opportunities for shared planning. In addition, you can be sure that the schedule you create for paraeducators working with you includes at least one planning period per week (Morgan & Ashbaker, 2001).

Day-to-Day Communication

Even if you have regularly scheduled planning periods with paraeducators, you still will need to use effective and efficient communication strategies to keep in touch with your paraeducator and to monitor their work and student progress (French, 2000). Of course, the communication skills outlined in Chapters 2, 3, and 4 are essential, as they are for all your professional interactions, but several other strategies can also be used. These are briefly described in the Putting Ideas into Practice feature on the next page.

Communication entails more than interactions about instruction and student concerns, however. One initial form of communication is the paraeducator's job description. This is the instrument through which you can discuss with paraeducators the expectations of the job. You may wish to check about the availability of a job description since not all school districts have these, and some that do have not updated them in many years (Riggs, 2001). You should also provide orientation at the beginning of the school year for paraeducators, including basic school policies and procedures on everything from parking to mailboxes to dress codes; your expectations for paraeducator interactions with students and other school staff; information about the school's philosophy (e.g., inclusive, problem-based learning); and steps to take if a problem arises either with a student or with a staff member. The more information that you formally communicate to a paraeducator, the less he or she will have to learn incidentally and the less likely it is that miscommunication will occur (Gerlach, 2001).

Supervising Paraeducators

It has been implied throughout this chapter, but at this point needs to be stated directly, that special education teachers, general education teachers, and other professionals have the responsibility of supervising paraeducators and the work they do with students (French, 1998). This may not be a formal responsibility; in many school districts, principals or special education supervisors are assigned the task of evaluating paraeducators. However, even when this is the case those administrators rely heavily on input from the day-to-day supervision that professionals have done in providing feedback to paraeducators.

PUTTING IDEAS INTO PRACTICE 9.2

Communicating with Your Paraeducator

In most schools, professionals and paraeducators have little, if any, time to formally meet, and they must become creative to maintain effective communication. Here are a few informal strategies for communicating about student academic and behavior programs with your paraeducator:

◆ Create for each of you a planning agenda that is laminated and can be used repeatedly. For example, the agenda might include sections for instructional issues, assistive technology matters, student behaviors, and team concerns. You and your paraeducator note items as you become aware of them, using a water-based marker. When you do have time to meet, you have a ready agenda to ensure your time is used wisely. After the meeting, the agendas can be wiped clean and used again. This system can also be used for paraeducators and general education teachers.

◆ Use a clipboard agenda. Hang or place a clipboard with a pad of paper in a location easily accessible to the paraeducator, special educator, and as appropriate, the general education teacher, but away from students (e.g., a teacher mailbox, in a special educator's office). Anyone lists agenda items on the paper, and when the meeting occurs, copies of the list are distributed and form the agenda.

◆ E-mail communication can also help professionals keep in touch with paraeducators. If you establish a routine—say, spending 5 or 10 minutes each morning or afternoon providing e-mailed directions to your assistant—you can be certain that you are documenting the assigned work. If the paraeducator also e-mails with notes about implementing the directions, a detailed record exists and communication is assured.

◆ If the paraeducator uses teacher's manuals or other materials in his or her work with students, you can use self-stick removable notes to provide directions and comments. Select one color to use for this purpose, and attach the note on the page where input is needed. The paraeducator could reply with notes in another color. Although this strategy is not shared planning, it can be an efficient and direct means of communication.

What have you learned in your other coursework about supervising paraeducators? Approximately 88 percent of special education teachers report that they learned to work with paraeducators from real-life experience; they did not receive any instruction on this topic in their formal professional preparation programs (Conderman & Stephens, 2000; Pickett, 1999) even though teacher educators think the topic should receive significant attention (Katisyannis et al., 2000). Paraeducators report that teachers are not proficient in guiding their work (Special Education News, 2000a). Further, teachers indicate that they are reluctant to think of themselves as supervisors or to function in that capacity; they believe that it interferes with their working relationship with paraeducators (French, 1998). Whether you share these perceptions or not, in today's schools special educators should assume that they will have supervisory responsibilities related to paraeducators such as these:

- Monitoring whether paraeducators are carrying out the specific tasks that have been assigned to them
- Providing feedback to paraeducators on their work with students, pointing out strategies or techniques they are using appropriately and redirecting them when the strategies they are using are not effective or are detrimental to the student
- Modeling effective ways to interact with students and instructional techniques to use with them
- Problem solving with general education teachers and paraeducators when disagreements arise about paraeducator roles in the general education setting
- Ensuring that paraeducators adhere to school policies
- Ensuring that paraeducators follow a code of ethics (such as that of the Council of Exceptional Children), particularly on matters such as confidentiality (Fleury, 2000)
- Supporting paraeducators by answering their questions regarding students, classroom practices, legal issues, and other related topics
- Arranging for some type of public acknowledgment of the work that paraeducators do (e.g., an appreciation day, having students make cards, conveying positive parent comments)

Of course, unless you are the formally identified supervisor for paraeducators, if significant issues arise related to paraeducator performance, you should alert the appropriate administrator so that more formal procedures can be implemented. A comprehensive listing of the skills you will need as a paraeducator supervisor are enumerated in Figure 9.3.

PARAEDUCATORS AND COLLABORATION

Perhaps you have been wondering if all of the information in this chapter is supposed to give a particular message about collaboration and working with paraeducators. The primary intent is to articulate the fact that your relationship with paraeducators is perhaps at this time the least understood and most complex of all the professional relationships you will have in your job.

Is it possible to collaborate with a paraeducator? Of course! Remember that collaboration is a style, and you may use the style when interacting with a paraeducator just as you use it with other professionals and parents/families. What is less clear, however, is the extent to which collaboration with paraeducators is appropriate and how special education professionals can balance their prefer-

---

**Figure 9.3   Recommended Competencies for Special Educators
Supervising Paraeducators**

A. Interviewing skills

B. Mentoring
   - Identifies and clarifies the roles and responsibilities of paraprofessionals
   - Delineates lines of authority
   - Demonstrates/models behavior

C. Communication
   - Applies interpersonal skills
   - Demonstrates effective listening skills
   - Uses team-building skills
   - Exhibits effective written and oral skills to provide team management

D. Problem Solving
   - Resolves conflicts
   - Identifies and clarifies a problem
   - Assumes the perspective of another

E. Motivation Skills
   - Creates a positive environment
   - Sets achievable goals
   - Rewards goal achievement
   - Shows respect and acknowledges achievement of others
   - Promotes change and growth

F. Coordination Skills
   - Demonstrates time-management skills
   - Designs effective meeting strategies
   - Implements scheduling techniques

G. Delegation Skills
   - Selects tasks to be delegated based on an individual's competence
   - Clarifies roles and clearly delegates responsibilities
   - Provides constructive feedback to the delegate

H. Feedback and Evaluation Skills
   - Monitors the performance of others
   - Provides constructive feedback
   - Participates in formal evaluation process
   - Describes and clarifies the evaluation process and content
   - Participates in individual personnel growth plans

---

*From National Joint Committee on Learning Disabilities. (1999). Learning disabilities: Use
of paraprofessionals [electronic version].* Learning Disability Quarterly, 22, *23–30.*

ence for collaborative interactions with paraeducators with their responsibility
to also supervise them.

This is an area in which clear guidelines simply do not exist, and the available
data is worrisome. Some professional literature suggests that teachers want to treat

Paraeducators may know the student better than any school staff, and they can make valuable contributions as team members.

paraeducators just like other teachers, to ask them to take over a class, to be peers (French, 1998). Even some administrative literature suggests this is acceptable practice (Daniels & McBride, 2001). At the same time, most paraeducators do not have professional credentials, they do not have a professional array of responsibilities in their jobs, and they do not make a professional salary. Taken together, these factors suggest that in some interactions, all the conditions for collaboration can be met, but that in others they cannot. You might want to review the defining characteristics of collaboration in Chapter 1 and discuss with your classmates when they fit in interactions with paraeducators and when they do not.

SUMMARY

With the increasing number of paraeducators employed to assist in the delivery of services to students with special needs, you are likely to be responsible for working with and guiding the activities of such an assistant. Although some paraeducators are used to assist teachers primarily with clerical tasks, most now spend the majority of their time completing instructional responsibilities and noninstructional responsibilities related to personal care and supervision. However assigned, the scope of a paraeducator's work should be clearly distinguished from that of individuals employed in a licensed capacity. To work effectively with paraeducators, special education professionals need a wide range of skills. They often arrange for necessary training for their assistants, they should ensure that systematic planning meetings and other strategies for clear communication are in place, and they provide supervision for their assistants. Collaboration between professionals and paraeducators is recommended, but it must be tempered with an understanding of the difference in status among the individuals participating.

ACTIVITIES AND ASSIGNMENTS

1. How common is it in the school districts in your area to employ paraeducators? What are the state and local qualifications to be a paraeducator? With your classmates, obtain job descriptions for paraeducators from several local school districts. How specific are they? How clearly would they guide your possible task of assigning tasks to the paraeducator?

2. Interview a general education teacher who works with a paraeducator about the instructional responsibilities the assistant assumes. How do those responsibilities compare with the ones discussed in this chapter? If you were working with the teacher, how would you try to increase or decrease the paraeducator's responsibilities?

3. Some professionals believe that paraeducators should assist professionals by duplicating, grading, keeping records, and performing other clerical tasks. The rationale is that this approach frees the licensed staff to work with students. What is your opinion on this issue?

4. Suppose you accept a position to be a special education teacher in an inclusive middle school. Your students with mild to moderate learning and behavior disabilities are on two teams, but you are assigned a teaching assistant to ensure that all students receive appropriate services. What factors would you consider in deciding how to assign tasks to your paraeducator? How would you ensure that you retained appropriate accountability for the progress of students served primarily by the paraeducator?

5. A critical issue in today's schools is training for paraeducators. What does your local school district do to meet the requirements of the federal law regarding paraeducator training? If you were responsible for training paraeducators you supervised, how would you go about creating time in their schedules for training?

6. Although most paraeducators are wonderful, committed individuals who truly make a significant contribution to student success, problems also can occur. Using the communication skills you have learned and your knowledge of effective problem solving, role-play the following situations with classmates and discuss appropriate ways to respond:

  ♦ The general education teacher mentions to you that your paraeducator, who is supposed to be in the classroom all morning, seems to disappear frequently for 15–20 minutes at a time.

  ♦ The paraeducator, who is nearly finished with a teaching credential, comments about today's lesson: "I just don't do much adapting on topics like that. I don't even see much point for him being there. The material being covered is just too hard for him. I'm thinking I'll start pulling him out."

◆ A parent informs you that you are not providing appropriate services for his daughter. In discussing the parent's dissatisfaction, you learn that a paraeducator, who baby-sits for the student and is a member of the family's church, has told the parents that you do not give enough attention to the student and should be providing more direct service.

◆ A general education teacher asks to meet with you and the paraeducator. The student in the classroom needs to be using assistive technology that you have demonstrated for the paraeducator. The teacher maintains the technology is not being used. The paraeducator says that she uses it when she can, but that the teacher often stops her, claiming it is too disruptive for the rest of the students.

7. If you were asked to provide a one-hour staff development session to school staff members on the roles and responsibilities of paraeducators, what topics would you prioritize for inclusion? How would you address the topic of collaboration between professionals and paraeducators?

8. Using the information in Figure 9.3, reflect on your preparation for and confidence to supervise paraeducators. If you were to design additional training for yourself, what would it include?

FOR FURTHER READING

Doyle, M. B., & Gurney, D. (2000). Guiding paraeducators. In Fishbaugh, M. S. E. (Ed.), *The collaboration guide for early career educators.* Baltimore: Brookes.

French, N. K. (2001). Supervising paraprofessionals: A survey of teacher practices. *Journal of Special Education, 35,* 41–53.

French, N. K., & Chopra, R. V. (1999). Parent perspectives on the role of the paraprofessional in inclusion. *Journal of the Association for Persons with Severe Handicaps, 24*(4), 1–14.

Giangreco, M. F., Edelman, S. W., Broder, S. M., & Doyle, M. B. (2001). Paraprofessional support of students with disabilities: Literature from the past decade. *Exceptional Children, 68,* 45–63.

Giangreco, M. F., Edelman, S. W., Luiselli, T. E., & MacFarland, S. Z. C. (1997). Helping or hovering? Effects of instructional assistant proximity on students with disabilities. *Exceptional Children, 64,* 7–18.

Katsiyannis, A., Hodge, J., & Lanford, A. (2000). Paraeducators: Legal and practice considerations. *Remedial and Special Education, 21,* 297–304.

National Joint Committee on Learning Disabilities. (1999). Learning disabilities: Use of paraprofessionals [electronic version]. *Learning Disability Quarterly, 22,* 23–30.

Pickett, A. L., & Gerlach, K. (Eds.). (1997). *Supervising paraeducators in school settings: A team approach.* Austin, TX: Pro-Ed.

Families

Connections

Thus far in this text, we have addressed concepts and skills important to collaboration and discussed partnerships with other professionals and with paraeducators. In this chapter, we consider special issues related to understanding families, your work with them, and their participation in educational decision making and program implementation. We examine professional responsibilities in working with families and suggest strategies for supporting and for collaborating with families.

Learner Objectives

After reading this chapter you will be able to:

1. Describe the historical and current roles of parents and families in the education of children and youth with disabilities.
2. Describe family systems theory and significant characteristics of four life stages of families.
3. Identify special considerations and challenges for families of children with disabilities at each of four life stages of families.
4. Identify cultural influences on families and list characteristics of culturally responsive services.
5. Outline major professional roles and responsibilities when working with families.
6. Identify strategies for promoting family participation in educational decision making.

INTRODUCTION

In Chapter 1 we noted that a number of IDEA provisions provide for parental representation and participation in developing and implementing educational programs for their children. For example, IDEA mandates that parents will be part of the team that makes eligibility, placement, and services decisions; that parents will be regularly informed of their child's progress; that parents will be given copies of evaluation reports and have a right to ask for reviews of IEPs; and that states will be required to offer no-cost mediation to parents to resolve disputes. Part C of the law mandates family-based early intervention services that may include parent education, support, and counseling as delineated in the Individualized Family Service Plan (IFSP). Parent Training and Information centers (PTIs) in each state and territory are also supported by the law to provide assistance so that parents and families may participate more in meeting the needs of their family member with disabilities. With each reauthorization of IDEA, originally passed in 1975, the role of parents and families in the education of their family member with disabilities has become increasingly more significant (Reyes, 1999; Wolfe & Harriott, 1998). The professional literature has also called for increased collaboration between families and schools (Parett & Petch-Hogan, 2000; Umansky & Hooper, 1998).

You are likely to have a different working relationship with each of the families with which you work. Your working relationships with parents and families will depend upon the needs of the student; the interests, resources, and needs of the families; and your skills, resources, and attitude. Consider these variations:

- Mrs. Wynott is a single parent who works full-time but is able to demonstrate her commitment to her son, Marcus, by interacting positively and constructively with adults at school and following through with the home-based behavior intervention program. Last week, Mrs. Wynott called to explain that Marcus's uncle, a significant father figure to the boy, had been hospitalized for a cardiac problem. This had upset Marcus, and he was acting out at home.

- Returning from overseas duty with the military, Mr. Johnson, William's father, has rejoined his family. He is a devoted father and is very concerned about his son's recently identified learning disability. Mr. Johnson has had a one-hour meeting with you each of the last three Mondays to learn more about learning disabilities and what he can do to help William at home. He suggested that you start meeting twice a week. Despite your commitment to working with parents, you are unable to schedule this much time for him because you have nearly 20 annual reviews and several eligibility meetings to schedule and complete in the next few weeks.

- Susan's parents are both professionals and working in high-pressure jobs. They rarely attend Back to School Night and never come in for conferences. When you call one of them, you receive a return call from a secretary or the nanny offering to convey your message to the parent. You have offered several dates for Susan's annual review meeting, but neither parent can schedule the time.

- Drew's mother has scheduled two conferences with you and has canceled both of them. She typically cancels meetings at the last minute because another child is ill, her car breaks down, or she is unable to get away from work. She calls you apologetically and wants to discuss the matters on the phone rather than coming to school. Yesterday she attended Drew's annual review meeting with her infant and preschool child, whose presence was disruptive to the meeting.

Every school professional can relate to the range of relationships these examples represent. Mrs. Wynott has many responsibilities and stressors in her life, but she has the emotional resources to manage them and collaborate with you in her son's educational program. She is sensitive to his needs and realizes that you need to know about significant family events that influence Marcus's school adjustment and performance. Mr. Johnson is a caring and involved parent who seems a little anxious about his son's school performance. You would like to work with him and feel that you could allay his fears and help him to understand and accept William's disability, but you do not have sufficient time available to devote

Often the presence of young children distracts the adults and requires their attention.

to him. Susan's parents seem uninterested and unwilling to commit to participating in their daughter's program. Drew's mother is committed to Drew, but the other children, pressures, and demands for her time make it exceptionally difficult for her to attend meetings at school. Nevertheless, she wants to know how he is doing and what she can do to support him at home.

When you consider the range of relationships professionals have with families, you will realize that in some cases collaboration is not an appropriate goal. If you are only going to talk with Susan's nanny or her mother's secretary, and if Drew's mother's job and family obligations make it impossible for her to meet at school, it may not be possible for you to get to know the parent well enough or for the parent to know you well enough for collaboration to occur. Similarly, some parents may have so many obligations and demands that collaboration is prohibited. For others, such as Mrs. Wynott, collaboration is appropriate and recommended. Collaboration with Mr. Johnson is also appropriate, but the limits of your schedule simply will not permit it at the level he wishes. In this case, you will have to communicate your situation to him and refer him to another professional, such as the school counselor, or to an information and referral resource.

Although collaboration is a worthy goal, your primary responsibilities in working with families are to understand the family and its needs and to facilitate family participation in making decisions about the educational program for their family member with a disability. Facilitating family participation will involve providing families with information about disabilities, educational concerns, and their rights, as well as assisting them to participate in conferences and team meetings. Oftentimes it involves collaboration.

UNDERSTANDING FAMILIES

It is critically important that professionals understand families and their perspectives in order to know how to support them and when and how to engage them in collaboration. While it is necessary to learn about each family individually, there are some special considerations that apply when you seek to understand any family. In Chapter 2 you considered prerequisites to effective interactions that involve your self-awareness and your ability to understand others. These concepts—frame of reference, cultural self-awareness, and selective perception—accompanied by nonverbal communication and listening skills, are important foundations for understanding others, including families. Here we augment that foundational information by (1) discussing a family systems framework that offers insights into functions and tasks of families at various developmental stages and (2) considering cultural influences on families.

Until relatively recently, professionals have focused on the roles and functions of parents in the care and education of children with disabilities. Turnbull and Turnbull (2001) describe seven major roles that parents have played over the years including parents as the source of their child's disability, organization members, service developers, recipients of professionals' decisions, teachers, political advocates, and educational decision makers. They add an eighth role, families as collaborators, as having emerged in the 1990s and stress that the emphasis on families signals a recognition that all family members, not just parents, are important to the care and education of children.

This shift in emphasis from parents to families occurred following the period from 1981 to 1989 when America's cultural diversity was expanded by the almost 6 million Asian, African, European, and Latin American people who became U.S. citizens. Entwisle (1994) has observed that increased cultural diversity and economic and social pressures led to considerable structural diversity among these families. Many of these changes, often nonnuclear in nature, have caused professionals to view families differently.

Family is defined many ways. Until recently, the narrow view of mother, father, and children has been the traditional view, sometimes expanded to include others who live in the home. Children of single-parent families, stepfamilies, ex-

Professionals need to understand the composition and membership of the families with whom they work. It is often informative to visit the child's natural environment.

tended families, families with same-sex parents, and families with adopted or foster children are all represented in today's schools. People from some ethnic groups view family quite narrowly, while others conceive of families in a much broader way and include grandparents, aunts, uncles, and even neighbors or community elders. One definition of family that is consistent with our thinking is

> two or more people who regard themselves as a family and who perform some of the functions that families typically perform. These people may or may not be related by blood or marriage and may or may not usually live together. (Turnbull, Turnbull, Shank, & Leal, 1995, pp. 24–25)

We encourage you to define family in the broadest fashion and accept the definition that parents and caregivers themselves use. For instance, if a mother suggests that her sister or aunt will be attending a parent conference in her place, it would be appropriate to accept that decision while continuing to encourage the mother's participation. Of course, legal matters such as taking a child from school require written permission from the child's parent or legal guardian.

Systems Theory

Although its influence has been recognized in related fields since the 1960s (Lambie, 2000), systems theory has become a major influence in how we view and respond to families of children with disabilities only over the last two decades. With systems theory, the family is seen as a complex and interactive social system in which all members' needs and experiences affect the others. The theory and its principles can help professionals to better understand a student's behavior, strengths, and challenges. Let's consider three key principles of systems theory.

Principle 1: No individual can be understood without recognizing how he or she fits within the entire family.

This is the central principle in systems theory. Each family member is a part of the whole, and it is important to understand how the members interact with one another and how their individual and collective histories have developed. Specifically, we need to see how each family member affects and is affected by the others and their situations. When a parent loses a job, the financial assets of the family change. Depending upon the reason for and the length of the unemployment period, the parent's attitudes, affect, and behavior may also change and have significant impact on the other family members. A teacher or counselor might view a behavioral or academic change in a student differently if he knew that the student's only parent had been laid off from her job, was unable to find work for several weeks, and was beginning to look for an alternative place to live.

Principle 2: Families need rules for structure and rules for change.

Rules for structure guide the family and its behavior in day-to-day events. For example, a single, working mother with two children may have a clear work schedule, specific household chores for the children or babysitter, a routine with a sister for sharing transportation to events, and arrangements with a neighbor or friend to share child-care responsibilities. If the mother's work schedule changes, or if she becomes unemployed and needs to seek a new job, many or all of the rules and arrangements must be renegotiated. If she is not able to renegotiate these matters, tensions will build and affect the other members of the family as well. Children might seem disoriented at school, tired from sleep missed due to schedule changes, and even display anxiety or other changes in affect if they sense and respond to these feelings from their parent.

Principle 3: Family interaction with the school, community, extended family, and friends is essential to the life of the family.

For families to be healthy and function well, members must have their external social and affiliation needs met. That is, although a family exists to meet the needs of its members, it is unlikely to be able to meet all of the needs of each family member. There are very real benefits to be derived through relationships with persons outside of the nuclear family, and family members need such interactions. Children need peer relationships, and adults need to interact with other adults. The importance of parents interacting with and deriving support from other parents is discussed later in this chapter. Here, let us just point out that families that isolate themselves are likely to become lonely, possibly hostile, and often dysfunctional.

Family Life Cycles

Much like human development, family systems theory views the family as undergoing a series of developmental tasks that vary along several life stages. W. C. Nichols (1996) describes the family life cycle as "being concerned with the developmental tasks of the family itself as it deals with the needs of the adult members and the developmental needs of the offspring" (p. 57). Many theorists have proposed family life cycle stages and advanced models that typically delineate from four to over 20 stages. In Figure 10.1, we summarize the typical functions and tasks advanced by several theorists and place them within a four-stage frame-work posited by Turnbull and Turnbull (2001). In the following section, we iden-tify special issues arising at each stage for families of children with disabilities and suggest actions that professionals can take to support families.

Birth and Early Childhood

For parents whose children's disabilities were identified at birth or during early childhood, the emphasis is on understanding the disability and working through their feelings about the diagnosis. Adjusting to a typically developing child cre-ates stress for most families, and a child with a disability creates additional stress.

Figure 10.1   Themes, Functions, and Tasks at Four Family Life Stages

Birth and Early Childhood

With the introduction of a child through birth or adoption, the primary family func-tions become nurturing and caring for the infant or young child and providing ap-propriate behavioral limits. Tasks are to realign family relationships and relationships with friends and extended families to accommodate the presence of the young child and the duties of parenthood.

Childhood

The primary themes for families with children in their elementary school years are af-filiation and allowing others to be brought within the family boundaries. The family functions are sensitivity to the child's developmental needs, encouraging the child's independence, and enjoying the child's experiences. Tasks to be accomplished are af-filiating with a peer network and establishing family responsibilities and sibling roles.

Adolescence

This stage is characterized by themes of decentralization and the relaxing of bound-aries. Parents' essential functions are to tolerate the efforts their child makes to "dis-tance" them and to provide the adolescent with support needed to establish his identity. The tasks that parents face include managing the adolescent's increasing in-dependence, refocusing their own careers and marriage, and developing more flexi-ble roles.

Adulthood

The stage of adulthood is characterized by themes of detachment, dissolving ties, and letting go. Family functions focus on supporting and facilitating independence while encouraging the young adult to accept more responsibility. The primary tasks for families at this time include renegotiating roles and relationships between or among parents and other family members, redefining roles with adult children, re-aligning relationships to include the adult child's housemate, assistant, spouse, and/or in-laws, and dealing with the death of family members.

Adapted from six stages presented by Lambie, R. (2000). Family systems within educational contexts: Understanding at-risk and special needs students *(2nd ed). Denver: Love.*

Kübler-Ross (1969) proposed a grief cycle model that has been used to describe the stages experienced by many parents as they learn of and grow to accept their child's disability. Not all parents go through the same process, and the stages may not be sequential or of equal duration, but they generally include shock, denial, guilt and anger, shame and depression, and acceptance. In addition to the grief cycle dynamics, families also experience stress in gaining a clear diagnosis, adjusting to the diagnosis, and informing family members and friends of the child's disability.

Shock and Denial.   When first learning of a child's disability, the family members initially do not accept the information given to them and may actively deny it or seek other opinions that are more to their liking. Like any family expecting a new child, they were anticipating the arrival of their dream child and may have spent many months, if not years, preparing for the arrival of what they expected to be a nearly perfect child.

Guilt and Anger.   Families are likely to experience anger and resentment with underlying guilt. They may feel somehow responsible for their child's disability and experience guilt as a result. They are likely to resent the professionals who are working with them and try to prove them wrong.

Shame and Depression.   Hopelessness and depression often become predominant themes at this stage. Parents may go through a process of mourning the loss of the child they expected; they need to "let go" of the ideal child they imagined. The period of depression may be of significant duration and interfere with the natural attachment or bonding process that normally occurs during infancy. This can interrupt the child's development and hinder the parent's ability to accept and nurture the child later. It is at this time that the family feels helpless, seeks assistance, and may begin to consider productive interventions.

Acceptance.   The final stage in the grief cycle is acceptance and represents resolution of many of the previous stages. Families accept the child's disability and recognize his needs. They are increasingly open to suggestions for productive actions for raising their child. They are likely to believe that there is much to be done, but they are also likely to commit to doing practical, useful things that they believe will make a difference.

Previously, interventions or supports that were thought to be helpful to families going through the grief cycle included patience, listening with acceptance, and providing resource and referral information (Cook, Tessier, & Klein, 1992). More contemporary family systems approaches also advocate "re-storying," or assisting families to externalize and separate from a "problem" orientation in order to construct a new story that will allow them to focus on possibilities and their ability to work actively to realize new possibilities for their child (Lambie, 2000). Professionals should provide a supportive and accepting environment for families and accept their feelings while also helping them to re-story and begin to see their family life in a new way. It is also incumbent upon professionals to provide access to parent support groups or parent-to-parent groups. As parents accept their child's disabilities, needs, and strengths, they will also need assistance in setting realistic goals for the child.

Childhood

The typical functions and tasks at this stage are more complex for the family of a child who is diagnosed with a disability. For children with disabilities who are not diagnosed at birth, the most common period for diagnosis is during the elementary school years. Regardless of when the diagnosis occurs, the family is likely to experience the grief cycle or some variation of it. Major stressors for families of elementary school age children are clarifying family goals for the child, deciding on appropriate services, and deciding on placement in self-contained, resource, or general education classrooms. Many issues associated with making decisions about inclusion for a child weigh heavily on families during this stage. Parents may have opinions, and certainly they have had advice from friends and other professionals, but they are likely to feel ill equipped to make decisions on this important topic. Many parents are reluctant to challenge or disagree with educators

PUTTING IDEAS INTO PRACTICE 10.1

Some Concerns about Inclusion

Many families have understandable concerns about the impact of inclusion on themselves and their family member with a disability. They may believe that inclusion benefits everyone and society in general. Or they may fear that inclusion is a means of saving money by "dumping" children with disabilities in general education classrooms or recreational programs. Parents may have little information about the characteristics and benefits of separate versus inclusive settings for special education services. The questions below are among those for which parents seek answers.

- What are the benefits of inclusion?
- Where can my child's IEP goals best be met?
- In which setting will his academic skills most develop?
- Will inclusion negatively impact the time and attention available to my child?
- Will my child receive the specialized instruction he needs?
- Will my child be able to manage his behavior in a group of 25?
- Will my child be "safer" in a separate setting?
- Where will my child's potential best be developed?
- Where will my child receive the most appropriate services?

for cultural reasons or for fear that their disagreement may result in bias against their child. Professionals can assist families with these decisions by listening with empathy to their concerns and by sharing objective information in response to their questions. It is also often helpful to assist parents in connecting with others who may provide information or take them to visit different programs that will contribute to their decision making.

Additional stressors that families with elementary school-age children face include handling the reactions of the child's peer groups and siblings to his disability. At this life cycle stage, in which affiliation is a primary theme, the potential ostracism by peers is especially worrisome. Professionals can help the child and his family to understand the disability and find appropriate and effective ways to talk with non-disabled peers about it. Affiliation is also a theme for other family members. This is a good time to encourage families to join support groups if they have not already done so. Information about such groups is presented later in this chapter. Parents who are engaged in parent support groups or receive other sorts of social support report the highest levels of enjoyment in parenting (Beach Center, 1999).

Adolescence

Adolescence is a tumultuous time. It is a period during which young people experience rapid maturation, hormonal changes, a newfound sexuality, and a need to challenge authority. Rebellion in one form or another is to be expected. Surely this is familiar to you. Perhaps you work or live with adolescents, or you may remember some challenges you posed for your own parents during that period of your life. Regardless, there are few people who would not agree that being an adolescent or having one in your home or classroom can be stressful.

Groce (1997) suggests that adolescence is more influenced by cultural context than is any other life cycle stage. European Americans typically view adulthood as beginning at age 18, while various ethnic or religious groups believe that adulthood commences earlier. As an example with which you are surely familiar, consider the Jewish bar and bat mitzvahs. In these rituals, 13-year-old adolescents become adult members of their congregations. Other, less familiar, examples exist in other world religions and in different ethnic and racial groups in which adolescents are perceived to be adults. Professionals are well advised to learn about the traditions and beliefs of a family toward adolescents and their roles and to respect those traditions in their interactions with the family.

Some daunting issues arise for adolescents with disabilities. One of the tasks of adolescence is to develop a sense of self or a personal identity. All adolescents begin to compare themselves with others during this stage, and they start to develop a sense of their own strengths and weaknesses. The presence of a chronic illness, physical impairment, behavior disorder, or other disability may negatively influence the adolescent's self-assessment, self-esteem, and identity. Typical adolescent resistance to authority may exhibit itself for adolescents with disabilities as noncompliance with medical treatments, such as refusal to monitor blood sugar or take insulin by an adolescent with diabetes or refusal to take prescribed medication by an adolescent with seizure disorders. The struggle between dependence and independence that characterizes many adolescent relationships is intensified for families of adolescents with disabilities. While developing independence is a primary task at this stage, there are often very real physical, cognitive, and emotional needs that make the struggle more precarious for adolescents with disabilities.

There are several significant educational issues that are likely to become the topic of discussion while families and professionals collaborate in planning programs and activities for adolescents with disabilities, including vocational planning and sexuality education. This is the stage at which planning for vocational development becomes particularly important (Downing, 2002). This topic will be addressed in Chapter 12, but its relationship to this developmental stage should be considered briefly. As the adolescent is assessing her strengths and weaknesses and developing her personal identity, consideration should be given to future goals and vocational options. For example: How limiting is her disability? What are her individual assets and needs? What are her and her family's dreams and expectations for the future? The family and school need to collaborate to help the student set appropriate and realistic goals consistent with the student's potential and interests. But we caution professionals and families to keep in mind the student's struggle for autonomy and independence at this stage. The range and number of options should not be reduced prematurely, and efforts should be made to enhance the student's self-determination skills (Agran, 1997; Wehmeyer & Sands, 1998).

It is also at this time that the adolescent becomes more involved in the decision making at his annual review and IEP meetings in preparation for assuming, at age 18, the role that has heretofore been held by his parents'. This is a move toward independence that may require the professional to provide support and guidance to the adolescent as well as to the other family members.

Adolescents' changes associated with maturation, puberty, and sexual development create a need for sexuality education (Whitehead, 1993). Sexuality curriculum should include maturation, sexually transmitted diseases, birth control, responsibility, same- and opposite-sex relationships, avoidance of sexual abuse, and marriage and family relationships and responsibilities (Cambridge, 1998; Walcott, 1997). Turnbull and Turnbull (2001) stress that sexuality issues may also represent educational needs for families. They note that parents are often unaware of their adolescent's sexual needs and interests. This suggests that professionals may also need to assist families to develop a better understanding of the sexuality issues commencing in adolescence.

Adulthood

Adulthood is the final stage we will consider. Many of the issues of adulthood are discussed, and strategies for addressing them are identified, in Chapter 12. Here we wish to call attention only to the significant educational and life decisions that occur at this stage. Families and professionals together must identify and access postsecondary educational and employment options and services. Depending upon his goals, abilities, and limitations, the individual might need assistance in selecting and preparing for postsecondary education, vocational training, or supported employment. Some individuals also may need to access supported living arrangements.

Transitions

These family life stages have been offered to help describe how families change over time. The theory suggests that each family experiences these predictable stages of development and that each stage represents changes the family undergoes (Lambie, 2000). As a family progresses from one stage to the next, family members' responsibilities shift, and the family is said to undergo transition. Transitions are the periods between stages when family members are readjusting their roles and interactions in order to meet the next set of expectations and tasks. These transitions are usually shorter in duration than are the stages, but they are characterized by confusion and often by increased stress. By attending to and being sensitive to the life stages of the families with which you collaborate and assisting them in taking appropriate steps to support their children, you can be especially effective in your collaboration with them.

Cultural Influences

The United States is one of the world's most culturally, ethnically, and linguistically diverse nations. It is unlikely that any professional practices in a school environment in which families of diverse cultures are not represented. The vast majority of professionals work in highly diverse settings where they interact with families from many different backgrounds. There is widespread agreement that professionals must become culturally competent (Lynch & Hansen, 1998) and able to offer culturally sensitive and relevant services (Chen, 2001; Harry, Kalyanpur, & Day, 1999; Trumbull, Rothstein-Fisch, Greenfield, & Quiroz, 2001).

As we begin to examine cultural influences, three points offered by Lynch (1998) are relevant.

◆ Culture is dynamic—always changing and evolving; it is not static. What individuals remember from a culture in which they were raised is probably not the way the culture is practiced in the same place today.
◆ Culture, language, ethnicity, and race are powerful influences on an individual's values, belief, and behaviors, but they are not the sole influences. One's socioeconomic status, education, socialization, education, and life experiences greatly influence his identity and frame of reference. These, in turn, influence how a family functions.
◆ No cultural, ethnic, linguistic, or racial group is homogeneous. There is great diversity in the attitudes, values, beliefs, and behaviors within groups of people who share a common culture.

Understanding the culture of a family is critically important to understanding the family. A family's culture is a significant determinant of its structure, values, and beliefs. Understanding these will increase your professional effectiveness. But how do you go about gaining such knowledge and developing cross-cultural com-

PUTTING IDEAS INTO PRACTICE 10.2

Enhancing Successful Transitions

Are you wondering what you can do in your professional role to assist families in making successful transitions from one life cycle stage to another? Here are some suggestions for each of the stages:

Early Childhood

◆ Begin preparing for the separation of preschool children by periodically leaving the child with others.

◆ Gather information and visit preschools in the community.

◆ Encourage participation in Parent-to-Parent programs. (Veteran parents are matched in one-to-one relationships with parents who are just beginning the transition process.)

◆ Familiarize parents with possible school (elementary and secondary) programs, career options, or adult programs so they have an idea of future opportunities.

Childhood

◆ Provide parents with an overview of curricular options.

◆ Ensure that IEP meetings provide an empowering context for family collaboration.

◆ Encourage participation in Parent-to-Parent matches, workshops, or family support groups to discuss transitions with others.

Adolescence

◆ Assist families and adolescents to identify community leisure-time activities.

◆ Incorporate into the IEP skills that will be needed in future career and vocational programs.

◆ Visit or become familiar with a variety of career and living options.

◆ Develop a mentor relationship with an adult with a similar exceptionality and an individual who has a career that matches the student's strengths and preferences.

Adulthood

◆ Provide preferred information to families about guardianship, estate planning, wills, and trusts.

◆ Assist family members in transferring responsibilities to the individual with an exceptionality, other family members, or service providers as appropriate.

◆ Assist the young adult or family members with career or vocational choices.

◆ Address the issues and responsibilities of marriage and family for the young adult.

Taken from Turnbull, A. P., & Turnbull, H. R. (2001). *Families, professionals, and exceptionality: Collaborating for empowerment* (4th ed., p. 173). Upper Saddle River, NJ: Merrill/Prentice Hall.

petence? The first step is gaining cultural self-awareness (Harry, 1992; Chan, 1990). This topic was discussed within the context of understanding one's own frame of reference in Chapter 2, and questions for increasing your cultural self-awareness were presented in Perspectives on Diversity 2.2.

Learning specific information about other cultures is a second step in the journey toward cultural competence (Chan, 1990; Lynch, 1998). This learning can be achieved through reading, travel, and interactions with representatives of the specific cultural groups. There are many useful texts, information briefs, and research summaries referenced in this chapter, but the most enjoyable learning will come from direct interaction and experience. Learning firsthand about the art, music, dance, foods, values, and traditions of a culture different from your own is an exciting and stimulating experience. Learning the language of another cultural group may be the best way of learning about that culture because many traditions and values are conveyed through language. While interesting and useful, language learning may not be feasible, and it is not necessary to learn another language for one to become culturally competent.

Developing a culture-generic awareness is the step that follows understanding your own and others' cultures. It is important to recognize that there are cultural values that are shared across cultures and that variations in values exist within cultural groups (Kalyanpur & Harry, 1999; Trumbull et al., 2001). This recognition will help you to understand that there may be values that are more characteristic of one cultural group than another but that no culture is monolithic, and hence, no culture should be viewed stereotypically. In Chapter 2 several dimensions of culturally based value orientations were suggested (e.g., human nature orientation, time orientation, and purpose of life orientation), and in Chapter 13 you will consider perspectives related to individualistic versus collectivistic orientations. These and other cultural variations are best viewed as continuous, rather than dichotomous, perspectives. Lynch (1998) proposes that we view many value sets as existing along a continuum and that we recognize that individuals' and family members' positions along the continuum are not static. They may vary at any given time based on such factors as age, education, life experiences, vocation, and socioeconomic status.

The final step toward cultural competence that we will consider here is the acquisition of specific information about cultural practices relative to children, childrearing, health, disability, and helpseeking (Hanson, Lynch, & Wayman, 1990; Umansky & Hooper, 1998). The views that a family holds toward disability and their beliefs about its causes are likely to affect how they respond to the child's disability and to the interventions that are recommended. You should also expect notable differences in the levels of involvement and collaboration with professionals that families desire.

Although we encourage you to develop awareness and knowledge of the cultures of families you work with professionally, it is not necessary for you to know everything about a particular culture in order to provide culturally sensitive and responsive services. If professionals are respectful of differences, open to learning, and committed to self-examination and change, they can develop culturally responsive and productive relationships with diverse families.

Suggestions have been made for providing culturally responsive services (Chen, McLean, Corso, & Bruns, 2001; Harry et al., 1999) and family-centered programs (Allen & Petr, 1996; Chan, 1998). Many of these are summarized here.

1. Focus on the family as the unit of attention.
2. Respect the uniqueness of each family system.

PUTTING IDEAS INTO PRACTICE 10.3

Cultural Continua

Reflect on the variations in values and beliefs along these continua. Think about which end of a continuum is closest to your values, then consider where you would place the values held by the families with which you work. Are they similar or different from yours? Professionals often need to schedule their interactions and meetings with families, and educational programs generally strive to increase a student's independence. Clearly, these issues may cause conflict for families whose values fall at the other end of the time or nurturance/independence continua. What issues may lead to potential misunderstandings or conflicts based on variations along other continua?

Family Constellation Continuum

Some families are large and have extended kinship networks that are intimately involved with nearly every aspect of the family's daily life. Others are smaller units of one or two adults who are responsible for all decisions and activities and operate independent of an extended family.

Interdependence/Independence Continuum

Interdependence is the primary value in some families. Contributions to the whole are more highly valued than expressing one's individuality, which could be seen as selfish and rejecting of the family. For other families, individuality, the expression of one's uniqueness, is the greatest value.

Nurturance/Independence Continuum

Although most people nurture young children, the behaviors viewed to be nurturing vary significantly from one individual or group to another. What one group sees as nurturing, another group may see as coddling or overindulgent.

Time Continuum

On one end of the continuum, the amount of time needed for a task or interaction is given to it. At the other end, the task or interaction is given only the amount of time that has been scheduled for it.

Tradition/Technology Continuum

From one perspective, respect for age, tradition, and ritual provide a solid base for contemporary life. The divergent perspective is one that places greater value on the future, technology, and youth.

Ownership Continuum

This continuum varies as to whether things are individually owned or are shared broadly.

(continued)

Rights and Responsibilities Continuum

The concept of equality is the fundamental concern. In some groups, equal and nondifferentiated roles are ascribed to both men and women. In others, women are the caretakers and men the providers and intermediaries between the family and community.

Harmony/Control Continuum

Some groups primarily value living in harmony and synchrony with their environments, and others believe it more important to control their environments and the events in their lives.

Adapted from Lynch, E. W. (1998). Developing cross-cultural competence. In E. W. Lynch & M. J. Hanson (Eds.), *Developing cross-cultural competence: A guide for working with young children and their families* (2nd ed., pp. 57–63). Baltimore: Brookes.

3. Develop a personalized, informal helping relationship.
4. Organize assistance in ways requested by the family.
5. Gather and provide information in culturally responsive ways.
6. Include a focus on family strengths and holistic family needs.
7. Give families complete and accurate information in a supportive manner.
8. Create alliances with community leaders and allies.
9. Develop a shared vision.
10. Provide families with choices from services that meet their needs.
11. Ensure accessibility of services with minimal disruption of family.
12. Obtain family evaluation of process and results.

Unique Factors and Barriers to Collaboration

In providing a framework for understanding families, we have considered specific needs based on the family's life stage and those that may arise from cultural differences. Now we look at the basic functions of families and how they may be affected by having a family member with a disability.

Families perform a number of functions that benefit their members. Successful families emphasize the importance of sharing affection with one another through the exchange of physical or verbal affection. Their interactions help each member to establish a self-identity and a sense of worth or self-esteem. They transmit cultural and personal spiritual beliefs across generations. Families also perform an economic function. They must earn income to provide for their basic needs. Families function to meet the day-to-day physical and health needs of their members. Social activity and affiliations as well as leisure and recreation activities are important functions for the health of individuals and their families.

Consider what the impact of a child with a moderate disability might be on these functions. First, certainly some families report that there is greater affection in their families as a result of having a child with a disability (Turnbull &Turnbull, 2001), but some families, when first learning of their child's disability, may have difficulty expressing affection. And, although the affection is likely to develop later, that initial response may cause a disruption in the bonding process. The family may have a difficult time helping the child with a disability to develop a positive self-identity. In fact, cultural and peer relations may also intervene, and the self-esteem of the parents or siblings may also be affected. Families also must earn and decide how to spend income. They report that they spend more money on a child with a disability, especially if he or she has health care needs or requires special equipment or clothing. Moreover, providing for the other daily care needs such as transportation, medical procedures, or behavioral management are often so demanding that the parents may not perform as well at work as they would otherwise, and they may lose economic or career opportunities. The same physical and emotional demands that sometimes lead to lost career opportunities may also interfere with family members' recreation and leisure activities.

We do not wish to imply that having a child with a disability is an overwhelming burden. In fact, many families believe that the child with a disability strengthens their families and the enjoyment they get from seeing their child succeed. Research on the positive contributions of having a child with a disability consistently finds that the child is a catalyst for increased spirituality of family members (Stainton & Besser, 1998; Turnbull & Turnbull, 2001). Nevertheless, a child with a disability requires more of a family's physical, emotional, temporal, and fiscal resources than do other children.

A number of variables that present challenges to family–professional interactions are outlined in Figure 10.2. Two additional types of barriers to family participation in children's educational programs are also identified by Bailey, Buysse, Edmondson, and Smith (1992). First, many parents of children with disabilities lack the knowledge and skills needed to contribute substantially to the education of their children. For example, parents of students with special needs may have limiting disabilities themselves. Similarly, they may be lacking the knowledge of programs and service options that are being discussed.

A second type of barrier is attitudinal, such as lack of confidence or assertiveness that prevents parents from active participation in the educational programs of their children. When such barriers are present, professionals must support families and help them feel valued and comfortable participating at whatever level possible in their child's education program. Given the tremendous range of parental abilities and preferences for involvement in interactions with school professionals, it is appropriate to ask whether collaboration is a reasonable expectation with particular parents. Knowing how to foster effective communication with parents is important, whether or not collaboration is the goal.

Educators need to be mindful of the many demands on families and consider them when they assess family strengths and set expectations for their work with families. Throughout this chapter and in most textbooks for teachers, you will read about the importance of parent participation and collaboration. We concur. But we also encourage you to recognize the very real demands on families as well

Figure 10.2	Variables That Make Family–Professional Interaction Challenging
Situation	**Impact**
Family structure	Loyalties, power, complex and varying rules under similar conditions, transitions between dwellings, availability of equipment
Child-care requirements	Availability of child care for infants, toddlers, and young children with disabilities, debates with child-care providers about the realities of serving children with disabilities, financial burdens
Single-parent families	Time and resource management, single-parent income, transportation issues, ill-child responsibilities, possible conflict with personal goals, increased need for respite care
Nontraditional partnerships	Prejudice of service providers and local community, debates over "proper parenting authority," legal authority issues
Poverty	Prejudice of service providers toward poor persons, lack of transportation to get to and from services, possible lack of phone services, possible lack of a permanent address
Substance abuse	Immediate impact on the person engaging in the abuse, subsequent impact on immediate and extended family members, inability to keep priorities in desired order, secondary health issues, guilt, shame
Foster care	No long-term goals or personal authority, lack of accurate history

Taken from Howard, V. F., Williams, B. F., Port, P. D., & Lepper, C. (1997). Very young children with special needs: A formative approach for the 21st century (p. 316). Upper Saddle River, NJ: Merrill.

as the challenges to family–professional interaction and gauge your expectations accordingly.

FACILITATING FAMILY PARTICIPATION IN DECISION MAKING

It is the professional's role to provide families with information they need to support their family member with a disability and to be effective participants in educational decision making. This includes communicating effectively, providing information about disabilities and educational concerns, and reporting evaluation results and student progress. The concepts and basic communication skills for providing information that were presented in Chapters 2, 3, and 4 are needed for effectively sharing information with families. You should review those skills and employ them as you provide families with information.

Providing Information to Families

Families have different information needs at different life stages to which professionals need to respond, as discussed earlier. When they learn of a child's disability, they need to understand the nature and consequences of the disability. They may need to learn about medical treatments or other related services as well as other physical care matters. As the child matures, they will need information on social, emotional, physical, and cognitive development. Families need to have clear and accurate information in these areas in order to adjust their expectations and goals for their child. Realistic expectations are central to setting appropriate educational goals.

In addition to basic information about the child's disability and its characteristics, families require procedural information regarding due process, placement, parent rights and responsibilities, and other legal provisions of the laws that affect their child. They further require information about educational and related services that may be appropriate for their child. In early years, the decisions may be focused on whether the toddler or young child receives services in a center or in a home-based program. During elementary and middle school years, choices of specific instructional approaches or different inclusionary practices become more focal. By adolescence, families need information about postsecondary employment and educational options so that they can begin planning for them.

Professionals have additional responsibilities for providing families with the results of diagnostic evaluations. This can be a highly sensitive matter, and you are advised to take care in communicating about evaluation results with parents. This is an especially sensitive matter when first communicating about the possible presence of a disability, but it remains a potentially emotional issue throughout the child's educational career. Thomas, Correa, and Morsink (2001) offer the following suggestions for providing diagnostic feedback:

- ◆ Provide feedback in a private, safe, comfortable environment.
- ◆ Keep the number of professionals to a minimum.
- ◆ Begin by asking parents their feelings about the child's strengths as well as weaknesses.
- ◆ Provide evaluation results in a jargon-free manner, using examples of test items and behavioral observations throughout.
- ◆ Provide the parents results from a variety of assessment activities, including standardized tests, criterion-referenced tests, direct behavioral observations, play-based or community-based assessment, and judgment-based approaches.
- ◆ Be sensitive to viewing the child as an individual and a "whole" child when reporting various evaluation results.

- Allow the parent time to digest the results before educational planning begins.
- Be sensitive to linguistically different families and the use of interpreters.
- Prepare for the session with the other team members, clarifying any possible conflicts before the meeting.
- Use conflict resolution strategies to clarify any possible conflicts with families. (p. 281)

Language Matters

Professionals must recognize these information needs, answer questions, and provide clear, useful information and referrals if appropriate. There is one additional communication strategy that we wish to point to here. Whenever possible, communication with families should be in a language in which they are fluent and preferably in their primary language. The written forms and materials used to communicate or plan programs, announcements from school, and fact sheets for information resources should all be translated into the family's primary language. Many of the website resources in this chapter offer materials in languages other than English or provide links to appropriate resources.

If the family uses a language other than that of the professionals, generally interpreters should be used. However, sometimes interpreters are not needed, particularly for informal communication, if the family has some proficiency in English. In informal communication with limited-English-proficient families, it may be sufficient to speak slowly and clearly and provide the family with written information (Ohtake, Fowler, & Santos, 2001). There are a number of matters to consider when selecting and using an interpreter. One of the most important recommendations we make is that you avoid using the student as the interpreter. This is an inappropriate role for the student, and it removes him or her from the appropriate role of participant. We also caution you to be sensitive to the confidentiality issues. Although professional interpreters have a code of ethics that honors confidentiality, the parents may not fully understand this and may be uncomfortable with the interpreter. In these cases, you will need to explain the interpreter's role and responsibility to maintain confidentiality. Many additional recommendations for the use of interpreters are offered by Ohtake, Fowler, and Santos (2001).

Communication Structures

Language considerations and communication skills learned in earlier chapters will be useful in your interactions with families, but planning the appropriate structure and mechanism for addressing family information needs can be almost as important. For example, it is worth your time to consider which information needs of families might best be met through such mechanisms as one-way information reporting, informal conferences, structured meetings, parent education or workshop sessions, or parent-to-parent groups.

PERSPECTIVES ON DIVERSITY 10.1

Recommended Practices for Working with Interpreters

Before the Meeting

◆ Have a list of interpreters.

◆ Encourage the family to choose an interpreter who is the most satisfactory to the family.

◆ Discuss the importance of neutrality.

◆ Encourage the interpreter to be self-reflective.

◆ Discuss how clear communication could be promoted with interpreters. Do not discuss attitudes of families toward the plan proposed by the team.

◆ Provide the interpreter with written documents as advanced organizers. Discuss the agenda of the meeting on the basis of the documents.

◆ Provide the interpreter a glossary that plainly explains terms used in special education.

◆ Encourage the interpreter to take an introductory course in special education at college level.

◆ Discuss the duties and vital roles of interpreters and other team members.

◆ Encourage the interpreter to be a cultural broker.

During the Meeting

◆ Create an informal atmosphere.

◆ Avoid using professional jargon.

◆ Use visual aids and concrete examples.

◆ Avoid idiomatic words, slang, and metaphors that are difficult to translate.

◆ Be aware of loan words.

◆ Use simple sentences.

◆ Speak slowly and clearly.

◆ Use consecutive interpretation.

◆ Encourage the interpreter to take notes and ask questions whenever he or she needs.

◆ Be sensitive to reactions shown by the interpreter to identify if interpretation process is going well. However, your eye-contact should be mainly with the family.

After the Meeting

◆ Evaluate the meeting with the interpreter using the guidelines described in "Before the Meeting" and "During the Meeting."

◆ Encourage the interpreter to ask questions and clarify issues about the meeting.

◆ Identify problems that the interpreter may have encountered during the meeting.

◆ Encourage the interpreter to advise you if you communicate with the family in a culturally inappropriate manner.

◆ Brainstorm ways to address those problems for future meetings.

Taken from Ohtake, Y., Fowler, S. A., & Santos, R. M. (2001). (p. 9). *Working with interpreters to plan early childhood services with limited-English–proficient families.* (Technical Report #12) [electronic version]. Champaign-Urbana, IL: Culturally and Linguistically Appropriate Services for Early Childhood Research (CLAS) Institute.

PUTTING IDEAS INTO PRACTICE 10.4

Families on the Web

Many resources for families of individuals with disabilities and for the professionals who work with them may be accessed on the World Wide Web. The websites listed here have been found useful and they provide links to many other valuable sites.

Beach Center on Disability
www.beachcenter.org/

This website provides research briefs and fact sheets on topics of interest to families and professionals, especially those that address information needs of families for educational, vocational, and adult-living decisions.

Children with Disabilities
www.childrenwithdisabilities.ncjrs.org

Jointly sponsored by nine federal agencies and maintained by the Coordinating Council on Juvenile Justice and Delinquency Prevention, this site supplies information about advocacy, education, employment, health, housing, recreation, technical assistance, and transportation. It offers useful links to federal and state resources.

Children's Defense Fund (CDF)
www.childrensdefense.org

CDF is an advocacy organization for children, especially poor and minority children and those with disabilities. Its website provides resources and information relating especially to issues of concern for people with low incomes.

Disability Resources
www.disabilityresources.org

This site provides valuable information about legal rights, financial resources, assistive technology, employment opportunities, housing modifications, child-rearing and educational options, transportation and mobility services, and related issues.

Family Voices**
www.familyvoices.org

Family Voices is a national clearinghouse for information and education about the health care of children with special health needs. The website includes a bimonthly newsletter, news updates, and information about the organization and its publications.

National Fathers Network**
www.fathersnetwork.org

NFN provides resources and support to men who have children with special needs through development of national and statewide databases of fathers from diverse ethnic, racial, and geographic backgrounds; provision of father support and mentoring programs; and provision of varied educational and technical assistance services.

National Information Center for Children and Youth with Disabilities (NICHCY)**
www.nichcy.org

NICHCY is a federally funded national information and referral center that provides information on disabilities and disability-related issues for families, educators, and other professionals. The website features its excellent fact sheets, resource guides, and other publications about specific disabilities and disability-related issues with a focus on children and youth from birth to age 22. Many website features and publications are available in Spanish.

National Parent Network on Disabilities (NPND)
www.npnd.org

This website is useful for current information and links relating to "hot topics" and legislation affecting children with disabilities.

Parents Helping Parents
www.php.com

This organization is a comprehensive resource and information center run by and for parents. Its website provides useful links to information about support groups for family members and information resources for families and professionals.

Sibling Support Project
www.seattlechildrens.org/sibsupp

This website offers resources and ideas for siblings of children with disabilities and their parents and service providers. It includes a national directory of sibling support programs and a newsletter.

T. A. Alliance for Parents (PACER Center)
www.taalliance.org

The Alliance for Parents provides technical assistance for establishing, developing, and coordinating parent training and information projects operated under IDEA. The website includes a national calendar, legislative information, links, and lists of organizations and parent centers. The site also features electronic study teams.

**These sites provide information in English and at least one other language, often Spanish.

One-way information sharing is often useful to keep the school and home aware of the child's experiences and performance in both settings. Typically, families and professionals use notes, progress reports, or school–home journals to share information about school assignments, schedule changes, homework, and behavior. With advances in technology, some schools have established websites for posting school and classroom information, and more families have access to and are comfortable with electronic mail. Voice mail offers another asynchronous method of communication (Cameron & Lee, 1997; Friend & Bursuck, 2002). One-way communication is often necessary for efficient information sharing, but two-way communication structures such as those discussed below are essential for effective communication and productive relationships with families.

Informal meetings are often spontaneous and may be more relaxed than meetings that are planned in advance. These meetings are sometimes characterized as informal "chats" or "visits." They may take place at school, in a parking lot, or during an accidental meeting in the community. Informal or casual meetings can be useful for sharing general information, clarifying a point of concern, and generally building rapport. This can help to prepare the participants for successful interactions in subsequent formal meetings (Jordan, Reyes-Blanes, Peel, & Lane, 1998). Another advantage of the casual conference or meeting is that it not only allows the educator to assess the child's interests and abilities but also affords opportunities to learn about the family's culture and how it is transmitted to family members (Harry, 1992).

Structured meetings, or purposeful conferences, are events scheduled to discuss a particular topic or agenda. Meetings with an agenda that is focused on one student and one family are discussed in the following section. The focus here is on structured or purposeful meetings that involve members from several families, such as parent information workshops or family support groups.

Several topics have been identified in the previous discussions that represent typical information needs of families at various stages. Most or all families need basic information about disability and appropriate interventions as their child is identified and as the child transitions from one stage to another. Workshops represent an efficient way of providing information about topics of interest to many families. This is a frequently used strategy in preschool programs and as families prepare for a student's transition to vocational and employment services. School professionals often offer these workshops or information seminars, but such training activities are also available from the Parent Training and Information centers as well as from other community and nonprofit groups.

Parent or family support groups are another type of purposeful meeting. Similar to informational groups, these are usually organized around some common element or family need such as groups with early childhood interests, groups for families of students with the same disability, or groups composed of persons with the same roles, such as fathers or siblings. Various structures exist for support groups as well. Some are groups of family members with a professional leader or facilitator, others are led by family members themselves, and still others provide one-to-one support. Research conducted by the Beach Cen-

Family needs are sometimes best met in support groups where professionals facilitate interactions and relationships among group members.

ter on Disability (1999) documented the effectiveness of one-to-one support in a program entitled Parent-to-Parent Support. This program, which matches parents with other parent support providers, was studied in five states and was rated by nearly 400 parents. The findings indicated that the program increases parents' acceptance of their situation and their coping strategies, and also helps parents to make progress on the need or problem that was their reason for participating in the program. Fifty-five percent of the respondents reported that they were satisfied with the companionship they derived from the program, and 18 percent reported that they received meaningful information services through the program. Parent-to-Parent programs exist in 29 states. Similar efforts to support siblings are conducted through the national Sibling Support Project. Many additional support groups can be identified through local and regional information and referral services.

Assisting Families to Participate in Student-Centered Meetings

We noted earlier that one of your primary responsibilities in working with families is to facilitate their effective participation in educational decision making, a sometimes difficult goal (Lazar & Slostad, 1999). Most of your interactions with families probably focus on understanding, planning for, and making decisions about their family member with a disability. Many of those interactions occur in meetings that are structured to focus on the child and family and discuss matters such as student progress, behavior, school–home program, or evaluation results. These meetings are often parent conferences, IEP meetings, or annual review meetings.

There are many examples in schools of the failure on the part of school professionals to ensure that family participation occurs. In some settings, for example, students' IEPs are written prior to conferring with families with the excuse that it takes too much time to discuss everything and write goals and objectives at a meeting. Sometimes this approach is used in order to have a draft document as an efficient starting point for a full discussion in which all participants will contribute to writing new material or modifying the draft. School professionals using this strategy risk communicating that they know what the student needs better than the family. In the worst case of this practice, someone at the meeting says to the parent, after all the prewritten information has been reviewed, "Do you have anything else you would like to add?" At best, this approach severely limits participation for most family members.

A second, more indirect example of limiting family participation also is common. School professionals informally (or even formally) touch base prior to a meeting with a family to be sure that everyone agrees with whatever is going to be said. This united front can create an adversarial climate in the interaction. What is even more unfortunate is that it indicates that controversy and alternative perspectives are not part of decision making when families are involved, unless the family member challenges decisions made by the educators as a group.

You should carefully reflect on how the formal and informal procedures for working with families in schools might constrain family participation, especially in interactions at IEP and other group meetings (Wolf & Stephens, 1990). If you can foster participation and collaboration, your interactions with families are more likely to be in the best interests of students.

Our primary suggestions for structuring and conducting these meetings were presented in the Chapter 6 section Conducting Meetings and in the Chapter 4 section Conducting Interviews. We recommend that you review that material and consider unique applications for family members in those situations. We also suggest that individuals and teams use the questions presented in Figure 10.3 to periodically assess themselves and their practices to ensure that they are using strategies that enhance family participation.

To augment the material in the previous chapters and the assessment questions, we offer a few simple ideas for fostering family participation.

1. In group meetings, create an environment that is welcoming and supportive. You can accomplish this in several ways. For example, prepare parents for meetings by sending home in advance a summary of the topics to be addressed and a list of possible questions they might want to ask. Suggest that they bring to school examples of their child's work that they would like to discuss, information about their child's friends and responsibilities at home, and other information that parents have (and school professionals do not) that can contribute to an understanding of the child. At the meeting, have professionals stay in the vicinity of the meeting room, chatting informally, until the parent arrives, and have all participants be seated at the same time, rather than having parents enter

Figure 10.3   Team Questions Designed to Enhance Family Participation in Decision Making

Assessment Design

- Have I individualized the team decision-making process for the family and the child?
- Have I taken the time to develop a trusting relationship with the family before starting the team decision-making procedures?
- Have I identified strategies for involving the family in the team decision-making process?
- Have I observed the child in a variety of naturalistic settings with and without caregivers?
- Have I included the extended family in the team decision-making process?
- Have I examined the team decision-making process for cultural biases?
- Do I know how or where to find cultural information that will help me during the team decision-making processes?

Professional Collaboration

- Have I made trained translators available to maintain communication with family members?
- Am I flexible when meeting with family members?
- Do I provide necessary assistance to the family members to ensure their participation in the team decision-making process?

- Is it possible to meet with the family members in their home before the team decision-making process?
- Have I informed family members of their rights in the decision-making process?
- Have I told family members about local support groups?
- Do I understand how the family feels about making direct contact with professionals involved in team decision making?
- Am I networking with other professionals to address cultural issues?

Cultural Issues

- Have I done a self-assessment of my own cultural background, experiences, values, and beliefs?
- Do my experiences, values, and beliefs allow me to interact with people from various cultures?
- Do I understand the family's values, beliefs, customs, and traditions?
- Have I modified the team decision-making process to ensure cultural competency?
- Do I try to achieve professional cultural competence?
- Can I train other staff members about cultural competence in the team decision-making process?

- Have I considered outreach organizations or individuals who can provide training?
- Do I communicate regularly with the cultural communities that I serve?
- Do I provide information and printed materials related to the team decision-making process in the language spoken by the family?
- Am I aware of the family's cultural rules regarding body language, eye contact, and proximity?
- Have I determined whether a community liaison would be the most appropriate contact through which to provide information to or receive information from the family?

Values

- Am I aware of the family's goals for the child and other family members?
- Am I aware of what the family expects out of me in the team decision-making process?
- Do I understand how family members may perceive a translator?
- Do I understand the family's attitude regarding disabilities?
- Do I know the key decision maker of the family?
- Do I understand the family's expectations of me as a professional?

(continued)

Figure 10.3 *(continued)*

- Do I understand the importance of the extended family?

- Am I aware of the family's approach to discipline?

- Do I understand the responsibilities of other siblings in the family setting?

- Does the family accept the idea of the team decision-making process as a tool to help their child?

- Does the family's religious affiliation influence their willingness to participate in or perceptions of the team decision-making process?

Family Factors

- Have I asked family members about their concerns for their child?

- Am I willing to pick up or arrange transportation for family members?

- Do I provide assistance to help family members when filling out forms necessary

for the team decision-making process?

- Do I allow family members to share cultural information about their child?

- Have I identified the family's primary caregiver?

- Does the socioeconomic status of the family impact on the child for whom the team decision-making process is being considered?

- Have I examined the home setting and determined how it might facilitate or inhibit the team decision-making process?

Acculturation

- Do I understand how acculturation has influenced the family's perceived need for the team decision-making process?

Ethnicity

- Have I examined ethnic factors that might affect

the child's or family's perception of the team decision-making process?

Social Influences

- Have I identified important social influences that might affect the child's or family's perception of the team decision-making process?

Past Experiences

- Have I identified past experiences of the child or family that could influence their current perception of the team decision-making process?

Developmental Expectations

- Have I determined the family's expectations regarding developmental milestones for the child that might influence the perception of the team decision-making process?

Note: From Cultural Competence in Screening and Assessment: Implications for Services to Young Children with Special Needs, Ages Birth Through Five *by M. Anderson & P. Goldberg, 1991, pp. 22–23. Chapel Hill, NC: National Early Childhood Technical Assistance System. Copyright 1991 by NECTAS. Adapted with permission.*

Taken from Parett, H. P., & Petch-Hogan, B. (2000). (p. 6). Approaching families: Facilitating culturally/linguistically diverse family involvement. Teaching Exceptional Children, 32(2), 4–10.

a room where everyone else has already been seated. A variation is to be sure that the professional the parents know best accompanies and sits next to them.

2. At meetings, have a file folder with samples of the student's work, copies of forms being discussed, and blank paper and a pen available for the

parents. The reason for this is straightforward: If you think about most meetings, all the school professionals arrive with folders, binders, reports, schedules, planbooks, and a plethora of other paperwork. Many parents arrive carrying nothing and are thus at a subtle but immediate disadvantage. Unobtrusively providing materials at least helps resolve this inequity.

3. Structure meetings so that parents have opportunities to provide input throughout. It is still too common in family interactions for the professionals to share their information or make their requests and only then to seek family input. For example, at IEP meetings, each professional often shares the results of his or her assessment, suggests goals, and then asks the family members if the goals are acceptable. An alternative strategy is to discuss issues related to students by domains. To do this, first address the student's academic strengths and needs, soliciting input from any team members who have pertinent information, including the family members. Then address social and emotional areas, using the same procedure, and so on through the domains that need to be addressed. This approach to a meeting can help ensure that a dialogue occurs rather than a series of report readings followed by a request for parental approval.

4. Maximize the opportunities for families to make informed decisions. Have a variety of choices for parents and students to make (for example, alternatives for elective classes, communication or self-help priorities, or social skill training options) and actively engage them in decision making. To the extent possible, make sure they understand the choices and how they will affect the student's program and future opportunities. When you are considering new program options for a student, such as a community-based instructional component or involvement in an after-school recreational program, ensure that family members are well informed and knowledgeable about the options. You can do this by arranging for them to tour a new setting, observe a program, or meet with other family members who are involved with the alternative. If they are unable to adjust their schedules for such meetings or observations, prepare written and visual materials to inform them about the alternatives. Photographs or videotapes are most useful for these purposes. Family members are more likely to invest in joint decision making and collaborate with you to set realistic goals and make future plans for their children when they have adequate information.

SUMMARY

Parent participation has been a key feature of education for individuals with disabilities, and it is guaranteed in IDEA. Over the years, the emphasis has moved from parent to family participation, and a broad definition of family has become accepted. Systems theory has been applied to the understanding of four family developmental life stages—birth and early childhood, childhood, adolescence, and adulthood. The importance of culture and its influence on family structure and values has been recognized, and the profession has emphasized the development of cultural competence and family responsive programs. Professional responsibilities include understanding families and their needs as well as facilitating family participation in making decisions about the educational program for the family member with a disability. A variety of strategies are used to maintain effective communication with families including one-way communication, casual meetings, and structured or purposeful meetings such as parent conferences and IEP meetings.

ACTIVITIES AND ASSIGNMENTS

1. Conduct an informational interview with the family members of a student with disabilities. Ask them about their experiences related to the eligibility, placement, and IEP processes, as well as their experiences working with school professionals. What have been the positive elements of their experiences? What have been the negative elements? What suggestions would they make for improving the collaboration between home and school?

2. Create an information packet to give to family members during IEP meetings. Include in the packet a clarification of educational jargon, information about their rights, an explanation of the IEP process, contact information for school personnel, and any additional information about expectations in your program such as a homework schedule, information about maintaining notebooks or study schedules, and more.

3. Review the "Conducting Meetings" section of Chapter 6 (pages 139–146). Prepare a summary of the suggestions to ensure that meetings facilitate family participation. Review the summary with classmates and decide how best to share it with colleagues on-site.

4. Review the culture-specific information resources provided on the websites suggested in this chapter and in Chapter 1. Consider the cultural groups represented among the students with whom you work. Identify what school-based or classroom-based practices you could institute that would make your environment more culturally appropriate for students and families.

5. Think of a recent meeting with a family of a child with a disability. Did you include more than one parent in the discussion or meeting? Even if only one parent attended the meeting, what explicit actions did you take to ensure that the roles and concerns of other family members were considered? List specific actions you will take at the next meeting to include other family members and/or address their information needs and concerns.

6. In this chapter, you read about family variables that may act as barriers to family–professional interaction. Consider the families with which you inter-

act. Are any of these variables factors in your situation? What strategies might you use to overcome them?

7. Family expectations and beliefs are important variables to consider in your work with students with disabilities. Consider the two scenarios below and identify the family variables that are surfacing and causing conflict, the information resources that might be helpful to the family in this situation, and the approach you should take to address the family concerns about the student. Discuss your responses with a classmate.

   ◆ Both parents, his brother Will, and Marvin attend his IEP meeting. At the meeting, you propose steps to begin including Marvin in age-appropriate general education classes and activities, starting with the possibility of Marvin's participating in a fifth-grade class during social studies instruction. Will, who is in fourth grade, gets angry and says that Marvin shouldn't be in that class. He is not smart enough.

   ◆ Mrs. Meyer is very anxious about the academic performance and future of her 14-year-old daughter, Barbara. She invests a lot of her time seeking information about instructional approaches and programs. Often as much as weekly, Mrs. Meyer sends you e-mail, telephones you, or stops at your school site to suggest new approaches to help her daughter with reading or to tell you about something she has instituted at home. At the upcoming IEP meeting, the team will be considering prevocational concerns and possible curriculum modifications.

FOR FURTHER READING

Entwisle, D. R. (1994). Subcultural diversity in American families. In L'Abate (Ed.), *Handbook of developmental family psychology and psychopathology* (pp. 132–156). New York: Wiley.

Harry, B., Kalyanpur, M., & Day, M. (1999). *Building cultural reciprocity with families: Case studies in special education.* Baltimore: Brookes.

Jordan, L., Reyes-Blanes, M. E., Peel, B. B., & Lane, H. B. (1998). Developing teacher–parent partnerships across cultures: Effective parent conferences. *Intervention in School and Clinic, 33*(3), 141–149.

Lynch, E. W. (1998). Developing cross-cultural competence. In E. W. Lynch & M. J. Hanson (Eds.), *Developing cross-cultural competence: A guide for working with young children and their families* (2nd ed). Baltimore: Brookes.

Parett, H. P., & Petch-Hogan, B. (2000). Approaching families: Facilitating culturally/linguistically diverse family involvement. *Teaching Exceptional Children, 32*(2), 4–10.

Rock, M. L. (2000). Parents as equal partners: Balancing the scales in IEP development. *Teaching Exceptional Children, 32*(6), 30–37.

Trumbull, E., Rothstein-Fisch, C., Greenfield, P. M., & Quiroz, B. (2001). *Bridging cultures between home and school: A guide for teachers.* Mahwah, NJ: Erlbaum.

Turnbull, A. P., & Turnbull, H. R. (2001). *Families, professionals, and exceptionality: Collaborating for empowerment* (4th ed.). Upper Saddle River, NJ: Merrill/Prentice Hall.

11

Difficult Interactions

Connections

In Chapter 5 you learned that problem solving is the most fundamental interaction process. In this chapter, you will explore the more specialized problem solving that occurs in resolving conflict and responding to resistance. The skills you have learned throughout this textbook, particularly for communication (Chapters 2, 3, and 4), are the means through which you can constructively manage difficult interactions.

Learner Objectives

After reading this chapter you will be able to:

1. Define *conflict* and *resistance*.
2. Appreciate the benefits that can occur when conflict and resistance are addressed in a respectful and productive manner.
3. Explain why conflict and resistance should be expected by special services professionals in today's schools.
4. Describe three major causes of conflict.
5. Explain the five response styles professionals typically use during interactions in which conflict occurs.
6. Outline the principles of negotiation as a strategy for addressing conflict.
7. Describe causes of resistance.
8. Recognize indicators of resistance.
9. Outline persuasion strategies that can be used to respond to resistance.

INTRODUCTION

Have you ever experienced a situation similar to one of these?

- You call the technology coordinator to ask for a copy of a new program to be put on your computer. The coordinator explains to you that you are welcome to have a copy, but that the district's policy is that you must first attend a one-hour after-school workshop on its use. You reply that you are very adept at using the computer and undoubtedly can figure out how to operate the program without having to take the workshop. The technology coordinator is sympathetic, but says that the program will only be installed after you attend the after-school session.
- The parents of a student refuse to give permission for an assessment, despite the student's failing grades. You are a member of the special services team that agrees the student should be considered for possible eligibility for special education services.
- You are meeting with your teaching assistant (TA) to discuss how to use the newly installed software to adapt instruction for a student with a mild cognitive disability with whom the assistant works in a general education setting. The assistant agrees with everything you say, but asks few questions. Two days later, the classroom teacher asks when you are going to meet with the TA because it's a shame to have all that software going unused in the classroom.
- You arrange a meeting with the assistant principal to discuss scheduling issues for next year. She cancels it at the last minute. You reschedule. She arrives, stating that she really can't meet because a crisis has occurred. You reschedule. She doesn't come at the scheduled time. You decide that for some reason the assistant principal does not want to discuss scheduling with you.

Each of these incidents and many others like them occur in schools each day. Some are relatively trivial and mostly annoying. Others concern the fundamental decisions made about students' educational needs. The first two scenarios are examples of conflict. The latter two are examples of resistance. In this chapter you will learn more about both of these difficult interactions and how to respond to them. Both conflict and resistance are natural occurrences in collaboration, but depending on your response to them, they can either enhance collaboration or impede it.

UNDERSTANDING CONFLICT

Conflict has been defined by numerous authors (e.g., Barsky, 2000; Capozzoli, 1999; Littlejohn & Domenici, 2001; Melamed & Reiman, 2000). The definitions offered tend to vary based on the theoretical perspective of the author

(Bell & Forde, 1999; Dalton, 1999; Isenhart & Spangle, 2000). For example, some view conflict as a situation that occurs when one party perceives that his or her status is no longer equitable to that of another party. Others see it as the result of attributions that some individuals assign to others. For our discussion, **conflict** can be defined as a struggle that occurs when individuals, interdependent with others, perceive that those others are interfering with their goal attainment. If you review the first two examples in the chapter introduction, you should be able to easily identify participants' needs and the perceived interference.

Traditionally, school professionals have been uncomfortable addressing conflict. In fact, Barsky (2000) notes that when compared to other professions such as business, law, and psychology, education has not evolved a systematic means of considering conflict as part of the work environment nor developed models for resolving it. Educators were particularly successful at avoiding conflict when school culture emphasized isolation. Now, however, it is unlikely that conflict can be avoided. The same approach that Tjosvold (1987) uses to analyze why conflict is inevitable in business settings can be applied to traditional schools to explain why this is so. First, each individual in traditional schools had clearly delineated tasks to accomplish and did these without relying to any great extent on others. As we discussed in Chapter 1, this picture accurately described special services providers, too. In today's schools, this isolation and delineation of individuals' tasks is outdated. Increasingly, staff members are expected to work together, and thus they are more likely to experience conflict just because they are in closer proximity (Cornille, Pestle, & Vanwy, 1999; Wood, 1998). An example of this happens on teams: When professionals from several disciplines with different frames of reference are making decisions about student needs, they are likely to differ occasionally about desired outcomes.

Second, the traditional value system of schools tended to downplay emotions and keep school somewhat impersonal. Emerging trends, however, support schools being nurturing environments for students and staff alike (Lee & Barnett, 1994). As more needs are expressed, conflict is likely to emerge, since meeting some individuals' needs can interfere with meeting the needs of others. For example, this may occur as professionals request smaller caseloads in order to implement innovative programs.

A third reason conflict is increasingly common in schools is that leadership approaches have changed (Kosmoski & Pollack, 2000). In traditional schools, principals were considered effective when they were strongly directive in school decision making. Now, however, participatory management approaches are preferred (Lambert, 1998). The resulting increased staff involvement in decision making also increases the opportunities for conflicts. For example, when special services staff gather to write mission statements or outline long-term plans for program development, they often find conflict integral to the activity.

Because you are likely to experience at least some conflict in your professional role, you should also understand how it can be beneficial (e.g., Bickmore, 1998; Margolis, 1999). By itself, conflict is neither good nor bad. *You* determine whether it will have positive or negative outcomes. Consider these potentially positive results from conflict.

1. Decisions made after addressing a conflict are often of high quality because of the intense effort invested in discussing perspectives and generating alternatives.

2. Professionals implementing decisions emerging from conflict are likely to have a strong sense of ownership for the decisions and for the commitment to carry them out.

3. Conflict typically causes professionals to sharpen their thinking about their points of view so that they can clearly communicate them. The result is a more carefully reasoned discussion that often includes a wider range of ideas and options.

4. Often, professionals who successfully manage conflict develop more open, trusting relationships with one another. This facilitates their subsequent interactions.

5. Practice in effectively communicating during conflict can make it easier to address future conflict situations.

Notice that we are not saying that interactions with conflict are simple or enjoyable; in fact, they are complex and often stressful (Kosmoski & Pollack, 2001). But conflict does not have to be viewed as exclusively negative. If you look upon it

As professionals work more closely with one another in schools, conflict is more likely to occur.

as an opportunity, it will be one. And expanding your understanding of why conflict occurs and how it can be managed will help you to view it this way.

Causes of Conflict

When you examine conflicts you experience in your professional role, you might identify different reasons why conflict occurs. We categorize these by the interaction of the goals of the individuals who are involved (Maurer, 1991).

Conflict between Individuals with Different Goals

One major cause of conflict occurs when two individuals want different outcomes but must settle for the same outcome (Brooks, 2001). For example, in a suburban school district, team members and parents disagree about the mission of a proposed program to include students with moderate disabilities. Some school professionals believe that few students will be able to be integrated because they cannot meet academic and social expectations. Others believe that the program's primary goal should be making any modifications that are needed in order to include all students for most of each school day. Some parents are not in favor of inclusion; they prefer the current service delivery system with limited mainstreaming. Others want their children with typical peers all day.

Each of the groups in this example wants a different outcome concerning the inclusive program; they have different goals. However, when a decision is made about the program, all the groups must abide by those guidelines. Only one group's goal can be attained. Other common examples of conflict between individuals with different goals include disagreements between parents and school professionals about the amount of service a student will receive and disagreements among professionals about how special education services should be arranged in their school. What additional examples of conflicts occurring for this reason have you observed in your professional role?

Conflict between Individuals with the Same Goals

The second major cause of conflict occurs when professionals all have the same goal, but not all of them can access it (e.g., DeVoe, 1999). The master school schedule offers an example of this cause of conflict. In a local high school, the master schedule is created by first blocking in the academic courses, then the vocational and special subjects, and finally the special education classes. However, with more students with disabilities enrolled in core academic classes, the special education teachers encounter problems arranging services. They request that the scheduling of special education classes occur immediately after the academic classes and before others. The special subject teachers argue that far more students are affected by art, music, and physical education classes and that those classes should thus have a higher priority. The teachers of the honors classes ask that other classes be arranged so that students who attend classes at the local university in the afternoons are not penalized.

In this example, the various parties have the same goal: receiving priority treatment in the scheduling process. However, when one group is given priority, the others cannot have it. One group is likely to be dissatisfied with the resolution of this conflict. You have probably witnessed or participated in many similar conflicts, such as when only two individuals could go to a professional conference and several requested to attend, when a position in a preferred school opened and several individuals requested a transfer, and so on. Scarce resources often result in competing goal conflicts (Morris & Su, 1999).

Conflict within Individuals

One additional cause of conflict is an internal discrepancy that you perceive within your own goals. We mention this cause of conflict for completeness, but this is an *intrapersonal* dilemma that does not necessarily affect others, although it can pose a very serious job stressor for special educators (Miller, Brownell, & Smith, 1999). For example, suppose you are responsible for scheduling a student for 60 minutes per week of direct services complemented by systematic consultation with his teacher. You know that you should not schedule the student for three such 60-minute periods each week, but you also believe strongly that by doing so you could deliver higher-quality services that would better meet the needs of the student. You delay finalizing your schedule for several days while you worry about the appropriate ethical decision to make. Internal causes of conflict such as these are extremely common in schools where professionals are changing their roles and where expectations for their services are evolving rapidly.

Intrapersonal conflict may cause unclear communication that negatively affects professional interactions. As you discuss the student with the teacher, for example, you may inadvertently convey the message that you believe the student should receive more intense direct services. If you do this while communicating that indirect services are the most appropriate approach, the teacher may wonder which message is accurate. If this same student is discussed at a team meeting, your internal conflict could even lead to interpersonal conflict. Although you agreed in a previous meeting that the team's recommendation for service was appropriate, you may vacillate in your opinion about the service's appropriateness and experience unanticipated disagreements with the teacher.

The Influence of Organizational Variables

Understanding the causes of conflict provides a framework for identifying and managing conflict situations; however, other factors interact with these causes to affect the frequency and intensity of conflicts in your school setting. One factor particularly important for school professionals concerns organizational variables.

School Administration and Organization

The conflict you encounter is influenced significantly by the organization and administration of your school (Goldman, 1998; Kosmoski & Pollack, 2000). For example your principal's leadership style affects conflict. If the principal tends to use a laissez-faire style, you and your colleagues may find yourselves in conflict with one another for scarce resources. Without leadership to set guidelines on the distribution of resources, you may disagree with their allocation and compete with one another for them.

Another cause of conflict in schools is lack of clarity in procedures (Isenhart & Spangle, 2000). For example, some professionals believe that permission to attend a staff development conference is to be given by the principal. Others know that the director of special education is responsible for paying the registration fees, and so they believe that the director must give permission. Various staff members contact these two individuals. In the confusion, more people initially receive approval to attend than funds exist to support. Some professionals express anger when they are later told that they cannot attend, and they question how attendees were selected from those who applied to attend.

Communication Patterns

Another critical organizational variable that affects conflict is the pattern of communication among the various components of the organization (Jehn, 2000). There are many different types of dysfunctional communication that create conflict situations. One type occurs when similar information is not available to all individuals. For example, the school psychologists and social workers receive information that the procedures for conducting multidisciplinary team meetings are changing, but the special education teachers do not receive this information. At a subsequent team meeting, the special education teachers challenge the change in procedures initiated by the social worker and question whether the change is mandatory or optional. Because the communication was dysfunctional, a conflict was caused.

Another dysfunctional communication pattern that affects the likelihood of conflict occurs when information is conveyed differently by the individuals who communicate with the same staff members (Kruk, 1997). You experience this when you attend a meeting with all the other members of your discipline and learn a new piece of information about how to write information on IEPs. A week later, you attend a meeting for all special services providers, and a different set of instructions is given on the same topic. Shortly after these meetings, several staff members experience conflict about the correct procedure for IEPs. Their differences are attributable to the conflicting information they received about the change.

Conflict Response Styles

The next component in learning to understand and respond to conflict concerns the style you are likely to use when participating in a conflict interaction. Figure 11.1 visually represents common conflict response styles. Notice that the styles vary along two dimensions: concern for others and concern for self. Avoidance has the least amount of both these characteristics, collaboration has the

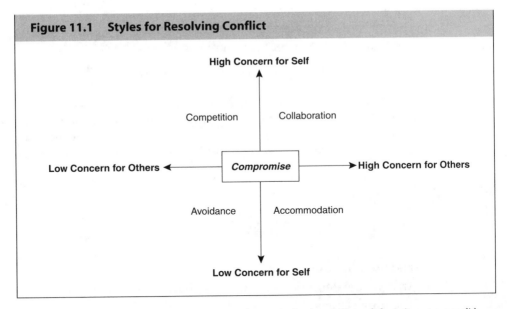

Figure 11.1   Styles for Resolving Conflict

Source: From Guilar, J. D. (2001). The interpersonal communication skills workshop *(transparency slide 3.9). New York: Amacom. Based on R. Kilmann & K. Thomas. (1975). Interpersonal conflict-handling behaviors as a reflection of Jungian personality dimensions.* Psychological Reports, 37, *971–980.*

greatest amount of each, and compromise has roughly equal, moderate amounts of both types of concern (Thomas & Kilmann, 1974). You can assess your style using the *Conflict Management Style Survey* included at the end of this chapter.

Most people have a preferred style for responding to conflict (Rudawsky & Lundgren, 1999). As each style is explained on the following pages, keep in mind that no style is entirely positive or negative. Depending on the situations in which a style is used, it has both merits and drawbacks.

Competitive Style

Some individuals address conflict using a competitive style. This style sometimes is associated with the use of power, as people who use it might attempt to over-power others. Their goal tends to be winning, regardless of the potential negative repercussions of their strategy.

A competitive conflict management style might be desirable when ethical issues are at stake or when you are certain that you are right. Occasionally, you may use this style when a decision must be made for which you alone have responsibility. The disadvantages of this style relate to its inappropriate use: If you frequently compete during conflict, others may stop interacting with you in a meaningful way. Too much use of a competitive style can seriously damage collaborative relationships. Also, few issues in schools have an absolute "right" solution; most are a matter of interpretation. If you often compete because you know you are right, you may be perceived by others as rigid and directive.

PERSPECTIVES ON DIVERSITY 11.1

Cultural Competence in Difficult Interactions

Although being aware of cultural differences and respecting others' values and priorities is important in all adult interactions, it is particularly important when conflict occurs. The following factors may affect how individuals from various cultural groups perceive conflict and how they wish to resolve it:

- The importance and legitimacy of preserving harmony
- The importance of face-saving
- The value of being other than confrontative or forthright
- The systemic roots of conflict and the need for systemic change
- The significance of time stretching far into the past and the future
- The usefulness of time in easing conflict
- An inclusive definition of parties (including extended family, for example)
- The importance of healing
- The significance of the differences between high- and low-context cultures
- The significance of the differences between individualist and collectivist cultures
- The importance of symbolism and ritual
- Visual and nonverbal cues
- The importance of involving "elders," gatekeepers, and "wise ones" in conflict resolution processes
- The legitimacy of advice giving in some cultural contexts
- The honor attached to indirectness and subtlety in various cultural contexts
- The lack of power experienced by members of some groups over a long period of time, such that techniques to "balance power" may be insufficient
- Varying needs for formality or informality
- The meaning of a contract or written agreement; this is considered evidence of bad faith in some cultural contexts and a necessity in others
- Different communication norms and styles in different cultural frameworks

  How might each of these factors influence your interactions with other professionals? Parents?

  How could you learn about another person's cultural preferences regarding how to interact during a conflict?

  What should you do if you recognize during the middle of an interaction that you are responding to a colleague or parent without cultural competence?

From LeBaron, M. (1997). Mediation, conflict resolution, and multicultural reality: Culturally competent practice (pp. 315–335). In E. Kruk (Ed.), *Mediation and conflict resolution in social work and the human services.* Chicago: Nelson Hall.

Avoidance Style

Individuals who prefer avoidance usually try to ignore the discrepancy between their own goals and those of others. They deal with conflict by turning away from it. If you have ever participated in a meeting in which an issue needed to be brought to the surface but everyone appeared to have tacitly agreed not to discuss it, you were experiencing avoidance. Notice that in this situation the conflict is not being resolved and may continue to plague the group.

In some instances, avoidance is advisable. If a conflict is extremely serious and emotion laden, temporary avoidance may enable the individuals involved to think about their positions and participate more constructively. Similarly, if there is not enough time to adequately address a conflict or if the issue is relatively inconsequential, avoidance may be the preferred strategy. However, using avoidance may create difficulties in your collaborative relationships. For example, if you and a colleague disagree on a teaching technique, avoiding discussion of the topic can exacerbate the conflict. Avoidance is a seductive strategy because it gives the appearance that all is well; its hidden danger is that a situation may become more conflicted by inaction.

Accommodative Style

Individuals who use an accommodative style set aside their own needs in order to ensure that others' needs are met. Their characteristic response to conflict is to give in. Occasionally, special services providers use this style because they believe it may help to initiate or preserve positive relationships with colleagues.

An accommodative style can be beneficial when the issue is relatively unimportant or when you cannot alter the situation. Accommodating has a distinct advantage in that it brings conflict to a quick close, enabling you to turn your attention to other issues. The drawbacks of accommodating include the risk of feeling as though others are taking advantage of you, the potential that the issue is one for which you have the best answer, and the possible devaluing of your ideas when you quickly accommodate on an important matter. Generally, accommodating can be especially appropriate for professionals who need to overcome the tendency to try to win every disagreement; it is often inappropriate for those who feel powerless in their professional relationships.

Compromising Style

Many school professionals use a compromising style in responding to conflict. They give up some of their ideas related to an issue while insisting that others do the same. They keep some of their ideas and go along with some of the ideas others have proposed. The result typically is an outcome that may not exactly meet everyone's needs, but is acceptable to all.

Because compromising is a style whose strength is expedience, it is often appropriate when limited time is available to manage a conflict. It is also useful when the issue at hand is not especially problematic and when two competitive individuals have a conflict. Although compromise seems like an ideal style since it infers that part of each individual's goal is achieved, it, too, has drawbacks. For example, sometimes when typically competitive professionals decide to compromise, they may feel that they have partly "lost" and so may be somewhat dissatisfied. As a result, additional conflict may occur later. The compromised resolution of an issue can be a bit like the agreement reached for a seaside vacation planned by two friends, one of whom wanted to go to the East Coast while the other wanted to go to the West Coast: They ended up in Kansas.

Collaborative Style

Collaboration in the context of responding to conflict is consistent with the conceptual foundation laid earlier in this text. Use of a collaborative style requires commitment to the defining elements we described, as well as to the emergent characteristics of collaboration. It often includes developing a completely new alternative to resolve the conflict situation. For example, a collaborative response to the vacation example might be for the friends to decide that the vacation was not the issue at all. Since both were looking for a relaxing experience near water, they could decide to spend a week in a lakeside retreat only 50 miles from their hometown.

Although collaboration has many positive aspects, in conflict situations it is not always the preferred approach. It is time-consuming, it requires that certain defining elements be in place, and it can only be undertaken as professionals learn about and come to trust one another. Thus, collaboration is sometimes not even an option for addressing conflict.

By learning to monitor the style you use to respond to conflict in your professional interactions, you will grow in your knowledge about how you handle such situations. Further, by knowing what causes conflict, understanding conflict response styles, and learning specific strategies such as those described below, you will be more successful in managing difficult interactions.

Resolving Conflict through Negotiation

Negotiation is a conflict management technique that has a long history of success in business settings (Bazerman & Neale, 1992; Cloke & Goldsmith, 2000) that can also help you resolve school conflict. Negotiation can be used in many types of conflict, as illustrated in this example of a principal and a special education teacher deciding on materials needed in a new classroom:

Principal: What are your needs for materials for your room?

Teacher: I've reviewed the records of my students and looked through the catalogues. I have a list here of the materials I need to begin the program, but I would like to be able to request an additional $500 for instructional supplies once I have the opportunity to work with the students. Also, I have concerns about equipment. I would like to have three computers in the classroom.

Principal: [*looking at the list and her notes*] I'd like to be able to provide all these items, but it's just not possible within the budget. How about if I managed to get funding for the top 20 prioritized items on this list and agreed that we would discuss additional resources next year?

Teacher: That's a problem. I'm concerned that in a new classroom I'll need more than the items with the highest priority. And the computer issue is important to me.

Principal: Perhaps we can resolve that one. You already have one computer. There are three loaner computers in the learning center. We could locate one in your classroom; the only time you would have to share it would be when the others were in use. That shouldn't happen too often. Then you have two computers, and you could use one of the laptops as a third.

Teacher: That's fine. But what about the other items?

Principal: I simply can't promise you the amount of money you are requesting for materials and supplies. What would be a reasonable solution?

Teacher: What if you furnished the initial materials and I prepared a request for the parent–teacher organization to assist in supplying additional materials I might need later in the year, especially computer software?

Principal: I can do that. I would want to work with you on the proposal though.

Teacher: Great! Then we've agreed you'll fund the initial list of needed supplies, I'll borrow the computer, and we'll approach the PTO about additional needs.

The key to successful negotiation, whether it is formal or informal, is to keep in mind that the object of the interaction is not for one person to win while the other loses. In their extensive work on this topic, Ury and his colleagues (Fisher, Ury, & Patton, 1997; Ury, 1991; Ury, Brett, & Goldberg, 1988) have derived these principles for successful negotiation:

1. Focus on issues, not people, whenever you experience conflict. Instead of saying, "You don't understand how changing the intervention will affect the entire class," you might say, "The strategy we're discussing now is problematic because it has the potential to affect classroom routine negatively." The former makes the disagreement an adversarial situation based on people; the latter acknowledges disagreement but anchors it on the proposed intervention instead of on the person who proposed it.

2. To the greatest extent possible, keep the conflict focused on issues that have the potential to be agreed upon. This reminds you as well as the others that you have a common ground from which to work to manage the conflict. For example, it is often more constructive to address specific interventions or approaches than to discuss individuals' underlying beliefs about how students should receive education services. The former can be addressed; in most cases, the latter cannot.

3. Reduce the emotional component of the conflict. If the issue in conflict has raised strong emotional responses, you may find that it is not possible

to proceed and temporary avoidance is needed. However, you can also sometimes defuse emotions by responding positively to others' negative comments, not responding to comments that might cause you to become angry, and by acknowledging others' feelings.

4. We would be remiss if we did not include a final strategy: the option for you to adapt to the issue or, if possible, to exit the situation. At some point it becomes self-defeating to continue to try to address a conflict if the other person does not view the matter as an issue or if you cannot influence the conflict situation. Resolving the matter within yourself so that you no longer fret about it may be the most viable option. If that is not possible and the issue is critical, you may choose to leave the situation or even the school setting. For example, a student with a moderate cognitive disability is transitioning from an early childhood special education program to first grade. The first-year special education teacher believes strongly that the child should spend most of the day with nondisabled peers. The first-grade teachers are adamant that they do not know how to meet the child's needs. The principal does not want to anger the first grade teachers, and so is tending to agree with their point of view. The parent is not strongly advocating for the included arrangement. In spite of her repeated efforts using superb communication skills and in light of so many factors constraining placement in a typical classroom, the special educator might decide that she should simply keep quiet about her beliefs. If this pattern of making decisions about children is common, she may decide that she would prefer to work in another school or another district.

Consider how each of the foregoing ideas can be applied to the exchange between the teacher and the principal at the beginning of this section. If you use these principles for effective negotiation and think of negotiation as specialized problem solving, you can use steps such as those in Putting Ideas Into Practice 11.1 to respond to conflict positively and constructively.

Resolving Conflict through Mediation

You have probably experienced formal negotiation if you have been involved in the discussion of teacher contracts through your local professional association. Perhaps you have informally negotiated with colleagues concerning the use of planning time or the clarification of roles in a co-taught class. However, what should you do if negotiation fails to resolve the conflict? What strategies remain when you cannot simply retreat from the situation and are not satisfied with the current situation? A specialized form of negotiation, *mediation* is a process in which a third party who is neutral in regard to the issue at hand guides the individuals in conflict through a voluntary discussion with the goal of settling the dispute (Covey, 1999; Isenhart & Spangle, 2000; Tamir, 1999). Some authors (e.g., Dana, 2001) even propose that professionals who study mediation and come to understand it and value its role in conflict resolution can learn to mediate even as one of the parties involved in a conflict.

PUTTING IDEAS INTO PRACTICE 11.1

Effective Negotiation

In addition to understanding the principles on which successful negotiation is based, you can use these steps to guide your negotiation to a positive conclusion:

♦ Understand your own motivation and that of others. What are the motivations of those involved in the conflict? Is the basis of the conflict a value difference? Is it an issue of limited resources and the stress caused by the situation? Is it a matter of differing opinions about interventions?

♦ Clarify the issues. If you and the other person(s) in a conflict do not have a mutual understanding of the issues, you are unlikely to resolve them.

♦ Set your expectations. This requires examining your ideal solution to the conflict and then tempering it with your understanding of motivations as well as other factors influencing the situation. This step is called *goal setting*.

♦ Discuss each issue involved in the conflict. Sometimes it is tempting to have a general discussion of all the issues related to the conflict. The result can be unclear communication and, sometimes, additional conflict.

♦ Make and respond to offers. This is the part of negotiation that includes give-and-take among participants.

♦ Monitor for ethics and integrity. Negotiation in conflict situations can only be successful if you work in good faith. If you withhold information or manipulate others' words, you may worsen the situation instead of improving it. At the same time, you should be aware of the ethical issues involved in serving the needs of students with disabilities. Your goal for concluding a negotiation should be to enable everyone to "save face," while at the same time resolving the dilemma in a professional manner.

Consider the situation mentioned above in which you and a colleague are unable to resolve your differences of opinion about the appropriate role for each professional in the co-taught class. The general education teacher is not comfortable with another adult contributing during large-group instruction and prefers that you remain seated and quiet during such times. You maintain that you are highly educated and experienced and that, with less large-group instruction and more use of small groups, you can actively participate in instruction and better provide a range of supports and services to students in the classroom. At an impasse, perhaps you ask your assistant principal to meet with both of you to discuss possible solutions. Alternatively, perhaps your school district employs a special education coordinator, a nonsupervisory staff member who has the responsibility of fostering collaboration and ensuring that students with special needs receive an appropriate education. This individual also might serve in the role of mediator.

In some situations, mediation is a constructive process for resolving conflict. IDEA requires that it be offered to parents.

You might also be involved in mediation in a more formal context. As you know, the reauthorization of IDEA in 1997 included the provision that mediation must be offered to parents who are in conflict with schools concerning their children's special education (Margolis, 1999). Although mediation may not be a successful strategy when the disputed issues concern a legal interpretation of the law or personnel changes (Fiedler, 2000), it has several advantages over due process hearings. For example, mediation is considered a much less formal approach that may prevent an adversarial climate from developing. Further, it is focused on the future, it emphasizes clear and direct communication, it keeps control of the process in the hands of the parties directly involved, and it is far less expensive than a due process hearing (Fiedler, 2000). Of course, if parents do not wish to engage in mediation, or if school professionals have a negative disposition toward the conflict situation and the potential of mediation, it is not the preferred option (Rhoades, Arnold, & Jay, 2001; Zerkin, 1999).

Many, many sources of information exist regarding how to successfully mediate during conflict. Some of the most helpful suggestions include these (Barsky, 2000):

1. In any type of mediation, preparation is the key. Whether this involves understanding the context in which a conflict is occurring, the frames of reference of participants, or the impact of the outcome on each individual, an effective mediator has a solid foundation of understanding from the very start.

2. Mediation begins with an orientation, that is, an explanation to all participants of the ground rules. Often, mediators emphasize the impor-

tance of clear communication, the priority given to making the situation feel "safe" to everyone, and the optimistic intent to resolve the conflict.

3. Early in mediation, each party explains his or her perspective, and the specific issues that comprise the conflict are articulated. The rationale for this process is that each person has a unique perspective regarding the conflict and that sharing perspectives sometimes helps to generate solutions.

4. The most critical step of mediation occurs when needs and interests are explored; each party looks for areas of shared needs and interests that might be elements of resolution. If this stage of mediation is not successful, the process is likely to flounder.

5. Once interests are identified, the strategies of negotiation and problem solving are used. An effective mediator will at this point subtly remind participants of the costs of failing to reach an agreement.

6. Once some type of agreement is reached, it should be clearly articulated, either in writing or through an oral point-by-point summary completed during the meeting. This prevents miscommunication.

7. Finally, it is often helpful in mediation for a follow-up meeting to be scheduled so that progress can be reviewed, the current situation assessed, and feedback obtained from the involved parties.

If you think about your roles and responsibilities in schools, you may have numerous opportunities to function as a mediator. You might first think of taking this role in assisting students to resolve disagreements. However, you might also serve as a mediator in a conflict among members of a multidisciplinary team, a grade-level, or a department team. You could mediate when parents of a student with special needs have a conflict with a teacher or specialist. Finally, you can use the thinking of mediation in your own interactions with your colleagues and the parents/families of the students with whom you work.

UNDERSTANDING RESISTANCE

Resistance has been a topic of concern in many fields, including business and the helping professions as well as education (e.g., Fairhurst & Sarr, 1997; Gardner & Cary, 1999; Kampwirth, 1999; Wagner, 1998). It most typically occurs as a response to an interpersonal change or an organizational change that has a personal impact. Karp (1984) provided a succinct but accurate characterization of **resistance** when he defined it as the ability to not get what is not wanted from the environment. The use of negatives in the definition is critical: Resistance only occurs in response to a perceived impending change. If no change exists, resistance vanishes.

The use of negatives in the definition, however, should not lead you to conclude that resistance itself is undesirable. In fact, the opposite is true. Resistance is a defense mechanism that prevents us from undertaking change that is too risky for our sense of safety. In addition, resistance sometimes leads to an appropriate decision not to participate in an activity or change. The concern in professional relationships arises when resistance becomes a barrier to effective interactions and needed innovation (Wade, Welch, & Jensen, 1994). Think about the issues that contribute to resistance in these two examples:

◆ The team of middle school teachers is discussing the options for an upcoming field trip. Mr. Matthews, the science teacher, has an idea he would like the group to consider. He says, "I've been thinking about the opportunities for teaching concepts of physics at an amusement park—you know, riding the roller coaster to explore the effects of gravity. I need to do some more checking, but going to an amusement park would accomplish two goals: keeping the students motivated for the spring and making science concepts come to life. Another team member immediately replies, "Right. There is not a chance that you'll catch me on a roller coaster. I've seen too many news stories recently about problems with safety on them; just thinking about it makes me queasy. And if we go to a park, there'll be too much pressure to ride. I don't like the idea at all."

◆ Ms. Hill, the school psychologist, is meeting with Mr. Neal, the fifth-grade teacher, shortly before the holidays about a behavioral contract for Reggie, a student with behavior disorders, who is inattentive and has been swearing at the teacher and other students. As Ms. Hill explains the contract as a possible intervention, Mr. Neal comments, "You know, I don't mind having Reggie in my class. But I don't know about this contract idea. It's not fair to the other kids to give Reggie special treatment. I predict I'll get parent phone calls about this." After more discussion, Mr. Neal reluctantly agrees to try the intervention.

A week later, Ms. Hill stops by Mr. Neal's classroom to check on Reggie. "How's the contract working for Reggie?"

"Well . . ."

"What's going on?"

"Actually," says Mr. Neal, "I tried it for two days and it just wasn't fitting into my classroom routine. Besides, Reggie probably didn't like being singled out. We need to change it, but for now, with the holidays coming, I just don't have the time to attend to this. Let's talk after the beginning of the year."

In the first example, the resistance to a trip to the amusement park is fairly straightforward: The teacher appears to be concerned about the *physical* safety of the proposed adventure. In the second example, the resistance is more difficult to discern clearly, but it is still related to safety: Mr. Neal's response might be interpreted as meaning that he is concerned with his *psychological* safety. Perhaps he is unfamiliar with the contracting approach Ms. Hill proposed, and he does not want to let her know this. Perhaps he is overwhelmed by the pressures of his job (which might include a new math curriculum, an overcrowded room, or several students with extraordinary needs), and he simply cannot manage one more demand.

Given the amount and pace of change currently taking place in schools, it is not surprising to find resistance common. And when you reflect on the changes occurring in the education of students with disabilities and other special needs, you should conclude that resistance is likely among special services providers as well as between special services providers and general education staff. The fact that many school changes result in increased adult–adult interactions only compounds the issue, because such interactions increase the likelihood that each individual's resistance will be known and will affect others.

Causes of Resistance

Although many causes of resistance have been described in the professional literature (e.g., Kampwirth, 1999; Piersal & Gutkin, 1983; Wickstrom & Witt, 1993), they can be summarized as addressing just one critical concept: Resistance is an emotional response based on a rational or irrational fear or concern related to whatever change is proposed or occurring (Carner & Alpert, 1995). These fears may pertain to (a) the change itself; (b) the impact of the change on the resistant person; (c) other persons initiating, participating in, or affected by the change; or (d) homeostasis.

Concerns about the Proposed Change

One common source of resistance is professionals' and parents' perceptions of the anticipated outcomes associated with a change. For example, parents may be resistant to moving their children's separate special education class into the local school; they believe that their children are receiving excellent services and should not be exposed to neighborhood school problems.

Another example of fear related to the change itself may be the philosophy or value system associated with the change. If you are a speech and language therapist who believes strongly in the value of therapy offered in separate settings, then the plan to have you work with students primarily in classes may cause you to be resistant. Alternatively, if you believe that integrative therapy should be the standard in your field, you are likely to be resistant to a plan in which you will provide only articulation therapy in a separate clinical setting. For general education teachers, this type of resistance may arise when considering adapting their learning materials and performance standards for students with disabilities. In each example, resistance is attached to a belief system that is associated with a specific change. This form of resistance is particularly likely to occur when change is not clearly explained.

Concerns about the Personal Impact of the Change

According to Fiedler (2000), fear about the personal impact of change is the category into which most professional resistance falls and includes the following issues:

1. Some individuals faced with changing their professional functioning are afraid of failing. They may anticipate that they do not have the skills to participate in the change, and they may perceive that they cannot acquire them.

2. Some professionals fear the frustration that may occur while learning new skills and practices. Whenever changes are undertaken in activities, programs, or services, professionals require time to adjust their practices. Because time is a luxury that simply cannot be afforded in many schools, however, they often are expected to assimilate change rapidly and to immediately function effectively, sometimes beyond the point of reasonable expectations.

3. Personal fear about change also relates to losing autonomy. Many school professionals are accustomed to completing their job responsibilities with little input from others. When a change is proposed, particularly one that appears to threaten this autonomy, fear sometimes results. Resistance is an expected outcome.

Concerns about Others Involved in the Change

The third category of concerns that may lead to resistance focuses on the other individuals. First, concern may be directed at the person initiating the change. Have you ever decided before hearing about a new strategy, service, or program that you probably did not want to participate just because you had a negative perception of the person whose idea it was? Perhaps you did not respect that individual, experienced a great deal of miscommunication with him, or had discrepant personal styles. It should be noted that this is another example of resistance that, in some cases, has a strongly rational basis.

The second major type of concern included in this category is the threat of change in your relationships with others. If you participate in a change, it may affect how other staff members view you and your status with them. For example, a newly hired special education teacher at the secondary level is asked by the special education director to begin developing a plan for co-teaching with the basic skills teachers. The basic skills teachers are opposed to the co-teaching idea, and the committee they were supposed to have formed to work on the project has met only once. If you were the special education teacher, how would you respond? One approach would be to develop the program alone, hoping to positively influence colleagues in the process. Another would be to let the basic skills teachers know about the request and then to collaborate with them to avoid meeting it. Even if this were not appropriate, the latter option might appeal to the special education teacher if he or she felt unaccepted by the other teachers and had concerns about how they would respond if the program were developed. This type of situation clearly has many alternative solutions. The point here is that the relationship issue may supersede others and lead to resistance.

Homeostasis

The tendency of some individuals and systems to prefer sameness to change is referred to as *homeostasis*. For individuals, once they become accustomed to a particular way of carrying out responsibilities, working with students, and otherwise fulfilling their professional obligations, they may be unable to consider alternative ways to do those tasks. The degree to which homeostasis plays a part in resistance varies greatly from person to person and with the nature of the change that is at issue.

Organizations also seek to maintain some level of homeostasis and in doing so may encourage resistance. In some school settings, it is considered the norm to resist *any* change, regardless of its source. We have worked in school settings in which staff members quickly stated that their schools were difficult places to initiate new programs because staff simply did not like change. Although this situation relates to individual homeostasis, it is distinguished from it because of its pervasiveness in the school's culture. Several staff in the school may be risk takers or change agents, but their individual characteristics are overshadowed by the norm.

Indicators of Resistance

Resistance often is indicated through subtle behaviors and can be difficult to clearly recognize. Most behaviors that indicate resistance have alternative, legitimate interpretations, but when examined closely, they actually function as means of avoiding change. Thus, in order to address resistance, you will need a clear picture of how resistance is likely to be manifested. The most common ways include (1) refusing to participate; (2) supporting a change with words but not actions; (3) displacing responsibility; (4) deferring change to a future time; and (5) relying on past practice. Each of these signals of resistance is presented with examples in Figure 11.2.

In considering signals of resistance, it is particularly important to look for patterns of behavior. Anyone can encounter a crisis that leads to the cancellation of a meeting. However, as with the assistant principal in the fourth opening vignette of this chapter, repeated cancellations could indicate resistance. Anyone could have a straightforward reason for delaying a change. However, repeated excuses may be an indicator of resistance. Your role in working with others is to distinguish between legitimate problems and resistance and to base your actions on such distinctions.

Assessing Whether to Address Resistance

The next consideration when you perceive resistance is to decide whether or not it should be addressed. Your deliberations should examine (1) the appropriateness of the resistance, (2) whether addressing it is warranted, and (3) others' commitment to change.

Determine Whether Resistance is an Appropriate Response

The concept that resistance is sometimes appropriate has already been mentioned, and overall you may have noticed that this chapter on resistance does not necessarily focus on making it go away. Instead, as you approach resistant interactions, you should first consider the situation from the other individual's point of view. If the change will place too great a burden on the person, resistance may be a positive reaction and should not be addressed. In general, if you remember

Figure 11.2	**Indicators of Resistance**
Indicator	**Explanation**
Refusing to participate	Response to change is "No thank you." Examples:
	I figure this is just a fad. By next year it'll be gone.
	I just can't deal with doing that right now. I have too many other responsibilities.
	I don't want to get involved with this issue. Please ask someone else.
Supporting without substance	Response to change is "puppies-on-the-dashboard" head nodding without meaning. Examples:
	Yeah—that's great.
	Okay—I see.
	That makes sense—uh-huh.
Displacing responsibility	Response to change is claiming others will not permit it. Examples:
	The other parents are going to complain.
	I understand that the state has said this is not legal.
	The principal doesn't allow it.
Deferring to a future time	Response to change is putting it off. Examples:
	[in September] Everything is so hectic with the start of the year. Let's give it a little time and then try it.
	[in November] The holidays are almost here and you know how disrupted the schedule gets.
Relying on past practice	Response to change is to call on tradition as a reason to retain the status quo. Examples:
	We've always done it this way.
	If it's not broken, don't fix it.
	This way has always been good enough for us.
	We can't just rush into this type of intervention. It's too different from what we're used to.

that addressing resistance should have as a goal respecting it, exploring it, and potentially (but not invariably) responding to it, you will be more effective in your professional relationships. Although our examples tend to make others the resistant people, also keep in mind a point made at the beginning of this chapter: We *all* resist, given the right circumstances.

Assess Whether Addressing Resistance is Warranted

Another consideration when deciding whether to respond to a resistant situation is the appropriateness of attempting to address it. The same questions presented in Chapter 5 for deciding whether to problem solve are applicable for resistance. In some instances, the best response to resistance, even if it is not rational, may be no response at all. For example, if a colleague is planning to leave her job at the end of the year, your efforts to address her resistance to a new technique may not be worth the effort. The same could be said for those who are transferring to other schools or retiring. Other situations that may not warrant addressing resistance are those in which administrative support is lacking or contextual variables (such as a lack of resources) make the proposed strategy unrealistic.

Consider the Extent of Others' Commitment to Change

Understanding the likelihood that others will change can assist you in gauging your own commitment to change. Individuals are more likely to participate in a change if they feel they have a moderate or low level of positive or negative feeling about the nature of the change (Fiedler, 2000). They are less likely to change if they have strong negative feelings about it. The implication is that change is less likely to be successful if offered when emotions are strong. A more constructive alternative would be to wait, if possible, until feelings are less intense and then use the strategies discussed in the following section.

Persuasion as a Strategy for Responding to Resistance

One critical strategy for addressing resistant situations is persuasion. **Persuasion** is your ability to convince another person to agree to your perception or plan regarding an issue or idea (Perloff, 1993). For example, you may be faced with the task of convincing a resistant colleague that change in the daily schedule is necessary and appropriate. Similarly, you may attempt to convince a parent that the educational services proposed by the team are in the best interests of the child.

Before considering a specific approach to persuasion, you should address the issue of personal qualities and their impact on persuasion (Raign & Sims, 1993). How do you think your colleagues perceive you? The answer to that question could be critical in understanding the extent to which you are able to persuade them. Individuals' personal qualities will in part determine whether they can convince others of their point of view. Kenton (1989) refers to these qualities as *credibility* and includes those presented in Figure 11.3.

Having positive personal persuasive qualities is only a prerequisite for using persuasion. Approaches for persuading are heavily influenced by theories that describe how individuals respond when faced with an idea or activity to which they are resistant (Shelby, 1986). For example, in a **behavioral approach** to persuasion the goal is to provide positive reinforcement to resistant individuals in order to convince them to change (Maital, 1996). This would occur if a teacher were offered a preferred classroom assignment in return for participating in a pilot co-teaching project.

A second theoretical orientation to persuasion is a **consistency approach,** which is based on the notion that individuals are more likely to change if they have a sense of cognitive dissonance (Festinger, 1957). For example, by suggesting to

Figure 11.3 **Personal Qualities Contributing to Credibility**	
Quality	**Examples**
Goodwill and fairness	Focused on the other person
	Concerned for the other person
	Unselfish
Expertise	Professionally prepared
	Experienced
	Qualified
	Competent
	Intelligent
Prestige	Rank
	Power
	Status
	Position
Self-presentation	Verbal ability
	Ability to "think on your feet"
	Similarity
	Dynamism
	Energy
	Confidence

Adapted from Kenton, S. B. (1989). Speaker credibility in persuasive business communication: A model which explains gender differences. Journal of Business Communication, 26, *143–157. Reprinted with permission.*

Ms. Boesche that she has already been successful with a student very much like the one she is currently expressing resistance about having in her class, you might plant a seed that eventually prompts her to be more accepting of the new student.

A **perceptual approach** is also considered a means for persuading others. Individuals applying this model recognize that individuals have a certain tolerance for change. If the proposed change is somewhat close to an activity a person is already comfortable doing, that person is more likely to accept the new activity than if it is perceived as radically different. For example, in discussing a new school initiative related to inclusive practices, a principal might explain that teachers in the school are already making many accommodations for students with special needs and that the initiative is simply an extension of work they are already doing.

Finally, a **functional approach** to persuasion suggests that the process of convincing someone to change must take into account adult learning characteristics. For example, if Ms. Schwartz complained that she dislikes the way students are constantly leaving the room to receive special services, you might suggest that she would prefer to have students stay in the room. This could acknowledge her desire for control over student movement and the sense of classroom community as well as creating an opportunity to discuss integrated, in-class services.

PUTTING IDEAS INTO PRACTICE 11.2

Using Communication Skills during Conflict

When you are faced with responding to conflict or resistance, you have the opportunity to use the communication skills you have learned to good advantage (Guilar, 2001). Consider this example: You have been trying to meet with a classroom teacher to follow up on a self-monitoring strategy you are trying to teach a student to use. The student is to keep an index card taped to her desk, and when she begins a requested task without making a comment out loud in class, she is to make a check on the card. In talking with the student, you realize that the teacher is not encouraging the student to use the strategy and sometimes seems to be going back to a pattern of confronting the student about callouts. In your conversation with the teacher, she claims that she is trying with the student, but that the student will not follow directions or accept guidance.

How might each of these aspects of positive communication help you at some point to talk to the teacher?

◆ *Frame of reference*
   When the teacher says, "I've been really careful about using the strategy and it's not working," what might the teacher mean?

◆ *Feedback and indirect question*
   You ask the teacher, "During the period when I had dropped by your class to observe Alesha using the strategy, I noticed that you asked her to not call out four times. I did not notice you direct her to the index card. I wonder if there is something about using the index card strategy that doesn't fit into your classroom routines?"

◆ *Presupposition*
   You ask the teacher, "In the two weeks that we've been trying this strategy in your class, what about it has been most effective? [after a reply] How does using the strategy break down?"

◆ *Open question*
   You ask the teacher, "What do you think we should do to make this strategy—or some other one that will accomplish the same purpose—more effective for Alesha and more workable for you?"

The knowledge base on theoretical approaches to persuasion leads to a number of suggestions for you to use in encouraging colleagues and others to change:

1. *Seek ways to provide incentives.* For special services providers, incentives could include a trade-off or reduction of workloads; for general education teachers they might involve assistance with classroom chores or the provision of paraprofessional assistance. If you think of any situation in

which you need to persuade others, you can probably identify incentives that could be offered to positively affect the outcome.

2. *Relate the proposed change issue to a positive image.* To many teachers, the word *change* is a negative stimulus; they immediately associate it with anxiety, stress, more work, and more meetings. One strategy for persuading others is to associate the change with a reduction of anxiety, work, and meetings. Obviously, this strategy is effective only to the extent that the reduction of workload can, in fact, be implemented.

3. *Provide opportunities for others to become familiar with the change through observation.* If a professional observes others successfully carrying out a change, he or she may sense it is feasible after all. For some educators, this could include visiting neighboring school districts where similar activities or services are offered. For others it may be just an observation period in a nearby colleague's classroom or therapeutic setting.

4. *Create discrepancies that can be brought to the attention of resistant individuals.* Imagine a history teacher who fears that a student with a disability will require too much of the teacher's attention. One strategy would be to arrange an informal meeting between the history teacher and another subject area teacher who has worked with the student and who can share the positive experiences the student had in a general education class. Knowing about the student's success creates a discrepancy and makes resistance less likely.

5. *Link the proposed change with the resolution of the discrepancy.* Persuasion involves more than simply creating dissonance; it also involves efforts to influence how the dissonance will be resolved. In the example just presented, the dissonance exists because of the history teacher's belief that the student cannot be successful and the other teacher's perspective that the student can be successful. To influence the history teacher to resolve the dissonance by agreeing the student could succeed, you might comment on the teacher's ability to work with other difficult students, the fact that he or she would be on the "cutting edge" for the district integration program and in compliance with emerging policy, and the satisfaction experienced by working with the student.

6. *Relate the change to others' knowledge and experience.* Keeping both the nature and the description of the proposed change within others' knowledge and experiential base is a basic strategy of persuasion. A simple illustration of this point concerns the use of technical vocabulary. If you have a strong background in behavioral approaches, you may tend to speak to others in the language of *reinforcers, extinction,* and *punishers.* If you change your language so that your message sounds more familiar to your colleagues—rewards, ignoring, and consequences, you may find that less resistance occurs.

7. *Propose changes within the value system of others.* This strategy is a powerful extension of the preceding strategy. Proponents of change should examine participants' value systems and tailor ideas to stay within those parameters.

Resistance to change is common among professionals and can be expressed in subtle or obvious ways.

8. *Gain public commitment.* One strategy for ensuring that a proposed change falls within individuals' tolerance levels is to obtain their overt commitment to the change. Once they have made such a commitment, they are more likely to try to expand their own levels of tolerance for the change. Public commitment raises significantly the probability of implementation.

9. *Involve others early in the planning stages.* Whether you are discussing a single intervention, a modification for a classroom, a program change, or the restructuring of an entire service delivery system, the change will be more readily accomplished if you include others in planning. Doing so enables you to be more responsive to others' needs. Change thus becomes less threatening, and the potential for resistance is decreased.

10. *Be sensitive to adult learning preferences.* As adults, certain conditions may make change easier for us. In fact, knowledge about adult learning is important when planning for change. Examples of adult learning preferences include incorporating ideas based on the life experiences of participants, using novelty to introduce an idea, and engaging participants in meaningful activities related to accomplishing the change. Although none of these techniques seems strongly persuasive, each has the potential to add enough appeal to the proposed change to make it attractive to the individuals affected by it.

11. *Clarify ownership of the task or activity.* Whenever people are working together toward a goal, they should specify how ownership will be assigned. If change is the issue, the more that individuals feel like they

have contributed to designing and implementing the change, the more likely it is that they will participate in it.

12. *Obtain and use feedback from participants.* Feedback is one type of information that participants can contribute to change. The obligation of professionals fostering change is to use this information in a meaningful way. For example, suppose you were working with a general education teacher on accommodations for a student with a mild disability. Before you discuss specific accommodations, you might ask what the classroom goals are, what the teacher's priorities are, and what approaches seem most suited to the class. Based on this input, the discussion of alternatives could proceed. In a second phase, the special educator and general educator should meet to discuss whether the accommodations are being successful. If the general education teacher mentions a problem, the appropriate response from the special education teacher is to explore how that feedback could be used to alter the arrangement. Counterproductive approaches would be for the special education teacher to defend the accommodation or explain how the teacher could make it more effective.

SUMMARY

As schools continue to emphasize collaboration among professionals, difficult interactions are likely to occur, often because of conflict or resistance. Conflict is any situation in which people perceive that others are interfering with their ability to meet their goals. Although school professionals, including special services providers, traditionally have tended to avoid conflict, it can be constructive and helpful. Conflict generally is caused when two individuals want different outcomes but must settle for the same one, when they want the same outcome but it cannot be available to both, or when one individual internally experiences conflicting reactions to a situation. These causes are influenced by a wide variety of organizational variables. Most individuals have a preferred style for responding to conflict, either competitive, avoiding, accommodative, compromising, or collaborative. Each of these has advantages and drawbacks. You should learn to use each style as appropriate in combination with specific negotiation and mediation strategies that may assist you to create constructive outcomes in conflict situations.

Resistance is the ability to avoid what is not wanted from the environment. It is an emotional response to change based on a variety of professional fears related to the change. Resistance may be demonstrated with many indicators, including refusal to participate, support without substance, displacement of responsibility, deferral to a future time, and reliance on past experience. However, resistance is subtle and should be looked for through patterns of behavior. Four approaches to conceptualizing persuasion—behavioral, consistency, perceptual, and functional—offer many strategies for addressing resistance.

ACTIVITIES AND ASSIGNMENTS

1. Many schools and school districts are continuing to make progress toward becoming more inclusive. As you think about the concerns that are often raised about inclusive practices, consider how they might lead to conflict. Try categorizing the conflicts that may arise using the three-part analysis of causes of conflict presented in this chapter. What conclusions does this activity lead you to regarding your school's move toward inclusive practices?

2. Select a conflict situation that is common among your colleagues or class members. First, role-play different styles for managing the conflict. Then discuss additional strategies for constructively addressing the conflict that are consistent with each style.

3. Special services professionals may not think of themselves as negotiators, despite the importance of negotiation in many of their activities. Describe instances in which you found yourself negotiating. Basing your answer on the information presented in this chapter, what did you do appropriately? What did you do that you would now do differently?

4. Suppose that a colleague working with your teaching assistant comes to you upset about the fact that the TA is deliberately ignoring teacher requests. The TA's perception is that the teacher treats her badly, asking her to do menial chores instead of working with students and "talking down" to her. What mediation strategies could you use to address this situation? Try role-playing this scenario with your classmates.

5. Recall a situation in which you perceived that a colleague was resisting a change. What types of fears or concerns may have caused the resistance?

6. Review the indicators of resistance described in this chapter. Generate an example you have experienced or observed in your work setting that illustrates each one. If you think about the colleagues with whom you most frequently interact, what do you find are their characteristic patterns of resistance?

7. Using the example you generated for the preceding activity, analyze it to determine whether it is a situation in which persuasion might be effective. That is, ask yourself these questions: Is resistance an appropriate response to the situation? Why or why not? Does the situation warrant a response to the resistance? Why or why not? How committed to change are the individuals involved? Given your analysis, what is the likelihood that the other person(s) can be persuaded?

8. Have each member of your class spend a few minutes writing about a situation encountered in which resistance played an important role. Then distribute these so that each class member has an unfamiliar situation to address. Role-play how to respond to the resistant individual using the strategies suggested in this chapter.

FOR FURTHER READING

Barsky, A. E. (2000). *Conflict resolution for the helping professions.* Belmont, CA: Brooks/Cole.

Bazerman, M. H., & Neale, M. A. (1992). *Negotiating rationally.* New York: Free Press.

Cornille, T. A., Pestle, R. E., & Vanwy, R. W. (1999). Teachers' conflict management styles with peers and students' parents [Electronic version]. *International Journal of Conflict Management, 10*(1), 69–79.

Fiedler, C. R. (2000). *Making a difference: Advocacy competencies for special education professionals.* Boston: Allyn & Bacon.

Fisher, R., Ury, W., & Patton, R. (1997). *Getting to yes: Negotiating agreement without giving in* (3rd ed.). Boston: Houghton Mifflin.

Isenhart, M. W., & Spangle, M. (2000). *Collaborative approaches to resolving conflict.* Thousand Oaks, CA: Sage.

Jehn, K. A. (2000). The influence of proportional and perceptual conflict composition on team performance. *International Journal of Conflict Management, 11*(1), 56–73.

Kosmoski, G. J., & Dennis, R. (2001). *Managing conversations with hostile adults: Strategies for teachers.* Thousand Oaks, CA: Corwin Press.

Perloff, R. M. (1993). *The dynamics of persuasion.* Hillsdale, NJ: Erlbaum.

Wood, M. (1998). Whose job is it anyway? Educational roles in inclusion. *Exceptional Children, 64*, 181–195.

APPENDIX: CONFLICT MANAGEMENT STYLE SURVEY

This Conflict-Management Style Survey has been designed to help you become more aware of your characteristic approach, or style, in managing conflict. In completing this survey, you are invited to respond by making choices that correspond with your typical behavior or attitudes in conflict situations.

This survey identifies twelve situations that you are likely to encounter in your professional lives. Please study each situation and the five possible behavioral responses or attitudes carefully and then allocate 10 points among them to indicate your typical behavior, with the highest number of points indicating your strongest choice. Any response can be assigned 0–10 points, as long as all five responses for the given situation add up to 10 total points, as shown in the following example:

EXAMPLE SITUATION: In responding to a request from another for help with a problem, you would:

1	A.	Clearly instruct him or her how to proceed.
4	B.	Enjoy the strategizing and the challenge.
4	C.	Help him or her to take responsibility for the problem.
1	D.	Find it unnerving but agree to help.
0	E.	Avoid the invitation at all costs.
10	**TOTAL**	

Please choose a single frame of reference (e.g., work-related conflicts, organizational conflicts) and keep that frame of reference in mind when responding to all the situations. And remember, as you complete the survey, that there are are no right or wrong answers. The survey will be helpful to you only to the extent that your responses accurately represent your characteristic behaviors and attitudes.

SITUATION 1: Upon experiencing strong feelings in a conflict situation, you:

_____ A. Enjoy the emotional release and sense of exhilaration and accomplishment.

_____ B. Enjoy the strategizing involved and the challenge of the conflict.

_____ C. Become serious about how others are feeling and thinking.

_____ D. Find it frightening because you do not accept that differences can be discussed without someone's feelings getting hurt.

_____ E. Become convinced that there is nothing you can do to resolve the issue.

10 **TOTAL**

SITUATION 2: Consider the following statements and rate them in terms of how characteristic they are of your personal beliefs:

_____ A. Life is conquered by those who believe in winning.

_____ B. Winning is rarely possible in conflict.

_____ C. No one has the final answer to anything, but each has a piece to contribute.

_____ D. In the last analysis, it is wise to turn the other cheek.

_____ E. It is useless to attempt to change a person who seems locked into an opposing view.

10 **TOTAL**

SITUATION 3: What is the best result that you expect from conflict?

_____ A. Conflict helps people face the fact that one answer is better than others.

_____ B. Conflict results in canceling out extremes of thinking so that a strong middle ground can be reached.

_____ C. Conflict clears the air and enhances commitment and results.

_____ D. Conflict demonstrates the absurdity of self-centeredness and draws people closer together in the commitment to each other.

_____ E. Conflict lessens complacency and assigns blame where it belongs.

10 **TOTAL**

SITUATION 4: When you are the person with the greater authority in a conflict situation, you:

_____ A. Put it straight, letting the other know your view.

_____ B. Try to negotiate the best settlement you can get.

_____ C. Ask to hear the other's feelings and suggest that a position be found that both might be willing to try.

_____ D. Go along with the other, providing support where you can.
_____ E. Keep the encounter impersonal, citing results if they apply.
10   **TOTAL**

SITUATION 5:   When someone you care for takes an unreasonable
position, you:

_____ A. Lay it on the line, telling him or her that you don't like it.
_____ B. Let him or her know in casual, subtle ways that you are not pleased;
possibly distract with humor; and avoid a direct confrontation.
_____ C. Call attention to the conflict and explore a mutually acceptable
solution.
_____ D. Try to keep your misgivings to yourself.
_____ E. Let your actions speak for you by indicating depression or lack of
interest.
10   **TOTAL**

SITUATION 6:   When you become angry at a friend or colleague, you:

_____ A. Just explode without giving it much thought.
_____ B. Try to smooth things over with a good story.
_____ C. Express your anger and invite him or her to respond.
_____ D. Try to compensate for your anger by acting the opposite of what you
are feeling.
_____ E. Remove yourself from the situation.
10   **TOTAL**

SITUATION 7:   When you find yourself disagreeing with other
members of a group on an important issue, you:

_____ A. Stand by your convictions and defend your position.
_____ B. Appeal to the logic of the group, in the hope of convincing at least
a majority that you are right.
_____ C. Explore points of agreement and disagreement and the feelings of
the group's members, and then search for alternatives that take
everyone's views into account.
_____ D. Go along with the rest of the group.
_____ E. Not participate in the discussion and not feel bound by any decision
reached.
10   **TOTAL**

SITUATION 8:   When a single group member takes a position
in opposition to the rest of the group, you:

_____ A. Point out publicly that the dissenting member is blocking the group
and suggest that the group move on without him or her if necessary.
_____ B. Make sure the dissenting member has a chance to communicate
his or her objections so that a compromise can be reached.
_____ C. Try to uncover why the dissenting member views the issue differently,
so that the group's members can reevaluate their own positions.

_____ D. Encourage the group's members to set the conflict aside and go on to more agreeable items on the agenda.

_____ E. Remain silent, because it is best to avoid becoming involved.

__10__ **TOTAL**

SITUATION 9: When you see conflict emerging in a group, you:

_____ A. Push for a quick decision to ensure that the task is completed.

_____ B. Avoid outright confrontation by moving the discussion toward a middle ground.

_____ C. Share with the group your impression of what is going on so the nature of the impending conflict can be discussed.

_____ D. Forestall or divert the conflict before it emerges by relieving the tension with humor.

_____ E. Stay out of the conflict as long as it is of no concern to you.

__10__ **TOTAL**

SITUATION 10: In handling conflict between your group and another, you:

_____ A. Anticipate areas of resistance and prepare responses to objections prior to open conflict

_____ B. Encourage your group's members to be prepared by identifying in advance areas of possible compromise.

_____ C. Recognize that conflict is healthy and press for the identification of shared concerns and/or goals.

_____ D. Promote harmony on the grounds that the only real result of conflict is the destruction of friendly relations.

_____ E. Have your group submit the issue to an impartial arbitrator.

__10__ **TOTAL**

SITUATION 11: In selecting a member of your group to represent you in negotiating with another group, you would choose a person who:

_____ A. Knows the rationale of your group's position and would press vigorously for your group's point of view.

_____ B. Would see that most of your group's judgments were incorporated into the final negotiated decision without alienating too many members of either group.

_____ C. Would best represent the ideas of your group, evaluate these in view of judgments of the other group, and then emphasize problem solving approaches to the conflict.

_____ D. Is most skillful in interpersonal relations and would be openly cooperative and tentative in his or her approach.

_____ E. Would present your group's case accurately, while not making commitments that might result in obligating your group to a significantly changed position.

__10__ **TOTAL**

SITUATION 12:   In your view, what might be the reason for the failure of one group to collaborate with another?

_____ A. Lack of a clearly stated position, or failure to back up the group's position.

_____ B. Tendency of groups to force their leadership or representatives to abide by the group's decision, as opposed to promoting flexibility, which would facilitate compromise.

_____ C. Tendency of groups to enter negotiations with a win/lose perspective.

_____ D. Lack of motivation on the part of the group's membership to live peacefully with the other group.

_____ E. Irresponsible behavior on the part of the group's leadership, resulting in the leaders placing emphasis on maintaining their own power positions rather than addressing the issues involved.

10   **TOTAL**

When you have completed all items in Section 1, write the number of points you assigned for each of the five responses for the twelve situations in the appropriate columns on the scoring form below. Add the total number of points for each column and make sure that they total 120 points. Then, transfer your column scores onto the style/approach form to discover the extent to which you model the different styles/approaches to managing conflict.

Scoring Form

Situation	Response A	Response B	Response C	Response D	Response E
1					
2					
3					
4					
5					
6					
7					
8					
9					
10					
11					
12					
TOTAL	____ +	____ +	____ +	____ +	____ = 120

Column	Points	Style/Approach	Column	Points	Style/Approach
A	____	Controller	D	____	Accommodator
B	____	Compromiser	E	____	Avoider
C	____	Collaborator			

Source: Conflict Management Style Survey. Macon, GA: Mercer University, Center for Student Involvement and Leadership. [http://www.mercer.edu/cs:l/leaps-resource-files.htm] Retrieved February 28, 2002.

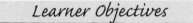

12

Perspectives and Issues

Connections

Preceding chapters have emphasized the applications in which collaboration occurs and the communication skills and interaction processes that you need to collaborate effectively. In Chapter 12, we turn to broader issues that also affect collaborative practice, including considerations related to specific participants and contexts for collaboration that may require special attention. The chapter concludes with a discussion of several ethical issues that occur when professionals collaborate.

Learner Objectives

After reading this chapter you will be able to:

1. Describe role-specific factors to take into account when collaborating with administrators, professionals from other disciplines (including related services professionals), transition specialists, and general education teachers.
2. Outline special issues that sometimes arise when professionals collaborate in early childhood settings, with private or public agencies other than school, and in multicultural contexts.
3. Discuss ethical issues that may arise in professional collaboration.

INTRODUCTION

As you have read this book, we hope you have recognized that collaboration is an immensely complex endeavor, in terms of both the subtleties that can make it effective or ineffective and the number of school activities and applications that benefit from it. Because of this complexity, it is often impossible to attend to all the significant factors that can influence collaborative practice, particularly in the typically frenetic daily lives of school professionals.

This chapter is intended to help you integrate what you have learned about collaboration—conceptually and technically—by highlighting three topics that require professionals to have clear and sophisticated understanding of their collaborative activities. First, we outline considerations for reflective collaboration with specific role groups, including general and special education teachers, related services providers, and administrators. Next, we explore issues that might arise in particular contexts (e.g., interorganizational situations, vocational settings, early childhood settings, multicultural environments). Finally, we discuss some of the ethical dilemmas that might occur as part of collaboration, in order to stimulate your own thinking about this crucial topic. As you read this chapter, we suggest that you analyze how your collaborative expertise can enhance or limit your professional interactions in these three areas.

ROLE-SPECIFIC CONSIDERATIONS IN COLLABORATION

Although the ideas and skills explained in this book are intended to be used whenever you collaborate, regardless of who the other participants are, it is also true that your interactions vary depending on those participants (Rogers & Steinfatt, 1999; Shoffner & Briggs, 2001). In this section, we offer information about some of the factors that might influence your interactions with administrators, related services professionals, and general education teachers. The information is not intended to form a prescription for your actions but rather to assist you in understanding why you need to make subtle changes in how you respond to different individuals in order to successfully collaborate.

Working with Administrators

Administrators face unique challenges when they are participants in the collaborative efforts at their schools because they have a dual role. They are colleagues and peers in collaboration, but they are also supervisors responsible for evaluating job performance and making other personnel decisions (Laud, 1998; Pandiscio, 1991; Terry, 1999). Keeping these two roles separate is often difficult, sometimes because of actions by other participants in collaboration.

Some school professionals find it difficult to nurture a collaborative relationship with their administrators because the administrator does not clearly indicate whether the decision making that might be occurring is intended to be collaborative. For example, consider the meeting one principal called to discuss the next steps for Julio, a student with emotional disabilities who had punched another student in the stomach during lunch. The special education and general education teachers, counselor, psychologist, and principal spent most of an hour discussing Julio's needs and the lack of follow-through on recommendations at home, and they considered various options—in-school suspension, a supervised lunch arrangement, and behavior contracts, among others. Both of the teachers supported the supervision option. Toward the end of the meeting, the principal said, "Thank you for all your input. I have decided that Julio has to be suspended from school—out-of-school suspension—because of this incident. Nothing you have said has made me change my mind. I'll arrange the necessary procedures, contact the central office since Julio receives special education, and call the parents." Needless to say, the professionals who had attended the meeting felt their time had been wasted.

When teachers and other professionals work with school administrators, it is important to ascertain whether the shared interaction is intended to be collaborative, whether they are functioning in an advisory (but not a decision-making) capacity, or whether they are really just being informed about a decision that has already been made. All of these options are sometimes appropriate. Principals do need information and, sometimes, advice even when they have to make decisions based on additional factors of which professionals may not be aware. They also sometimes inform staff about decisions that have already been reached. And sometimes they collaborate (Hargreaves & Fullan, 1998; Sergiovanni, 1994). Your responsibility is to recognize the place and impact of each type of situation and gauge your communication accordingly. To do this, you might have to ask directly whether an interaction is collaborative or advisory, or you might need to ask your administrator to clarify the purpose of a meeting in which you are a participant.

Understanding the distinctions in interactions with administrators can help you put some administrative actions in the proper perspective. We encourage you to do so and set expectations accordingly. We are sometimes struck by professionals' frustration about not having their input used by an administrator, even though the administrator had clearly stated that the input will be considered but not necessarily acted upon.

The other dilemma that sometimes arises when administrators are participants in collaboration, especially at team meetings, IEP meetings, or conferences attended by several individuals, is inappropriate reliance by professionals on administrative authority. For example, consider what occurred at this team meeting.

◆ Ms. Sanchez, a general education teacher; Mr. Klupchek, a special education teacher; Ms. Andersen, a reading specialist; Ms. Maroney, a speech and language therapist; and Mr. Weinberg, a principal, were meeting to decide whether a student should be referred for an individual assessment. Ms. Andersen commented, "Of course he needs it. I've screened for reading problems and they're clearly there. He needs this assessment."

Ms. Maroney said, "All our information indicates that this student is achieving at his expected level. He is struggling with reading because he has difficulty learning. He is also struggling with math, but in both areas he is doing as well as we would expect, and socially he is okay."

The conversation continued, with Ms. Andersen speaking repeatedly for assessment, stating that she spoke for all the teachers, both general education and special education. Eventually, a decision was reached to assess the student, but several team members, including Ms. Sanchez and Mr. Klupchek, thought it was inappropriate. Later, they confronted Mr. Weinberg, blaming Ms. Andersen for the outcome. The team members asked Mr. Weinberg to talk to Ms. Andersen about being more careful to take into account others' points of view.

Mr. Weinberg wisely avoided the trap of saying, "I'll take care of it," an administrative rather than a collaborative response. Rather, he noted that if a poor decision had been made, it was a team responsibility and that if increasing sensitivity to others' points of view needed to be discussed, it should occur with the entire team, not with one person. He suggested that they initiate it at the next meeting.

At a subsequent meeting, the team talked about the decision, analyzed what had happened, and recommitted themselves to speaking up when they had differing points of view. Mr. Weinberg averted the problem of team members overly relying on administrative authority when not appropriate.

Two other administrative issues related to collaboration merit mention. First, in some schools the dilemma faced in collaborating with administrators is not a matter of how the principal participates or how others react to that individual's presence. Instead, it is a matter of the administrator's absence during crucial interactions, especially those requiring an administrative representative for the purpose of special education decision making. Although this problem is not widespread, our experiences in schools have taught us that in some schools it is a chronic issue. In interactions that are likely to be especially difficult or those in which the decisions being made are far-reaching, your responsibility is to remind your administrator of your need for his or her presence, inform your special education supervisor if your administrator does not attend meetings as needed, and document your efforts to ensure administrative participation.

The second issue is much broader and concerns administrators' understanding of topics related to collaboration (Barth, 1990; Leonard & Leonard, 1999). This includes general understanding of the importance of collaboration, the role of the administrator in fostering a school climate supportive of collaboration, and enough knowledge about collaborative activities to help make them a reality. Perhaps the clearest example of this issue occurs in schools that are beginning co-teaching programs as part of their service delivery system for special education. It is crucial that principals understand that co-teaching involves far more than special educators popping into classrooms to help the students with IEPs. They need to recognize the importance of shared planning time, feasible scheduling, and the importance of not assigning huge numbers of students with IEPs or other extraordinary needs into classrooms just because co-teaching is available there.

Recognizing that collaboration with its related activities is only one of many items competing for an administrator's attention, one strategy you can use to facilitate your interactions with your administrator is to help provide as much

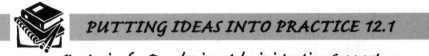

PUTTING IDEAS INTO PRACTICE 12.1

Strategies for Developing Administrative Support

Principals have many, many issues and concerns that demand their attention. To help your principal learn about and develop a commitment to collaboration, try the strategies below.

- Share journal articles on pertinent topics. You might have as a goal to provide at least one article or clipping each month.

- Alert your administrator to professional development activities related to collaboration. Request permission to attend with a general education teacher, and encourage your principal or assistant principal to accompany you.

- Share with your principal handouts about collaboration received at professional conferences. You might even suggest that particularly relevant ones be distributed to the entire staff for discussion at a faculty, team, or department meeting.

- Discuss with your principal the elements of collaboration you have or wish to include in your program. Decide with your principal what support and resources you can expect for the program.

- Take a few moments on a regular basis to chat about the opportunities and challenges of your collaborative activities. This type of face-to-face interaction is sometimes more effective than written communication. Further, it can provide your administrator with enough information that he or she can make better decisions and be more supportive of your collaborative efforts.

- Invite your principal or assistant principal to visit another school with you to observe a particularly good program emphasizing collaboration.

- Maintain an ongoing log or list of topics relative to your collaborative efforts that you wish to discuss with your administrator. Determine the priority of each topic, and discuss one or two at each meeting.

relevant information as you can. Some strategies for providing such information are given in the Putting Ideas into Practice feature.

Working with General Education Teachers

Much of what is presented in the preceding chapters included an emphasis on interacting with general education teachers. However, as with the other specific groups addressed in this section, additional considerations should be kept in mind when working with this group of professionals.

First, as with some special educators, few general education teachers have been prepared for collaborative roles and responsibilities (Howard et al., 2001;

Landers & Weaver, 1997; Welch, 1998). Some intuitively understand what is required or actively seek information, and others are receptive to input from colleagues, but a few are uncomfortable working with others in part because they have no orientation to this approach to teaching and related responsibilities. In one school, middle school teachers who attended a professional development workshop on co-teaching heard ideas that they later used to rescue and revitalize their failing program. They even contacted the presenter to get additional advice to help them design an effective model for their setting. Contrast that example to an elementary school where a group of teachers met to plan an innovative language arts program in which students work in different classrooms on different days and general educators and special educators share instructional responsibilities. The idea had tremendous potential, but it soon became clear that each teacher firmly believed that he or she had the best approach to teaching language arts and was unwilling to make changes in that approach to accommodate the innovative program. The teachers soon reverted to their separate programs.

General education teachers may experience other challenges based on their perception of their role in interactions involving students with disabilities (Kay, Sherrer, & Fitzgerald, 1992; Vaughn, 1994). For many reasons, including a long history of general education teachers being told that students with disabilities needed something that only a special educator could provide, some general education teachers collaborate on many issues—but not about students with IEPs. Teachers make comments such as, "I didn't study to become a special education teacher," "She needs more specialized help than I can give her," or "I don't know how to teach this student."

With new emphases in teacher preparation and professional development, this perception is fading. Nonetheless, general educators' concerns about their roles and responsibilities relative to students with disabilities may continue to present roadblocks to effective collaboration. Specific dilemmas may occur around topics that are already issues of concern to all teachers, such as curriculum standards and proficiency assessment. Standards-based education is a central focus across the nation, and the Elementary and Secondary Education Act (ESEA) requires increased use of curriculum standards and a system of proficiency assessment to determine student learning and to make teachers accountable for it. There is active debate in the field about the benefits and dangers associated with this initiative. And, even though the IDEA requires that all students with disabilities participate in state- and districtwide assessment programs unless an IEP team determines that the student requires an alternative assessment, many teachers are especially resistant to the inclusion of students with disabilities in the assessment programs.

General education teachers often believe that students with IEPs either should not be required to take such tests, or that they as classroom teachers should not be responsible for the achievement of those students. Collaboration may become difficult, especially when special educators explain that the same movement for accountability is occurring for students with disabilities and that many such students should be expected to take the same tests as other students (with appropriate accommodations) and succeed on them, or should take an alternative test with the same purpose in mind (Kearns, Kleinert, & Kennedy, 1999).

General education teachers experience yet another dilemma in collaborating on behalf of students with disabilities—a dilemma that will be discussed in Chapter 13 (see the "Coordinating Services for Collaboration" section on pages 316–317). Especially in schools using inclusive practices, a single elementary classroom could have a special education teacher, a paraprofessional, an occupational therapist, a speech and language therapist, and a social worker coming in to the classroom to work collaboratively. In addition, the teacher may be working with adult volunteers, student teachers or interns, and a reading specialist. Not surprisingly, the sheer number of individuals coming to the classroom and the amount of meeting time required cause some general education teachers to become protective of their class groups and of their time. Chapter 13 presents some ideas on reducing this stressor for collaboration.

One final topic needs to be mentioned concerning general education teachers and collaboration. In many schools, one—or perhaps two, three, or more—individuals make it excruciatingly clear through their words and actions that they will not collaborate on behalf of students with disabilities. Even when special educators make the best use of communication skills and interaction processes and use appropriate strategies for responding to conflict and resistance, such individuals refuse to meet with a team, to co-teach, or to confer for shared problem solving or consultation. Sadly, these few individuals drain a disproportionately high amount of energy from the positive efforts of other staff members, and the rest of the school staff sometimes plan all their activities around them. We mention this small but critical group of educators for two reasons: First, we wish to acknowledge realistically that even with the best skills some situations that could and should be collaborative will not be. Second, we find that special educators often feel it is their responsibility to convince such individuals to work collaboratively. We would like to remind you gently that collaboration cannot be coerced; it is a professional choice. If a teacher is not carrying out his or her responsibilities in terms of working appropriately with students, it is not the role of a special educator to remedy the situation singlehandedly. That is an administrative issue and one for which we encourage you to seek administrative support.

Sometimes when a school staff is working to increase collaborative activities they are helped by taking the time to better understand each other's roles and responsibilities (Hargreaves & Fullan, 1998; Pounder, 1998). One way to do this is to spend time at a faculty or department meeting not only discussing the contributions each group makes in collaboration but also noting the constraints on each group's participation. Another strategy is to experiment with some in-school job sharing, in which special education teachers take responsibility for a class group and general educators work with students with IEPs for a brief period of time. It is especially important that both general education and special education teachers raise any issues on roles and responsibilities as they occur so that they can be resolved as small matters instead of major professional disagreements.

Working with Professionals from Other Disciplines

Although this textbook is intended to address the participation in collaboration by a wide range of special services providers, professionals who are not teachers often have several unique issues that directly and profoundly influence their collaborative interactions (Downing, 2002; Howard, Williams, Port, & Lepper, 2001) both among themselves and with general education and special education teachers. This group of professionals includes related services personnel—psychologists, social workers, speech and language therapists, counselors, occupational and physical therapists, itinerant specialists (e.g., orientation and mobility specialists or inclusion facilitators), adaptive physical educators, nurses, and others. Their issues have to do with professional preparation and orientation, the limited amount of time that related services personnel are able to spend at a single school, and other role-specific constraints they may experience.

Many related services professionals do not have teaching credentials, nor do they have experience in working with large groups of students in a classroom environment. Further, some of them have training that is highly clinical or medical in its orientation, and they may have had considerable experience with adults and little coursework or internship experience with school-age children or education settings. The result is that some related services providers seem to work from an orientation significantly different from that of general education or special education teachers and other staff. During collaborative activities, the difference in preparation and orientation can lead to misunderstandings and miscommunication, and sometimes to conflict and resistance. For example, an occupational therapist may propose working with a student on grasping and other fine motor skills in a pullout model. The teachers may argue that grasping and related skills can be addressed during coloring, writing, cutting, eating, playing with clay, and an entire array of other school activities and do not need to be taught through isolated tasks. Although the occupational therapist might

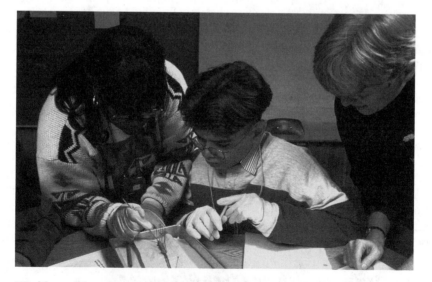

Working with professionals from different disciplines promotes a holistic approach to the child's learning.

see the value in those practice activities, he or she maintains that only an occupational therapist can really provide the instruction and that this needs to occur in a quiet and separate location. In another example, some speech and language therapists assert that most of their services should be delivered in small, quiet settings away from peers. Many teachers (and other speech and language therapists) note that the classroom is the best location for students to learn speech and language skills.

A second dilemma for collaboration involving related services personnel as well as itinerant teachers is their limited time at a single school site. This factor alone suggests that collaboration will be difficult and sometimes simply not possible. These professionals frequently comment that they never know quite what is happening at any of their schools because they are never there long enough to become part of the school community. This leads to innumerable problems. For example, sometimes they arrive at a school to provide services only to find that all the students are at a special assembly. Or they are available to meet with a team only on Thursday mornings, and if the team meets at another time, they cannot be present and they miss the discussion. Even when they do attend meetings, they may be late because they have to drive from another location and were delayed. Conversely, school-based professionals sometimes express frustration with related services and itinerant personnel because of their scarce presence at the school, their rigid scheduling requirements, and their tardiness. Even though often unavoidable, these issues can constrain the development of collaborative work relationships. For example, at one school where general education teachers were discussing dissatisfaction with related services personnel, one teacher very honestly noted, "Intellectually I understand that their time limits are not their doing and that they get here whenever they can. But emotionally I still get angry about how our entire schedule has to revolve around *their* schedules."

A third set of issues for related services professionals, also related to time, concerns their other professional obligations. Many individuals in these professional groups may have extremely high caseloads and, as a result, may have extraordinary numbers of meetings and conferences to attend and assessments to complete. Some may also be obligated to preserve time in their schedules for writing reports and attending discipline-specific meetings. They may also be assigned to help with other school programs such as kindergarten screenings. Further, they may have extensive responsibilities for working with families, community agencies, the juvenile justice system, and other groups. In addition to creating rigid schedules and limited time in schools, these responsibilities fragment the attention of these professionals and limit the depth of their involvement in school-based collaboration. They also severely constrain the feasibility of delivering collaborative services and sometimes even preclude their contribution to problem solving because they lack the necessary knowledge of school context and the student.

Any or many of the above factors may limit the extent to which related services professionals are able and willing to undertake collaborative endeavors. It may be necessary for these professionals and special and general education teachers to prioritize situations in which active participation on the part of related services professionals is needed. It is also critical that the personnel in a single school maintain awareness of the constraints under which these professionals work and take that into account in scheduling meetings and professional development activities. Finally, if you hear dissatisfaction from other colleagues about some or all related services or itinerant professionals, you might want to find out the nature and extent of the issues and either work to resolve them or assist others in understanding the challenges involved.

CONTEXT CONSIDERATIONS FOR COLLABORATION

In addition to considering issues that arise for specific role groups in collaboration, we want to mention that in certain contexts, regardless of the individuals involved, collaboration may have distinct qualities. Three contexts in which this is true are interagency collaboration, collaboration in early childhood settings, and collaboration in vocational and community settings.

Public or Private Agencies

Collaboration is a challenging endeavor when professionals from within the same organization work together. It can be an even more ambitious goal when it involves interacting with individuals from one or sometimes several organizations (Fowler, Donegan, Lueke, Hadden, & Phillips, 2000; Hord, 1986). Despite the difficulty, however, interorganizational collaboration plays an important role in the education of students with disabilities. Examples of interorganizational collaboration you may experience include working with staff from a residential or hospital setting to transition a student back to a public school environment; participating on a team that includes professionals from mental health, juvenile justice, public school, and family services to create options for students for whom no traditional educational approach has been successful; or just working with a private service provider who is counseling or teaching a student you also serve.

A number of issues can arise as part of interorganizational collaboration. First, the decision to collaborate might be reached by one set of professionals although the implementation of a collaborative effort is the responsibility of a different set of individuals (Quinn & Cumbland, 1994). For example, the director of a public preschool and a special education director may reach an agreement to collaborate in serving students with disabilities in a preschool setting. However, neither the teachers nor the itinerant staff of the preschool have participated in the decision. Some staff may support the decision and work together enthusiastically, but others may misunderstand the purpose of the decision or disagree with it entirely and undermine it through their actions. Clearly, communication among the staff within an organization is as important as communication among organizations in interorganizational collaboration.

A second issue that can arise in this type of collaboration concerns the blending of sometimes very different organizations (Klapstein, 1994; Morse, 1994).

For example, the policies and rules that guide each organization may vary considerably. Teachers in public schools routinely stay after school for meetings with parents and others; the clinical staff from a hospital setting often work in a culture in which staff may come to the hospital very early for "rounds" but leave as soon as their workday has ended. Professionals from the juvenile justice system may be accustomed to enforcing decisions reached by requesting a court order; professionals from public schools and family services more frequently rely on negotiating instructional arrangements and enforcing them by offering encouragement, providing incentives, and staying in close contact. The two approaches are strikingly different, and when professionals share problem solving, they sometimes approach the task from almost opposite perspectives. The following list includes six ways in which medical, especially hospital, services differ from those offered by public school agencies (Gilkerson, 1990):

1. *Acute versus chronic care orientation.* Medical personnel typically address medical crises for relatively short periods of time. School personnel have as a goal long-term, in-depth services.

2. *Individual versus systems approach.* Medical personnel have as their task identifying illness based on symptoms and, on that basis, designing treatment. School-based intervention works from a perspective that includes the family and the environment as well as the child for designing an educational program.

3. *Medical science versus social science base for decision making.* Medical personnel are perceived as precise and scientific and thus may have higher status and authority for decision making than educators, who work from a social sciences perspective that is often, appropriately, a matter of judgment and consensus.

4. *Horizontal versus vertical institutions.* Hospital and other medical facilities tend to have cultures that are highly stratified, and membership in them is controlled. Education, on the other hand, seeks to involve the community and sometimes depends on other agencies for funding of its efforts.

5. *Asymmetrical versus symmetrical relationships.* Doctor–patient relationships appropriately assume that the doctor is the expert but then extend that perspective to assume that the patient (child and parents) neither understands the problem nor can develop the solution. Education programs assume that parents are partners in their child's programs and that they have a contribution to make that is different from but as valuable as that of the professionals.

6. *Reactive versus proactive process.* In general, medical professionals often respond to patients' immediate needs. In public school programs, the goal incorporates a much more proactive focus that includes planning for the future and averting problems.

Generally, the challenges of interorganizational collaboration derive from the differences in organizational cultures of the sort described above. To lessen dilemmas in interorganizational collaboration, you should keep in mind ideas such as those below.

1. Explain your expectations for meeting a student's needs and your concerns about designing an appropriate educational environment with examples, sample schedules, and other specific information. Encourage your counterparts from other organizations to do the same. The communication skills presented throughout this text are particularly critical when working across organizations, especially those pertaining to being clear and concrete in the messages you send. This care in creating clear communication can avert problems during program implementation.

2. Expect a "getting to know you" period. You have learned that collaboration is developmental and that your practice of it will mature as you learn about one another. This is even more true for interorganizational collaboration. We recommend that you allow time for general conversations about expectations from everyone involved and that you move gradually into the partnership.

3. Use negotiation skills to clarify any agreements. As you work with others, you might find it necessary to negotiate the use of facilities, materials and equipment, personnel time, funds, or any number of other resources. The representatives from each organization may have as an agenda contributing the fewest resources possible. If you are unsure of your role or degree of authority in this facet of interorganizational collaboration, you may need to involve an appropriate administrator.

4. Recognize that the nature and extent of your partnership may be determined partly by factors you do not control. Sometimes, professionals are frustrated because they recognize that a student would benefit from a particular service, because they would like to contribute funds to purchase a piece of equipment, or because they want an action to be taken—now. However, they are constrained because of organizational agreements. We sympathize with the dilemma, but we also recognize that it is simply part of the complexity of working across organizations.

Interorganizational collaboration has tremendous potential to multiply our effectiveness in serving the needs of students with disabilities and other special needs. Despite its complexities, you are likely to be a participant in this type of collaboration and to experience both its power and its frustration as schools and other settings become increasingly collaborative.

Early Intervention and Preschool Settings

Collaboration is now central to all of special education, but it has long been a defining feature of early childhood programs that meet the needs of young children with disabilities. The strong emphasis on parental involvement makes collaboration especially integral to early childhood services (Cavallaro & Haney, 1999). *Collaboration* often is used to describe the philosophy that underlies service delivery for young children with disabilities. A rationale for the commitment to collaboration is presented in the Putting Ideas into Practice feature that follows.

Perhaps the best illustration of collaboration at the core of early intervention and preschool services is found in the IDEA rules and regulations that specify who participates on the team to develop the Individualized Family Service Plan (IFSP). In addition to the professionals serving the child, the team includes the parents, other family members the parents request, an advocate, an interim service coordinator who has been working with the family, professionals who have assessed the child, and professionals who might provide services to the child. These individuals jointly design a service plan to meet the needs of the child and his family (Noonan & McCormick, 1993).

Collaboration in early childhood education simultaneously exists at the personal/professional level and at the interorganizational or systems level. At the personal level, professionals and parents make joint decisions as they collaboratively plan, implement, and evaluate programs for young children with disabilities. At the systems level, agencies strive for collaboration as they jointly work to provide coordinated and comprehensive programs for children and

PUTTING IDEAS INTO PRACTICE 12.2

Rationale for the Collaborative Commitment in Early Childhood

Collaboration is a crucial aspect of service delivery in the early childhood arena. Here is one author's succinct summary of why a commitment to collaboration is so essential.

- Because the needs of individuals requiring support are often multiple;
- Because many of the multiple family needs and subsequent sources of intervention often overlap and potentially compete with one another;
- Because parents and other family members working in concert with service providers should be able to expect coordination and valid prioritization and clarity;
- We therefore commit ourselves, as professionals who work on behalf of infants and young children with disabilities, to working with each other toward a common goal;
- The outcome of this commitment shall be a unified approach to service provision which has as its purpose the health and growth of the person being served.

From McGuigan, C. (1985). *Presentation to the governor of Minnesota's blue ribbon panel for early childhood, special education services.* Minneapolis, MN. As presented in Howard, V. F., Williams, B. F., Port, P. D., & Lepper, C. (1997). *Very young children with special needs: A formative approach for the 21st century.* Upper Saddle River, NJ: Merrill.

their families. Both levels of collaboration are needed to provide appropriate and well-designed services.

Services for young children and their families can be classified as belonging to one of three models: home-based, center-based, or a combination of the two. In all three approaches, cooperation and collaboration are essential. In home-based services, professionals work with parents and other family members, who become the child's primary teachers. The professional typically goes into the home two or three times weekly and teaches the parents and other family members to implement the appropriate interventions, monitor the child's progress, and evaluate the outcomes. Being able to collaborate effectively with parents and have them work as partners with the professionals is critical in this approach.

Center-based services also require collaboration skills, as the teacher must work as a member of a team that consists of staff members with expertise in several related disciplines. Typically the team includes speech and language specialists, medical personnel, special education and early childhood teachers, occupational therapists, adaptive physical education teachers, physical therapists, and social workers. A comprehensive program is developed for children that is likely to involve a number of service providers from the other disciplines. Collaboration with parents is still important, but increased demands for professional collaboration often are the central issue.

Combination services are exactly what the name implies—a combination of home- and center-based services. The children come to a center two or three times weekly, and the professionals also visit their homes and work with the families two to four times monthly. These programs are multifaceted and require flexibility on the part of the teacher. They also require extraordinary collaboration skills on professionals' parts, since they combine the services and demands of the other two models.

From these observations and your understanding of parental participation, you can see that collaboration in early childhood is essential but that it can be complex. Your role is to recognize the factors of collaboration that are especially important in these situations and to use your communication and interaction process skills to foster appropriate interactions, while at the same time using your knowledge of frame of reference to understand the challenges that may be faced.

Vocational and Community Settings

Transition specialists, vocational educators, vocational rehabilitation counselors, secondary teachers, and related personnel in public schools and adult service agencies spend considerable time placing students with disabilities in school and community sites for prevocational and vocational services. Planning, placing, training, and supporting students as they develop functional skills and prepare for adult living and employment are key responsibilities for these educators and related professionals (Harvey, 2001; Johnson, 2002; Moon & Inge, 2000). Increasingly, these specialists are collaborating to plan for and support a student's community-based educational program and transition to postschool employment. There is value to having students involved in all of the decisions made about their school programs, and their role as team members was discussed in Chapter 6. In the case of transition planning, however, it is essential that students be actively involved in their own program planning, and they need to acquire the knowledge and skills to collaborate in the process.

In this section, we discuss collaboration in vocational and community settings. We do so using a framework in which prevocational, vocational, and transition services exist on a continuum that involves increasing student participation in community settings and increasing involvement of other adult agencies and services as the student prepares for and makes the transition to postschool employment or educational options.

Prevocational and Vocational Services

The Individuals with Disabilities Education Act (IDEA) requires a formal transition plan for students with disabilities beginning at the age of 14 or younger. The importance of these IDEA provisions cannot be overstated. There is significant evidence of the need for effective preparation for postsecondary educational, community, employment, and recreational involvement (Wagner & Blackorby, 1996), but the appropriate implementation of this provision is uneven and still evolving in many settings. For the most part, prevocational skills such as following directions, timeliness, completion of assignments, and appropriate group behaviors can be addressed in the school curriculum. Similarly, career awareness and exploration activities can be incorporated into the school curriculum. Some advanced prevocational skills are best acquired through community-based instructional programs.

The use of community-based instruction is not without controversy. Although the community is seen as the most effective environment in which students can learn appropriate community-based skills (McDonnell, 1997), some criticize such programming as promoting isolation and segregation (Tashie, Jorgensen, Shapiro-Barnard, Martin, & Schuh, 1996). Therefore, clear communication and collaboration among professionals, parents, and the student during program planning and implementation is especially critical. Successful collaboration in this context is predicated upon the articulation of shared goals and expectations and a commitment to honoring individual values, needs, and beliefs. It is indisputable that as students get older and approach the end of their public school educations, they need to learn about postschool options, including jobs—how to get, perform, and keep them. They also need to learn how to use public facilities and services, prepare for safe and healthy adult living, and develop leisure and recreational skills. For many students, most notably those with moderate and severe disabilities, this will require community-based instruction.

Effective community-based instruction, like appropriate special education, is individualized. The extent and nature of the appropriate community-based program is dependent upon student needs and reflects the student's age, abilities and limitations, goals, and the community context. In deciding upon the amount of community-based instruction, teams need to determine the appropriate balance of learning skills for successful community living and attending classes with students who do not have disabilities. As the emphasis on integrated recreational activities and service learning increases in the general education community (Kesson & Oyler, 1999), opportunities for integrated community experiences also increase. However, in many cases, teams still must balance a student's participation in classrooms with peers who do not have disabilities and his participation in community settings that may be less integrated.

When community-based options are selected, collaborative planning and work is required of secondary teachers, transition specialists, and often related service providers to provide appropriate learning experiences. A number of challenges face these professionals, and they center largely on coordination of services, communication, and the delineation of responsibilities.

A specific challenge in the coordination of services arises from the sometimes competing pressures for students to meet requirements for graduation and to benefit from community-based instruction. The relationship between community-based instruction and the traditional academic skills emphasized in the general education curriculum has not been clearly established (Langone, Langone, & McLaughlin, 2000), yet educators are often able to describe this relationship for a given student. Collaborative assessment and articulation of the academic skills to be derived from a student's community placement and identification of the student's place in the general education curriculum are necessary tasks for professionals involved in community-based instruction.

Many of the communication challenges for professionals in community-based settings are similar to those associated with interagency collaboration. For example, the school schedule does not necessarily coordinate with the schedule for community activities. The immediate implications of this are challenges for

The schedules of community-based professionals sometimes require them to participate in school meetings by telephone.

the professionals in scheduling real-time communication through meetings or phone calls. The community-based professionals are often working with clients and community agencies after school hours when teachers and other school personnel are available for meetings or phone conferences. The transition specialist or job coach is likely to have a very irregular working schedule that may include supporting clients who have vocational placements at night or on weekends. In these cases, it is incumbent upon the professionals to develop communication strategies that allow them to share information regularly. Popular options are using pagers and cellular telephones with scheduled conference times. Asynchronous communication through electronic mail or voice mail is also increasingly used. For meaningful collaboration, however, we encourage you to make some scheduled face-to-face meetings a priority, especially when problem solving or decision making is needed.

Additional challenges to communication occur as a result of the number and diversity of individuals from the community who are involved in the placement and supervision of students. In developing placements and then placing students, the transition specialist may meet with employers, human resources personnel, and potential coworkers as well as observe the work setting to assess the requisite skills and abilities and to prepare the setting for the student's participation. The logistics of arranging these communications are often daunting, but they are made even more complex by the challenge of understanding the differing cultures, vocabularies, and values of the various professionals and community settings. The transition specialist, knowledgeable about both school and community cultures and expectations, becomes the critical player in facilitating effective communication and understanding among these professionals, the student, and the student's family. It is the transition specialist to whom the team turns to ensure that clear and accurate information is being shared across all team members, including the student and family.

Closely related to communication and coordination is the matter of concretely delineating functions and responsibilities for the professionals involved. Clearly described professional roles and responsibilities can facilitate effective communication by specifying the individuals with responsibility and accountability for distinct programmatic functions. Perhaps the area that is most frequently a matter of concern is the assessment and record keeping for community and vocational placements (Dowdy, 1996; Sitlington & Neubert, 1998). Assigning a professional the responsibility for maintaining a transition profile or similar summary of information about a student's secondary school vocational needs and experiences may provide a mechanism for developing a database upon which effective communication and transition planning can be built. One such profile was developed by Neubert, Moon, Leconte, and Lowman (1998) in collaboration with transition specialists and vocational rehabilitation counselors to summarize important information acquired during secondary years that would be useful in determining eligibility for vocational rehabilitation services. The profile includes 17 brief sections addressing general student information, goals, functional levels, self-advocacy skills, community access, worker characteristics, and specific job or volunteer experience. Implementation of this process in Maryland has proven successful as a means of summarizing data for parents and teachers and improving the communication and eligibility certification processes with vocational rehabilitation and other adult service agencies. Delineation of responsibilities and processes for these and similar functions are likely to facilitate your collaborative efforts with community-based professionals and agencies.

Transition Services

Although state and federal rehabilitation programs have long helped to achieve employment for individuals with disabilities, the collaboration of education agencies and rehabilitation services has been limited. Just as the responsibility

PUTTING IDEAS INTO PRACTICE 12.3

Strategies for Enhancing Collaboration with Vocational Rehabilitation Counselors

- ◆ Invite vocational rehabilitation counselors to present an in-service for educational personnel and parents on the eligibility and service provision requirements. Include students when appropriate.

- ◆ Encourage vocational rehabilitation counselors to become involved with appropriate cases as early as possible. The age at which a student becomes eligible for services varies by state, but school personnel should invite vocational rehabilitation counselors to visit classrooms, interact with students and parents, and become involved in cases at the earliest opportunity.

- ◆ Learn about appropriate transition activities for the age levels and needs of the students you teach. Infuse transition activities into subject matter classes and school programs.

- ◆ Invite the vocational rehabilitation counselor to speak in or co-teach some classes with a focus on transition to postsecondary options including college education and job market or career alternatives.

- ◆ Discuss specific disabilities and legal rights guaranteed by IDEA, Section 504 of the Rehabilitation Act, and the Americans with Disabilities Act with students and parents. They need to be able to describe the student's abilities and weaknesses and discuss service options if they are to be coequal partners in the decision-making processes.

- ◆ Prepare students to participate in vocational rehabilitation processes by teaching them to use self-advocacy strategies and equipping them with personal portfolios that include assessments and reports of their medical status, academic achievement, work history, career interest inventories, IEPs and transition plans, and other relevant information.

of schools for transition planning is made clear in IDEA, recent amendments to legislation governing the federal Rehabilitation Services Administration (RSA) include mandates that should lead to greater collaboration with schools in the area of transition. In fact, the Individualized Written Rehabilitation Program (IWRP) has many of the same elements and provisions of the IEP and is developed under a similar process. Since the 1992 Amendments to the Rehabilitation Act, RSA has used the same definition of "transition services" used in IDEA, and both vocational rehabilitation counselors and school professionals must agree on a coordinated set of activities that comprise an appropriate transition plan for an eligible student. These and many additional provisions require collaboration between the schools and rehabilitation agencies. Yet the collaboration is not easily achieved as it is influenced by many of the barriers confronting any interagency collaboration, including differences between IDEA and the Rehabilitation Act requirements relative to eligibility for services, assessment techniques and standards, diagnostic criteria, and availability of services.

Among the immediate concerns for collaborating with vocational rehabilitation colleagues is the need for professionals from both agencies to understand the different contexts in which they operate, the similarities and variations in their governing legislation, and the different professional orientations they bring to their work. In addition to learning definitional, assessment, and eligibility issues, it is important to understand the transition processes and resources of each agency. Based on this understanding, professionals can develop a shared language and understanding of the opportunities and constraints of both systems.

As is the case with IDEA, the Rehabilitation Act emphasizes collaboration with families and participation of individuals with disabilities. For this reason, it is important that school personnel educate and prepare students and their families for effective participation as partners in the process as they implement transition plans for students. Several suggestions for facilitating collaboration with vocational rehabilitation counselors are offered in the Putting Ideas into Practice feature.

MULTICULTURAL CONTEXTS

The increasing diversity in the population of this country has an impact on the use of collaborative strategies for educating students with disabilities (Miller, 2002). It is certainly far beyond the scope of this textbook to adequately explore the interaction issues that occur in multicultural and/or bilingual environments, but we would like to at least raise several issues for your consideration.

If you work in an area represented by racial and cultural diversity, you understand that each student, each family, and each colleague is unique, regardless of racial or cultural heritage. However, if you are unaccustomed to such diversity, you inadvertently might treat racial or cultural groups as monolithic and attribute to them stereotypic characteristics. For example, much is currently written about African American families and Asian American families. These phrases do not give you an accurate picture of a specific family because they do not take into account the geographic area in which the family lives, their religious preferences, their lifestyles, or their economic status (Tobias, 1993).

At the same time that you work to base your collaboration on understanding your colleagues or your students and their families as individuals, you also need to be aware that culture does influence individuals' interactions in many ways that can positively or negatively influence collaborative activities. (See the Chapter 2 section on frame of reference in multicultural settings for a review.) For example, the directness of your conversations and the topics they address might be influenced by cultural expectations. Some cultural groups turn to their extended families in times of need and may be reluctant to share information with school professionals (Correa & Tulbert, 1993). This could be viewed by school professionals as resistance. Another example is based on individuals' perceptions of themselves in relation to the rest of society. If colleagues or family members see themselves primarily as part of a minority group, they may interact in a way that conveys powerlessness, thus undermining the essential collaborative characteristic of parity. Conversely, such individuals may interact so assertively that others feel powerless; this may be an attempt to override their own sense of not having control. Most professionals have experienced this in interactions with a family member who begins by making many accusatory statements and extraordinary demands. This can occur because of the family member's sense of powerlessness.

A final consideration about collaboration with racially or culturally diverse groups concerns understanding, respect, and valuing. Every individual who participates in a collaborative activity should begin with the understanding that the only culture one understands is one's own. This critical frame of reference can lead all involved to strive for better understanding and more patience if miscommunication does occur.

In your role as a school professional, the contexts in which you are likely to experience the greatest diversity are in interacting with families and in communities where students live. These topics were addressed in Chapter 10. Many of the challenges or dilemmas you will encounter as you collaborate in multicultural settings will reflect your frame of reference and the cultural perspectives you hold as well as those held by those with whom you interact. This topic was discussed in Chapter 2, but specific resources and activities to help you examine your cultural perspectives and gain new knowledge about cultural influences are presented in the Perspectives on Diversity box that follows. Specifically, the awareness activities and introspection exercises referenced on the Multicultural Pavilion website will provide meaningful experiences that should make you more aware of your own cultural perspectives and how they influence your relationships and interactions.

Student-to-Student Collaboration

A number of strategies that promote student–student interaction can serve as important mechanisms for supporting student success in inclusive environments. Differing approaches that emphasize student–student interaction are used as strategies for teaching social skills, promoting academic achievement, and increasing the social acceptance of diverse students (Fisher, 2001; Kassner,

PERSPECTIVES ON DIVERSITY 12.1

Resources for Expanding Your Cultural Knowledge and Competence

Culturally and Linguistically Appropriate Services (CLAS)
http://clas.uiuc.edu/index.html

The CLAS Early Childhood Research Institute collects and describes early childhood/early intervention resources that reflect the intersection of culture and language, disabilities and child development.

Multicultural Pavilion: Awareness Activities
http://curry.edschool.virginia.edu/go/multicultural/activityarch.html

This site offers structured activities for students and adults to begin discussion and exploration of multicultural perspectives.

CA Department of Education
www.cde.ca.gov/iasa/cooplrng2.html

Cooperative learning: Response to diversity.

National Multicultural Institute
http://www.nmci.org

Through its initiatives, NMCI leads efforts to increase communication, understanding, and respect among people of diverse backgrounds. It addresses some of the important issues of multiculturalism facing our society.

Fiesta Educativa
http://latino.sscnet.ucla.edu/community/fiesta2.html

This organization works to educate and assist Latino families in obtaining services and in caring for their children with special needs. It provides training, technical assistance, and referral services.

WWW Hmong Homepage
http://www.hmongnet.org

This site provides online resources, translation services, demographic data, referrals, and links to documents such as the English-Hmong Dictionary of Special Education.

National Black Child Development Institute (NBCDI)
http://www.nbcdi.org

NBCDI exists to improve and protect the quality of life of African American children and their families. It works to influence children to reach their full potential, to train professionals, and to empower parents.

2002). The importance of student acceptance, friendships, and student support networks cannot be overstated. These are critical considerations when designing educational programs for students with disabilities (Turnbull & Turnbull, 2001; Walther-Thomas, Korinek, McLaughlin, & Williams, 2000). But social acceptance and friendships are not synonymous with collaboration. To be sure, students who acquire appropriate social skills and skills of cooperation and collaboration are more likely to be accepted and to develop friendships, but we can all think of at least one of our own friends whom we value and enjoy, but might not describe as highly collaborative. In this context, it is not difficult to recognize that there are many important and supportive student–student interaction activities in schools that may not be collaborative, but are nonetheless supportive of student success. We recommend that educators learn about and implement such supports to promote student success, but our focus here is on student collaboration. Certainly one of the most important applications of collaboration in the schools is that which occurs between and among students.

Cooperative group learning is probably the most direct and clear-cut example of an approach that teaches students to collaborate and then uses and reinforces those collaborative skills to also improve academic achievement. There are many cooperative learning models that have evolved over the years. Most involve dyadic or small-group work to achieve an academic outcome or goal. The pairs or groups are generally composed of students with heterogeneous learning skills and needs, and the learning environment is structured to include five essential components: positive interdependence, interaction, individual accountability, interpersonal and small-group interaction skills, and group processing skills (Johnson & Johnson, 1999). These are described in box 12.4.

There are several models for cooperative group learning including various student team learning structures (Slavin, 1986), Learning Together (Johnson & Johnson, 1999), Jigsaw (Aronson, Blaney, Stephan, Sikes, & Snapp, 1978), and Group Investigation (Sharan & Sharan, 1994). The research and meta-analyses supporting these structures has consistently demonstrated that cooperative group learning arrangements lead to improved student achievement, increase student self-esteem, respond to cultural diversity, and promote student success in general education classrooms (see reviews by Slavin, 1991; Stevens & Slavin, 1995; and Qin, Johnson, & Johnson, 1995).

The need for improved social skills of many students with varying disabilities is one of the reasons for the popularity of cooperative learning as a strategy for including students with disabilities in general education classrooms (Prater & Bruhl, 1998). The lack of appropriate social skills has been identified for all categories of students with disabilities, including those with behavior disorders (Nelson & Pearson, 1991), learning disabilities (Vaughn, Zaragoza, Hogan, & Walker, 1993), hearing impairments (Gaustad, 1999), and visual impairments (Dote-Kwan & Chen, 1995). Cooperative learning has been widely promoted as one approach to improving students' social skills and their acceptance by peers (Quinn, Jannasch-Pennell, & Rutherford, 1995). There is general acceptance of the notion that for collaboration to be achieved and for students to benefit from it, teachers will need to explicitly teach the interpersonal and collaborative skills needed for effective team or group work (Johnson & Johnson, 1999; Pomplun, 1997).

PUTTING IDEAS INTO PRACTICE 12.4

Five Essential Components of Cooperative Group Learning

Positive Interdependence

The goal structure emphasizes teamwork and the value of individual team member contributions. Rather than an individualistic or competitive orientation, team members adopt an orientation of interconnectedness. Individual efforts are valued for what they contribute to the team.

Interaction

Positive face-to-face interactions also involve students praising, assisting, supporting, and encouraging each other. This also involves greater opportunity for students to produce and comprehend language and encourages use of higher-order thinking skills as students explain and elaborate ideas.

Individual Accountability

There is clearly group accountability and recognition for group accomplishments in cooperative learning. Individual accountability is needed so that each student contributes to the group by doing a fair share of the work. Sometimes this is best achieved by structuring a task to ensure that each individual has a task to complete without which the group's work cannot be completed or its goal cannot be achieved.

Interpersonal and Small-Group Skills

Social skills, communication and interaction skills, and interpersonal process skills are necessary for students to be successful in group work. The structure of the cooperative group learning tasks provides authentic reasons for using communication and interaction skills such as listening, clarifying, asking questions, explaining, and paraphrasing.

Group Processing Skills

Groups need to discuss how well they are working together and progressing toward or meeting their goals. Group processing enables members to discuss which behaviors or actions are helpful or unhelpful to the group. Processing helps facilitate the development of collaborative skills and provides students with feedback on their participation.

The skills advocated for students are not universally agreed upon, but there is general consensus that they should include those communication skills described in Chapters 2 and 3, such as listening, paraphrasing, and giving feedback, and the interpersonal process skills presented in Chapters 5 and 11 such as managing conflict, decision making, and problem solving. As you prepare to use cooperative learning strategies and teach students the collaborative skills needed, we suggest you review the chapters indicated as well as the related readings at the

Collaboration among students can enhance their achievement and their attitudes toward school.

end of this chapter. As students develop collaborative skills through cooperative learning or other explicit teaching strategies, they will be able to apply them in a wider range of student–student interactions.

In one of the first papers published in the early stages of our collaboration, we discussed the developmental stages of collaboration and wrote:

> When we look to an anticipated adulthood for collaboration . . . We are hopeful that we will see the implementation of recommendations like this one, by the 1989 Commission on Workforce Quality and Labor Market Efficiency: "Techniques emphasizing less interpersonal competition, more cooperative effort, and increased problem-solving abilities, should be used throughout a child's entire education" (p. 10). (Cook & Friend, 1991, p. 27)

It is encouraging for us to reflect on the advances that have been made in such a short time, for now collaborative work is not uncommon in pre-K–12 classrooms and in colleges and universities, and in many schools the competitive atmosphere among students is notably diminished. Collaboration among students is truly becoming an accepted practice.

ETHICS IN COLLABORATIVE PRACTICE

It seems that a particularly fitting final topic for this chapter is ethics. A number of authors have expressed concern over the past several years about the scant attention paid to ethics in the field of special education (e.g., Howe & Miramontes,

1992; Paul, French & Cranston-Gingras, 2001). Even though the Council for Exceptional Children, the American Speech and Hearing Association, the National Association for School Psychologists, and other professional organizations have codes of ethics and standards of practice, in schools the topic is too often ignored. When the dimension of working collaboratively is added to the other ethical issues professionals face, it becomes critical to recognize potential ethical dilemmas and to consider how you will address them. Three of several possible ethical issues are confidentiality, feasibility, and accountability.

Common Ethical Issues

One of the most frequent and basic ethical considerations in collaborative practice concerns confidentiality (Taylor & Adelman, 1998). While it is true that educators have been cautioned for many years about preserving confidentiality related to student information, collaboration brings an entirely new dimension to this ethical issue. For example, suppose that two teachers are co-teaching and the general education teacher shares his favorite teaching idea with the special educator. The latter individual sees that the idea has tremendous potential in several classrooms and enthusiastically but naively shares it with several other teachers. The special educator is startled when the teacher confronts her about giving away "trade secrets." This example of a breach of confidentiality is not so much about teaching or learning as it is about developing and maintaining trusting relationships with colleagues.

A second ethical dilemma concerns feasibility. We work in many schools in which professionals profess belief in the power of collaboration yet have virtually no time or other supports for collaborative practice. Whether a collaborative effort involves a special education teacher and general education teacher planning interventions for a student with a mild learning disability, a transdisciplinary team preparing for the inclusion of a student with multiple disabilities, or a multiagency and parental effort to create wraparound services for a high school student with serious emotional disabilities, if time does not exist to meet, the effort is unlikely to be successful. As such it may be unethical to create assumptions about working collaboratively if feasibility issues are not addressed.

A third ethical dilemma can occur regarding accountability (Cook, Weintraub, & Morse, 1995; Friend & Cook, 1992). Special educators are responsible for ensuring that the needs of students receiving special education and related services are met. In collaboration, there often can be disagreement on the nature of a student's needs and the strategies necessary to address them. A general education teacher may perceive a student as unmotivated, while a special educator perceives that student as overwhelmed by the academic environment. A speech and language therapist may see that a language-based program in an inclusive setting would best address a student's needs, but the special educator may identify the priority as offering the student a highly structured, small-group environment such as that found in a special education classroom. What are other ethical dilemmas related to accountability that may occur?

Professionals need to reflect on and clarify their own ethical standards regarding students with disabilities and their own professional behaviors. By doing this before entering into collaborative interactions and continuing during them, it is possible to recognize practices that you might not be comfortable with but can live with, versus those that you cannot justify. We encourage you to continue the conversation about ethics as it relates to collaboration so that you can balance your commitment to collaboration with your responsibilities to meet the needs of the students you serve.

SUMMARY

The purpose of this chapter is to address issues that have been implied throughout the text but not made explicit. One set of issues relates to individuals in specific role groups, including administrators, related services professionals, general education teachers, and professionals in the community. For each of these groups, collaboration may be influenced by job or role constraints, environmental factors, or the potentially uneven relationships between participants in collaborative activities. A second set of issues concerns the contexts in which collaboration occurs. Four common contexts that influence collaboration are interorganizational situations, early childhood settings, vocational settings and multicultural environments. Professionals who collaborate in these four domains need to be cognizant of the assumptions of their practice and how these assumptions may be problematic for the specific context. A third set of issues to consider relates to ethics. Professionals who work closely with one another as well as with paraprofessionals and parents face ethical issues more complex than those that typically occur when professionals work alone.

ACTIVITIES AND ASSIGNMENTS

1. Interview parents of a child with a disability about their expectations for interacting with school professionals. Ask them to relate their most positive and negative experiences. Compare your interview results with those of your classmates. What patterns can you discern? How do parents' perspectives relate to the basic characteristics of collaboration described in Chapter 1? Are there differences between parents whose children were in preschool programs and those who were not?

2. Write a memo to a building administrator outlining the key elements in a collaborative program you are offering or would like to offer. Include a brief description of the program and its rationale and note any fiscal or resource implications. Then suggest the areas in which you will need administrative support and describe the nature of that support. Finally, propose that you meet with the administrator to discuss these points and offer a brief agenda

for that meeting. Have classmates or colleagues critique the memo and offer suggestions that clarify it.

3. Make a chart of the roles of individuals who typically participate in collaboration in your setting. For each, list the factors that foster their participation and those that constrain it. What does your analysis suggest about the potential for expanding collaboration in your setting?

4. Select a colleague from another discipline with whom you work. Ask your colleague to do the same. Compare your lists, clarify your roles and make plans to eliminate unnecessary overlap, and identify any responsibilities that are not assigned.

5. In small groups, discuss which of the contextual situations presented in this chapter most affect your collaborative practice. How does your school or district work to ensure that collaboration in these contexts is optimized?

6. Write a journal entry about ethical dilemmas you have faced, currently face, or anticipate facing as a school professional. On what basis would you make a decision about whether or not to take action because of an ethical issue? What supports are provided in your school or school district to help teachers who encounter ethical dilemmas? What assistance might your professional organization provide?

FOR FURTHER READING

Cavallaro, C. C., & Haney, M. (1999). *Preschool inclusion* (pp. 65–104). Baltimore: Brookes.

Dowdy, C. A. (1996). Vocational rehabilitation and special education: Partners in transition for individuals with learning disabilities. *Journal of Learning Disabilities, 29,* 137–147.

Johnson, D. W., & Johnson, R. T. (1999). *Learning together and alone* (5th ed.). Boston: Allyn & Bacon.

Leonard, L. J., & Leonard, P. E. (1999). Reculturing for collaboration and leadership. *The Journal of Educational Research, 92,* 237–242.

Miller, S. P. (2002). *Validated practices for teaching students with diverse needs and abilities* (pp. 235–285). Boston: Allyn & Bacon.

Neubert, D. A., & Moon, M. S. (2000). How a transition profile helps students prepare for life in the community. *Teaching Exceptional Children, 33*(2), 20–25.

Vernon, D. S., Schumaker, J. B., & Deshler, D. D. (1993). *The SCORE skills: Social skills for cooperative groups.* Lawrence, KS: Edge Enterprises.

13

Practical Matters

Throughout this textbook, you have learned about the importance of collaboration, ways to design collaborative services for students with special needs, and strategies for making collaborative initiatives effective and efficient. Chapter 13 is an essential companion to the rest of the book. It describes an entire range of practical matters that must be addressed in order to take collaboration from a pleasant concept to a realistic way of doing business in schools. Topics include time—finding it and using it wisely; scheduling and service coordination; program development; and staff development, that is, strategies for sharing information about collaboration and other topics with colleagues. Although you are unlikely to face all of the pragmatic issues raised in this chapter, you undoubtedly will have to address at least several of them.

Learner Objectives

After reading this chapter you will be able to:

1. Describe strategies for finding, prioritizing, and effectively using time for participation in collaborative activities.
2. Identify critical considerations for scheduling collaborative activities and coordinating them with other service delivery options in a school.
3. Describe the major stages of program development and apply these to collaborative activities, including strategies for successfully developing collaborative programs.
4. Describe five models of staff development, and use these with effective presentation strategies to share information about collaboration with colleagues and others.
5. Reflect on the importance of addressing practical matters for the creation and maintenance of collaborative culture in schools.

INTRODUCTION

Increasingly, school professionals are being given the responsibility for developing new programs or for revitalizing existing programs to increase opportunities for professional collaboration. If you do not currently have this responsibility, you might have it in the future, since many collaborative programs evolve in support of inclusive schools and involve special education staff members. For example, you could be asked to initiate a schoolwide mentoring program, teacher assistance team, or integrated therapy program. Or you could work with general education teachers to expand a co-teaching project from an informal arrangement between two teachers to a schoolwide option for delivery of special education services. Whatever your focus, you are faced with several critical issues. First, you probably will need to work with your administrators to ensure that participants in any collaborative program have adequate shared planning and that the time is used wisely. In addition, as you develop a collaborative program, you may have to coordinate it with existing programs and resolve scheduling problems, including avoiding the assignment of several professionals and/or paraprofessionals to a single classroom at one time. Third, you may face the challenge of simultaneously managing all these practical issues as you go through a systematic program development process. Finally, you may be asked to explain a collaborative initiative by providing staff development for your colleagues. The purpose of this chapter is to assist you in succeeding at these rather formidable tasks.

TIME FOR PLANNING

School professionals repeatedly express dismay that collaboration is not possible without time for shared planning (Friend, Reising, & Cook, 1993; Hackman & Berry, 2000; Walther-Thomas, Korinek, & McLaughlin, 1999), and that they seldom, if ever, have enough planning time to enable their collaborative efforts to reach their full potential. These concerns are not without some validity: American teachers spend more time in direct contact with their students and have significantly less time for planning in their schedules than teachers in most other industrialized countries (Darling-Hammond, 1999). In the current climate of school reform and accountability, no simple prescription exists for solving the problem of limited time, but there are some considerations you can take into account, and there are some suggestions for maximizing time use that others have found successful (Brownell, Yeager, Rennells, & Riley, 1997; Bryant & Land, 1998; Dufour, 1999).

We advocate allocating specific time in the school day for the collaborative interactions of professionals—whether those interactions concern students with disabilities or other school matters. However, before suggesting how to find time, we feel obligated to acknowledge some related issues. First, we have found that time alone is seldom the problem in fostering collaboration. Nearly all school professionals have a "relative yardstick" on the topic of time: No matter what their caseloads or other responsibilities, they find they need more time for collaboration. We hear nearly the same number of comments about time from special education teachers with caseloads of eight students with high-incidence disabilities as we do from special educators with caseloads of 28 in a fully inclusive school. It is partly a perception of time and partly the priorities educators give to their various tasks that influence the time available for collaboration (Peterson, 1999).

Second, experienced co-teachers have raised a time issue (Adams, Tomlan, Cessna, & Friend, 1995): When time is available it needs to be used to its fullest advantage. Because many educators spend much of the day working in isolation, when they have the opportunity to interact with another adult outside the presence of students, they tend to want to chat about the day's events, vent concerns about school district and school issues, and socialize. Although such conversations serve a purpose, they need to be limited to ensure that time is available for collaboration (Schumm, Vaughn, & Harris, 1997). If chatting takes one-third of a planning session, it is difficult to justify a request for additional time!

Third, whether teachers are meeting to plan for co-teaching or to problem solve about meeting a student's needs in an upcoming unit of instruction, they should pay careful attention to the procedures they use for planning. It is helpful to think of planning as a three-part process. The general education teacher does the first part prior to the meeting by thinking about and outlining upcoming curricular content and typical related instructional activities. The second part of the planning occurs with both the general education teacher and the special services provider. They jointly review the curricular material, and if they are co-teaching, they decide how to arrange teachers and students in order to accomplish the learning goals. They also make judgments about topics or activities that are likely to be easily understood by students with special needs as well as those likely to be challenging. The special educator carries out the third part of the planning process after the joint meeting. This professional is responsible for preparing any significantly adapted materials or alternative materials that will be needed by the students. This combination of shared planning and an appropriate division of the planning labor results in efficient and effective use of time.

Finally, many issues about time are more problematic in new programs and diminish as programs mature. While it is true that time for intervention assistance team meetings, middle school team meetings, and other group interactions will need to be scheduled, the time required for planning for co-teaching and informal problem solving decreases as professionals develop collaborative work relationships, learn specific interaction skills, and refine their time management skills. Eventually, many time needs, especially those related to planning in-class services, can be met partly through the use of quarterly or even summer meetings supplemented by brief planning meetings on an ongoing basis.

Options for Creating Shared Planning Time

The following three general ideas offer great promise for providing long-term solutions to creating planning time for individuals engaged in collaborative service delivery. They also represent three very different points on a continuum of cost and need for community support.

Early Release/Late Arrival

In school districts across the country, there is increased recognition that schools are adult workplaces as well as places where children go to learn. With this recognition is the understanding that time needs to be allocated in the school day for adults to conduct the professional "business" needed for schools to be effective, including collaborating on behalf of students. One straightforward means of incorporating this time into the school schedule is the use of early release or late arrival days (Hackman & Berry, 2000; National Staff Development Council, 1994).

In this approach, students arrive late or are dismissed early on a regular basis. The professionals use the time to meet, attend professional development activities, confer with parents, and so on. In some schools, these shortened school days occur each week. In others, they happen once each month. A few districts restrict their use to once each grading period. Typically, the instructional time lost on these shortened days has been compensated for through an overall slightly longer instructional day. For example, in the Merryville School District, students leave school each Thursday at about 1:50 P.M. Teachers then have one hour for collaboration. However, each of the other school days has been lengthened by 15 minutes so that students are not losing instructional time. In the Hobart Community Schools, early release occurs once each month, with students

Collaboration requires that teachers and other professionals find time to share planning and discuss student concerns.

leaving school at approximately 1:00 P.M. This gives teachers one and a half hours of time for collaboration. The school day has been lengthened by just five minutes to accommodate this time for collaboration.

Small rural districts, large urban districts, and suburban and small-town districts are all using early release to create time for collaboration. For it to be successful, these guidelines should be kept in mind:

1. Community support must be developed. Since this approach has implications for parents who must arrange child care and for transportation in locales in which students ride buses, the members of the community must see a need for the time created because it also has a cost for them. It is reasonable that community members will expect teachers to be accountable for this time as well.

2. The time created should be preserved for collaborative interactions. It should not be treated as extra preparation time during which teachers work in isolation, nor should it be used for staff meetings or other administrative purposes.

3. It is important to leave some flexibility in the time allocated for collaboration. For example, at one elementary school, all grade-level teams meet on the first week of the month during the late arrival time. The special education staff meet with each team for approximately 20 minutes to address concerns about students with IEPs and other students experiencing difficulty. All the teams have agreed that when the special educator arrives at the team meeting, other business is set aside and resumed later.

Use of Substitutes

Another common alternative for creating shared planning time is to employ substitute teachers to release professional staff members for collaboration. Many creative systems facilitate the maximum use of this type of resource. For example, in one district a permanent substitute is employed and is scheduled at each school one day every other week. If additional time is needed, a school administrator can request the time. In an elementary school in another district, a substitute is employed once each week. The special educators post a schedule of when they are available to meet with teachers. Teachers sign up to meet with the special educator, and the substitute moves from class to class, releasing general education teachers as needed. In a high school, two substitutes are employed once per month. One substitute releases special education staff; the other releases general education staff.

Although funding for substitute teachers can be problematic, this is a relatively low-cost option for creating shared planning time. In some school districts, substitutes are provided just for general education teachers; the time special educators allocate to planning is considered part of students' special education services. In other districts, special educators have made the argument that their time away from their other responsibilities also warrants a substitute. This is a matter for local negotiation. If funding is very restricted, you might be able to use creative strategies for obtaining substitutes. One district has provided a small financial incentive to qualified paraprofessionals who can then work in their schools one day per week as a substitute teacher instead of as a paraprofessional.

Your parent–teacher organization might be able to assist in funding substitutes, or a disability advocacy group might be willing to provide "volunteer" substitutes. Student groups from your local university might also serve as "volunteer" substitutes, as might recently retired teachers. Be aware that local policies may determine whether you can seek alternative funding sources for substitute teachers and whether volunteers can serve in this role. Of course, you are obligated to follow those policies.

These guidelines can help make the use of substitute teachers to create time for collaboration successful:

1. It is important for the substitutes working in these types of teacher-release programs to be comfortable moving from class to class throughout the day. They should clearly understand that this is the expectation for the assignment.

2. Teachers sometimes worry that it takes more time to plan for a substitute teacher than the amount of release time this provides. One easy solution is for teachers to create notebooks of review activities as they deliver their instruction. When a substitute is in the classroom, he or she uses one of the review activities instead of attempting to continue the teacher's instructional program.

3. Procedures for requesting and confirming the use of a substitute teacher should be established. For example, teachers may need to sign up for sub time three days before the planning time occurs. They might also be expected to keep a log of the interactions that occur as a result of the availability of sub time.

4. In some areas of the country, the issue is not getting funding for substitute teachers, it is finding individuals who are willing to substitute teach. If your school faces this dilemma, try to convince administrators to specify dates a favorite substitute will fill in for collaborating teachers in April or May of the preceding year. By doing this, the substitute has a commitment for his or her time, and the staff benefits by knowing their students are in the hands of a competent individual.

Instructional Strategies that Facilitate Planning

One interesting approach to reduce the need for arranged planning time can be used when co-teaching is the selected collaborative activity. Special educators who provide in-class services frequently lament that they walk into classrooms not knowing exactly what their role will be, and as a result they can end up functioning more like classroom helpers than like professional colleagues. When release time is nonexistent, teachers can plan as part of instruction in a no-frills approach to creating time.

- In Ms. Mardell's English class, Ms. Lesson co-teaches three times each week. On these days, Ms. Mardell begins the class by explaining how each teacher will be working with students. This lets Ms. Lesson know how the class will operate and makes her feel more comfortable with co-teaching. It is not the same as having a shared planning time each week, but since Ms. Lesson co-teaches in six classrooms, that would not be possible anyway. Mr. Eliott uses a similar approach in his fourth-grade class. When Ms. Razmoski enters the room, he stops the instruction and asks the class to review what they have covered so far. He then has the class explain what he had told them they would do when Ms. Razmoski arrived. This is sound instructional practice—the mid-lesson review helps students check their understanding; it also helps orient Ms. Razmoski. In both these instructional arrangements, the general education teacher's planning is shared through student interactions.

When it comes to creating time for collaboration, we endorse the idea that working together is a legitimate professional responsibility for educators. We also suggest that time issues need to be raised with your administrator since that individual can often provide a tremendous amount of assistance in finding ways to make collaboration time available. Specific examples of additional shared planning time ideas are included in box 13.1 on page 314.

SCHEDULING AND COORDINATING SERVICES

Any discussion of finding the time for collaborative planning and using it wisely leads to the companion conversation about the matter of scheduling special education teachers and related services personnel time and coordinating all the services offered through special education and other specialized school programs (e.g., reading tutorial programs, enrichment programs). Finding feasible scheduling options and creating services that complement rather than compete with other programs often requires setting aside some assumptions about how students receive services and what professional role responsibilities should be (Fox & Yssldyke, 1997; Rieck & Wadsworth, 2000).

Establishing Schedules in a Collaborative School
Scheduling Issues for Special Educators

Several scheduling issues arise when school professionals move to increased collaborative practice. Three scheduling issues common for special education staff will be addressed here: (1) scheduling teacher by teacher or collectively; (2) arranging co-teaching schedules on a daily or less-than-daily basis; and (3) creating flexibility in a special educator's daily schedule.

Some special education teachers, particularly at the elementary school level, arrange their schedules the way they used to arrange traditional special education services: by going from teacher to teacher, generally beginning with the least cooperative, and building a schedule based on when they are "willing" to work together. Many special educators know firsthand the futility of this approach in a school that stresses collaboration, whether the scheduling issues surround co-teaching, teaming, or consultation. An alternative that can help is to schedule by grade level, or at the middle school level, to schedule by team. For example, Mr. Lowes is the special education teacher at Fielder Elementary. He alerts the third-grade team that he would like to meet with them once each week and requests that meeting for Thursdays. Since all grade-level teams meet twice each week, this request can be accommodated, and the teachers spend time at that meeting discussing the general problems and concerns that arise about students as well as planning upcoming units and needed adaptations. Mr. Lowes follows a similar pattern in each grade level in which he has students. In some high schools, special educators are disbanding their departments and assigning themselves to the academic departments. Thus, one special educator attends English department meetings, problem solves with those teachers, and does most of the English co-teaching. The special educators meet as a group only as needed.

A second scheduling matter concerns co-teaching. Many special education teachers plan for co-teaching to be a daily service delivery option, and then they encounter difficulties meeting all the competing demands for their time. The schedule created by the special education staff of one junior high illustrates the dilemmas daily services can pose: The special education teachers were each spending four instructional periods every day rotating among eight different classrooms in order to provide services to all the students with IEPs. Neither the special education teachers nor the general education teachers sensed that students were getting individualized instruction. When resources and staff are readily available, daily co-teaching permits both teachers to have a higher sense of ownership in the co-taught class and assists in maintaining the continuity of instruction. However, other options can be more viable. For example, in the junior high just described, the program was modified so that co-teaching occurred every other day in each class for an entire class period. Thus, the teachers reduced from eight to four the number of classrooms in which they co-taught daily. In a high school, another special education teacher addressed the problem in this way: He identified two fourth-period classes in which co-teaching was appropriate, then he co-taught in each class twice each week, with the fifth day being left open for flexible scheduling. Keeping less-than-daily co-teaching as a program option is one specific strategy for reaching more students and increasing service intensity. Of course, the extent to which this can occur depends on the nature and extent of students' needs and the requirements for services outlined in their IEPs.

A third scheduling issue for special education teachers concerns retaining some flexibility in the daily schedule. Many special educators have every minute of each day scheduled, and when an emergency meeting is called, a new student requires attention, or an assessment needs to be completed, some service has to be canceled, often to the understanding but annoyance of general education colleagues. It is important for special educators to keep a bit of flexibility so that if they have to cancel a service, another option might be available (Luckner, 1996). For example, in some schools, co-teaching occurs in paired classes as described above, but the fifth day can be available for meetings or as an alternative service delivery time. In elementary schools, some special educators schedule

PUTTING IDEAS INTO PRACTICE 13.1

Finding Shared Planning Time

Professional educators struggle to find the time needed to create and sustain collaborative work relationships. Here are 10 examples of how some schools address the issue of time:

◆ Teachers working together are scheduled for a shared lunch and preparation period. By scheduling these times back-to-back, teachers have a 90-minute block of shared planning time.

◆ In a junior–senior high school, students spend one morning per week in community service. Teachers use this time for shared planning.

◆ In a large school district, increasing class size by one or two students can provide enough additional resources to hire a permanent substitute teacher who is then available to release teachers for planning.

◆ In a year-round school, the three weeks between each quarter are used by teachers for day-long meetings. Teachers receive compensation for this time.

◆ Instead of using professional development days for large-group workshops, one district permits teachers to use this time for two-hour release periods throughout the school year for collaborative activities.

◆ In an elementary school, students are dismissed 45 minutes early once each week so that teachers can jointly plan. The instructional time is added to the other school days.

◆ A variation of the above includes lengthening one school day by 20 minutes and releasing students at noon one day per week. The gained time is used for teacher collaboration.

◆ In a large school, fine and related arts staff (e.g., art, music, and physical education) work with each other and with teachers to arrange schedules so that teachers receive a half day of collaboration time every two or three weeks.

◆ In a variation of the above, in some schools, fine and related arts occur in one grade level at one time in order to release the team of teachers for collaboration.

◆ In an alternative high school, classes are scheduled from 7:30 to 3:30. Even though the earliest classes are special (e.g., tutoring, clubs), the school can meet minimum time requirements in 4.5 days. They use the additional time to collaborate.

Adapted from Raywid, M. A. (1993). Finding time for collaboration. *Educational Leadership, 51*(1), 30–34.

their lunch and preparation periods back-to-back so that they can flip-flop them as the need to meet with colleagues arises. Yet others keep two blocks of time (for a total of 45 minutes to one hour) reserved each week for flexible use. The time is used for student observation, additional consultation, team meetings, adaptations of instructional materials, or "makeup" sessions if a regularly scheduled in-class service has to be canceled during the week.

Many appropriate strategies exist for creating a professional schedule that both meets the needs of students and promotes professional collaboration. One sample teaching schedule is shown in Figure 13.1, but it must also be acknowledged that in schools that value collaboration as a strategy for meeting diverse student needs, professional schedules typically are periodically revised to reflect shifting priorities. They may change as often as once per month, but often at the end of each grading period.

School Scheduling Issues

A second type of scheduling problem concerns the overall schedule on which the school operates. Although informal collaboration often occurs in spite of a difficult school schedule, if collaboration is a valued professional activity and an expectation for teachers and other staff members, the school schedule might need to be modified to make it feasible (Idol, 1997; Lehr, 1999).

One common scheduling matter in elementary schools concerns the time of day when language arts is taught. Most general education teachers prefer co-teaching during language arts instruction, but all the teachers may be teaching language arts at the same time, thus making it impossible to deliver services in a timely manner in every place it is needed. However, if teachers stagger the schedule for teaching language arts, it is far more likely that in-class services can be a feasible option.

Another scheduling matter for some elementary schools concerns art, music, and physical education. As noted in the Putting Ideas Into Practice Feature, "Finding Shared Planning Time" on page 314, in some schools principals are working with central office administrators to arrange these classes simultaneously

Figure 13.1   Sample Teaching Schedule for a Middle School Special Educator

Period	Monday	Tuesday	Wednesday	Thursday	Friday
1	Co-taught English	Co-taught English	Co-taught English	Testing/ Accommodations	Co-taught English
2	Co-taught math	Co-taught math	Co-taught math	Co-taught math	Co-taught math
3	Co-taught social studies	Co-taught science	Co-taught social studies	Co-taught science	Co-taught social studies
4	Lunch	Lunch	Lunch	Lunch	Lunch
5	Planning	Team planning	Planning	Team planning	Planning
6	Co-taught English	Co-taught English	Co-taught math	Co-taught math	Staffings
7	Resource	Resource	Resource	Resource	Resource

at one grade level. This creates an opportunity for team planning, and it allows for a special educator to meet with a grade-level team.

At the high school level, scheduling issues often concern arranging shared preparation time for teachers and special educators. One strategy for doing so is to assign this time first, before other preparation times are established. This often disrupts traditional seniority-based scheduling approaches but does help teachers be successful in their collaborative efforts. As noted earlier, another high school option is to assign a special educator to each department. In addition to solving a scheduling problem, doing this has the advantage of ensuring that any general education teacher need contact only one person regarding a student concern, rather than try to figure out who the responsible special services person happens to be.

Coordinating Services for Collaboration

Arranging a schedule that encourages collaboration is not sufficient in many cases. It is also important to consider that schedule in terms of its impact on the schedules of other service providers in a school and the programs and services they are operating (Lugg & Boyd, 1993). This matter of service coordination becomes especially important in schools in which most, if not all, individualized services for students are delivered in the general education classroom.

Consider this list of individuals who could be going into a classroom to work with teachers and students:

- special education teachers (could be several, depending on school size and student needs)
- speech/language therapists
- counselors
- social workers
- psychologists
- paraprofessionals (special education or from other programs)
- Title I math or reading teachers
- paid tutors
- parent volunteers
- interns or student teachers
- members of Future Teachers of America
- bilingual educators

Would you want to be a general education teacher trying to coordinate the work of even half of these individuals coming to the classroom? One teacher we know was given just such a task. After one particularly grueling day, she told her principal to get everyone out, that she wanted just her classroom and her students by herself. She had had too much of a good thing.

Professionals delivering in-class services may need to coordinate their efforts and assist each other in meeting student needs. For example, if a speech and language therapist is co-teaching in a first-grade classroom and there is one student in the class with a learning disability, the therapist may be able to meet that student's needs instead of the special educator going into the classroom. If a Title I reading specialist or a bilingual educator is spending an hour each day in a fourth-grade class, this specialist may be able to include students with IEPs who need reading instruction. In other words, care must be taken to prevent individual classrooms from being overrun by many service providers coming and going or otherwise disrupting instruction. This is especially true if the classroom already has a paraprofessional assigned to it because of either large class size or identified student needs. At the same time, high-quality services often can be delivered and personnel resources used more efficiently if the professionals are flexible in their approaches and their willingness to share their responsibilities for service delivery with each other as appropriate. Of course, all these ideas can be viewed as applicable only if the needs of students with IEPs or other specialized services are being met.

PROGRAM DEVELOPMENT TASKS

All of the issues and concerns raised thus far in this chapter are parts of a whole. They are considerations that must be taken into account when planning or refining programs emphasizing collaboration. The next practical matter addressed here directly concerns how to go about planning, implementing, and maintaining programs.

Many authors have proposed models to facilitate the successful implementation of innovations in schools, including collaborative programs (Kruse, 1999; Loucks-Horsley & Hergert, 1985; Sparks, 1999; Sparks, Nowakowski, Hall, Alec, & Imrick, 1985). The stages for program development depicted in Figure 13.2 incorporate key elements from these models and comprise the five-stage framework we recommend for school professionals. The stages apply both to new programs and to those being refined.

Stage 1: Establishing the Program and Its Goals

Much of what you accomplish in the initial stage of program development consists of communicating your preliminary plans while determining receptivity and commitment for the program. The critical components include clarifying intent, establishing a planning structure, and assessing needs and setting goals.

Clarify Intent

Once you have decided to undertake program development, fundamental questions are, What is the purpose of this project? and What would this program look like in operation? Having a picture of what you want the program to accomplish enables you to better communicate about it and promotes necessary dialogue about topics such as program feasibility and resource allocation.

Clarifying your program's purpose also can help you to identify the key stakeholders—those individuals or groups who will be most affected by your project. Stakeholders probably include at least one administrator and some of your colleagues, students, and their parents. You and these stakeholders need to

---

Figure 13.2   Stages for Program Development

Stage 1: Establishing the Program and Its Goals

1.1   Clarify intent
1.2   Establish a planning structure
1.3   Assess needs and set goals

Stage 2: Planning for Implementation

2.1   Identify and describe the ideal outcome
2.2   Match the context and resources
2.3   Design implementation strategies
2.4   Specify component parts
2.5   Establish timelines

Stage 3: Preparing for Implementation

3.1   Create awareness
3.2   Select implementers
3.3   Make logistical arrangements
3.4   Train personnel
3.5   Design an evaluation plan

Stage 4: Implementing the Program

4.1   Expand professional development activities
4.2   Carry out program activities
4.3   Evaluate the program

Stage 5: Maintaining the Program

5.1   Refine the program
5.2   Plan for ongoing support

---

reach a shared understanding of and agreement about program purpose (Schwahn & Spady, 1998). For example, if you are proposing to co-teach with a general education teacher, you, the principal, and the teacher all need to have the same understanding of what co-teaching involves. The principal could assume that you and the other teacher are dividing responsibility for the existing curriculum. The general education teacher may think the arrangement will result in reduced class size because you will divide the students and each teach some of them. You might be envisioning you and your colleague both teaching the whole group with one person presenting and the other supporting. These are three valid but very different interpretations, and they demonstrate the importance of achieving shared understanding of program purpose.

Establish a Planning Structure

As you clarify the purpose of the program and begin the crucial task of building a base of relationships, forming a planning team and process is the next activity.

Often schools use a task force structure and involve 5–12 people. This is particularly important if the program affects many people, since teams that include a representative group of stakeholders can ensure that diverse perspectives are considered and create a broad base of support. Recognize, too, that other types of diversity on a planning team are an asset. Thus, you should include veteran teachers, new teachers, teachers from different ethnic groups, and men and women. The team is often well served by having at least one skeptical member who will point out problems in the program and otherwise represent potential opposition to it.

Assess Needs and Set Goals

The final task in the initial program development stage is goal setting based on needs assessment. This task requires taking all the information gleaned during preliminary conversations and clearly articulating it. For example, consider the project described below that Mr. Martin, a middle school resource teacher, proposes to implement with his colleagues Ms. Linden and Mr. Kent.

◆ Ms. Linden and Mr. Kent both teach eighth-grade social studies using the district-adopted text and following district curriculum guidelines. Ms. Linden has five students who receive learning strategies assistance one period each day from Mr. Martin in the resource room. Mr. Kent has four students in his class who also receive these services, but he also has two students who are being assessed for special education eligibility. Ms. Linden and Mr. Kent each have an additional four to six students who consistently fail unit tests and have many learning problems, although they do not qualify for special education. Mr. Kent and Ms. Linden are proficient teachers with strong organizational and presentation skills who work diligently to reach their students. They are frustrated because they do not feel they are succeeding.

Mr. Martin also is frustrated because he knows that the students from these classes with whom he works are falling further behind even though they could learn most of the information with some additional adaptations. Mr. Martin believes that co-teaching is a preferable approach for serving these students as well as for assisting the high number of other students struggling in social studies. Although he would like to co-teach in every general education classroom, Mr. Martin has decided to begin with only Mr. Kent and Ms. Linden, treating their effort as a pilot for possible later expansion.

An analysis of this project and the initially identified goals are shown in Figure 13.3. The analysis illustrates a needs assessment and goal-setting process in a pilot activity involving a limited number of people. The same process also can be used to set goals for larger projects or programs.

Whether you are developing a program with limited or broad impact, goal setting should derive from the assessment of needs. One of the most important questions to ask is, What needs are we trying to address? At first glance this question may seem simplistic, but it is essential, since it eventually guides the evaluation of the program. A team that emphasizes intervention assistance to general education teachers, for example, may address the need either to reduce referrals

Figure 13.3	Needs Analysis and Goals for a Collaborative Project
Kind of Program	Curriculum and instruction Student inclusion with co-teaching
Who Is Affected	Resource teacher Two sections of eighth-grade social studies Two social studies teachers Nine students with IEPs Eight to 12 students in general education

Current Situation	Students
	   Some unable to keep up
	   Some repeating material
	   Some tuning out and ditching classes
	Students with IEPs
	   Isolated from peers in resource service
	   Little access to class discussion
	Teachers
	   Frustrated by barriers to student learning
	   Unable to vary instruction for student needs

Evidence	Teacher observation of students' special education class Record of 6 to 8 students failing unit tests in each class

Goals	Improved student performance on unit tests
	Increased teacher knowledge of ways to modify
	   instruction to meet student needs
	Opportunities for enrichment activities
	Improved student attitudes toward social studies
	Improved student attendance
	Learning assistance for resource students in general
	   education classes
	Interest in co-teaching on the part of teachers in
	   other classes

to special education, to increase general education teacher skills for responding to student learning and behavior problems, or to individualize services for all students. In other collaborative programs, needs addressed could include improved professional morale, increased skills, or expanded teacher empowerment. The clarification of needs helps you to specify appropriate program goals, but these goals should be stated explicitly so that the expectations are clear.

Stage 2: Planning for Implementation

The second stage of program development is to systematically plan a course of action to achieve the desired program goals. This involves several tasks, including identifying and describing in detail the desired program outcomes, matching context and resources, designing implementation strategies derived from the program analysis, specifying program components, and establishing timelines.

Identify and Describe the Ideal Outcome

There are many ways to describe the ideal outcome for the program you are developing. One strategy is to determine who will benefit directly from the program and for whom the program is appropriate. For example, the program might include special education professionals serving students who do not have IEPs or providing services to students with IEPs in innovative ways, with the outcome being an increase in the number of students receiving assistance or an increase in contacts between students with and without disabilities. This type of outcome should be specific so that any legal or procedural issues can be addressed. Another reason for clarifying the appropriateness of the program for different students is that this information gives an indication of how many students will be served and thus assists in allocating appropriate amounts of teacher time and other resources.

A second strategy for specifying ideal outcomes is to set the criteria for selecting participants. Because it is often advisable to start new programs on a small-scale pilot basis, this selection may determine the ultimate success or failure of the effort. Planning teams should delineate criteria for selecting professionals who have the attitudes and skills to participate effectively, to work collaboratively, and to help disseminate information about the pilot to others. In programs that serve students, the question also concerns establishing entry and exit criteria. Many times, general professional judgment has been the primary criterion used for students' entry into and exit from programs. Although this approach may have some intuitive appeal, the necessity of establishing parameters that can be documented seems self-apparent.

Match the Context and Resources

A new program cannot exist as an add-on to the already extensive responsibilities of school professionals. Establishing a new program or initiating a new project requires the careful assessment and allocation or reallocation of appropriate resources and may necessitate securing some outside resources. Many of the role requirements, time issues, and scheduling and coordination concerns already described in this chapter should be articulated during this part of program development. Decisions eventually should be reached based on what is possible balanced against what is ideal.

Design Implementation Strategies

After you analyze the context in which your program will operate, you can reconceptualize the previously specified ideal outcome, making clearer decisions about feasible parameters for your program. As you refine your program design and develop a plan for implementing it, you will be considering and selecting the implementation strategies that offer the most promise for success. The importance of considering a school's ecology to determine ongoing adaptations of your original plan cannot be overemphasized, because the sense of ownership and commitment that develops during the adaptation process is critical to the success of these endeavors (e.g., Berman & McLaughlin, 1978; Phillips, McCullough, Nelson, & Walker, 1990; Schwahn & Spady, 1998).

Staying open to adapting your program and implementation strategies can sometimes turn presumed barriers into opportunities. For example, you might be contemplating a project that the professional literature and experts claim requires extensive teacher preparation and curriculum development time. The situation in your school may prohibit making any significant new demands for teacher time. Yet your context analysis may reveal that funds are available in particular budget lines to purchase new materials (thus reducing or eliminating the need for teachers to develop new materials) and that two previously scheduled inservice days can be used for teacher preparation time. In this circumstance, money may be more readily available than time, and you may be able to use it to reduce some of the time requirements and enhance the potential for program implementation and success.

Specify Component Parts

Another important element in the implementation plan is to specify the program's component parts. These might include the types of services or activities involved or the procedures needed to support the program. This specification provides guidance for carrying out the program and sets appropriate expectations for the individuals involved.

An example may assist in clarifying this concept: In one local district, a pilot project to provide teachers with assistance in developing interventions for their students with learning or behavior difficulties was undertaken at five elementary school sites. One of the first activities completed by the planning team was to articulate these services as part of the project: individual assistance in developing strategies to improve student performance in classes, assistance in implementing alternative classroom grouping arrangements such as cooperative learning and peer tutoring, social worker and psychologist assistance for social skills training, arrangement of in-service training for teachers as requested, and development of supplemental materials for students. By creating this list, one of the most common sources of discomfort in new programs was eliminated: The intervention team members knew what they could and should do, and classroom teachers knew what services were available. In another district in which this was not done, the same questions are still occurring after two years of implementation: "Okay, so exactly what do I *do* when I work with a classroom teacher?" "So there's a team that is supposed to help me. What kind of help am I supposed to be getting and what do *I* have to do to get it? Will I just get more advice about what I should do?"

Establish Timelines

A time line for program implementation facilitates planning and effective implementation, clarifies goals, and communicates realistic expectations for the program. However, overly ambitious time lines cause frustration and stress, and so they should be sufficiently long to allow both for inevitable delays and adaptations and for demonstration of a program's success before expansion occurs.

Stage 3: Preparing for Implementation

Once an implementation plan is developed, a number of other developmental tasks remain. These tasks—creating awareness, selecting implementers, making logistical arrangements, preparing personnel, and designing an evaluation plan—collectively represent a stage for detailed preparation for implementation.

Create Awareness

When individuals are first confronted with the possibility of changing their practices or roles, they are likely to have very self-oriented concerns: What is the new practice? What will it mean to me? Only after the concerns of a self-oriented nature are resolved do individuals progress to other concerns about managing the new practice (How do I implement it effectively?) or about its impact on students (How is this affecting students?) (Guskey & Peterson, 1996; Hall & Loucks, 1978).

Because professionals' first level of concern is typically self-oriented, initial preparation should focus on increasing their awareness and providing them with introductory information. Some schools have used staff meetings, grade-level meetings, or small-group briefings to familiarize personnel with new programs. You will learn more about conducting this and other types of staff development later in this chapter. In addition, information also can be shared in written form through school bulletins, faculty memos, fact sheets, school newspapers, and the like. Whatever approach is used, the emphasis should be on brevity, since personnel are not likely to want detailed procedures or skill development at this point.

Since this text is about school-based special services providers and their collaborative activities with colleagues, we should mention some of the unique initial concerns these professionals may experience. For example, the shifts in professional roles and responsibilities in collaborative programs are likely to be significant. Special educators newly involved in collaborative service delivery programs may fear that their professional positions are gradually being eliminated. Another concern relates to professional self-confidence. Some special services providers question whether or not they have valuable information to share with general education teachers. They have specific expertise, but they wonder how it applies to students in another context. A third fear specifically concerns co-teaching programs. Special services providers sometimes fear they will become glorified paraprofessionals, a clearly inappropriate role for them. Other concerns of special services providers include ability to deal with the personalities of many other colleagues and apprehension about working with colleagues who are disinterested in collaborative approaches.

General education teachers, too, may have concerns about the implementation of programs stressing collaboration with special services providers. For example, they may fear that others will be coming into their classrooms to tell them what to do, and teachers used to working autonomously may resent this invasion of their "turf." Other concerns include a conviction that many special services providers do not understand the limitations on teachers' time for implementing highly individualized interventions and fear that the dubious reward for participating in collaborative programs will be further requests to work with students with special needs.

These and similar concerns are real and should be expected elements of the awareness level in the preparation stage. It is these concerns and the information they require that will assist implementors in providing an adequate foundation.

Select Implementers

One early task—describing ideal outcomes—included a strategy to establish criteria for selecting participants. As you prepare to implement the program, you apply those criteria to identify the personnel and students to be involved. Generally, it is preferable during early program implementation to select implementers from among individuals who volunteer to participate. However, there are some drawbacks to voluntary implementation, particularly if the program is meant to have an eventual schoolwide effect. The distinction between implementers and nonimplementers in a voluntary project may lead to divisions in staff and may create dissention. Awareness of this potential, emphasis on the pilot nature of new programs, and communication of selection criteria may help to reduce this. The principal also should periodically clarify that after the pilot project, many or all teachers may be expected to participate.

Make Logistical Arrangements

Securing needed resources and arranging for their use is part of preparing for implementation. Logistical arrangements may involve arranging for and scheduling the needed training for staff, determining room and other space assignments, selecting and ordering materials, and otherwise arranging program details.

One logistical arrangement that merits additional discussion here is to develop reporting forms and record-keeping procedures. When professionals become involved in programs that require them to interact with others, time accountability sometimes becomes an issue, and so procedures for time accounting should be created. A simple log is usually sufficient, yet not burdensome on your time.

Prepare Personnel

You should be aware, particularly if you are involved in a pilot program, that while implementers are receiving skill-based professional development, many others in the school or district probably require awareness activities so that they can implement the program as appropriate. If the pilot implementers are to be involved in expanding the project in the future, skills they will need for this activity should also become part of a professional development plan. As noted earlier, the topic of staff development is addressed in the next section of this chapter.

Design an Evaluation Plan

Determining whether or not a collaborative endeavor is successful depends on the assessment of many variables, both those addressing the program's outcomes and those considering the satisfaction of individuals affected by it. Any evaluation plan should, of course, be based on the goals set for the program as determined by the needs assessment. Thus, topics for evaluation might include systematic assessment of student achievement, the number of referrals for other services, personnel satisfaction, and parent and student perceptions. Eventually, cost (time, financial resources, number of students served versus benefits for students, teachers, and parents) should be examined. In some cases, personnel evaluation procedures will need to be modified to reflect the program's emphasis on collaboration. Standard evaluation practices should be used for evaluating a small-scale, pilot, or districtwide program.

The following section on implementation and the next on program maintenance are described only briefly because everything that is hoped to occur at these points should have been planned for and anticipated in earlier stages. The strategies designed, the training provided, and the logistics arranged all come together as a well-planned program. The major tasks of these two stages are professional development and evaluation.

Stage 4: Implementing the Program

Expand Professional Development Activities

Professional development at this stage shifts to match the new level of participant concern, often including management issues. Implementers may want to learn how to effectively participate in the new program and how to acquire the specific skills they need. In addition, considerable attention should be paid to assisting professionals to develop positive communication skills, since they have been well prepared to work with students but may know surprisingly little about adult–adult interactions.

Carry Out Program Activities

This is the task that is left to you. Whether you have planned a formal program that requires major changes in professionals' roles and responsibilities or you and a colleague or two are taking a first step toward sharing a program, the benefits of the detailed efforts you have taken to prepare will become apparent as you carry out your program.

Evaluate the Program

The importance of evaluation has already been discussed. You should only have to implement the evaluation design that was developed earlier. Both formative and summative evaluation strategies should be used. The formative evaluation can be coupled with progress-monitoring strategies for the project to assist you in obtaining valuable information during project implementation.

Stage 5: Maintaining the Program

Refine the Program

Reviewing evaluation data should assist you and the planning team to review progress and identify the program's problems and strengths. This review should lead to recommendations for program refinement and continuation. Of course, if data continually indicate that the program is not successful, termination should also be considered.

Plan for Ongoing Support

Assuming that program refinements can be successfully designed and implemented, the next and final task is to arrange ongoing program maintenance. Ideally, planning for maintenance was built into every stage of program development. It requires attention to all of the same issues reviewed throughout this chapter. Timelines, awareness, logistics, context assessment, and all of the other tasks need to be reconsidered and possibly reexecuted. Administrative support that facilitated development at earlier stages becomes particularly critical. Administrators or others with leadership skills and authority should take responsibility for troubleshooting and helping to obtain needed resources to ensure program continuation (Mamlin, 1999; Whitworth, 1999). Without deliberate attention to maintenance, you may find that support for your program deteriorates over time.

STAFF DEVELOPMENT

A discussion of practical matters related to building school collaboration would not be complete without at least a brief mention of staff development, since it is through staff development that professionals usually become aware of initiatives such as collaborative programs and learn the skills to make them successful. Staff development is much more than single workshops or lectures by experts. It is results-driven, standards-based, school-focused, job-embedded, matched to desired professional practices, focused on specific pedagogy, and built on a core set of ideas and beliefs (Sparks & Hirsch, 1997). In twenty-first-century schools, professionals have more and more opportunities to design staff development for themselves and their colleagues. The models and suggestions that follow should assist you in meeting these reasonabilities.

Models of Staff Development

Sparks and Loucks-Horsley (1989) have suggested five models of staff development for teachers. These models are not entirely exclusive of one another, yet they represent generally independent approaches to staff development and offer a means for organizing principles and validated practices. In Figure 13.4 we have summarized the models to highlight key characteristics, underlying assumptions, and aspects of the research base or theoretical orientation that support each one. They are elaborated here.

Figure 13.4	Models of Staff Development for Teachers		
Model	**Key Characteristics**	**Assumptions**	**Theory/Research**
Individually Guided Staff Development	◆ Teachers set own goals. ◆ Learning activities designed by teachers.	◆ Teachers are best judges of own needs. ◆ Teachers are capable of self-directed learning.	◆ Adult learning theorists and stage theory: Individuals have different needs.
Observation/ Assessment	◆ Regular observation and feedback on teaching.	◆ Observation data stimulate reflection and analysis and promote professional growth.	◆ Teaching can be objectively observed and analyzed. ◆ Improvement can result from feedback.
Development/ Improvement Process	◆ Teachers involved in developing or adapting curriculum or other activities to improve instruction.	◆ Demands of problem solving drive teacher learning. ◆ Teachers know best how to improve their performance.	◆ Engagement in curriculum development/school improvement sharpens teachers' thinking.
Training	◆ Workshop type activity conducted by expert. ◆ High participant–trainer ratio.	◆ There are behaviors or techniques worthy of replication by teachers.	◆ Critical training elements are exploration of theory, demonstration or modeling, practice, feedback, and classroom coaching.
Inquiry	◆ Teachers formulate questions about their practice and search for answers.	◆ Teachers are intelligent and have legitimate expertise and experience. ◆ Teachers tend to search for data and reflect to find solutions. ◆ New understanding results from formulating and answering self-generated questions.	◆ Action research and self-monitoring develop teachers' thought.

Adapted from Sparks, D., & Loucks-Horsley, S. (1989). Five models of staff development for teachers. Journal of Staff Development, 10*(4), 40–57.*

Individually Guided Staff Development

In this model, teachers choose and manage their own development program. The phases of activity in this model are (1) identification of a learning need or an interest for an individual teacher, (2) articulation of a learning goal that responds to the teacher's need or interest, (3) design of a plan to meet the goal, (4) implementation of the learning experience(s), and (5) assessment of learning in relation to the teacher's goal. Individually guided staff development may be as straightforward as reading one or more journal articles or attending a professional conference. A significantly more elaborate example is found in teacher-designed and teacher-implemented professional projects, such as those supported by district or other "teacher incentive" grants. These projects generally involve research, curriculum development, program development, or similar learning experiences.

Observation/Assessment

Teachers receive surprisingly little feedback on their teaching performance. In some school systems teachers are observed and given feedback by supervisors as infrequently as every three years if they have tenure and annually if they do not. In contrast with these practices, the overriding assumption of the observation/assessment model is that reflection and analysis are the central processes in professional growth. Reflection is stimulated by receiving feedback from others and by observing others in peer coaching, peer observation, and clinical supervision approaches. The phases of activity in the observation/assessment model are (1) pre-observation conference to determine the focus and methods for observation, (2) observation, (3) analysis of observation data, and (4) post-observation conference.

Development/Implementation Process

The primary difference between individually guided staff development and the development/implementation process model is that the latter has a school improvement focus and is driven by a school problem or initiative while the former approach is based on the needs or interests of an individual teacher. The belief that staff development should enhance the abilities of teachers to think and solve problems is central to this model. Illustrative approaches are curriculum development projects and school improvement teams. Phases of activity for the development/implementation process model are (1) identification of and agreement on a problem by a group (such as a department, committee, grade-level team or general faculty), (2) formulation of a response using problem-solving steps, (3) implementation of the plan or development of the product, and (4) assessment of the success of the response or program. The emphasis is on teachers' professional development and learning within the context of problem solving.

Training

The training model is the one with which most teachers have the greatest familiarity. It generally is a large group activity with the primary objectives being to promote awareness, change attitudes, or advance general knowledge and skills. The objectives usually are set by the expert who conducts the training or by those who arranged the event. The trainer must select the methods of delivery (e.g., lecture, simulation, role-playing, and demonstration) that will produce the desired outcomes.

The training model is cost-effective because of the high participant-to-trainer ratio, and it may be the most efficient way for large numbers of teachers to become aware of new information or approaches. Joyce and Showers (1995) suggest that this is also a cost-effective way for groups of teachers to view demonstrations and have the opportunity for skill practice under the guidance of an objective observer.

In the training model, phases of activity include (1) determination of the scope of the training (content, objectives, schedules), (2) conduct of the training, including modeling and demonstrating skills, (3) skill practice with feedback and discussion under simulated conditions, and (4) in-classroom assistance through observation and coaching to promote transfer of learning. This final activity phase is highly similar to the observation/assessment model described on the previous page and makes use of similar procedures.

Inquiry

The inquiry model is perhaps the most difficult of the five staff development models to describe. Through it teachers design and conduct their own research to find answers to questions they have about their practice. It can take a great many forms and may be conducted by a single teacher, a small group, or a school faculty. Inquiry might be formal or informal and may occur in any number of

Staff development can be a strategy for innovation, an innovation in its own right, or a means for institutional development.

settings, including a classroom, library, university, or community. The underlying assumptions stress that teachers are inclined to search for objective answers to their own questions and that they will develop new understandings by doing so.

In the inquiry model, the phases of activity include (1) identification and articulation of a question related to teaching or school practices, (2) selection of data collection approaches, with options ranging from library research to original data collection in the classroom or other school settings, (3) collection of data, and (4) analysis and interpretation of data by an individual or group. Depending on the nature of the inquiry, these activities may lead to a change in the classroom that then requires further data collection and analysis. Examples of this model are seen in current trends toward collaborative research involving teachers and classroom action research (Dilworth & Imig, 1995).

Of the five models presented here, which has the greatest appeal to you as a learner? Which would you prefer to use when you have responsibility for providing others with staff development opportunities? No model fits every kind of learning situation or every type of learner. Moreover, resource issues of time, cost, and personnel often restrict the kinds of staff development opportunities that are possible. We encourage you to keep these models and the differing perspectives on staff development in mind as you design and participate in staff development programs.

Participant Involvement

As you think about effective models of staff development, it is important to keep in mind how all participants will be involved. Based on more than three decades of research on staff development (e.g., Garmston & Wellman, 1992; Joyce & Showers, 1995; Sparks, 1986), the following suggestions should assist you in your efforts:

1. Link staff development to the school culture. The relationship of staff development, school culture, and innovation was discussed earlier in this chapter. Simple strategies such as conducting staff development programs in school settings may help to achieve this. But more significant efforts, such as ensuring that staff development is an integral aspect of existing schoolwide initiatives, are required to truly connect to school culture.

2. Involve teachers in all aspects of the staff development program. As pointed out in discussions of needs assessment and adult learners, teachers should be involved in identifying their own learning needs and in planning to meet them. They can be involved even further by engaging them as facilitators and coaches for one another.

3. Combine effective training strategies with strategies derived from knowledge about adult learners. Specific connections between demonstration, practice, and feedback are known to be effective for skill acquisition. Knowledge about adult learning and alternative models of staff development suggests that other elements are also necessary for effective staff

PUTTING IDEAS INTO PRACTICE 13.2

Refining Your Skills as a Staff Developer

Effective staff developers modify their practices to respond to the character-istics of adult learners. Here are a few adult learner characteristics and some practices that are responsive to them.

Adults as Learners	Effective Practice
Adults have considerable experience, knowledge, and skills.	Tap participants' experience as a learning resource.
Adults seek learning experiences in order to address specific problems or life changes.	Provide learning experiences that give adults specific tools to cope with change.
Adults tend to prefer single-concept, single-theory workshops that focus on application.	Balance theory and application. Create learning opportunities so new concepts can be integrated with existing concepts/practices.
Adults approach learning with a set of expectations.	Clarify leader's and participants' expectations at the beginning.
Adults need to be physically comfortable for effective learning.	Attend to adult needs with breaks, comfortable chairs, and adequate lighting and ventilation.
Adults have many commitments and demands on their time.	Provide learning experiences within an appropriate time frame. Begin and end on time.
Adults have established various ways to resist authority.	Provide for a balance of control between leader and participants.

development. Whatever the model, it should allow for some level of self-directed learning activities with a breadth of opportunities. Opportunities and structures must also be provided that cause teachers to reflect on what they have learned perhaps through structured discussions or journaling.

Design and Delivery

Regardless of the scope of your responsibilities for providing staff development to colleagues, you should keep in mind several core concepts for making it effective. These include (1) basing staff development on needs assessment data, (2) specifying objectives for the staff development, (3) selecting a format complementary to the objectives, and (4) making any presentations that are part of the staff development with careful attention to detail.

Need Assessment

School professionals share some characteristics, but their individuality is undeniable. Recognition of these differences and the uniqueness of each school's culture serve as a rationale for assessing needs of a group before planning staff development with them. Several principles can guide needs assessment:

1. Needs assessment must be linked clearly to the subsequent staff development program. Ideally, needs assessment should be designed to provide useful information that can advise the design and content for staff development efforts.

2. Teachers' perceptions about their needs and ways of meeting them should be a central concern of needs assessment.

3. Needs assessment should be an ongoing process. As teachers become more knowledgeable about a topic and more proficient in a skill, their awareness of their needs changes.

4. Valid, reliable, and comprehensive data are essential. Whenever possible, needs data should be collected from multiple sources using different methods of data collection (e.g., interviews, surveys, focus groups, and observation). This improves the validity and credibility of the results.

5. The information gathered in the needs assessment should be reported back to the participants and to others who may have a legitimate interest in it (e.g., PTA, school board, and local university personnel).

When possible, needs assessment should be interactive. The process used should include opportunities for interaction with those participating in it. In addition to obtaining data, interactive strategies serve to inform or instruct the participants of how data will be used and the intent of the questions or tasks.

Objectives

The needs assessment data you gather should help you decide the objectives for the staff development. You may wish to address one or more of these four types of staff development outcomes (Harris, 1989; Joyce & Showers, 1995; Sparks & Hirsch, 1997):

1. *Knowledge* or *awareness* concerns understanding educational practices, curriculum, concepts, academic content to be taught, educational theories, and legal or procedural requirements.

2. *Attitude change* concerns one's disposition toward one's self (confidence, role changes), others (colleagues, parents, students), academic content (math, English as a second language), or new requirements (teaming, paperwork, inclusion).

3. *Skill development* refers to the acquisition and refinement of discrete proficiencies and strategies.

4. *Adoption* refers to embracing the innovation that is the basis for the staff development and consistently using it, including transferring the training to appropriate use in the learning environment.

Considering these types of outcomes helps to specify the intended results of select activities or a full staff development program. However, also it is important to recognize the existing knowledge, skills, attitudes, and practices of teachers when designing staff development. Is the training needed to help teachers refine or enhance existing practices? Or is it needed to introduce and develop something new that is not in their current repertoire? Answering these questions will help to clarify the type, intensity, and duration of the training that may be required.

Formats

Once the objectives are determined, the next task is to select instructional strategies and formats to include as you design training components that will achieve the intended outcomes. For example, to increase knowledge or awareness a lecture or lecturette is straightforward and laborsaving but has the disadvantage of leaving participants in a passive role. **Listening teams** in which small groups of

PUTTING IDEAS INTO PRACTICE 13.3

Effective Presenting Techniques

Successful presenters adopt a number of attitudes and practices for effectively conveying their messages.

Format

Simplicity	For your audience: ◆ Say what you are going to say. ◆ Say it. ◆ Say what you have said.
Memory Capacity	Present no more than seven concepts during the presentation; four to five concepts would be even better.
Visuals/Graphics	◆ Use graphics and visuals frequently; let visuals guide the message. ◆ Use transition statements between visuals. ◆ Use a title to introduce yourself and your presentation.
Organization	Draft your summary first; work back from that point. Lay out a storyboard to help ensure continuity and completeness of thought and information.
Practice	Practice, polish, and refine your presentation.

Delivery

Make Visuals Legible	There is a limit to the amount of information any one visual can carry. For a room 25 feet long, letters on the screen should be one inch high; for 48 feet, two inches high, etc.
Credibility	Convey authority, expertise, and credible sources in the material presented.
Control	Keep in control of the presentation. Move forward to capture attention; do not stand in one place.
Variation	Vary your "speaking" voice. Provide equal presenter/ media emphasis.
Summarize	Use transition statements with brief summaries of points just made. State conclusions specifically.

Evaluation

Feedback	Prepare a short evaluation form to be filled out by your audience after each presentation. Use their comments to assist you in preparing for future presentations.
Self-Evaluation	Ever wonder how others see you? Try videotaping yourself and evaluate your own performance.

Adapted from materials of the Professional Development Department, Council for Exceptional Children.

participants are assigned particular topics to listen for and discuss later can address this problem. Likewise, a group from the audience may be asked to form a *reaction panel* that offers its perception of the information provided and facilitates participant discussion.

Another format that can be used in staff development is **simulation.** For example, co-teachers might place themselves in the situation of introducing each other to students and rehearse how they will accomplish this task to maintain parity. Team members might simulate an IEP meeting in which each professional receives a case study and directions on the perspective to be taken.

Various forms of discussion groups also can be effective means for delivering staff development. A **group buzz** is one variation of this format. A group buzz is a short discussion of a defined topic. Groups normally are comprised of three to five members who report back to a larger group when they have completed their buzz. **Brainstorming** is a second variation of a group discussion. In this application group members suggest in rapid-fire order all the possible solutions or ideas that come to mind. Criticism and discussion are prohibited until a time limit is reached or ideas are no longer being offered.

Finally, sequence of **model, practice,** and **feedback** is recommended for skill instruction (Joyce & Showers, 1995). Demonstration or modeling of the skill is used to present a clear example of the desired behavior. Practice under simulated circumstances follows demonstration. This may be accomplished through simulated teaching situations with other participants in the workshop or other training setting, or it may be done with small groups of children or a full classroom group. The more complex the skill, or the more it differs from other skills in the teacher's repertoire, the more practice it will require.

Presentation

Whether you are making a presentation in a self-contained workshop or as part of an ongoing professional development program, the attention you give to the design, preparation, and delivery of the session may well determine the success of the event. Conducting training is a complex process that requires practice and feedback to perfect, but a number of essentials will help you prepare and deliver presentations. These are summarized in the box on page 334. As you can see, the secrets of being a successful presenter often have to do with paying careful attention to detail, checking everything related to the presentation to be sure that any possible glitches can be avoided, and then being prepared to handle glitches that arise anyway!

SUMMARY

Whether you participate in collaborative activities involving just one or two colleagues or are involved in redesigning the entire service delivery structure for your school, practical matters related to collaboration will have to be addressed. One set of pragmatic issues concerns finding time for shared planning. Three common solutions for this dilemma are early release/late arrival days, the use of substitute teachers, and instructional strategies as a means of communicating about planning. A second set of pragmatic issues relates to scheduling and coordinating services. Matters to be addressed include establishing individual and school schedules and distributing personnel resources in order to meet all students' needs effectively and efficiently. Practical matters often are addressed through a program development process. The five-stage process recommended includes establishing the program's purpose, planning for implementation, detailed preparation for implementation, implementation, and program maintenance. Finally, staff development, including model selection, participant involvement, and design and delivery, is frequently a significant component of fostering collaboration in schools.

ACTIVITIES AND ASSIGNMENTS

1. Using the list of options for finding time for shared planning, create a questionnaire you can use to poll your colleagues about this important matter. Share the results with others. If possible, interview at least three principals about the feasibility of each option for your locale.

2. Duplicate copies of one of your weekly teaching/service schedules. With a small group, find ways to enhance the amount of time that could be available for collaborative activities. Discuss how changes in your schedule would affect the schedules of other professionals and programs at your school. If you are not in a school setting, create what you would consider to be an ideal schedule.

3. If you currently are teaching or doing a field experience in a school in which special services providers go into classrooms on a regular basis, experiment with alternatives for increasing service efficiency. Begin by listing every individual (including paraprofessionals) who goes into classrooms. Obtain copies of their schedules and a list of the students in those classrooms. Then look for overlaps in services and ways to eliminate these. See if you can devise a plan for increasing the amount of time service providers spend in any particular classroom by blending their roles and eliminating duplication of services.

4. Interview a principal of a school with a strong culture of collaboration. Ask that person how pragmatic and logistical matters are addressed. Write a reflective essay summarizing your findings and relating them to effective collaboration in schools.

5. Based on your evaluation of a situation in your school or in school with which you are familiar, describe a schoolwide program that emphasizes collaboration that you would like to see implemented. With a classmate or colleague, develop a plan for implementing the program.

6. Review the five models of staff development presented in the chapter and answer these questions: Which model has the greatest appeal to you as a learner? Which would you prefer to use when you have responsibility for

providing others with staff development opportunities? Consider your answers and identify principles or tenets common to your preferred models. Discuss your thinking with a colleague.

7. Design an awareness-level presentation for a one-hour workshop to teach the general education teachers in your school about the characteristics and types of instructional modifications needed by a particular group of students.

FOR FURTHER READING

Darling-Hammond, L. (1999). Target time toward teachers. *Journal of Staff Development, 20*(2), 31–36.

Garmston, R. J., & Wellman, B. M. (1992). *How to make presentations that teach and transform.* Alexandria, VA: Association for Supervision and Curriculum Development.

Hackman, D. G., & Berry, J. E. (2000). Cracking the calendar. *Journal of Staff Development, 21*(3), 45–47.

Lynn, L., & Sparks, D. (1999). Time: Squeeze, carve, apply, target, use, arrange, for adult learning [special issue]. *Journal of Staff Development, 20*(2), 1–73.

Peterson, K. D. (1999). Time use flows from school culture. *Journal of Staff Development, 20*(2), 16–19.

Pounder, D. G. (1998). *Restructuring schools for collaboration: Promises and pitfalls.* Albany: State University of New York Press.

Schwahn, C., & Spady, W. (1998). Why change doesn't happen and how to make sure it does. *Educational Leadership, 55*(7), 45–47.

References

Abelson, M. A., & Woodman, R. W. (1983). Review of research on team effectiveness: Implications for teams in schools. *School Psychology Review, 12,* 125–136.

Adams, L., Tomlan, P., Cessna, K., & Friend, M. (1995). *Co-teaching: Lessons from practitioners.* Unpublished manuscript, Colorado Department of Education, Denver.

Agran, M. (1997). *Student directed learning: Teaching self-determination skills.* Pacific Grove, CA: Brooks/Cole.

Alessandra, T., & Hunsaker, P. (1993). *Communicating at work.* New York: Fireside.

Allen, M., & Petr, C. G. (1996). Toward developing standards and measurements for family-centered practice in family support programs. In G. H. S. Singer, L. E. Powers, & A. L. Olsen (Eds.), *Redefining family support: Innovations in public-private partnerships* (pp. 57–86). Baltimore: Brookes.

Allen-Malley, M., & Bishop, P. A. (2000). The power of partners: Two-teacher teams [electronic version]. *Schools in the Middle, 9*(8), 26–30.

Allen, R. I. & Peter, C. G. (1996). Toward developing standards for family-centered practice in family support programs. In G. H. S. Singer, L. E. Powers, & A. L. Olsen (Eds.), *Redefining family support: Innovations in public-private partnerships* (pp. 57–86). Baltimore: Brookes.

American Federation of Teachers. (1999a). AFT renews push for para certification [electronic version]. *American Teacher, 83*(4), 3.

American Federation of Teachers. (1999b). Johns Hopkins study shows positive role of paras [electronic version]. *American Teacher, 84*(1), 3.

Appl, D. J., Troha, C., & Rowell, J. (2001). Reflections of a first-year team. *Teaching Exceptional Children, 33*(3), 4–8.

Argüelles, M. E., Hughes, M. T., Shay, & Schumm, J. S. (2000). Co-teaching: A different approach to inclusion [electronic version]. *Principal, 79*(4), 48, 50–51.

Argyle, M. (1999). *Psychology of interpersonal behavior* (5th ed.). London: Penguin.

Armer, B., & Thomas, B. K. (1978). Attitudes towards interdisciplinary collaboration in pupil personnel service teams. *Journal of School Psychology, 16,* 168–177.

Aronson, E., Blaney, N., Stephan, C., Sikes, J., & Snapp, M. (1978). *The jigsaw classroom.* Beverly Hills, CA: Sage.

Ashbaker, B. Y., & Morgan, J. (2001). Growing roles for teachers' aides. *Education Digest, 66*(7), 60–64.

Austin, V. L. (2001). Teachers' beliefs about co-teaching. *Remedial and Special Education, 22,* 245–255.

Baggs, J. G., Ryan, S. A., Phelps, C. E., Richeson, J. F., & Johnson, J. E. (1992). Collaboration in critical care. *Heart and Lung, 21*(1), 18–24.

Bahamonde, C., & Friend, M. (1999). Teaching English language learners: A proposal for effective service delivery through collaboration and co-teaching. *Journal of Educational and Psychological Consultation, 10,* 1–24.

Bailey, D. B., Buysse, V., Edmondson, R., & Smith, T. M. (1992). Creating family-centered services in early intervention: Perceptions of professionals in four states. *Exceptional Children, 58*(4), 298–309.

Banks, J. A., & McGee-Banks, C. A. (Eds.). (1999). *Multicultural education.* New York: Wiley.

Barsky, A. E. (2000). *Conflict resolution for the helping professions.* Belmont, CA: Brooks/Cole.

Barth, R. S. (1990). *Improving schools from within.* San Francisco: Jossey-Bass.

Bassi, L. J., & Van Buren, M. E. (1999). Sharpening the leading edge. *Training and Development Journal, 53*(1), 23–33.

Bay, M., Bryan, T., & O'Connor, R. (1994). Teachers assisting teachers: A prereferral model for urban educators. *Teacher Education and Special Education, 17,* 10–21.

Bazerman, M. H., & Neale, M. A. (1992). *Negotiating rationally.* New York: Free Press.

Beach Center on Disability. (1999). *Effectiveness of parent to parent support* (Beach Center Research Brief). Lawrence: University of Kansas.

Behring, S. T., Cabello, B., Kushida, D., & Murguia, A. (2000). Cultural modifications to current school-based consultation approaches reported by culturally diverse beginning consultants [electronic version]. *School Psychology Review, 29,* 354–367.

Bell, C. R., & Nadler, L. (1985). Clients and consultants: Meeting and exceeding expectations (2nd ed.). Houston, TX: Gulf.

Bell, M. L., & Forde, D. R. (1999). A factorial survey of interpersonal conflict resolution [electronic version]. *Journal of Social Psychology, 139*(3), 369–377.

Bennis, W., & Biederman, P. W. (1997). *Organizing genius: The secrets of creative collaboration.* Reading, MA: Addison-Wesley.

Bergan, J. R., & Tombari, M. L. (1975). The analysis of verbal interactions occurring during consultation. *Journal of School Psychology, 13,* 209–226.

Bergin, J. W., & Bergin, J. J. (2000). Consultation and counseling strategies to facilitate inclusion [electronic version]. *Counseling and Human Development, 33,* 1–12.

Berman, P., & McLaughlin, M. W. (1978). *Federal programs supporting educational change: Vol. 8. Implementing and sustaining innovation.* Santa Monica, CA: Rand.

Bickmore, K. (1998). Teacher development for conflict resolution. *Alberta Journal of Educational Research, 44*(1), 53–69.

Bishop, K., & Larimer, N. (1999). Collaboration: Literacy through collaboration [electronic version]. *Teacher Librarian, 27*(1), 15–20.

Blanchard, K., & Johnson, S. (1982). The one minute manager. New York: William Morrow.

Bloor, M., Frankland, J., Thomas, M., & Robson, K. (2001). *Focus groups in social research.* Thousand Oaks, CA: Sage.

Bondy, E., & Brownell, M. T. (1997). Overcoming barriers to collaboration among partners-in-teaching [electronic version]. *Intervention in School and Clinic, 33,* 112–115.

Boyd, S. D. (2001). The human side of teaching: Effective listening. *Techniques: Connecting Education and Careers, 76*(7), 60–62.

Braithwaite, C. A. (1997). Sa'ag Naaghai Bik'eh Hozhoon: An ethnography of Navajo educational communicatio practices. *Communication Education, 46,* 219–33.

Brammer, L. M., & MacDonald, G. (1999). *The helping relationship: Process and skills* (7th ed.). Boston: Allyn & Bacon.

Briggs, M. H. (1999). Systems for collaboration: Integrating multiple perspectives. *Comprehensive Psychiatric Assessment of Young Children, 8,* 365–377.

Brinkley, R. C. (1989). Getting the most from client interviews. *Performance and Instruction, 28*(4), 5–8.

Brooks, M. (2001). How to resolve conflict in teams [electronic version]. *People Management, 7*(16) 34–35.

Brown, D., Pryzwansky, W. B., & Schulte, A. C. (1995). *Psychological consultation: Introduction to theory and practice* (3rd ed.). Boston: Allyn & Bacon.

Brownell, M. T., Yeager, E., Rennells, M. S., & Riley, T. (1997). Teachers working together: What teacher educators and researchers should know. *Teacher Education and Special Education, 20,* 340–359.

Bryant, M., & Land, S. (1998). Co-planning is the key to successful co-teaching. *Middle School Journal, 30*(1), 28–34.

Burdette, P. J., & Crockett, J. B. (1999). An exploration of consultation approaches and implementation in heterogeneous classrooms. *Education and Training in Mental Retardation and Developmental Disabilities, 34,* 432–452.

Burns, M. K. (1999). Effectiveness of special personnel in the intervention assistance team model. *Journal of Educational Research, 92*(6), 354–356.

Cambridge, P. (1998) Challenges for safer sex education and HIV prevention services for people with intellectual disabilities in Britain. *Health Promotion International, 13*(1), 67–74.

Cameron, C. A., & Lee, K. (1997). Bridging the gap between home and school with voice-mail technology. *Journal of Educational Research, 90*(3), 182–190.

Caplan, G. (1970). *The theory and practice of mental health consultation.* New York: Basic Books.

Capozzoli, T. K. (1999). Conflict resolution: A key ingredient insuccessful teams [electronic version]. *Supervision, 60*(11), 14–16.

Carner, L. A., & Alpert, J. A. (1995). Some guidelines for consultants revisited. *Journal of Educational and Psychological Consultation, 6,* 47–57.

Carpenter, S. L., King-Sears, M. E., & Keys, S. G. (1998). Counselors + educators + families as a transdisciplinary team = More effective inclusion for students with disabilities, *Professional School Counseling, 2*(1), 9.

Carroll, D. (2001). Considering paraeducator training, roles, and responsibilities. *Teaching Exceptional Children, 34*(2), 60–64.

Cavallaro, C. C., & Haney, M. (1999). *Preschool inclusion.* Baltimore: Brookes.

Chalfant, J. C., Pysh, M. V., & Moultrie, R. (1979). Teacher assistance teams: A model for within building problem solving. *Learning Disability Quarterly, 2,* 85–96.

Chan, S. (1998). Families with Asian roots. In E. W. Lynch & M. J. Hanson (Eds), Developing cross-cultural competence: A guide for working with young children and their families (2nd ed., pp. 251–354). Baltimore: Brookes.

Chan, S. Q. (1990). Early interventionists and culturally diverse families of infants and toddlers with disabilities. *Infants and Young Children, 3*(2), 78–87.

Chen, D., McLean, M., Corso, R., & Bruns, D. (2001). *Working together in EI: Cultural considerations in helping relationships and service utilization* (Technical Report No. 11). [electronic version]. Champaign-Urbana, IL: Culturally and Linguistically Appropriate Services for Early Childhood Research (CLAS) Institute.

Chrispeels, J. H., Strait, C. C., & Brown, J. H. (1999). The paradoxes of collaboration [electronic version]. *Thrust for Educational Leadership, 29*(2), 16–19.

Christie, L. S., McKenzie, H. S., & Burdett, C. S. (1972). The consulting teacher approach to special education: Inservice training for regular classroom teachers. *Focus on Exceptional Children, 4,* 1–10.

Clark, D. L., & Astuto, T. A. (1994). Redirecting reform: Challenges to popular assumptions about teachers and students. *Phi Delta Kappan, 75,* 512–520.

Cloke, K., & Goldsmith, J. (2000). Conflict resolution that reaps great rewards [electronic version]. *Journal for Quality and Participation, 23*(3), 27–30.

Coben, S. S., Thomas, C. C., Sattler, R. O., & Morsink, C. V. (1997). Meeting the challenge of consultation and collaboration: Developing interactive teams. *Journal of Learning Disabilities, 30,* 427–432.

Conderman, G., & Stephens, J. T. (2000). Reflections from beginning special educators. *Teaching Exceptional Children, 33*(1), 16–21.

Conoley, J. C., & Conoley, C. W. (1988). Useful theories in school-based consultation. *Remedial and Special Education, 9*(6), 14–20.

Conoley, J. C., & Conoley, C. W. (1992). *School consultation: Practice and training* (2nd ed.). Boston: Allyn & Bacon.

Constantinides, H. (2001). Organizational and intercultural communication. *Technical Communication Quarterly, 10*(1), 31–59.

Cook, L., & Friend, M. (1990a, April). *A conceptual framework for collaboration in special education.* Preconvention keynote paper presented at the 68th annual convention of the Council for Exceptional Children, Toronto.

Cook, L., & Friend, M. (1990b). Pragmatic issues in the development of special education consultation programs. *Preventing School Failure, 35*(1), 43–46.

Cook, L., & Friend, M. (1991). Collaboration in special education: Coming of age in the 1990s. *Preventing School Failure, 35*(2), 24–27.

Cook, L., & Friend, M. (1995). Co-teaching guidelines for creating effective practices. *Focus on Exceptional Children, 28*(2), 1–12.

Cook, L. H., Weintraub, F. J., & Morse, W. C. (1995). Ethical dilemmas in the restructuring of special education. In J. L. Paul, D. Evans, & H. Rosselli (Eds.), *Integrating school restructuring and special education reform* (pp. 119–139). Fort Worth, TX: Harcourt Brace.

Cook, R. E., Tessier, A., & Klein, M. D. (1992). *Adapting early childhood curricula for children with special needs.* Upper Saddle River, NJ: Merrill/ Prentice Hall.

Cornille, T. A., Pestle, R. E., & Vanwy, R. W. (1999). Teachers' conflict management styles with peers and students' parents [electronic version]. *International Journal of Conflict Management, 10*(1), 69–79.

Correa, V. I., & Tulbert, B. (1993). Collaboration between school personnel in special education and Hispanic families. *Journal of Educational and Psychological Consultation, 5,* 283–308.

Covey, S. (1999). Resolving differences [electronic version]. *Executive Excellence, 16*(4), 5–6.

Crespin, B. J. (1971). Means of facilitating education sought. *Education, 92*(2), 36–37.

Cui, G., Van den Berg, S., & Jiang, Y. (1998). Cross-cultural adaptation and ethnic communication: Two structural equation models. *The Howard Journal of Communications, 9*(1), 69–85.

daCosta, J. L., Marshall, J. L., & Riordan, G. (1998, April). *Case study of the development of a collaborative teaching culture in an inner city elementary school.* Paper presented at the annual meeting of the American Educational Research Association, San Diego, CA. (ERIC Documentation Reproduction Service No. ED420630)

Dalton, D. (1999). Ten pointers worth considering in conflict resolution [electronic version]. *Security: For Buyers of Products, Systems, and Services, 36*(10), 72.

Dana, D. (2001). *Conflict resolution.* Washington, DC: McGraw-Hill.

Daniels, V. I., & McBride, A. (2001). Paraeducators as critical team members: Redefining roles and responsibilities [electronic version]. *NASSP Bulletin, 85*(623), 66–74.

Darling-Hammond, L. (1999). Target time towards teachers. *Journal of Staff Development, 20*(2), 31–36.

Darling-Hammond, L. (1999). Target time towards teachers. *Journal of Staff Development, 20*(2), 31–41.

Darling-Hammond, L. (2001). The challenge of our schools. *Educational Leadership, 58*(8), 12–17.

DeBoer, A., & Fister, S. (1995). *Working together: Tools for collaborative teaching.* Longmont, CO: Sopris West.

Delbecq, A. L., Van de Ven, A. H., & Gustafson, D. H. (1986). *Group techniques for program planning: A guide to nominal group and Delphi processes.* Middleton, WI: Green Briar.

Dettmer, P., Dyck, N., & Thurston, L. (2002). *Consultation, collaboration, and teamwork for students with special needs* (4th ed.). Boston: Allyn & Bacon.

Dettmer, P., Dyck, N., & Thurston, L. P. (1999). *Consultation, collaboration, and teamwork for students with special needs* (3rd ed.). Boston: Allyn & Bacon.

DeVito, J. A. (2001). *The interpersonal communication book* (9th ed.). New York: Longman.

DeVoe, D. (1999). Don't let conflict get you off course [electronic version]. *InfoWorld, 21*(32), 69.

Dilworth, M. E., & Imig, D. G. (1995). Professional teacher development and the reform agenda. *ERIC Digest* (ED 383694).

Dinnebeil, L. A., Hale, L., & Rule, S. (1999). Early intervention program practices that support collaboration [electronic version]. *Topics in Early Childhood Special Education, 19*, 225–235.

DiSibio, R. A., & Gamble, R. J. (1997). Collaboration between schools and higher education: The key to success [electronic version]. *College Student Journal, 31*, 532–536.

Dote-Kwan, J., & Chen, D. (1995). Learners with visual impairments and blindness. In M. C. Wang, M. C. Reynolds, & H. J. Walberg (Eds.), *Handbook of special and remedial education: Research and practice* (2nd ed., pp. 205–228). New York: Elsevier Science.

Dowdy, C. A. (1996). Vocational rehabilitation and special education: Partners in transition for individuals with learning disabilities. *Journal of Learning Disabilities, 29*, 137–147.

Downing, J. E. (1999). *Teaching communication skills to students with severe disabilities.* Baltimore: Brookes.

Downing, J. E. (2002). *Including students with severe and multiple disabilities in typical classrooms: Practical strategies for teachers* (2nd ed.). Baltimore: Brookes.

Downing, J. E., Ryndak, D. L., & Clark, D. (2000). Paraeducators in inclusive classrooms: Their own perceptions. *Remedial and Special Education, 21*, 171–181.

Doyle, M. B., & Gurney, D. (2000). Guiding paraeducators. In Fishbaugh, M. S. E. (Ed.), *The collaboration guide for early career educators.* Baltimore: Brookes.

DuFour, R. (1999). Game plan. *Journal of Staff Development, 20*(2), 61–62.

Egan, G. (2001). Skilled helper: A problem-management and opportunity-development approach to helping (7th ed.). Belmont, CA: Wadsworth.

Elksnin, L. K., & Elsknin, N. (2000). Teaching parents to teach their children to be prosocial. *Intervention in School and Clinic, 36*(1), 27–32.

Elliott, D., & McKenney, M. (1998). Four inclusion models that work. *Teaching Exceptional Children, 30*(4), 54–58.

Elliott, S. N., & Sheridan, S. M. (1992). Consultation and teaming: Problem solving among educators, parents, and support personnel. *Elementary School Journal, 92*, 315–338.

Entwisle, D. R. (1994). Subcultural diversity in American families. In L'Abate (Ed.), *Handbook of developmental family psychology and psychopathology* (pp. 132–156). New York: Wiley.

Erchul, W. P. (1999). Two steps forward, one step back: Collaboration in school-based consultation [electronic version]. *Journal of School Psychology, 37*, 191–203.

Erchul, W. P., & Martens, B. K. (1997). *School consultation: Conceptual and empirical bases.* New York: Plenum.

ERIC Clearinghouse on Language and Linguistics. (2000, December). *Examining Latino paraeduca-*

tors: Interactions with Latino students. Washington, DC: Author.

Evans, R. (1990). Making mainstreaming work through prereferral consultation. *Educational Leadership, 48*(1), 73–77.

Evans, S. B. (1980). The consultant role of the resource teacher. *Exceptional Children, 46,* 402–404.

Fairhurst, G. T., & Sarr, R. A. (1997). *The art of framing: Managing the language of leadership.* San Francisco: Jossey-Bass/Pfeiffer.

Feldman, R. S. (1985). *Social psychology: Theories, research, and applications.* New York: McGraw-Hill.

Fennick, E. (2001). Co-teaching: An inclusive curriculum for transition. *Teaching Exceptional Children, 33*(6), 60–66.

Fenton, K. S., Yoshida, R. K., Maxwell, J. P., & Kaufman, M. T. (1979). Recognition of team goals: An essential step toward rational decision-making. *Exceptional Children, 45,* 638–644.

Festinger, L. (1957). *A theory of cognitive dissonance.* Stanford, CA: Stanford University Press.

Fiedler, C. R. (2000). *Making a difference: Advocacy competencies for special education professionals.* Boston: Allyn & Bacon.

Fiedler, F. E. (1967). *A theory of leadership effectiveness.* New York: McGraw-Hill.

Fishbaugh, M. S. E. (1997). *Models of collaboration.* Boston: Allyn & Bacon.

Fishbaugh, M. S. E. (2000). *The collaboration guide for early career educators.* Baltimore: Brookes.

Fisher, D. (2001) Cross age tutoring: Alternatives to reading resource room for struggling adolescent readers. *Journal of Instructional Psychology, 28,* 234–240.

Fisher, D., & Frey, N. (2001). Access to the core curriculum: Critical elements for student success. *Remedial and Special Education, 22,* 148–157.

Fisher, R., Ury, W., & Patton, R. (1997). *Getting to yes: Negotiating agreement without giving in* (3rd ed.). Boston: Allyn & Bacon.

Fleming, G. P. (2000). The effects of brainstorming on subsequent problem-solving (Doctoral dissertation, St. Louis University 2000). *Dissertation Abstracts International, 61,* 2804.

Fleury, M. L. (2000). Confidentiality issues with substitutes and paraeducators. *Teaching Exceptional Children, 33*(1), 44–45.

Foley, G. (1990). Portrait of the arena evaluation. In E. Gibbs & D. Teti (Eds.), *Interdisciplinary assessment of infants: A guide for early intervention professionals* (pp. 271–286). Baltimore, MD: Brookes.

Fowler, S. A., Donegan, M., Lueke, B., Hadden, D. S., & Phillips, B. (2000). Evaluating community collaboration in writing interagency agreements on the age 3 transition. *Exceptional Children, 67,* 1–50.

Fox, N. E., & Ysseldyke, J. E. (1997). Implementing inclusion at the middle school level: Lessons from a negative example. *Exceptional Children, 64,* 81–98.

Freer, P., & Watson, T. S. (1999). A comparison of parent and teacher acceptability ratings of behavioral and conjoint behavioral consultation [electronic version]. *School Psychology Review, 28,* 672–684.

French, N. K. (1998). Working together: Resource teachers and paraeducators. *Remedial and Special Education, 19,* 357–368.

French, N. K. (1999). Paraeducators and teachers: Shifting roles. *Teaching Exceptional Children, 32*(2), 69–73.

French, N. K. (1999). Paraeducators: Who are they and what do they do? *Teaching Exceptional Children, 32*(1), 65–69.

French, N. K. (2000). Taking time to save time: Delegating to paraeducators. *Teaching Exceptional Children, 32*(3), 79–83.

French, N. K. (2001). Supervising paraprofessionals: A survey of teacher practices. *Journal of Special Education, 35,* 41–53.

French, N. K., & Chopra, R. V. (1999). Parent perspectives on the role of the paraprofessional in inclusion. *Journal of the Association for Persons with Severe Handicaps, 24*(4), 1–14.

Friend, M. (1984). Consultation skills for resource teachers. *Learning Disability Quarterly, 7,* 246–250.

Friend, M. (1988). Putting consultation into context: Historical and contemporary perspectives. *Remedial and Special Education, 9*(6), 7–13.

Friend, M. (2000). Perspectives: Collaboration in the twenty-first century. *Remedial and Special Education, 20,* 130–132, 160.

Friend, M., & Bursuck, W. (1999). *Including students with special needs: A practical guide for classroom teachers* (2nd ed.). Boston: Allyn & Bacon.

Friend, M., & Bursuck, W. (2002). *Including students with special needs: A practical guide for classroom teachers* (3rd ed.). Boston: Allyn & Bacon.

Friend, M., & Cook, L. (1988). Pragmatic issues in school consultation. In J. F. West (Ed.), *School consultation: Interdisciplinary perspectives on theory, research, training, and practice* (pp. 127–142). Austin:

Research and Training Project on School Consultation, University of Texas.

Friend, M., & Cook, L. (1990). Collaboration as a predictor for success in school reform. *Journal of Educational and Psychological Consultation, 1,* 69–86.

Friend, M., & Cook, L. (1992). It's my turn: The ethics of collaboration. *Journal of Educational and Psychological Consultation, 3,* 181–184.

Friend, M., & Cook, L. (1997). Student-centered teams in schools: Still in search of an identity. *Journal of Educational and Psychological Consultation, 8*(1), 3–20.

Friend, M., Reising, M., & Cook, L. (1993). Co-teaching: An overview of the past, a glimpse at the present, and considerations for the future. *Preventing School Failure, 37*(4), 6–10.

Fullan, M. G. (1994). Coordinating top-down and bottom-up strategies for educational reform. In R. F. Elmore & S. H. Fuhrman (Eds.), *The governance of curriculum: 1994 yearbook of the Association for Supervision and Curriculum Development* (pp. 186–202). Alexandria, VA: Association for Supervision and Curriculum Development.

Gallessich, J. (1982). The profession and practice of consultation. San Francisco: Jossey-Bass.

Gallivan-Fenlon, A. (1994). Integrated transdisciplinary teams. *Teaching Exceptional Children, 26*(3), 16–20.

Gamble, T. K., & Gamble, M. (1999). *Communication works* (6th ed.). New York: McGraw-Hill.

Gamble, T. K., & Gamble, M. (2001). *Communication works* (7th ed.). New York: McGraw-Hill.

Garcia, S. B., Mendez-Perez, A., & Ortiz, A. A. (2000). Mexican American mothers' beliefs about disabilities: Implications for early childhood intervention. *Remedial and Special Education, 21,* 90–102.

Gardner, D. B., & Cary, A. (1999). Collaboration, conflict, and power: Lessons for case managers [electronic version]. *Family and Community Health, 22*(3), 64–77.

Garmston, R. J., & Wellman, B. M. (1992). *How to make presentations that teach and transform.* Alexandria, VA: Association for Supervision and Curriculum Development.

Gately, S. E., & Gately, F. J. (2001). Understanding co-teaching components. *Teaching Exceptional Children, 33*(4), 40–47.

Gaustad, M. G. (1999). Including the kids across the hall: Collaborative instruction of hearing, deaf, and hard-of-hearing students. *The Journal of Deaf Studies and Deaf Education, 4,* 176–190.

Geen, A. G. (1985). Team teaching in the secondary schools of England and Wales. *Educational Review, 37,* 29–38.

Gentry, M., & Ferriss, S. (1999). StATS: A model of collaboration to develop science talent among rural students [electronic version]. *Roeper Review, 21,* 316–320.

Gerber, P. J., & Popp, P. A. (2000). Making collaborative teaching more effective for academically able students: Recommendations for implementation and training [electronic version]. *Learning Disability Quarterly, 23,* 229–236.

Gerlach, K. (2001). *Let's team up! A checklist for paraeducators, teachers, and principals* [NEA checklist series]. Washington, DC: National Education Association.

Giangreco, M. F., Edelman, S. W., Broer, S. M., & Doyle, M. B. (2001). Paraprofessional support of students with disabilities: Literature from the past decade. *Exceptional Children, 68,* 45–63.

Giangreco, M. F., Edelman, S. W., Luiselli, T. E., & MacFarland, S. Z. C. (1997). Helping or hovering? Effects of instructional assistant proximity on students with disabilities. *Exceptional Children, 64,* 7–18.

Gilkerson, L. (1990). Understanding institutional functioning style: A resource for hospital and early intervention collaboration. *Young Children, 2*(3), 22–30.

Glickman, C. D., Gordan, S. P., & Ross-Gordan, J. M. (1998). The significance of leadership style. *Educational Leadership, 55*(7), 20–22.

Goldman, E. (1998). The significance of leadership style. *Educational Leadership, 55*(7), 20–22.

Gomez, G. G. (2001). Sources and information: Creating effective collaboration between high school and community colleges [electronic version]. *New Directions for Community Colleges, 113,* 81–86.

Gonzalez-Mena, J., & Bhavnagri, N. P. (2000). Diversity and infant/toddler caregiving. *Young Children, 55*(5), 31–35.

Goodlad, J. (1984). *A place called school.* New York: McGraw-Hill.

Goodman, G. (1978). *SASHA tape user's manual.* Unpublished manuscript, Department of Psychology, University of California, Los Angeles.

Goodman, G. (1984). SASHA tapes: Expanding options for help-intended communication. In D. Larson (Ed.), *Teaching psychological skills:*

Models for giving psychology away (pp. 271–286). Monterey, CA: Brooks/Cole.

Graden, J. L., (1989). Redefining prereferral intervention as intervention assistance: Collaboration between general and special education. *Exceptional Children, 56,* 227–231.

Graham, D. S. (1998). Consultant effectiveness and treatment acceptability: An examination of consultee requests and consultant responses [electronic version]. *School Psychology Quarterly, 13,* 155–168.

Groce, N. E. (1997). *Adolescence and disability.* Paper presented at the Thematic Discussionon Childhood Disability, Sixteenth Session of the Committee on the Rights of the Child, Palais des Nations, Geneva.

Guilar, J. D. (2001). *The interpersonal communication skills workshop.* New York: Amacom.

Gursky, D. (2000). From para to teacher [electronic version]. *American Teacher, 84*(8), 8.

Guskey, T. R., & Peterson, K. D. (1996). The road to classroom change. *Educational Leadership, 53*(4), 10–14.

Gutkin, T. B. (1999). Collaborative versus directive/prescriptive/expert school-based consultation: Reviewing and resolving a false dichotomy [electronic version]. *Journal of School Psychology, 37,* 167–189.

Hackman, D. G., & Berry, J. E. (2000). Cracking the calendar. *Journal of Staff Development, 21*(3), 45–47.

Hadley, P. A., Simmerman, A., Long, M., & Luna, M. (2000). Facilitating language development for inner-city children: Experimental evaluation of a collaborative, classroom-based intervention [electronic version]. *Language, Speech, and Hearing Services in Schools, 31,* 280–295.

Hall, E. T. (1966). *The hidden dimension.* Garden City, NY: Doubleday.

Hall, E. T. (1981). *The silent language.* New York: Anchor Books.

Hall, G. E., & Loucks, S. F. (1978). Teacher concerns as a basis for facilitating and personalizing staff development. *Teachers College Record, 80*(1), 36–53.

Hall, L. J., McClannahan, L. E., & Krantz, P. J. (1995). Promoting independence in integrated classrooms by teaching aides to use activity schedules and decreased prompts. *Education and Training in Mental Retardation and Developmental Disabilities, 30,* 208–217.

Hanson, M. J., Lynch, E. W., & Wayman, K. I. (1990). Honoring the cultural diversity of families when gathering data. *Topics in Early Childhood Special Education, 10*(1), 112–131.

Hargie, O., Saunders, C., & Dickson, D. (1994). *Social skills in interpersonal communication* (3rd ed.). New York: Routledge.

Hargreaves, A., & Fullan, M. (1998). *What's worth fighting for in education.* Buckingham: Open University Press.

Haring, N. G., & McCormick, L. (1990). *Exceptional children and youth.* Upper Saddle River, NJ: Merrill/Prentice Hall.

Harris, A. M., & Cancelli, A. A. (1991). Teachers as volunteer consultees: Enthusiastic, willing or resistant participants? *Journal of Educational and Psychological Consultation, 2,* 217–238.

Harris, B. M. (1989). *In-service education for staff development.* Boston: Allyn & Bacon.

Harris, K. C. (1995). School-based bilingual special education teacher assistance teams. *Remedial and Special Education, 16,* 337–343.

Harry, B. (1992). Developing cultural awareness: The first step in values clarification for early interventionists. *Topics in Early Childhood Special Education, 12,* 333–350.

Harry, B., Kalyanpur, M., & Day, M. (1999). *Building cultural reciprocity with families: case studies in special education.* Baltimore: Brookes.

Harvey, M. (2001) Vocational-technical education: A logical approach to dropout prevention for secondary special education. *Preventing School Failure, 45*(3), 108–114.

Henning-Stout, M., & Meyers, J. (2000). Consultation and human diversity: First things first [electronic version]. *School Psychology Review, 29,* 419–420.

Heron, T. E., & Harris, K. C. (2001). *The educational consultant: Helping professionals, parents, and mainstreamed students* (4th ed.). Austin, TX: Pro-ed.

Hersey, P. (1984). *The situational leader...The other 59 minutes.* Escondido, CA: The Center for Leadership Studies.

Hobbs, T., & Westling, D. L. (1998). Promoting successful inclusion through collaborative problem-solving. *Teaching Exceptional Children, 31*(1), 12–19.

Hord, S. (1986). A synthesis of research on organizational collaboration. *Educational Leadership, 43*(5), 22–26.

Hourcade, J. J., & Bauwens, J. (2001). Cooperative teaching: The renewal of teachers [electronic version]. *Clearinghouse, 74,* 242–247.

Howard, V. F., Williams, B. F., Port, P. D., & Lepper, C. (1997). *Very young children with special needs: A formative approach for the 21st century.* Upper Saddle River, NJ: Merrill.

Howard, V. F., Williams, B. F., Port, P. D., & Lepper, C. (2001). *Very young children with special needs: A formative approach for the 21st century* (2nd ed.). Upper Saddle River, NJ: Merrill/Prentice Hall.

Howe, K. R., & Miramontes, O. B. (1992). *The ethics of special education.* New York: Teachers College Press.

Howells, K. D. (2000). Boldly going where angels fear to tread [electronic version]. *Intervention in School and Clinic, 35,* 157–160.

Huefner, D. S. (2000). The risks and opportunities of the IEP requirements under IDEA 97. *Journal of Special Education, 33,* 195–204.

Hutchinson, D. J. (1978). The transdisciplinary approach. In J. B. Curry & K. K. Peppe (Eds.), *Mental retardation: Nursing approaches to care* (pp. 65–74). St. Louis, MO: Mosby.

Huxham, C. (Ed.). (1996). *Creating collaborative advantage.* Thousand Oaks, CA: Sage.

Idol, L., Nevin, A., & Paolucci-Whitcomb, P. (1994). *Collaborative consultation* (2nd ed.). Austin, TX: Pro-Ed.

Idol, L., Nevin, A., & Paolucce-Whitcomb, P. (2000). *Collaborative consultation* (3rd ed.) Austin, TX: Pro-Ed.

Institute of Medicine. (1996). *Healthy communities: New partnerships for the future of public health: A report of the first year of the committee on public health.* Washington, DC: National Academy Press.

Isenhart, M. W., & Spangle, M. (2000). *Collaborative approaches to resolving conflict.* Thousand Oaks, CA: Sage.

Ivey, A. E., & Ivey, M. B. (1999). *Intentional interviewing and counseling: Facilitating client development in a multicultural society* (4th ed.). Belmont, CA: Wadsworth.

Jacobson, J. W., & Mulick, J. A. (2000). System and cost research issues in treatments for people with autistic disorders [electronic version]. *Journal of Autism and Developmental Disorders, 30,* 585–593.

Jayanthi, M., & Friend, M. (1992). Interpersonal problem solving: A selected literature review to guide practice. *Journal of Educational and Psychological Consultation, 3,* 147–152.

Jehn, K. A. (2000). The influence of proportional and perceptual conflict composition on team performance. *International Journal of Conflict Management, 11*(1), 56–73.

Johnson, D. R. (2002). Challenges facing secondary education and transition services for youth with disabilities. *Teaching Exceptional Children, 34*(3) 86–88.

Johnson, D. W., & Johnson, F. P. (1997). *Joining together: Group theory and group skills* (6th ed.). Boston: Allyn & Bacon.

Johnson, D. W., & Johnson, F. P. (2000). *Joining together: Group theory and group skills* (7th ed.). Boston: Allyn & Bacon.

Johnson, D. W., & Johnson, R. T. (1999). *Learning together and alone: Cooperative, competitive, and individualistic learning* (5th ed.). Boston: Allyn & Bacon.

Johnson, S. D., & Roellke, C. F. (1999). Secondary teachers' and undergraduate education faculty members' perceptions of teaching-effectiveness criteria: A national survey [electronic version]. *Communication Education, 48,* 127–138.

John-Steiner, V. (2000). *Creative collaboration.* New York: Oxford University Press.

Johnston, M., Brosnan, P., Cramer, D., & Dove, T. (Eds.). (2000). *Collaborative reform and other improbable dreams.* Albany: State University of New York Press.

Johnston, S. S., Tulbert, B. L., Sebastian, J. P., Devries, K., & Gompert, A. (2000). Vocabulary development: A collaborative effort for teaching content vocabulary [electronic version]. *Intervention in School and Clinic, 35,* 311–315.

Jordan, J. B., Gallagher, J. J., Hutinger, P. L., & Karnes, M. B. (1988). *Early childhood special education: Birth to three.* Reston, VA: Council for Exceptional Children and Its Division for Early Childhood.

Jordan, L., Reyes-Blanes, M. E., Peel, B. B., & Lane, H. B. (1998). Developing teacher–parent partnerships across cultures: Effective parent conferences. *Intervention in School and Clinic, 33*(3), 141–149.

Joyce, B., & Showers, B. (1995). *Student achievement through staff development: Fundamentals of school renewal* (2nd ed.). White Plains, NY: Longman.

Jung, B. (1998). Mainstreaming and fixing things: Secondary teachers and inclusion [electronic version]. *Educational Forum, 62,* 131–138.

Kaiser, S. M., & Woodman, R. W. (1985). Multi-disciplinary teams and group decision-making techniques: Possible solutions to decision-making problems. *School Psychology Review, 14,* 457–470.

Kalyanpur, M., & Harry, B. (1999). *Culture in special education.* Baltimore: Brookes.

Kalyanpur, M., & Harry, B. (1999). *Culture in special education: Building reciprocal family-professional relationships.* Baltimore, MD: Brookes.

Kampwirth, R. J. (1999). *Collaborative consultation in the schools: Effective practices for students with learning and behavior problems.* Upper Saddle River, NJ: Merrill.

Karp, H. B. (1984). Working with resistance. *Training and Development Journal, 38*(3), 69–73.

Kassner, K. (2002). Cooperative learning revisited: A way to address the standards. *Music Educators Journal, 88*(4), 17–23.

Katisyannis, A., Hodge, J., & Lanford, A. (2000). Paraeducators: Legal and practice considerations. *Remedial and Special Education, 21,* 297–304.

Kay, P. J., Sherrer, M. K., & Fitzgerald, M. (1992, November). *Involving special educators in school reform: The development of peer leadership.* Paper presented at the conference of the Teacher Education Division of the Council for Exceptional Children, Cincinnati. (ERIC Document Reproduction Service No. 365 029).

Kearns, J. F., Kleinert, H. L., & Kennedy, S. (1999). We need not exclude anyone. *Educational Leadership, 56*(6), 33–38.

Kenton, S. B. (1989). Speaker credibility in persuasive business communication: A model which explains gender differences. *Journal of Business Communications, 26,* 143–157.

Kersh, M. E., & Masztal, N. B. (1998). An analysis of studies of collaboration between universities and K–12 schools [electronic version]. *Educational Forum, 62,* 218–225.

Kesson, K., & Oyler, C. (1999). Integrated curriculum and service learning. *English Education, 31,* 135–49.

Kew, D. W. (2000). Middle level teaming—Strength in collaboration [electronic version]. *Schools in the Middle, 9*(9), 39–40.

Killoran, J., Templeman, T. P., Peters, J., & Udell, T. (2001). Identifying paraprofessional competencies for early intervention and early childhood special education. *Teaching Exceptional Children, 34*(1), 68–73.

Kinlaw, D. C. (1993). *Team-managed facilitation.* San Diego: Pfeiffer & Company.

Klapstein, S. (1994). A collaborative interagency diagnostic classroom. *Intervention in School and Clinic, 29,* 180–183.

Kluckhorn, F. R. (1968). Variations in value orientations as a factor in education planning. In E. M. Bower & W. G. Hallister (Eds.), *Behavioral science frontiers in education* (pp. 289–314). New York: Wiley.

Kluwin, T. N. (1999). Co-teaching deaf and hearing students: Research on social integration [electronic version]. *American Annals of the Deaf, 144,* 339–344.

Knoff, H. M., Sullivan, P., & Liu, D. (1995). Teachers' ratings of effective school psychology consultants: An exploratory factor analysis study [electronic version]. *Journal of School Psychology, 33,* 39–57.

Kosmoski, G. J., & Pollack, D. R. (2000). *Managing difficult, frustrating, and hostile conversations: Strategies for savvy administrators.* Thousand Oaks, CA: Corwin Press.

Kosmoski, G. J., & Pollack, D. R. (2001). *Managing conversations with hostile adults: Strategies for teachers.* Thousand Oaks, CA: Corwin Press.

Kotkin, R. A. (1995). The Irvine paraprofessional program: Using paraprofessionals in serving students with ADHD. *Intervention in School and Clinic, 30,* 235–240.

Kratochwill, T. R., & Stoiber, K. C. (2000). Uncovering critical research agendas for school psychology: Conceptual dimensions and future directions [electronic version]. *School Psychology Review, 29,* 591–603.

Krebs, C. S. (2000). Beyond blindfolds: Creating an inclusive classroom through collaboration [electronic version]. *RE:view, 31,* 180–186.

Kronick, R. F. (2000). *Human services and the full service school: The need for collaboration.* Springfield, IL: Thomas.

Kruger, L. J., Struzziero, J., Watts, R., & Vaca, D. (1995). The relationship between organizational support and satisfaction with teacher assistance teams. *Remedial and Special Education, 16,* 203–211.

Kruk, E. (Ed.). (1997). *Mediation and conflict resolution in social work and the human services.* Chicago: Nelson-Hall.

Kruse, S. D. (1999). Collaborate. *Journal of Staff Development, 20*(3), 14–16.

Kübler-Ross, E. (1969). *On death and dying.* New York: Macmillan.

Kurpius, D. J., & Brubaker, J. C. (1976). *Psycho-educational consultation: Definition, functions, preparation.* Bloomington: Indiana University.

Lambert, L. (1998). How to build leadership capacity. *Educational Leadership, 55*(7), 17–19.

Lambie, R. (2000). *Family systems within educational contexts: Understanding at-risk and special needs students* (2nd ed). Denver: Love.

Landers, M. F., & Weaver, H. R. (1997). *Inclusive education: A process, not a placement.* Swampscott, MA: Watersun.

Langone, J., Langone, C. A., & McLaughlin, P. J. (2000). Analyzing special educators' views on commumnity-based instruction for students with mental retardation and developmental disabilities: Implications for teacher education. *Journal of Developmental and Physical Disabilities, 12*(1), 17–34.

Lasater, M. W., Johnson, M. M., & Fitsgerald, M. (2000). Completing the education mosaic. *Teaching Exceptional Children, 33*(1), 46–51.

Laud, L. E. (1998). Changing the way we communicate. *Educational Leadership, 55*(7), 23–25.

Lawson, H. A. (1999). Two new mental models for schools and their implications for principals' roles, responsibilities, and preparation [electronic version]. *NASSP Bulletin, 83*(611), 8–27.

Lazar, A., & Slostad, F. (1999). How to overcome obstacles to parent–teacher partnerships. *Clearinghouse, 72*(4), 206–211.

LeCapitaine, J. (2000). Role of the school psychologist in the treatment of high-risk students [electronic version]. *Education, 121,* 73–79.

Lee, G. V., & Barnett, B. G. (1994). Using relective questioning to promote collaborative dialogue. *Journal of Staff Development, 15*(1), 16–21.

Lehr, A. E. (1999). The administrative role in collaborative teaming [electronic version]. *NASSP Bulletin, 83*(611), 105–111.

Leonard, L. J., & Leonard, P. E. (1999). Reculturing for collaboration and leadership [electronic version]. *Journal of Educational Research, 92,* 237–242.

Lewin, K. (1951). *Field theory in the social sciences: Selected theoretical papers.* New York: Harper & Row.

Little, J. W. (1982). Norms of collegiality and experimentations: Workplace conditions of school success. *American Educational Research Journal, 5,* 325–340.

Littlejohn, S. W., & Domenici, K. (2001). *Engaging communication in conflict: Systemic practice.* Thousand Oaks, CA: Sage.

Lloyd, J. W., Crowley, E. P., Kohler, R. W., & Strain, P. S. (1988). Redefining the applied research agenda: Cooperative learning, prereferral, teacher consultation, and peer-mediated interventions. *Journal of Learning Disabilities, 21,* 43–52.

Lopez, E. C. (2000). Conducting instructional consultation through interpreters [electronic version]. *School Psychology Review, 29,* 378–388.

Lortie, D. C. (1975). *School teacher: A sociological study.* Chicago: University of Chicago Press.

Loucks-Horsley, S., & Hergert, L. (1985). *An action guide to school improvement.* Alexandria, VA: Association of Supervision and Curriculum Development.

Lovelace, K. A. (2000). External collaboration and performance: North Carolina local public health departments, 1996. *Public Health Reports, 115*(3).

Luckner, J. L. (1999). An examination of two co-teaching classrooms [electronic version]. *American Annals of the Deaf, 144,* 24–34.

Lugg, C. A., & Boyd, W. L. (1993). Leadership for collaboration: Reducing risk and fostering resilience. *Phi Delta Kappan, 75,* 253–258.

Lustig, M. W., & Koester, J. (1999). *Intercultural competence: Interpersonal communication across cultures* (3rd ed.). New York: Longman.

Lynch, E. W. (1998). Developing cross-cultural competence. In E. W. Lynch & M. J. Hanson (Eds.), *Developing cross-cultural competence: A guide for working with young children and their families* (2nd ed.). Baltimore: Brookes.

Lynch, E. W., & Hanson, M. J. (1998). Steps in the right direction: Implications for interventionists. In E. W. Lynch & M. J. Hanson (Eds.), *Developing cross-cultural competence: A guide for working with young children and their families* (2nd ed, pp. 491–512). Baltimore: Brookes.

MacIver, D. J. (1990). Meeting the needs of young adolescents: Advisory groups, interdisciplinary teacher teams, and school transition programs. *Phi Delta Kappan, 71,* 458–464.

Maeroff, G. (1993). Building teams to rebuild schools. *Phi Delta Kappan, 71,* 512–519.

Maital, S. L. (1996). Integration of behavioral and mental health consultation as a means of overcoming resistance. *Journal of Educational and Psychological Consultation, 7,* 291–303.

Mamlin, N. (1999). Despite best intentions: When inclusion fails. *Journal of Special Education, 33,* 36–48.

Man, D. (1999). Community based empowerment programme for families with a brain injured survivor: An outcome study. *Brain Injury, 13*(6), 433–445.

Marans, S., Berkowitz, S. J., & Cohen, D. J. (1998). Police and mental health professionals: Collaborative response to the impact of violence on children and families. *Child and Adolescent Psychiatric Clinics of North America, 7,* 635–650.

Margolis, H. (1999). Meditation for special education conflicts: An opportunity to improve family-school relationships. *Journal of Educational Psychological Consultation, 10,* 91–100.

Marks, S. U., Schrader, C., & Levine, M. (1999). Paraeducator experiences in inclusive settings: Helping, hovering, or holding their own? *Exceptional Children, 65,* 315–328.

Martinez, M. E. (1998). What is problem solving? *Phi Delta Kappan, 79,* 605–609.

Mattison, R. E. (2000). School consultation: A review of research on issues unique to the school [electronic version]. *Journal of the American Academy of Child and Adolescent Psychiatry, 39,* 402–413.

McCaleb, J. G. (1987). Review of communication competencies used in statewide assessments. In J. L. McCaleb (Ed.), *How do teachers communicate? A review and critique of assessment practices* (pp. 7–28). Washington, DC: American Association of Colleges for Teacher Education.

McCroskey, J. C., Fayer, J. M., Richmond, V., Sallinen, A., & Barraclough, R. A. (1996). A multicultural examination of the relationship between nonverbal immediacy and affective learning. *Communication Quarterly, 44,* 297–307.

McDonnell, J. (1997). Isn't it about achieving a balance? *TASH Newsletter, 23*(2), 23–24, 29.

McGinn, D., & McCormick, J. (1999, February 1). Your next job. *Newsweek,* 42–45.

McKenzie, H. S. (1972). Special education and consulting teachers. In F. Clark, D. Evans, & L. Hammerlynk (Eds.), *Implementing behavioral programs for schools and clinics.* Champaign, IL: Research Press.

Medved, M. (2001, August 8). Good teamwork outshines superstar systems. *USA Today,* 13A.

Mehrabian, A. (1971). *Silent messages.* Belmont, CA: Wadsworth.

Melamed, J. C., & Reiman, J. W. (2000). Collaboration and conflict resolution in education [electronic version]. *High School Magazine, 7*(7), 16–20.

Menninger, W. C. (1950). Mental health in our schools. *Educational Leadership, 7,* 520.

Miller, M. D., Brownell, M. T., & Smith, S. W. (1999). Factors that predict teachers staying in, leaving, or transferring from the special education classroom. *Exceptional Children, 65,* 201–218.

Miller, S. P. (2002). *Validated practices for teaching students with diverse needs and abilities* (Chapter 6, pp. 235–285). Boston: Allyn & Bacon

Mitchell, A. (1997). Teacher identity: A key to increased collaboration. *Action in Teacher Education, 19*(3), 1–14.

Moon, M. S., & Inge, K. (2000). Vocational preparation and transition. In M. Snell & F. Brown (Eds.), *Instruction of student s with severe disabilities* (5th ed., pp. 591–628).Upper Saddle River, NJ: Merrill/Prentice Hall.

Morgan, J., & Ashbaker, B. Y. (2001). Work more effectively with your paraeducator [electronic version]. *Intervention in School and Clinic, 36,* 230–231.

Morris, M. W., & Su, S. K. (1999). Social psychological obstacles in environmental conflict resolution [electronic version]. *American Behavioral Scientist, 42,* 1322–1349.

Morse, W. (1994). Mental health professionals and teachers: How do the twain meet? *Beyond Behavior, 3*(2), 12–20.

Mueller, P. H., & Murphy, F. V. (2001). Determining when a student requires paraeducator support. *Teaching Exceptional Children, 33*(6), 22–27.

Nadler, D. J., Hackman, R., & Lawler, E. E. (1979). *Managing organizational behavior.* Boston: Little, Brown.

Nastasi, B. K., Varjas, K., Bernstein, R., & Jayasena, A. (2000). Conducting participatory culture-specific consultation: A global perspective on multicultural consultation [electronic version]. *School Psychology Review, 29,* 401–413.

National Joint Committee on Learning Disabilities. (1999). Learning disabilities: Use of paraprofessionals [electronic version]. *Learning Disability Quarterly, 22,* 23–30.

Nelson, C. M., & Pearson, C. A. (1991). *Integrating services for children and youth with emotional and behavioral disorders.* Reston, VA: Council for Exceptional Children.

Nelson, J. R., Smith, D. J., Taylor, L., Dodd, J. M., & Reavis, K. (1992). A statewide survey of special education administrators regarding mandated prereferral interventions. *Remedial and Special Education, 13*(4), 34–39.

Nelson, M. G. (2001, September). Capitalizing on collaboration [electronic version]. *Information Week, 855,* 109–111.

Neubert, D. A., & Moon, M. S. (2000). How a transition profile helps students prepare for life in the community. *Teaching Exceptional Children, 33*(2), 20–25.

Neubert, D. A., Moon, M. S., Leconte, P. J., & Lowman, M. (1998). Transition profile. Unpublished manuscript, University of Maryland at College Park.

Nezu, A., & D'Zurilla, T. J. (1981). Effects of problem definition and formulation on the generation of alternatives in the social problem-solving process. *Cognitive Therapy and Research, 5,* 265–271.

Nichols, W. C. (1996). *Treating people in families: An integrative framework.* New York: Guilford Press.

Niebuhr, K. E., & Niebuhr, R. E. (1999). Principal and counselor collaboration [electronic version]. *Education, 119,* 674–678.

Noell, G. H., & Witt, J. C. (1999). When does consultation lead to intervention implementation? Critical issues for research and practice. *Journal of Special Education, 33,* 29–35.

Noonan, M. J., & McCormick, L. (1993). *Early intervention in natural environments: Methods and procedures.* Pacific Grove, CA: Brooks/Cole.

Ogletree, B. T., Bull, J., Drew, R., & Lunnen, K. (2001). Team-based service delivery for students with disabilities: Practice options and guidelines for success, *Intervention in School and Clinic, 36,* 138–145.

Ohtake, Y., Fowler, S. A., & Santos. R. M. (2001). *Working with interpreters to plan early childhood services with limited-English–proficient families* (Technical Report No. 12) [electronic version]. Champaign-Urbana, IL: Culturally and Linguistically Appropriate Services for Early Childhood Research (CLAS) Institute.

Okhuysen, G. A. (2001). Structuring change: Familiarity and formal interventions in problem-solving groups [electronic version]. *Academy of Management Journal, 44,* 794–808.

Olson, J., Murphy, C. L., & Olson, P. D. (1998). Building effective successful teams: An interactive training model for inservice education, *Journal of Early Intervention, 21*(4), 339.

Orelove, F., & Sobsey, D. (1987). *Educating children with multiple disabilities: A transdisciplinary approach.* Baltimore: Brookes.

Ormsbee, C. K. (2001). Effective preassessment team procedures: Making the process work for teachers and students, *Intervention in School & Clinic, 36*(3), 146.

Ormsbee, C. K., & Haring, K. A. (2000). Rural preassessment team member perceptions of effectiveness. *Rural Special Education Quarterly, 19,* 17–26.

O'Sullivan, P. B. (2000). What you don't know won't hurt me: Impression management functions of communication in relationships. *Human Communication Research, 26,* 403–431.

Palma, G. M. (1994). Toward a positive and effective teacher and paraprofessional relationship. *Rural Educator, 13*(4), 46–48.

Palmer, J. D. (1988). For the manager who must build a team. In W. B. Reddy & K. Jamison (Eds.). *Team building: Blueprints for productivity and satisfaction* (pp. 137–149). San Diego: University Associates.

Palsha, S. A., & Wesley, P. W. (1998). Improving quality in early childhood environments through on-site consultation [electronic version]. *Topics in Early Childhood Special Education, 18,* 243–253.

Pandiscio, H. F. (1991). The risky business of collaboration. *School Administrator, 48*(4), 24, 27.

Parett, H. P., & Petch-Hogan, B. (2000). Approaching families: Facilitating culturally/linguistically diverse family involvement. *Teaching Exceptional Children, 32*(2), 4–10.

Park, E. (1999). Making a team effort [electronic version]. *Schools in the Middle, 8*(7), 35–38.

Parker, C. A. (Ed.). (1975). *Psychological consultation: Helping teachers meet special needs.* Minneapolis: University of Minnnesota Leadership Training Institute.

Parsons, M. B., & Reid, D. H. (1999). Training basic teaching skills to paraeducators of students with severe disabilities. *Teaching Exceptional Children, 31*(4), 48–54.

Paul, J., French, P., & Cranston-Gingras, A. (2001). Ethics and special education. *Focus on Exceptional Children, 34*(1), 1–16.

Perloff, R. M. (1993). *The dynamics of persuasion.* Hillsdale, NJ: Erlbaum.

Peterson, J. V., & Nisenholz, B. (1998). *Orientation to counseling* (4th ed.). Boston: Allyn & Bacon.

Peterson, K. D. (1999). Time use flows from school culture. *Journal of Staff Development, 20*(2), 16–19.

Petress, K. C. (1999). Listening: A vital skill. *Journal of Instructional Psychology, 26*(4), 261–263.

Pfeiffer, S. I. (1981). The school based interprofessional team: Recurring problems and some possible solutions. *Journal of School Psychology, 18,* 388–394.

Phillips, V., McCullough, L., Nelson, C. M., & Walker, H. M. (1990). Teamwork among teachers: Promoting a statewide agenda for students at risk for school failure. *Special Services in the Schools, 6,* 3–4.

Pickett, A. L. (1996). *A state of the art report on paraeducators in education and related services* (Report No. SP 398 188). New York: City University of New York, Center for Advanced Studies in Education. (ERIC Document Reproduction Services No. ED398188)

Pickett, A. L. (1997). Paraeducators in school settings: Framing the issues. In A. L. Pickett & K. Gerlach (Eds.), *Supervising paraeducators in school settings: A team approach* (pp. 1–24). Austin, TX: Pro-Ed.

Pickett, A. L. (1999). *Paraeducators: Factors that influence their performance, development, and supervision* (ERIC Digest E587) [electronic version]. Reston, VA: ERIC Clearinghouse on Disabilities and Gifted Education, Council for Exceptional Children. [Available online: http://ericec.org/digests/e587.htm]. Retrieved September 17, 2001.

Piersel, W. C., & Gutkin, T. B. (1983). Resistance to school-based consultation: A behavioral analysis of the problem. *Psychology in the Schools, 20,* 311–320.

Pillari, V., & Newsome, M. (1997). *Human behavior in the social environment: Families, groups, organizations, and communities.* Belmont, CA: Wadsworth.

Pipho, C. (1997). The possibilities and problems of collaboration. *Phi Delta Kappan, 79,* 261–262.

Pomplun, M. (1997). When students with disabilities participate in cooperative groups. *Exceptional Children, 64,* 49–58.

Pounder, D. (1998). *Restructuring schools for collaboration: Promises and pitfalls.* New York: SUNY Press.

Prater, M. A., & Bruhl, S. (1998). Acquiring social skills through cooperative learning and teacher-directed instruction. *Remedial and Special Education, 19*(3), 160–172.

Pryzwansky W. B. (1974). A reconsideration of the consultation model for delivery of school based psychological service. *American Journal of Orthospychiatry, 44,* 579–583.

Pryzwansky, W. B., & Rzepski, B. (1983). School-based teams: An untapped resource for consultation and technical assistance. *School Psychology Review, 12,* 174–179.

Pugach, M. C. (1988). The consulting teacher in the context of educational reform. *Exceptional Children, 55,* 273–275.

Pugach, M. C., & Johnson, L. J. (1995). *Collaborative practitioners, collaborative schools.* Denver: Love.

Pugach, M. C., & Johnson, L. J. (2002). *Collaborative practitioners, collaborative schools* (2nd ed.). Denver: Love.

Qin, Z., Johnson, D. W., & Johnson, R. T. (1995). Cooperative versus competitive efforts and problem solving. *Review of Educational Research, 65,* 129–143.

Quinn, K., & Cumbland, C. (1994). Service providers' perceptions of interagency collaboration in their communities. *Remedial Special Education, 2,* 109–116.

Quinn, M. M., Jannasch-Pennell, A., & Rutherford, R. B. (1995). Using peers as social skills training agents for students with antisocial behavior: A cooperative learning approach. *Preventing School Failure, 39*(4), 26–31.

Raign, K. R., & Sims, B. R. (1993). Gender, persuasion techniques, and collaboration. *Technical Communication Quarterly, 2*(1), 89–104.

Ray, K. P., Skinner, C. H., & Watson, T. S. (1999). Transferring stimulus control via momentum to increase compliance in a student with autism: A demonstration of collaborative consultation [electronic version]. *School Psychology Review, 28,* 622–628.

Redditt, S. (1991). Two teachers working as one. *Equity and Choice, 8*(1), 49–56.

Reyes, E. I. (1999). Parents, families and communities ensuring children's rights. *Bilingual Review, 24*(1–2), 53–63.

Reynolds, C. R., Gutkin, T. B., Elliott, S. N., & Witt, J. C. (1984). *School psychology: Essentials of theory and practice.* New York: Wiley.

Rhoades, J. A., Arnold, J., & Jay, C. (2001). The role of affective traits and affective states in disputants' motivation and behavior during episodes of organizational conflict. *Journal of Organizational Behavior, 22,* 329–345.

Rieck, W. A., & Wadsworth, D. E. D. (2000). Inclusion: Administrative headache or opportunity? [electronic version]. *NASSP Bulletin, 84,* 56–62.

Riggs, C. G. (2001). Ask the paraprofessionals. *Teaching Exceptional Children, 33*(3), 78–83.

Riggs, C. G., & Mueller, P. H. (2001). Employment and utilization of paraeducators in inclusive settings. *Journal of Special Education, 35,* 54–62.

Rock, M. L. (2000). Parents as equal partners: Balancing the scales in IEP development. *Teaching Exceptional Children, 32*(6), 30–37.

Rock, M. L., & Zigmond, N. (2001). Intervention assistance: Is it substance or symbolism? *Preventing School Failure, 45*(4) 153.

Rogers, C. (1972). *On becoming a person.* New York: Dell.

Rogers, C. R. (1951). *Client-centered therapy: Its current practice, implications, and theory.* Boston: Houghton Mifflin.

Rogers, E. M., & Steinfatt, T. M. (1999). *Intercultural communication.* Prospect Heights, IL: Waveland Press.

Rogers, M. R. (2000). Examining the cultural context of consultation [electronic version]. *School Psychology Review, 29,* 414–418.

Rosenfield, S. A., & Gravois, T. A. (1996). *Instructional consultation teams: Collaborating for change.* New York: Guilford Press.

Rudawsky, D. J., & Lundgren, D. C. (1999). Competitive responses to negative feedback [electronic version]. *International Journal of Conflict Management, 10,* 172–190.

Salend, S. J. (2001). *Creating inclusive classrooms: Effective and reflective practices* (4th ed.). Upper Saddle River, NJ: Merrill/Prentice Hall.

Salisbury, C. L., Evans, I. M., & Palombaro, M. M. (1997). Collaborative problem-solving to promote the inclusion of young children with significant disabilities in primary grades. *Exceptional Children, 63,* 195–209.

Samaha, N. V., & DeLisi, R. (2000). Peer collaboration on a nonverbal reasoning task by urban, minority students [electronic version]. *Journal of Experimental Education, 69,* 5–21.

Sarason, S. B. (1982). *The culture of the school and the problem of change* (2nd ed.). Boston: Allyn & Bacon.

Schamber, S. (1999). Ten practices for undermining the effectiveness of teaming. *Middle School Journal, 30,* 10–14.

Schmuck, R. A., & Runkel, P. J. (1994). *The handbook of organizational development in schools* (4th ed.). Prospect Heights, IL: Waveland Press.

Schumm, J. S., Vaughn, S., & Harris, J. (1997). Pyramid power for collaborative planning. *Teaching Exceptional Children, 29*(6), 62–66.

Schwahn, C., & Spady, W. (1998). Why change doesn't happen and how to make sure it does. *Educational Leadership, 55*(7), 45–47.

Scott, J. J., & Smith, S. C. (1987). *Collaborative schools* (ERIC Digest Series No. 22). Eugene, OR: ERIC Clearinghouse on Educational Management, University of Oregon. (ERIC Document Reproduction Service No. ED290233)

Secules, T., Cottom, C., Bray, M., & Miller, L. (1997). Creating schools for thought. *Educational Leadership, 54*(6), 56–63.

Sergiovanni, T. J. (1994). *Building community in schools.* San Francisco: Jossey-Bass.

Sharan, Y., & Sharan, S. (1994). Group investigation in the cooperative classroom. In S. Sharan (Ed.), *Handbook of cooperative learning methods* (pp. 191–214). Westport, CT: Greenwood Press.

Shelby, A. N. (1986). Theoretical bases of persuasion. *Journal of Business Communication, 25,* 5–29.

Shen, J. (1998). Do teachers feel empowered? *Educational Leadership, 55*(7), 35–36.

Sheridan, S. M., Kratochwill, T. R., & Bergan, J. R. (1996). *Conjoint behavioral consultation: A procedural manual.* New York: Kluwer/Plenum.

Sheridan, S. M., Welch, M., & Orme, S. F. (1996). Is consultation effective? A review of outcome research. *Remedial and Special Education, 17,* 341–354.

Sherif, M., & Sherif, C. (1956). *An outline of social psychology.* New York: Harper & Row.

Shoffner, M. F., & Briggs, M. K. (2001). An interactive approach for developing interprofessional collaboration: Preparing school counselors. *Counselor Education & Supervision, 40,* 193–200.

Simmons, K. H., Ivry, J., & Sletzer, M. M. (1985). Agency-family collaboration. *Practice Concepts, 25,* 343–346.

Sindelar, P. T., Griffin, C. C., Smith, S. W., & Watanabe, A. K. (1992). Prereferral intervention: Encouraging notes on preliminary findings. *Elementary School Journal, 92,* 245–259.

Sitlington, P. L., & Neubert, D. S. (1998). Assessment for life: Methods and processes to determine students' interests, abilities and preferences. In M. Wehmeyer & D. J. Sands (Eds.), *Making it happen: Student involvement in educational planning, decision making, and instruction* (pp. 75–98). Baltimore: Brookes.

Slavin, R. E. (1986). *Using student team learning* (3rd ed.). Baltimore: Center for Research on Elementary and Middle Schools, Johns Hopkins University.

Slavin, R. E. (1991) Synthesis of research on cooperative learning. *Educational Leadership, 48*(5), 71–82.

Slavin, R. E. (1995). *Cooperative learning: Theory, research, and practice* (2nd ed.). Boston: Allyn & Bacon.

Snell, M. E., & Janney, R. (2000). *Collaborative teaming*. Baltimore: Brookes.

Snell, M. E., & Janney, R. (2000). Improving communication and handling conflicts. In M. E. Snell, R. Janney, J. Elliot, & C. C. Burton (Eds.), *Collaborative teaming* (pp. 107–131). Baltimore: Brookes.

Snell, M. E., & Janney, R. E. (2000). Teachers' problem-solving about children with moderate and severe disabilities in elementary classrooms. *Exceptional Children, 66*, 472–490.

Snow, D. A., Zurcher, L. A., & Sjoberg, G. (1982). Interviewing by comment: An adjunct to the direct question. *Qualitative Sociology, 5*, 285–311.

Sodowsky, G. R., & Johnson, P. (1994). World views: Culturally learned assumptions and values. In P. Pedersen & J. C. Carey (Eds.), *Multicultural counseling in schools: A practical handbook* (pp. 59–79). Boston: Allyn & Bacon.

Sparapani, E. R., & Norwood, J. E. (1997). Collaborating with a university [electronic version]. *Principal, 77*(2), 53–54.

Sparks, D. (1997). Maintaining the faith in teachers' ability to grow: An interview with Asa Hilliard. *Journal of Staff Development, 18*(2), 24–25.

Sparks, D. (1999). Try on strategies to get a good fit. *Journal of Staff Development, 20*(3), 56–60.

Sparks, D., & Hirsh, S. (1997). *A new vision for staff development*. Alexandria, VA: Association for Supervision and Curriculum Development.

Sparks, D., & Loucks-Horsley, S. (1989). Five models for staff development for teachers. *Journal of Staff Development, 10*(4), 40–57.

Sparks, D., Nowakowski, M., Hall, B., Alec, R., & Imrick, J. (1985). School improvement through staff development. *Educational Leadership 42*(6), 59–61.

Sparks, G. (1986). The effectiveness of alternative training activities in changing teaching practices. *American Educational Research Journal, 23*(2), 217–225.

Special Education News. (2000a). Many teachers say they are not prepared to coach paraeducators. [Available online: http://specialednews.com/educators/ednews/parateams051900.html]. Retrieved January 7, 2002.

Special Education News. (2000b). Paraeducator's role is changing amid teacher shortage. [Available online: http://spedialednews.com/educators/ednews/paraeds051900.html]. Retrieved January 7, 2002.

Stainton, T., & Bessler, H. (1998). The positive impact of children with an intellectual disability on the family. *Journal of Intellectual and Developmental Disability, 23*(1), 57–70.

Stevens, R. J., & Slavin, R. E. (1995). Effects of a cooperative learning approach in reading and writing on academically handicapped and nonhandicapped students. *The Elementary School Journal, 95*, 241–262.

Stewart, C. J., & Cash, W. B. (2000). *Interviewing: Practices and principles* (9th ed.). New York: McGraw-Hill.

Sullivan, T. J. (1998). *Collaboration: A health care imperative*. New York: McGraw-Hill.

Tamir, L. (1999). Conflict mediation [electronic version]. *Executive Excellence, 16*(6), 15–16.

Tarver-Behring, S. & Spagna, M. E. (1999). Counseling with exceptional children. In A. Vernon, (Ed.), *Counseling children and adolescents*. Denver, CO: Love.

Tashie, C., Jorgensen, C., Shapiro-Barnard, S., Martin, J., & Schuh, M. (1996). High school inclusion: Strategies and barriers. *TASH Newsletter, 22*(9), 19–22.

Taylor, L., & Adelman, H. (1998). Confidentiality: Competing principles, inevitable dilemmas. *Journal of Educational and Psychological Consultation, 9*, 267–275.

Terry, P. M. (1999). Essential skills for principals. *Thrust for Educational Leadership, 29*, 28–32.

Tharp, R., & Wetzel, R. (1969). *Behavior modification in the natural environment*. New York: Academic Press.

Thomas, C. C., Correa, V. I., & Morsink, C. V. (2001). *Interactive teaming: Consultation and collaboration in special programs* (3rd ed.). Upper Saddle River, NJ: Prentice Hall.

Thomas, K. W., & Kilmann, R. H. (1974). *Thomas–Kilmann conflict mode instrument*. Tuxedo, NY: Xicom.

Thousand, J. S., & Villa, R. A. (2000). Collaborative teaming: A powerful tool in school restructuring. In R. A. Villa & J. S. Thousand (Eds.), *Restructuring for caring and effective education: Piecing the puzzle together* (2nd ed.). Baltimore: Brookes.

Tichenor, M. S., Heins, B., & Piechura-Couture, K. (2000). Parent perceptions of a co-taught inclusive classroom [electronic version]. *Education, 120,* 569–574, 546.

Tjosvold, D. (1987). Participation: A close look at its dynamics. *Journal of Management, 13,* 739–750.

Tobias, R. (1993). Underlying cultural issues that affect sound consultation/school collaboratives in developing multicultural programs. *Journal of Educational and Psychological Consultation, 4*(3), 237–251.

Toffler, A. (1980). *The third wave.* New York: Morrow.

Tourse, R. W. C., & Mooney, J. F. (Eds.). (1999). *Collaborative practice: School and human service partnerships.* Westport, CT: Praeger.

Tractman, G. M. (1961). New directions for school psychology. *Exceptional Children, 28,* 159–162.

Trenholm, S. (2001). *Thinking through communication: An introduction to the study of human communication* (3rd ed.). Boston: Allyn & Bacon.

Trent, S. C. (1998). False starts and other dilemmas of a secondary general education collaborative teacher [electronic version]. *Journal of Learning Disabilities, 31,* 503–513.

Trentin, G., & Gibelli, C. (1998). Distance collaboration for studying history in lower secondary schools: The storybase project [electronic version]. *International Journal of Instructional Media, 25*(1), 11–27.

Trumbull, E., Rothstein-Fisch, C., Greenfield, P. M., & Quiroz, B. (2001). *Bridging cultures between home and school: A guide for teachers.* Mahwah, NJ: Erlbaum.

Trump, J. L. (1966). Secondary education tomorrow: Four imperatives for improvement. *NASSP Bulletin, 50*(309), 87–95.

Turnbull, A. P., & Turnbull, H. R. (2001). *Families, professionals, and exceptionality: Collaborating for empowerment* (4th ed.). Upper Saddle River, NJ: Merrill/Prentice Hall.

Turnbull, A. P., Turnbull, H. R., Shank, M., & Leal, D. (1995). *Exceptional lives: Special education in today's schools.* Englewood Cliffs, NJ: Merrill/Prentice Hall.

U.S. Department of Education. (n.d.). *Roles for education paraprofessionals in effective schools: An idea book.* Washington, DC: U.S. Department of Education, Planning and Evaluation Service.

Umansky, W., & Hooper, S. R. (1998). *Young children with special needs* (3rd ed). Upper Saddle River, NJ: Merrill/Prentice Hall.

Van Meter, P., & Stevens, R. J. (2000). The role of theory in the study of peer collaboration [electronic version]. *Journal of Experimental Education, 69,* 113–127.

Vargo, S. (1998). Consulting teacher-to-teacher. *Teaching Exceptional Children, 30*(2), 54–55.

Vaughn, S. (1994, April). *Teachers' views of inclusion: "I'd rather pump gas."* Paper presented at the annual meeting of the American Educational Research Association, New Orleans. (ERIC Document Reproduction Service No. ED370928)

Vaughn, S., Zaragoza, N., Hogan, A., & Walker, J. (1993). A four-year longitudinal investigation of the social skills and behavior problems of students with learning disabilities. *Journal of Learning Disabilities, 26,* 404–412.

Villegas, A. M., & Clewell, B. C. (1998). Increasing teacher diversity by tapping the paraprofessional pool [electronic version]. *Theory into Practice, 37,* 121–130.

Wade, S. E., Welch, M., & Jensen, J. B. (1994). Teacher receptivity to collaboration: Levels of interest, types of concern and school characteristics as variables contributing to successful implementation. *Journal of Educational and Psychological Consultation, 5,* 177–209.

Wadsworth, D. E., & Knight, D. (1996). Paraprofessionals: The bridge to successful full inclusion. *Intervention in School and Clinic, 31,* 166–171.

Wagner, M., & Blackorby, J. (1996). Transition from high school to work or college: How special education students fare. *The Future of Children, 6*(1), 103–120.

Wagner, T. (1998). Change as collaborative inquiry: A constructivist methodology for reinventing schools. *Phi Delta Kappan, 79,* 512–517.

Walcott, D. D. (1997, July–August). Education in human sexuality for young people with moderate and severe mental retardation. *Exceptional Children, 29*(6), 72–74.

Walker, W. (1999). Collaboration: "The faint of heart need not apply" [electronic version]. *Peabody Journal of Education, 74,* 300–305.

Walther-Thomas, C. S. (1997). Co-teaching experiences: The benefits and problems that teachers and principals report over time. *Journal of Learning Disabilities, 30,* 395–407.

Walther-Thomas, C., Korinek, L., & McLaughlin, V. L. (1999). Collaboration to support students' success. *Focus on Exceptional Children, 32*(3), 1–18.

Walther-Thomas, C., Korinek, L., McLaughlin, V., & Williams, B. T. (1999). *Collaboration for inclusive education.* Boston: Allyn & Bacon.

Walther-Thomas, C., Korinek, L., McLaughlin, V., & Williams, B. T. (2000). *Collaboration for inclusive education: Developing successful programs.* Boston: Allyn & Bacon.

Warwick, D. (1971). *Team teaching.* London: University of London.

Wehmeyer, M. L., & Sands, D. J. (1998). *Making it happen: Student involvement in education planning, decision-making, and instruction.* Baltimore: Brookes.

Welch, M. (1999). The DECIDE strategy for decision making and problem solving: A workshop template for preparing professionals for educational partnerships. *Journal of Educational and Psychological Consultation, 10,* 363–375.

Welch, M. (2000). Descriptive analysis of team teaching in two elementary classrooms: A formative experimental approach. *Remedial and Special Education, 21,* 366–376.

Welch, M., & Tulbert, B. (2000). Practitioners' perspectives of collaboration: A social validation and factor analysis. *Journal of Educational and Psychological Consultation, 11,* 357–378.

Welch, M., Brownell, K., & Sheridan, S. (1999). What's the score and game plan on teaming in schools? *Remedial and Special Education, 20*(1), 36–49.

Welch, M. (1998). Collaboration: Staying on the bandwagon. *Journal of Teacher Education, 49*(1), 26–37.

Wesson, L., & Kudlacz, J. M. (2000). Collaboration for change [electronic version]. *Principal Leadership, 1*(3), 50–53.

Westby, C. E., & Ford, V. (1993). The role of team culture in assessment and intervention. *Journal of Educational and Psychological Consultation, 4,* 319–341.

Westmyer, S. A., DiCioccio, R. L., & Rubin. R. B. (1998). Appropriateness and effectiveness of communication channels in competent interpersonal communication. *Journal of Communication, 48*(3), 27–48.

White, J., & Mullis, F. (1998). A systems approach to school counselor consultation [electronic version]. *Education, 119,* 242–252.

Whitehead, B. (1994). The failure of sex education. *American Educator, 18,* 22–29, 44–52.

Whitten, E., & Dieker, L. (1995). Intervention assistance teams: A broader vision. *Preventing School Failure, 40*(1), 41–45.

Whitworth, J. (1999). *Seven steps to successful inclusion.* (ERIC Document Reproduction Service No. ED436040)

Wickstrom, K. F., & Witt, J. C. (1993). Resistance with school-based consultation. In J. Zins, T. R. Kratochwill, & S. N. Elliott (Eds.), *Handbook of consultation services for children* (pp. 159–178). San Francisco: Jossey-Bass.

Widrick, G., Whaley, C., DiVenere, N., Vecchione, E., Swartz, D., & Stiffler, D. (1991). The medical education project: An example of collaboration between parents and professionals. *Children's Health Care, 20,* 93–100.

Wilczynski, S. M., Mandal, R. L., & Fusilier, I. (2000). Bridges and barriers in behavioral consultation. *Psychology in the Schools, 37,* 495–504.

Wineburg, S., & Grossman, P. (1998). Creating a community of learners among high school teachers. *Phi Delta Kappan, 79,* 350–353.

Wolf, J. S., & Stephens, T. M. (1990). Friends of special education: A parent training model. Journal of Educational and Psychological Consultation, 1, 343–356.

Wolf, R. (1979). *Strategies for conducting naturalistic evaluation in socio-educational settings: The naturalistic interview.* Kalamazoo, MI: Occasional Series, Evaluation Center, Western Michigan University.

Wolfe, P. S., & Harriott, W. A. (1998). The reauthorization of the Individuals with Disabilities Act (IDEA): What educators and parents should know. *Focus on Autism and Other Developmental Disabilities, 13*(2), 88–95.

Wood, M. (1998). Whose job is it anyway? Educational roles in inclusion. *Exceptional children, 64,* 181–195.

Index

Photo Credits